Yakitate!! Japan

23

TAKASHI HASHIGUCHI

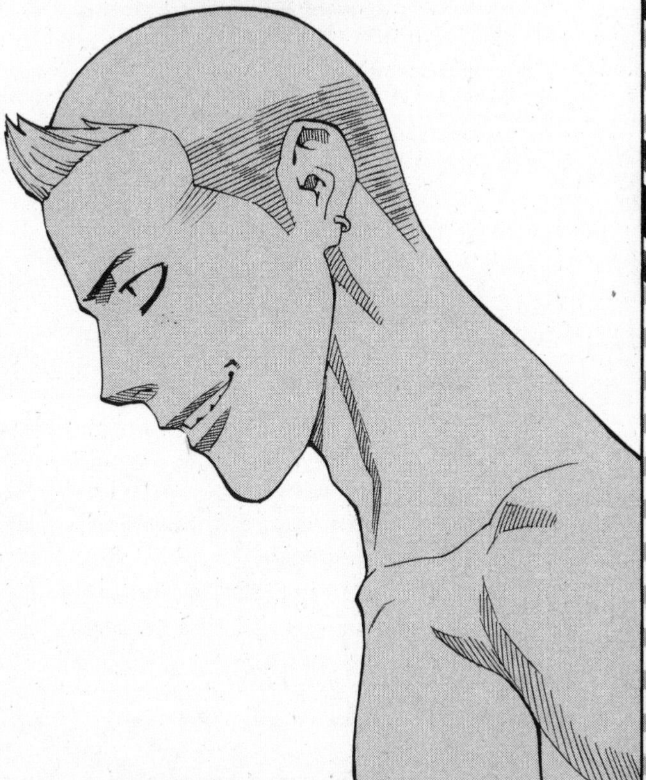

YAKITATE!! JAPAN 23
Shonen Sunday Edition
★The Story Thus Far★

In order to save Pantasia from being taken over by rival bakery St. Pierre, Azuma and his team compete to make the best use of unique products from various regions of Japan in the hotly contested television bakeoff, "Yakitate!! 25."

In the ninth round of the competition, the team faces prodigal pizza-maker Marco, who came from Italy. In an upset, Pantasia wins with a "Petticoat Method" pizza (innovated by Azuma and named by judge Kuroyanagi). The technique is so strong that it turns Kuroyanagi into a bird and Marco into a turtle!

In the tenth round, their opponent is Tsukino's sister Yukino! Her tart-making skills are top-notch, and she combines the reverse fold and tarte tatin techniques to produce a Reverse Tart that creates an astounding rift in reality! All of Pantasia's wins thus far are reversed, and the "Yakitate!! 25" scores now favor St. Pierre! Can Pantasia ever catch up?

CONTENTS

Research Assistance: Nichirei Foods Inc.
Special Assistance: Kanto Tsukuba Bank
Information supplied by Tsukuba Circuit
"Pan No Mimi," Koichi Uchimura/Writer, Shigeyuki Kimura/
Scenario Creator

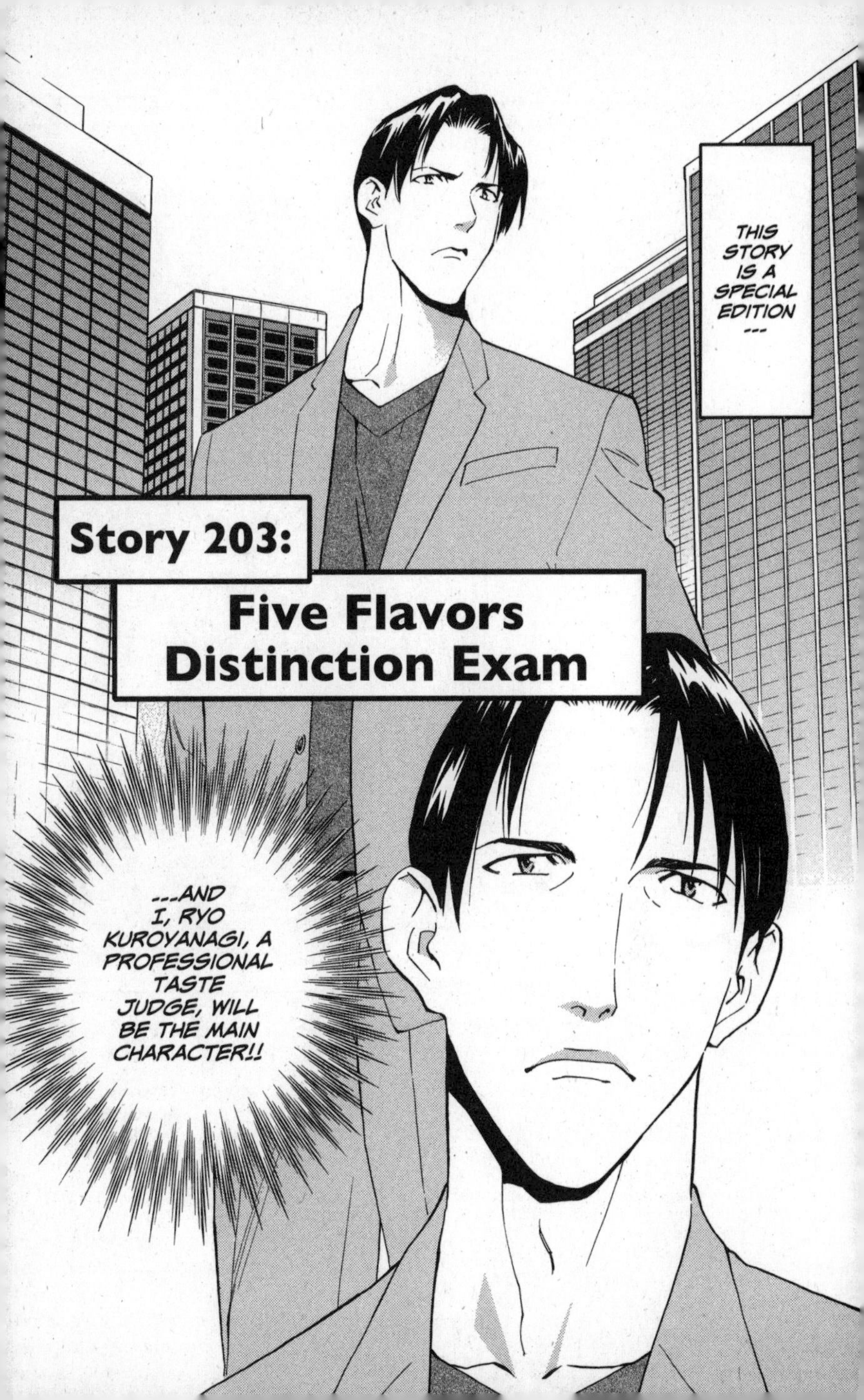
THIS STORY IS A SPECIAL EDITION---
Story 203:
Five Flavors Distinction Exam
---AND I, RYO KUROYANAGI, A PROFESSIONAL TASTE JUDGE, WILL BE THE MAIN CHARACTER!!

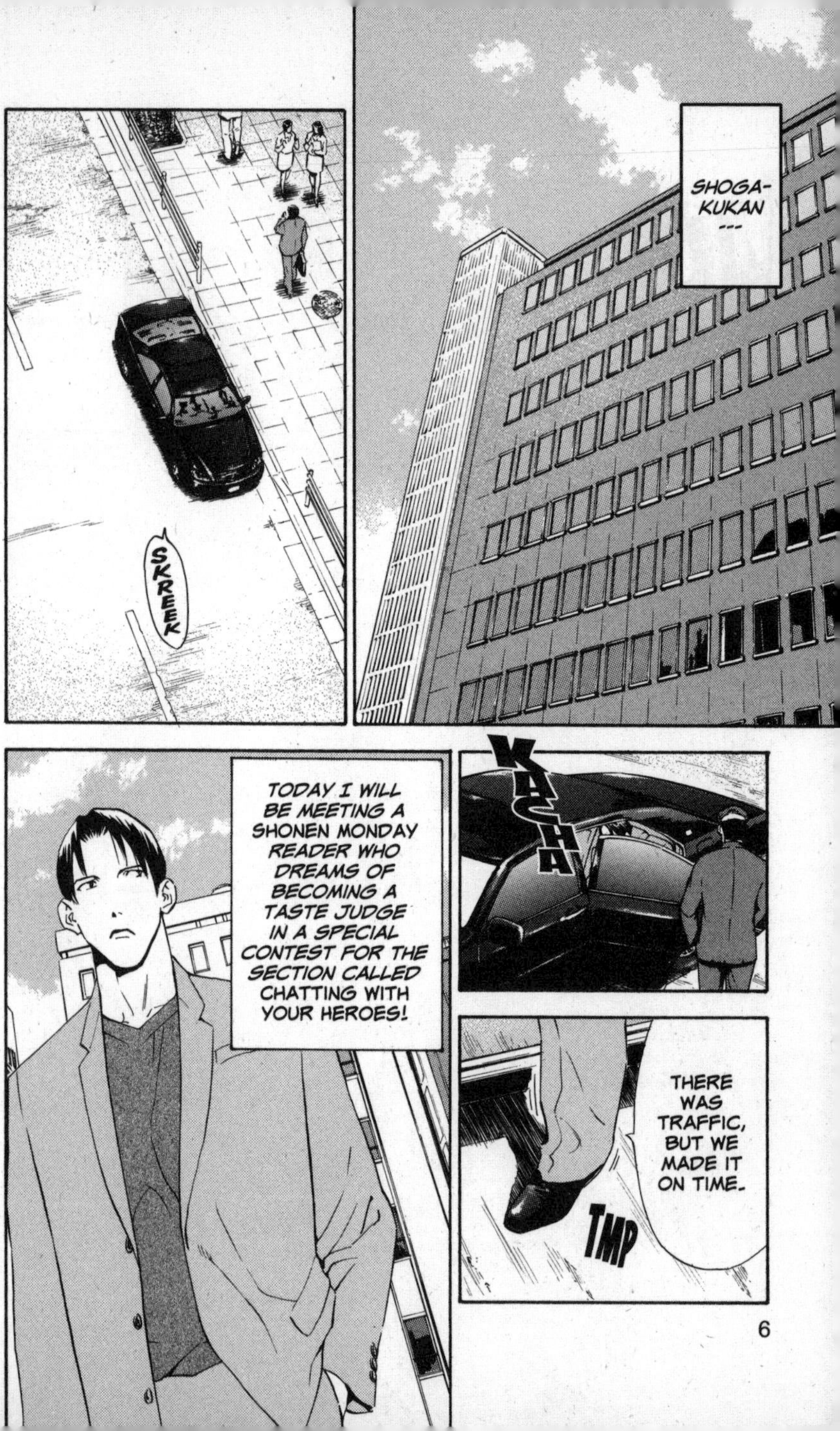
SHOGA-KUKAN ---
SKREEK
KACHA
THERE WAS TRAFFIC, BUT WE MADE IT ON TIME.
TMP
TODAY I WILL BE MEETING A SHONEN MONDAY READER WHO DREAMS OF BECOMING A TASTE JUDGE IN A SPECIAL CONTEST FOR THE SECTION CALLED CHATTING WITH YOUR HEROES!

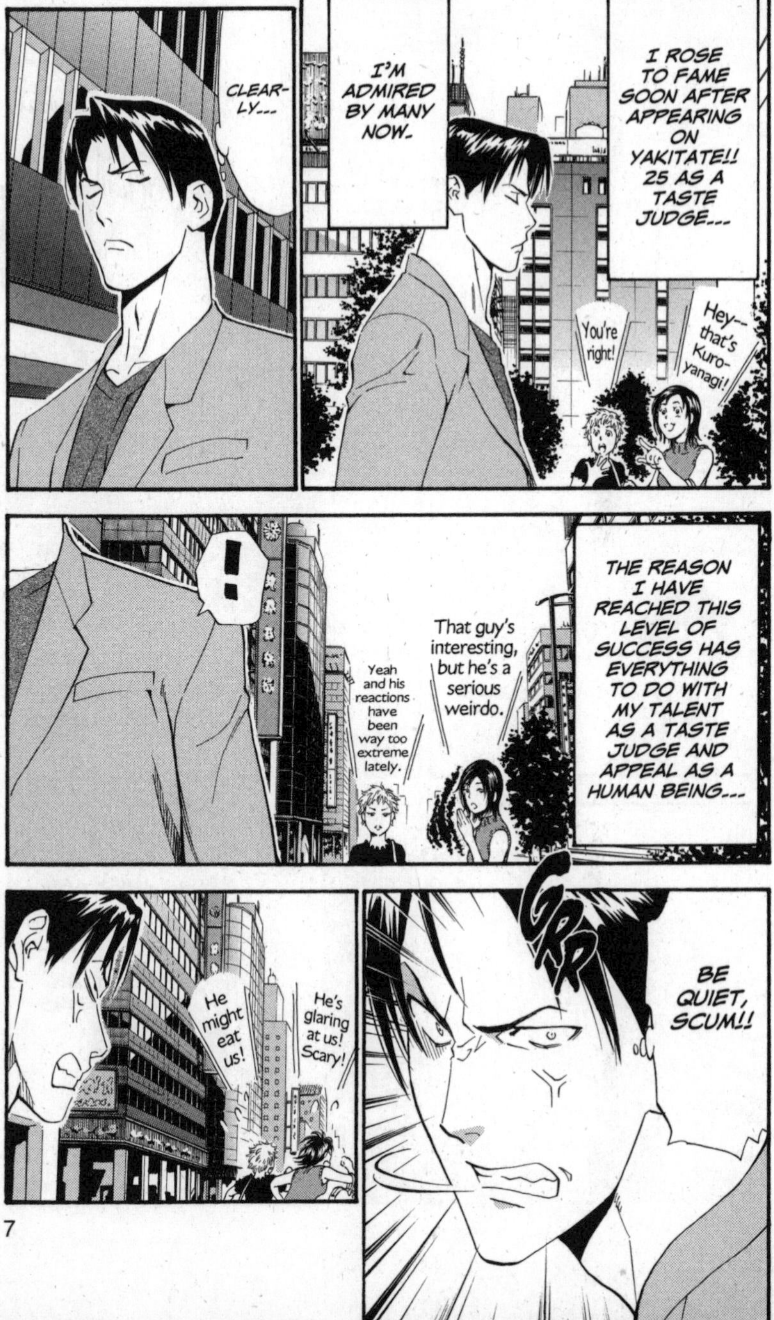
I ROSE TO FAME SOON AFTER APPEARING ON YAKITATE!! 25 AS A TASTE JUDGE...
I'M ADMIRED BY MANY NOW.
Hey-- that's Kuroyanagi!
You're right!
CLEARLY...
THE REASON I HAVE REACHED THIS LEVEL OF SUCCESS HAS EVERYTHING TO DO WITH MY TALENT AS A TASTE JUDGE AND APPEAL AS A HUMAN BEING...
That guy's interesting, but he's a serious weirdo.
Yeah and his reactions have been way too extreme lately.
!
GRR
BE QUIET, SCUM!!
He's glaring at us! Scary!
He might eat us!

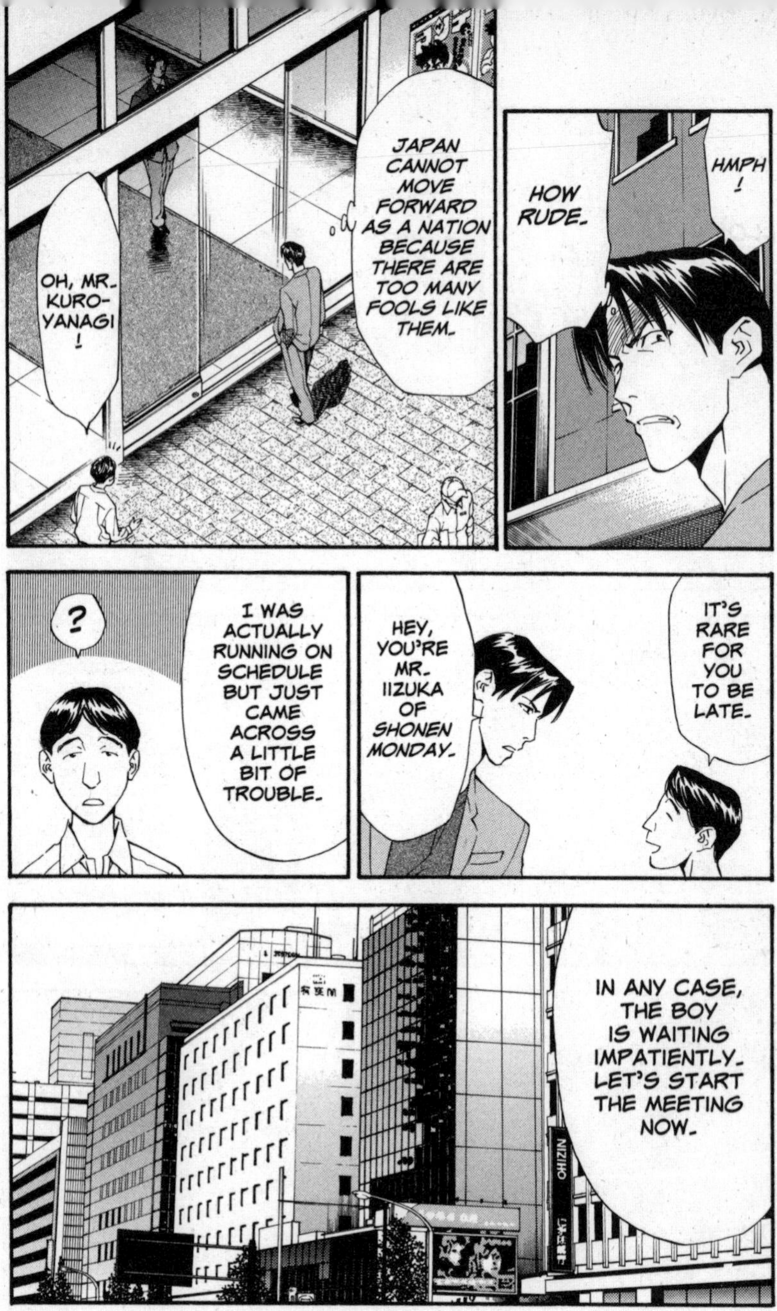
HMPH!
HOW RUDE.
JAPAN CANNOT MOVE FORWARD AS A NATION BECAUSE THERE ARE TOO MANY FOOLS LIKE THEM.
OH, MR. KURO-YANAGI!
IT'S RARE FOR YOU TO BE LATE.
HEY, YOU'RE MR. IIZUKA OF SHONEN MONDAY.
I WAS ACTUALLY RUNNING ON SCHEDULE BUT JUST CAME ACROSS A LITTLE BIT OF TROUBLE.
?
IN ANY CASE, THE BOY IS WAITING IMPATIENTLY. LET'S START THE MEETING NOW.

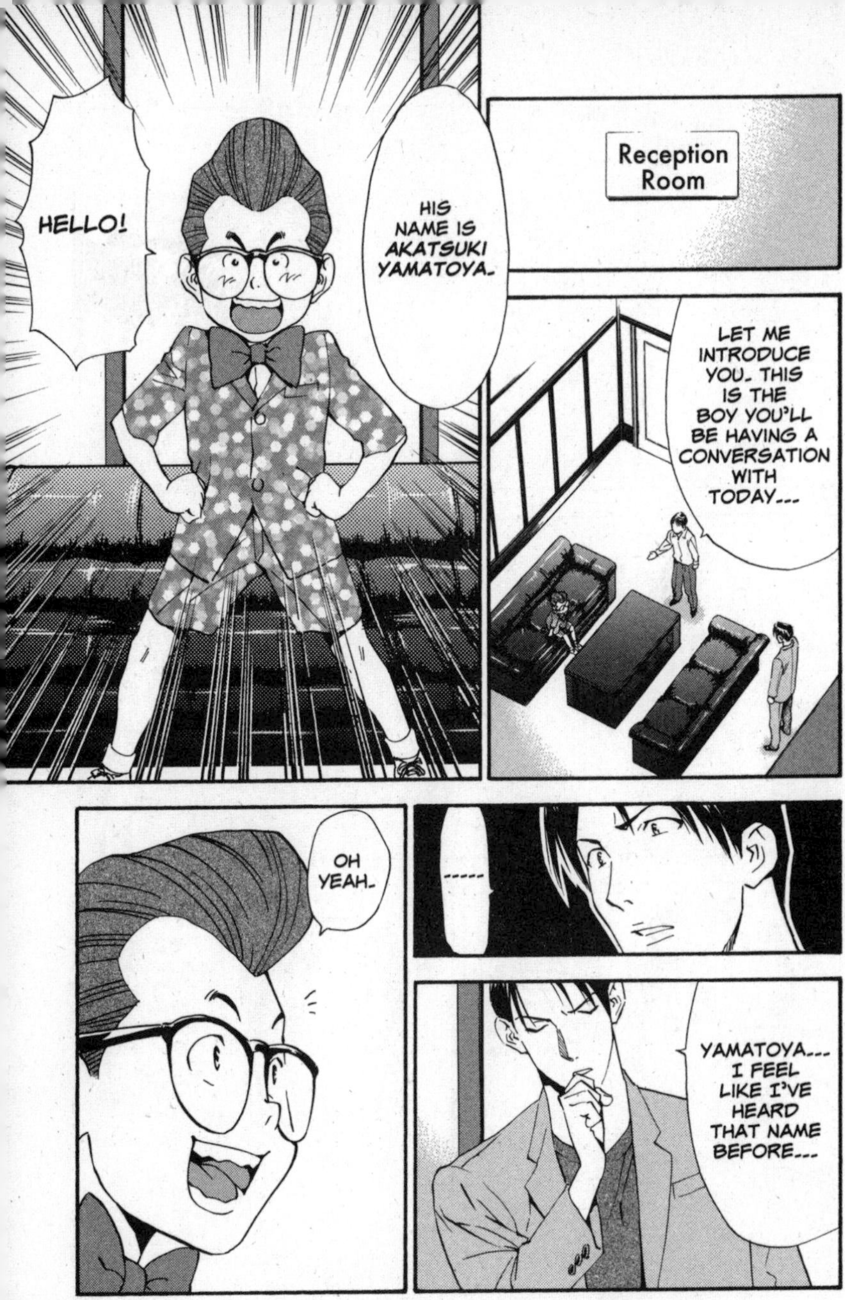
Reception Room
LET ME INTRODUCE YOU. THIS IS THE BOY YOU'LL BE HAVING A CONVERSATION WITH TODAY...
HIS NAME IS AKATSUKI YAMATOYA.
HELLO!
.....
YAMATOYA... I FEEL LIKE I'VE HEARD THAT NAME BEFORE...
OH YEAH.

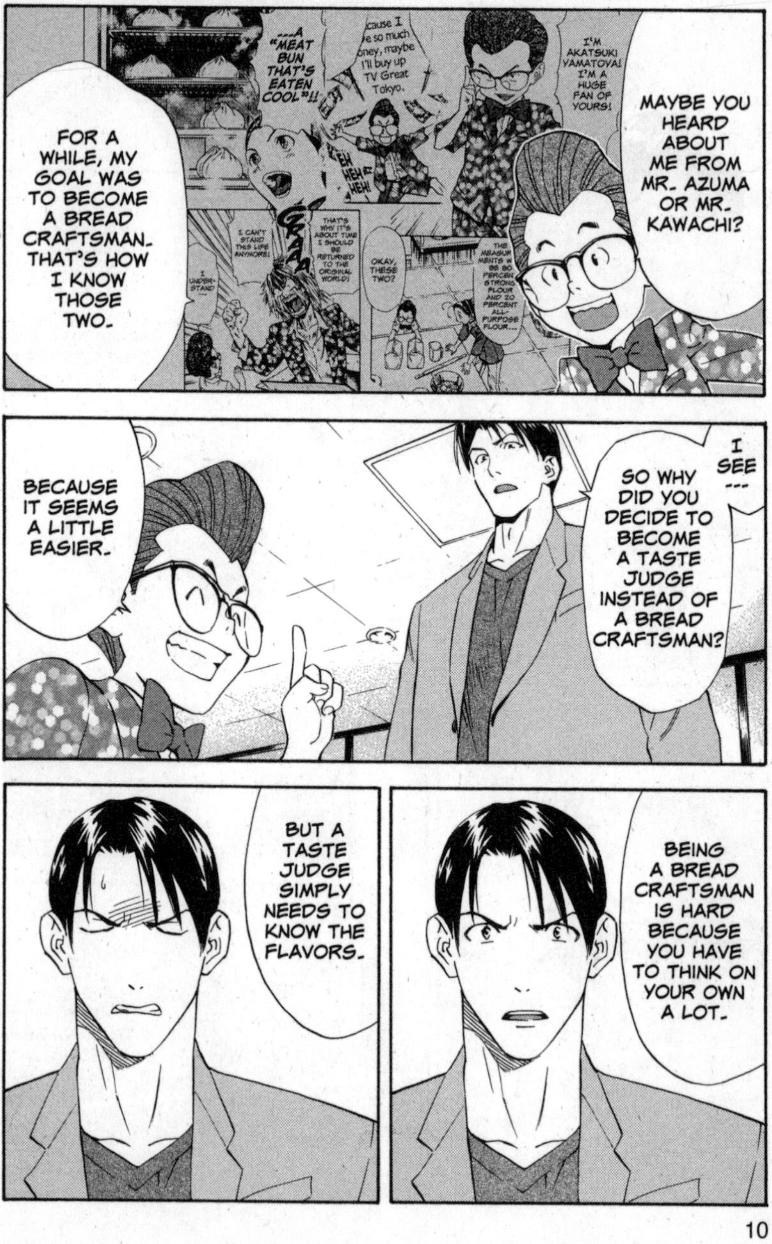
MAYBE YOU HEARD ABOUT ME FROM MR. AZUMA OR MR. KAWACHI?
I'M AKATSUKI YAMATOYA! I'M A HUGE FAN OF YOURS!
...A "MEAT BUN THAT'S EATEN COOL"!!
EH HEH HEH HEH!
THAT'S WHY IT'S ABOUT TIME I SHOULD BE RETURNED TO THE ORIGINAL WORLD!
I CAN'T STAND THIS LIFE ANYMORE!
OKAY, THESE TWO?
FOR A WHILE, MY GOAL WAS TO BECOME A BREAD CRAFTSMAN. THAT'S HOW I KNOW THOSE TWO.
I SEE...
SO WHY DID YOU DECIDE TO BECOME A TASTE JUDGE INSTEAD OF A BREAD CRAFTSMAN?
BECAUSE IT SEEMS A LITTLE EASIER.
BEING A BREAD CRAFTSMAN IS HARD BECAUSE YOU HAVE TO THINK ON YOUR OWN A LOT.
BUT A TASTE JUDGE SIMPLY NEEDS TO KNOW THE FLAVORS.

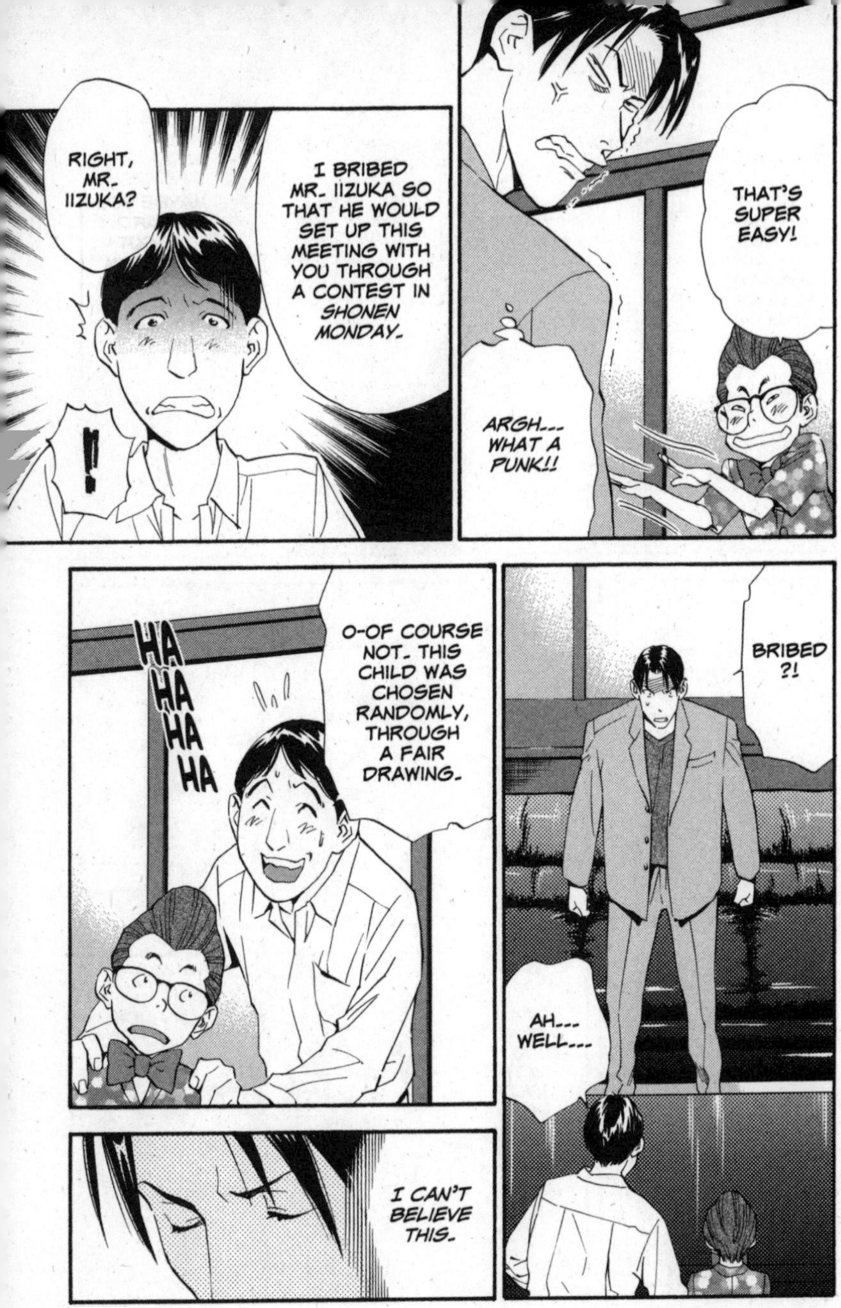
THAT'S SUPER EASY!
ARGH... WHAT A PUNK!!
I BRIBED MR. IIZUKA SO THAT HE WOULD SET UP THIS MEETING WITH YOU THROUGH A CONTEST IN *SHONEN MONDAY*.
RIGHT, MR. IIZUKA?
!
BRIBED ?!
AH... WELL...
O-OF COURSE NOT. THIS CHILD WAS CHOSEN RANDOMLY, THROUGH A FAIR DRAWING.
HA HA HA HA
I CAN'T BELIEVE THIS.

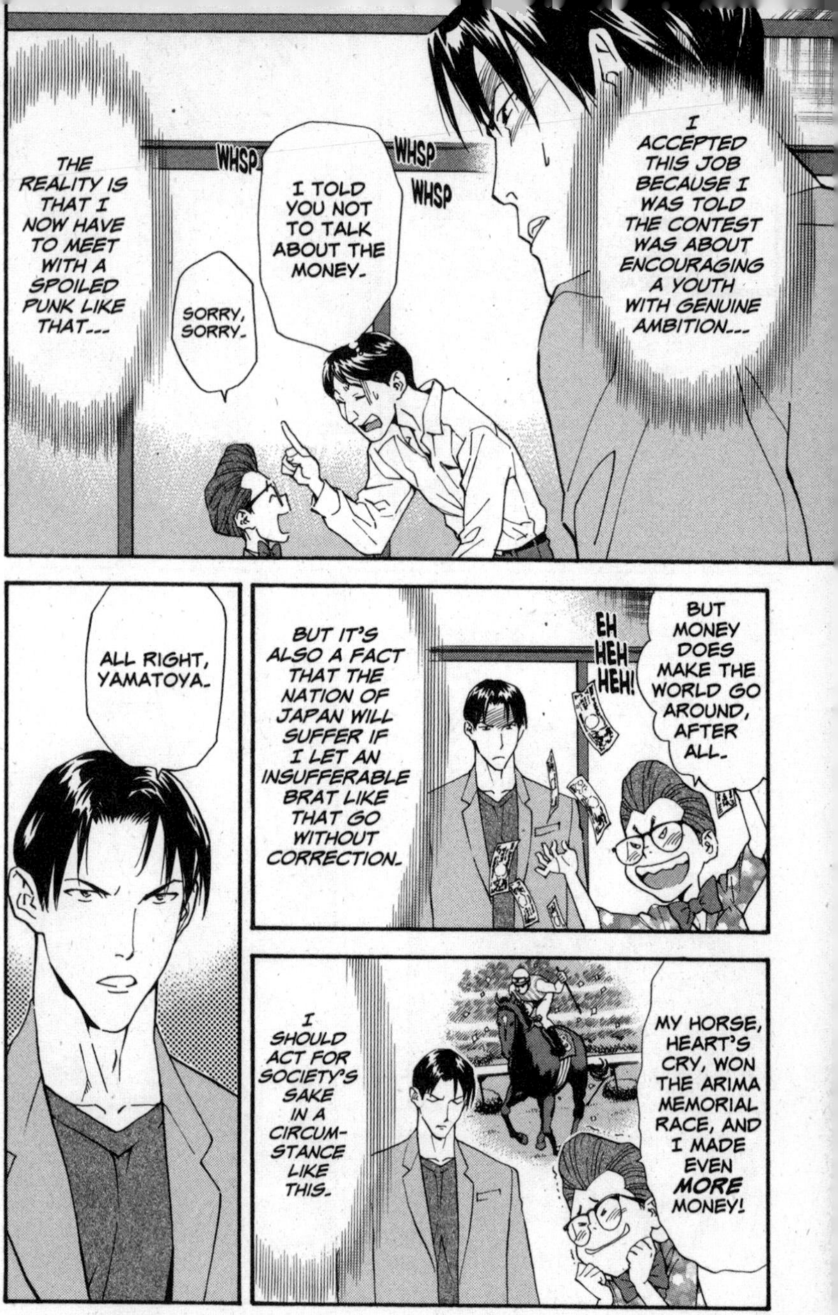
I ACCEPTED THIS JOB BECAUSE I WAS TOLD THE CONTEST WAS ABOUT ENCOURAGING A YOUTH WITH GENUINE AMBITION...
WHSP WHSP WHSP
I TOLD YOU NOT TO TALK ABOUT THE MONEY.
THE REALITY IS THAT I NOW HAVE TO MEET WITH A SPOILED PUNK LIKE THAT...
SORRY, SORRY.
BUT MONEY DOES MAKE THE WORLD GO AROUND, AFTER ALL.
EH HEH HEH!
BUT IT'S ALSO A FACT THAT THE NATION OF JAPAN WILL SUFFER IF I LET AN INSUFFERABLE BRAT LIKE THAT GO WITHOUT CORRECTION.
MY HORSE, HEART'S CRY, WON THE ARIMA MEMORIAL RACE, AND I MADE EVEN ***MORE*** MONEY!
I SHOULD ACT FOR SOCIETY'S SAKE IN A CIRCUMSTANCE LIKE THIS.
ALL RIGHT, YAMATOYA.

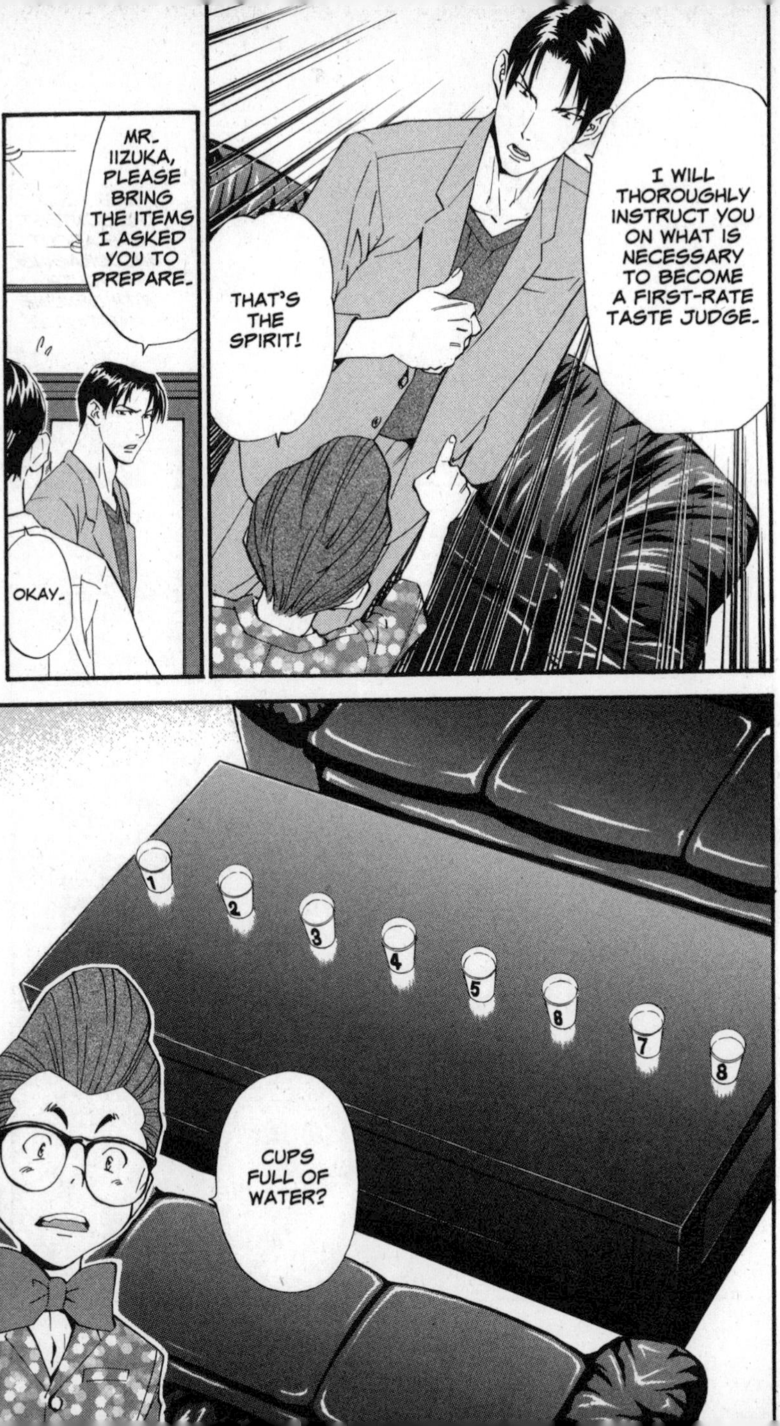
I WILL THOROUGHLY INSTRUCT YOU ON WHAT IS NECESSARY TO BECOME A FIRST-RATE TASTE JUDGE.
THAT'S THE SPIRIT!
MR. IIZUKA, PLEASE BRING THE ITEMS I ASKED YOU TO PREPARE.
OKAY.
CUPS FULL OF WATER?

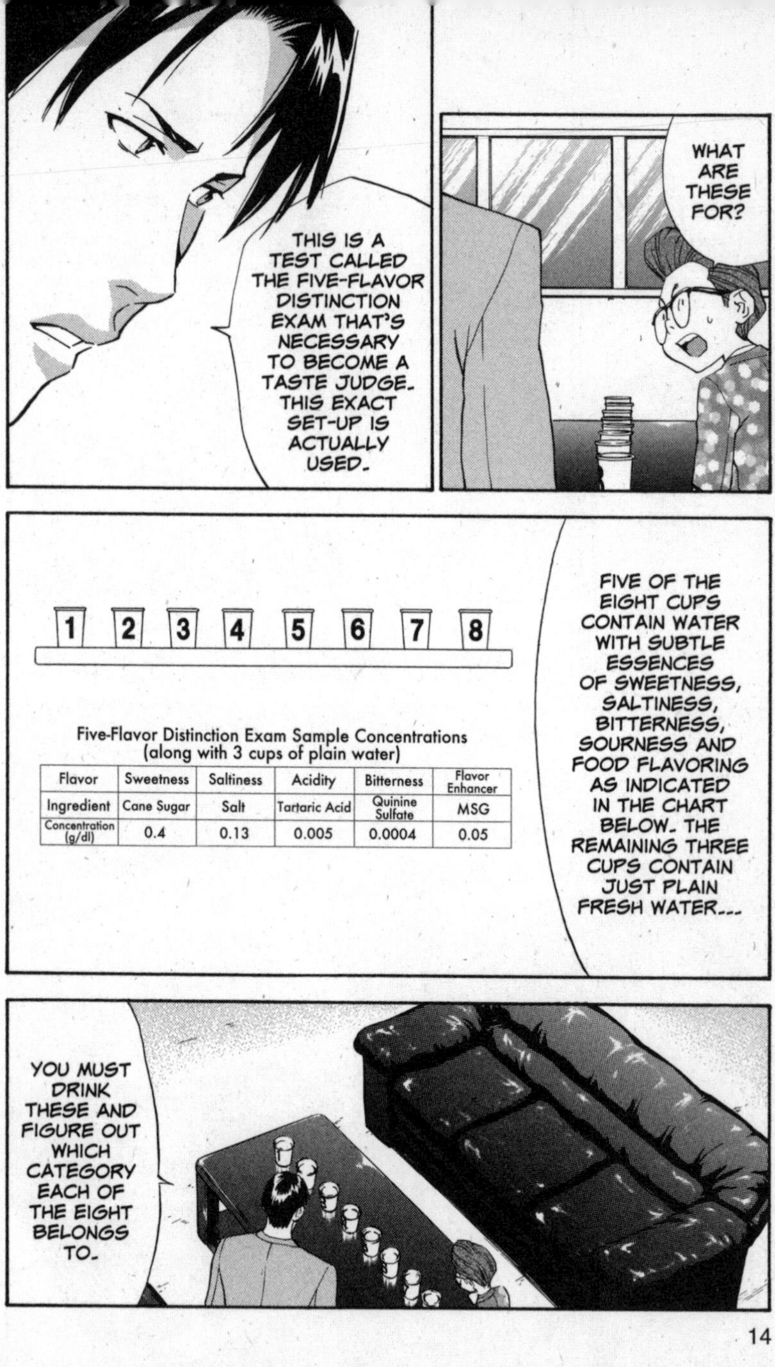
WHAT ARE THESE FOR?
THIS IS A TEST CALLED THE FIVE-FLAVOR DISTINCTION EXAM THAT'S NECESSARY TO BECOME A TASTE JUDGE. THIS EXACT SET-UP IS ACTUALLY USED.
FIVE OF THE EIGHT CUPS CONTAIN WATER WITH SUBTLE ESSENCES OF SWEETNESS, SALTINESS, BITTERNESS, SOURNESS AND FOOD FLAVORING AS INDICATED IN THE CHART BELOW. THE REMAINING THREE CUPS CONTAIN JUST PLAIN FRESH WATER...
1 2 3 4 5 6 7 8
Five-Flavor Distinction Exam Sample Concentrations
(along with 3 cups of plain water)
YOU MUST DRINK THESE AND FIGURE OUT WHICH CATEGORY EACH OF THE EIGHT BELONGS TO.

Flavor	Sweetness	Saltiness	Acidity	Bitterness	Flavor Enhancer
Ingredient	Cane Sugar	Salt	Tartaric Acid	Quinine Sulfate	MSG
Concentration (g/dl)	0.4	0.13	0.005	0.0004	0.05

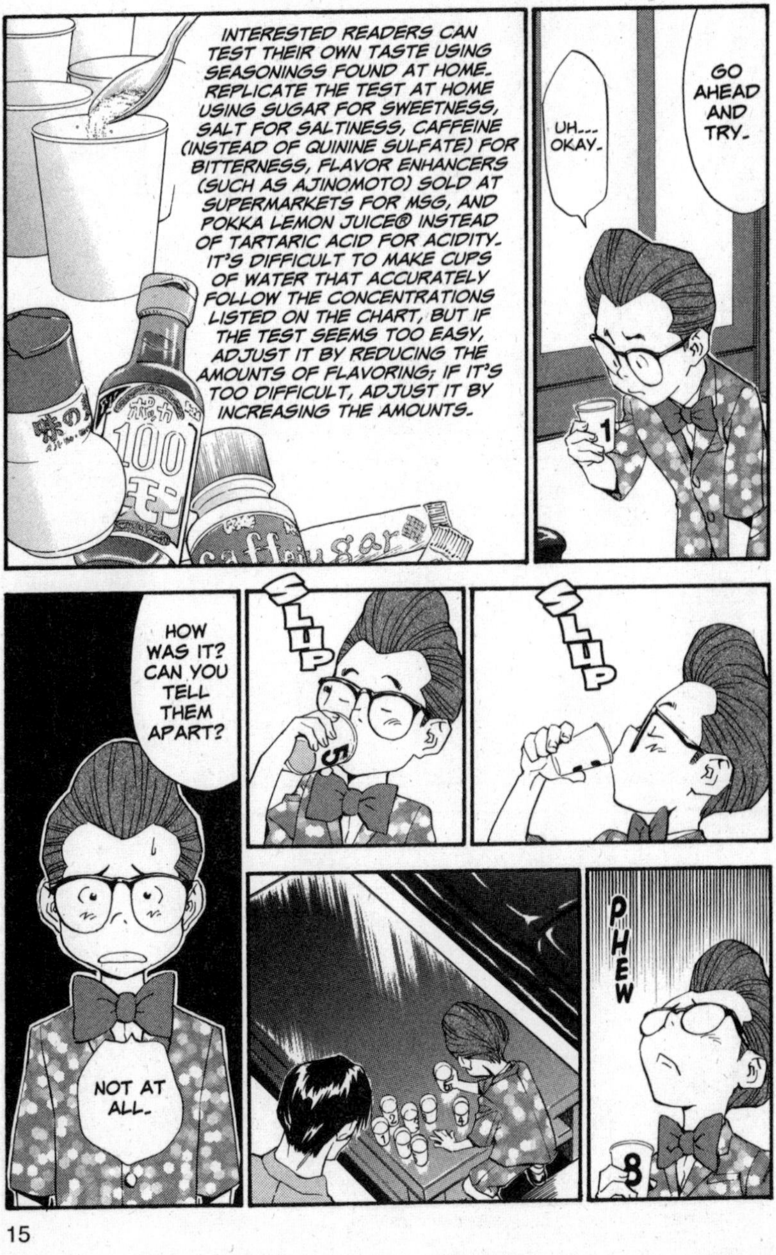
GO AHEAD AND TRY.
UH... OKAY.
INTERESTED READERS CAN TEST THEIR OWN TASTE USING SEASONINGS FOUND AT HOME. REPLICATE THE TEST AT HOME USING SUGAR FOR SWEETNESS, SALT FOR SALTINESS, CAFFEINE (INSTEAD OF QUININE SULFATE) FOR BITTERNESS, FLAVOR ENHANCERS (SUCH AS AJINOMOTO) SOLD AT SUPERMARKETS FOR MSG, AND POKKA LEMON JUICE® INSTEAD OF TARTARIC ACID FOR ACIDITY. IT'S DIFFICULT TO MAKE CUPS OF WATER THAT ACCURATELY FOLLOW THE CONCENTRATIONS LISTED ON THE CHART, BUT IF THE TEST SEEMS TOO EASY, ADJUST IT BY REDUCING THE AMOUNTS OF FLAVORING; IF IT'S TOO DIFFICULT, ADJUST IT BY INCREASING THE AMOUNTS.
SLUP
SLUP
PHEW
HOW WAS IT? CAN YOU TELL THEM APART?
NOT AT ALL.

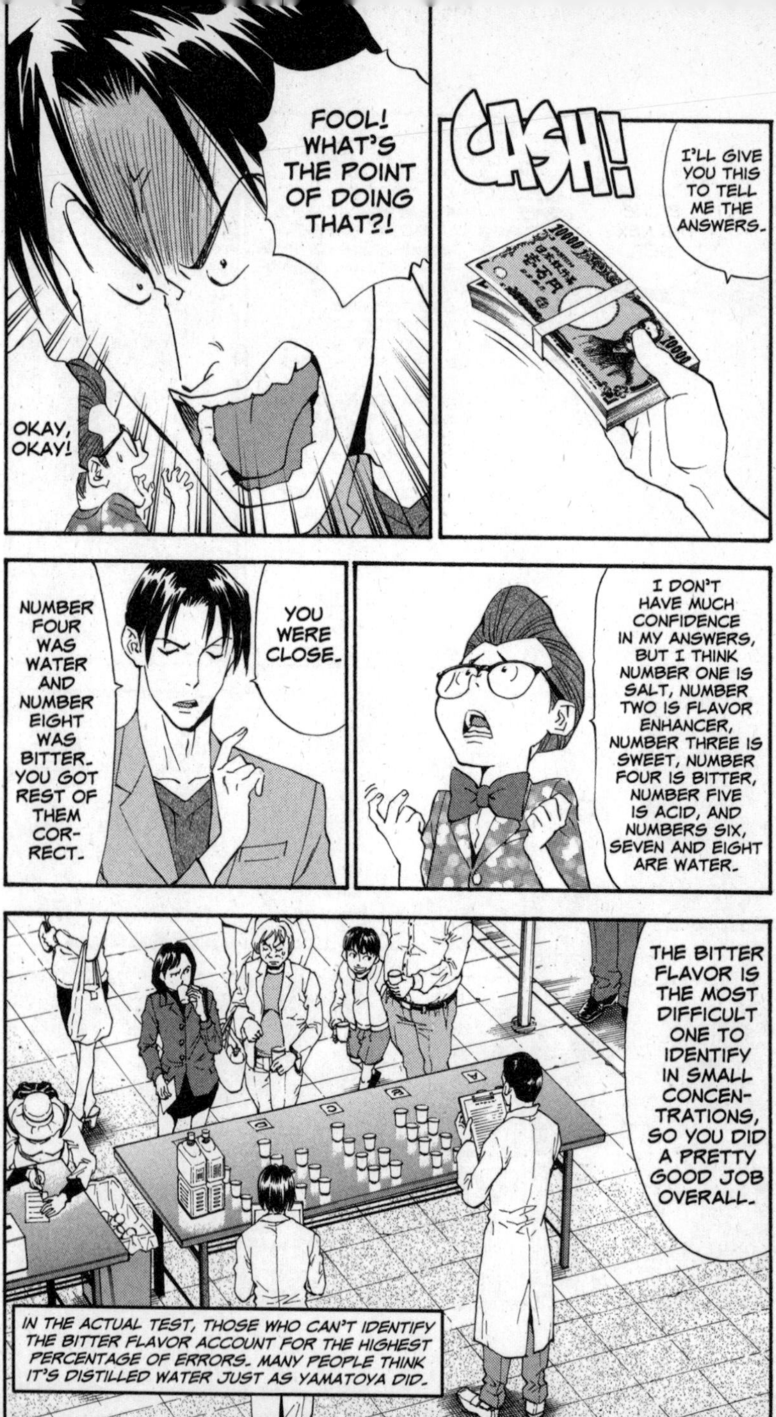
CASH!
I'LL GIVE YOU THIS TO TELL ME THE ANSWERS.
FOOL! WHAT'S THE POINT OF DOING THAT?!
OKAY, OKAY!
I DON'T HAVE MUCH CONFIDENCE IN MY ANSWERS, BUT I THINK NUMBER ONE IS SALT, NUMBER TWO IS FLAVOR ENHANCER, NUMBER THREE IS SWEET, NUMBER FOUR IS BITTER, NUMBER FIVE IS ACID, AND NUMBERS SIX, SEVEN AND EIGHT ARE WATER.
YOU WERE CLOSE.
NUMBER FOUR WAS WATER AND NUMBER EIGHT WAS BITTER. YOU GOT REST OF THEM CORRECT.
THE BITTER FLAVOR IS THE MOST DIFFICULT ONE TO IDENTIFY IN SMALL CONCENTRATIONS, SO YOU DID A PRETTY GOOD JOB OVERALL.
IN THE ACTUAL TEST, THOSE WHO CAN'T IDENTIFY THE BITTER FLAVOR ACCOUNT FOR THE HIGHEST PERCENTAGE OF ERRORS. MANY PEOPLE THINK IT'S DISTILLED WATER JUST AS YAMATOYA DID.

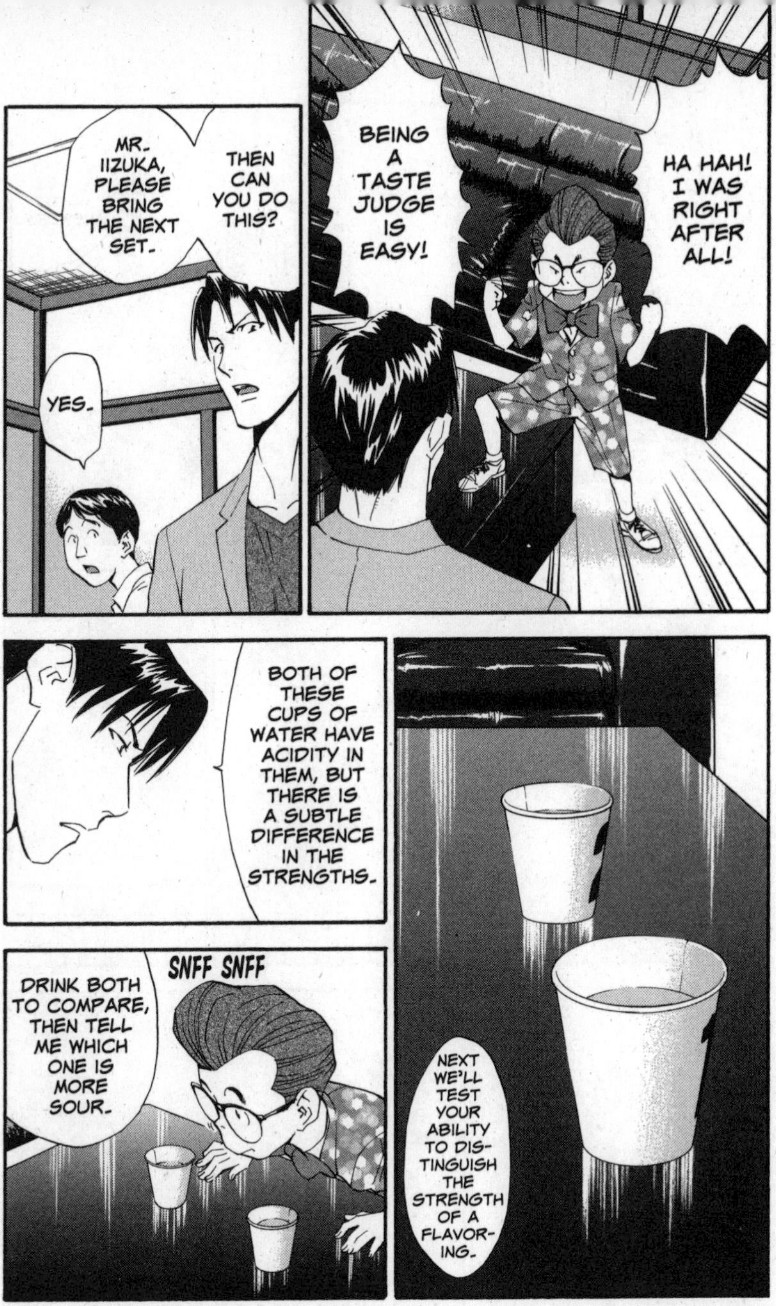
HA HAH! I WAS RIGHT AFTER ALL!
BEING A TASTE JUDGE IS EASY!
THEN CAN YOU DO THIS?
MR. IIZUKA, PLEASE BRING THE NEXT SET.
YES.
NEXT WE'LL TEST YOUR ABILITY TO DIS-TINGUISH THE STRENGTH OF A FLAVOR-ING.
BOTH OF THESE CUPS OF WATER HAVE ACIDITY IN THEM, BUT THERE IS A SUBTLE DIFFERENCE IN THE STRENGTHS.
SNFF SNFF
DRINK BOTH TO COMPARE, THEN TELL ME WHICH ONE IS MORE SOUR.

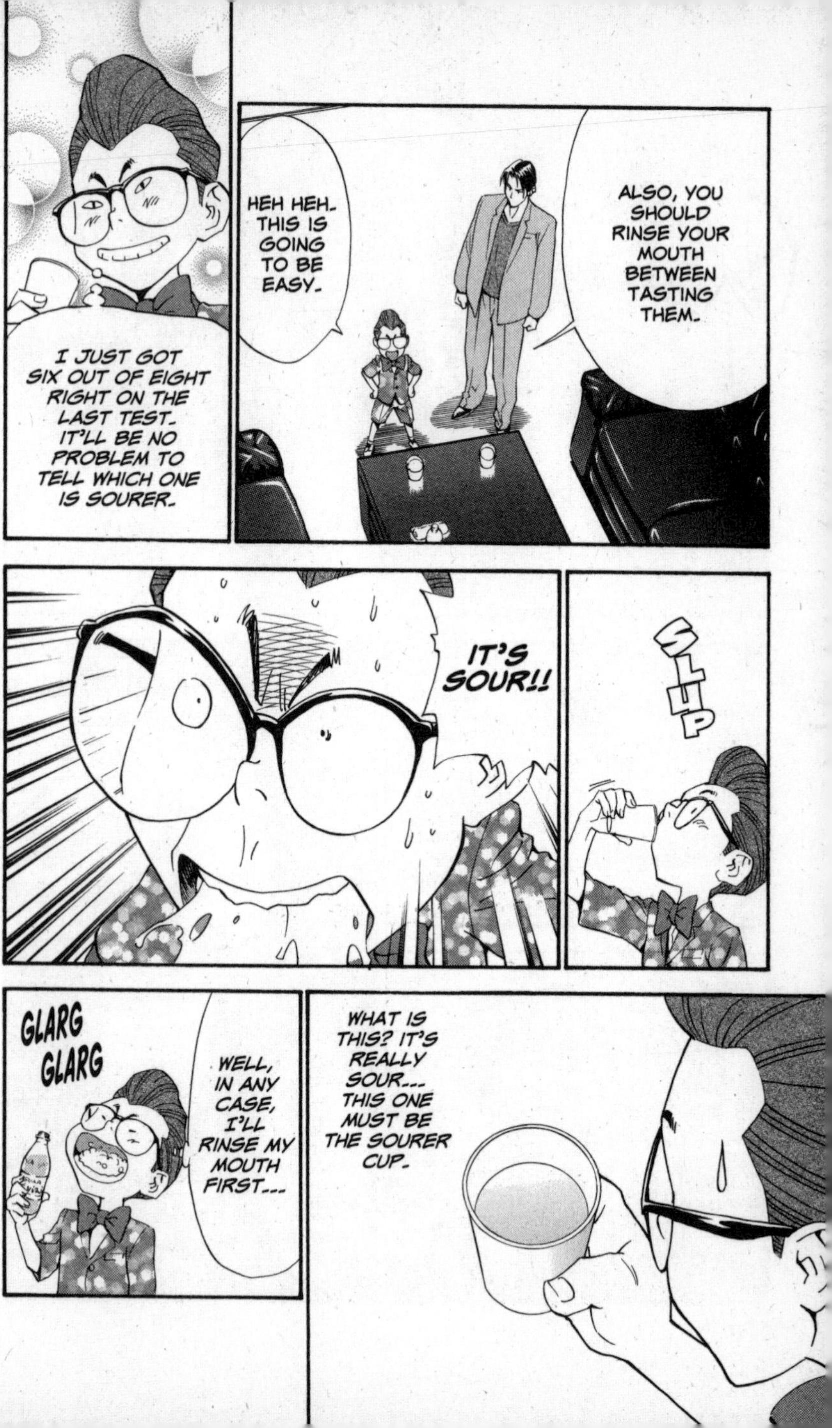
ALSO, YOU SHOULD RINSE YOUR MOUTH BETWEEN TASTING THEM.
HEH HEH. THIS IS GOING TO BE EASY.
I JUST GOT SIX OUT OF EIGHT RIGHT ON THE LAST TEST. IT'LL BE NO PROBLEM TO TELL WHICH ONE IS SOURER.
SLUP
IT'S SOUR!!
WHAT IS THIS? IT'S REALLY SOUR... THIS ONE MUST BE THE SOURER CUP.
WELL, IN ANY CASE, I'LL RINSE MY MOUTH FIRST...
GLARG GLARG

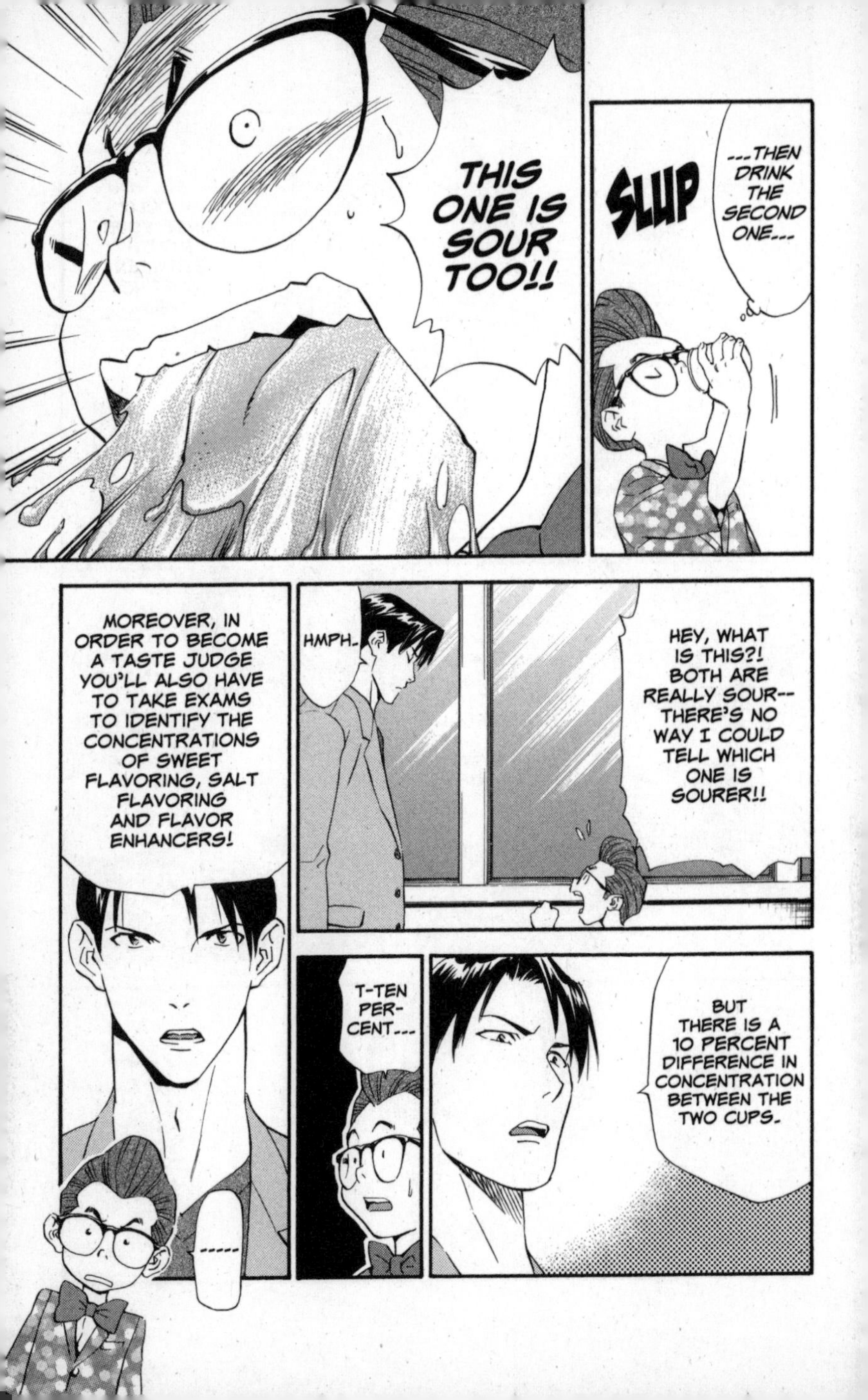
---THEN DRINK THE SECOND ONE---
SLUP
THIS ONE IS SOUR TOO!!
HEY, WHAT IS THIS?! BOTH ARE REALLY SOUR-- THERE'S NO WAY I COULD TELL WHICH ONE IS SOURER!!
HMPH.
BUT THERE IS A 10 PERCENT DIFFERENCE IN CONCENTRATION BETWEEN THE TWO CUPS.
T-TEN PER-CENT---
MOREOVER, IN ORDER TO BECOME A TASTE JUDGE YOU'LL ALSO HAVE TO TAKE EXAMS TO IDENTIFY THE CONCENTRATIONS OF SWEET FLAVORING, SALT FLAVORING AND FLAVOR ENHANCERS!

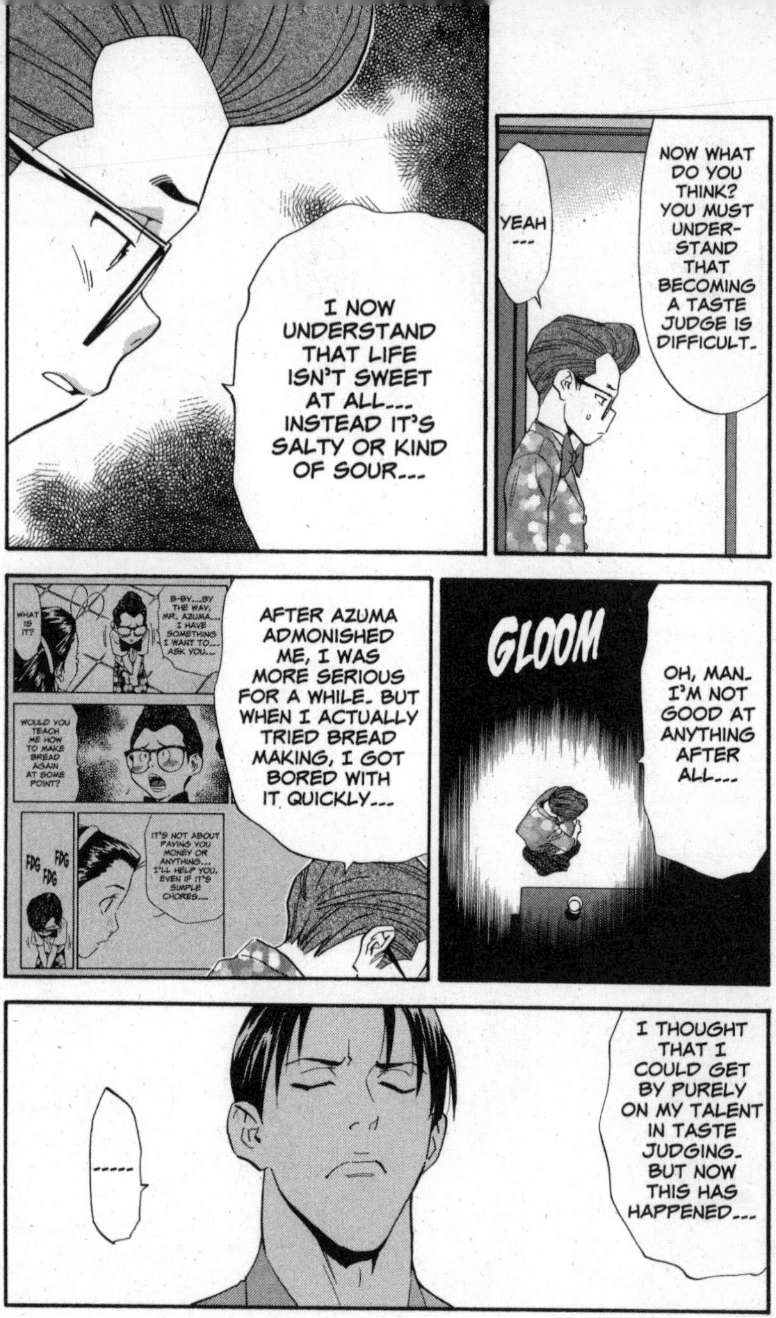
NOW WHAT DO YOU THINK? YOU MUST UNDER-STAND THAT BECOMING A TASTE JUDGE IS DIFFICULT.
YEAH ...
I NOW UNDERSTAND THAT LIFE ISN'T SWEET AT ALL... INSTEAD IT'S SALTY OR KIND OF SOUR...
GLOOM
OH, MAN. I'M NOT GOOD AT ANYTHING AFTER ALL...
AFTER AZUMA ADMONISHED ME, I WAS MORE SERIOUS FOR A WHILE. BUT WHEN I ACTUALLY TRIED BREAD MAKING, I GOT BORED WITH IT QUICKLY...
B-BY...BY THE WAY, MR. AZUMA... I HAVE SOMETHING I WANT TO... ASK YOU...
WHAT IS IT?
WOULD YOU TEACH ME HOW TO MAKE BREAD AGAIN AT SOME POINT?
IT'S NOT ABOUT PAYING YOU MONEY OR ANYTHING... I'LL HELP YOU, EVEN IF IT'S SIMPLE CHORES...
FDG FDG FDG
I THOUGHT THAT I COULD GET BY PURELY ON MY TALENT IN TASTE JUDGING. BUT NOW THIS HAS HAPPENED...

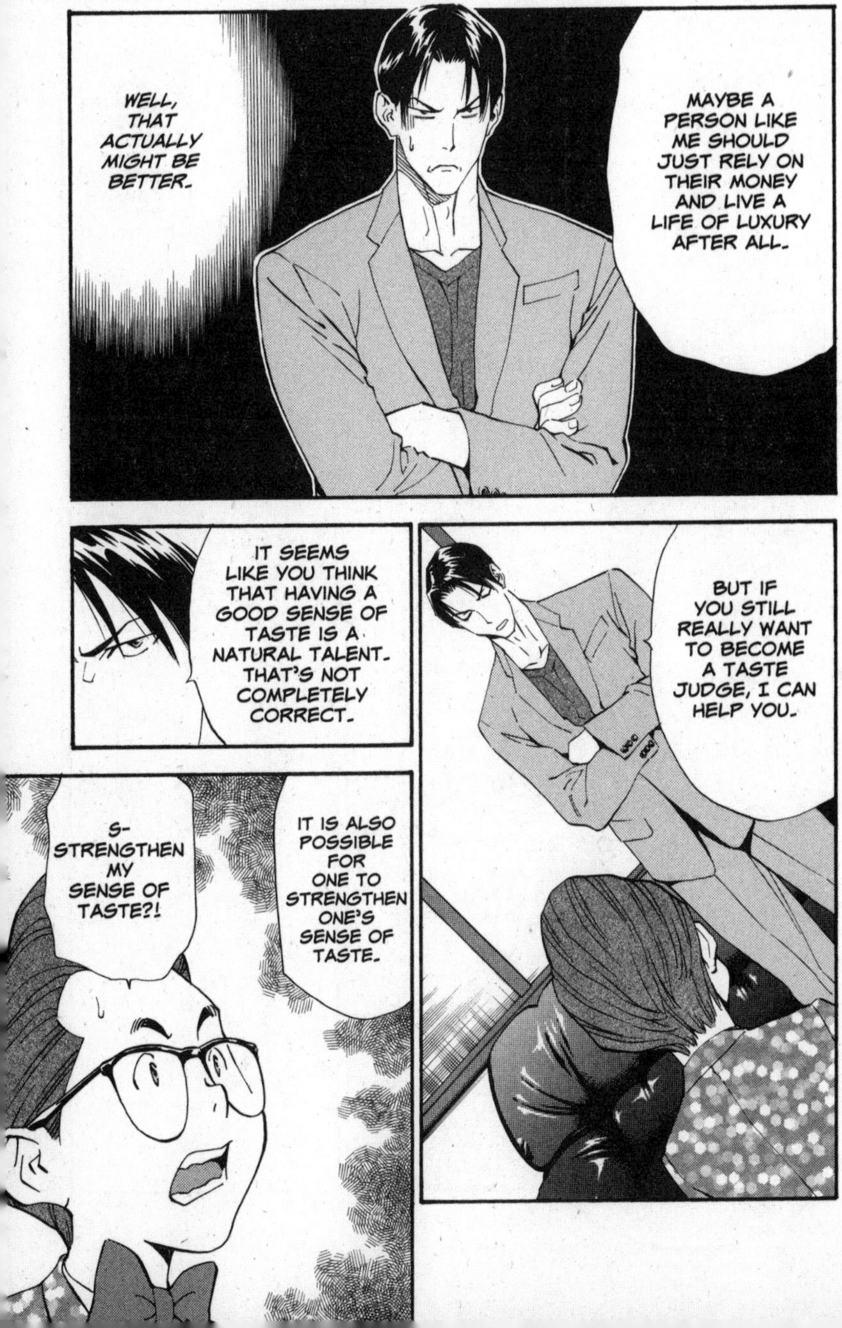
MAYBE A PERSON LIKE ME SHOULD JUST RELY ON THEIR MONEY AND LIVE A LIFE OF LUXURY AFTER ALL.
WELL, THAT ACTUALLY MIGHT BE BETTER.
BUT IF YOU STILL REALLY WANT TO BECOME A TASTE JUDGE, I CAN HELP YOU.
IT SEEMS LIKE YOU THINK THAT HAVING A GOOD SENSE OF TASTE IS A NATURAL TALENT. THAT'S NOT COMPLETELY CORRECT.
IT IS ALSO POSSIBLE FOR ONE TO STRENGTHEN ONE'S SENSE OF TASTE.
S-STRENGTHEN MY SENSE OF TASTE?!

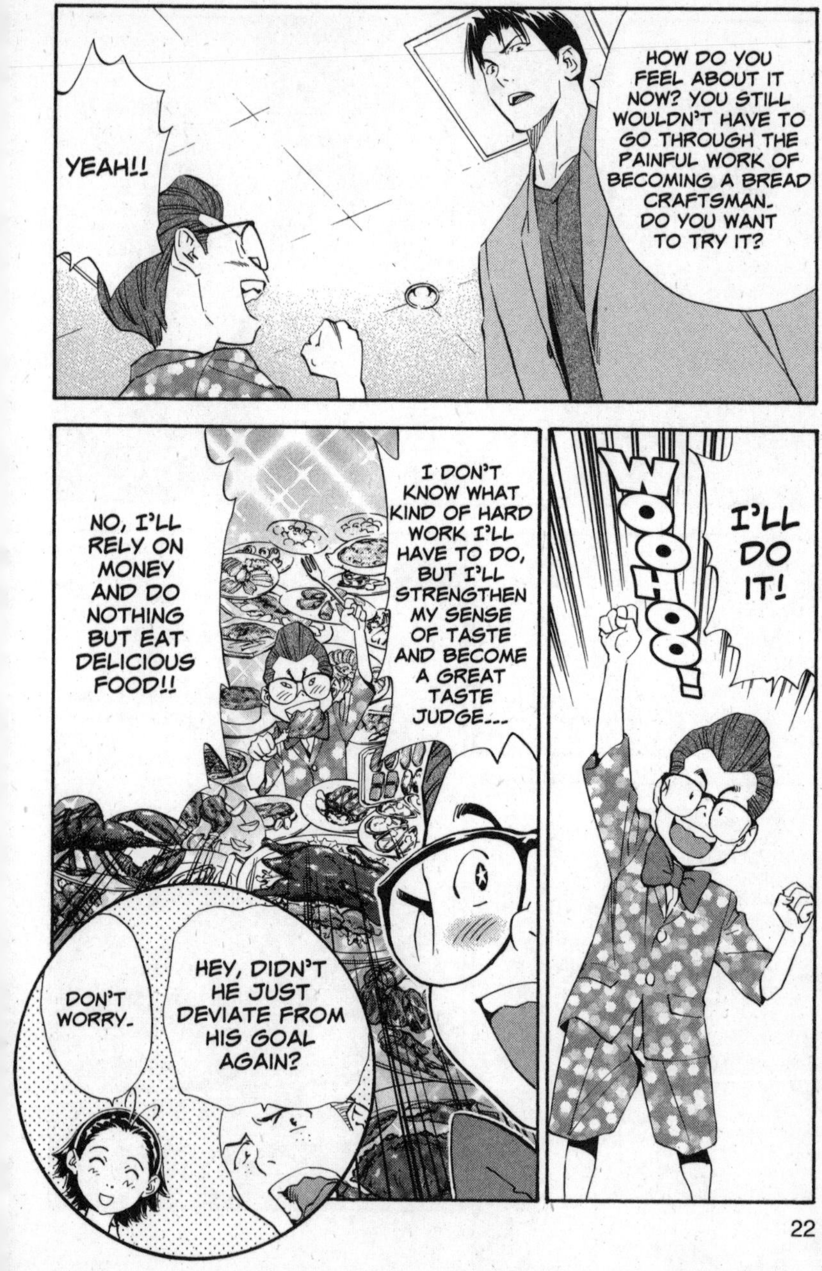

HOW DO YOU FEEL ABOUT IT NOW? YOU STILL WOULDN'T HAVE TO GO THROUGH THE PAINFUL WORK OF BECOMING A BREAD CRAFTSMAN. DO YOU WANT TO TRY IT?
YEAH!!
WOOHOO!
I'LL DO IT!
I DON'T KNOW WHAT KIND OF HARD WORK I'LL HAVE TO DO, BUT I'LL STRENGTHEN MY SENSE OF TASTE AND BECOME A GREAT TASTE JUDGE...
NO, I'LL RELY ON MONEY AND DO NOTHING BUT EAT DELICIOUS FOOD!!
HEY, DIDN'T HE JUST DEVIATE FROM HIS GOAL AGAIN?
DON'T WORRY.

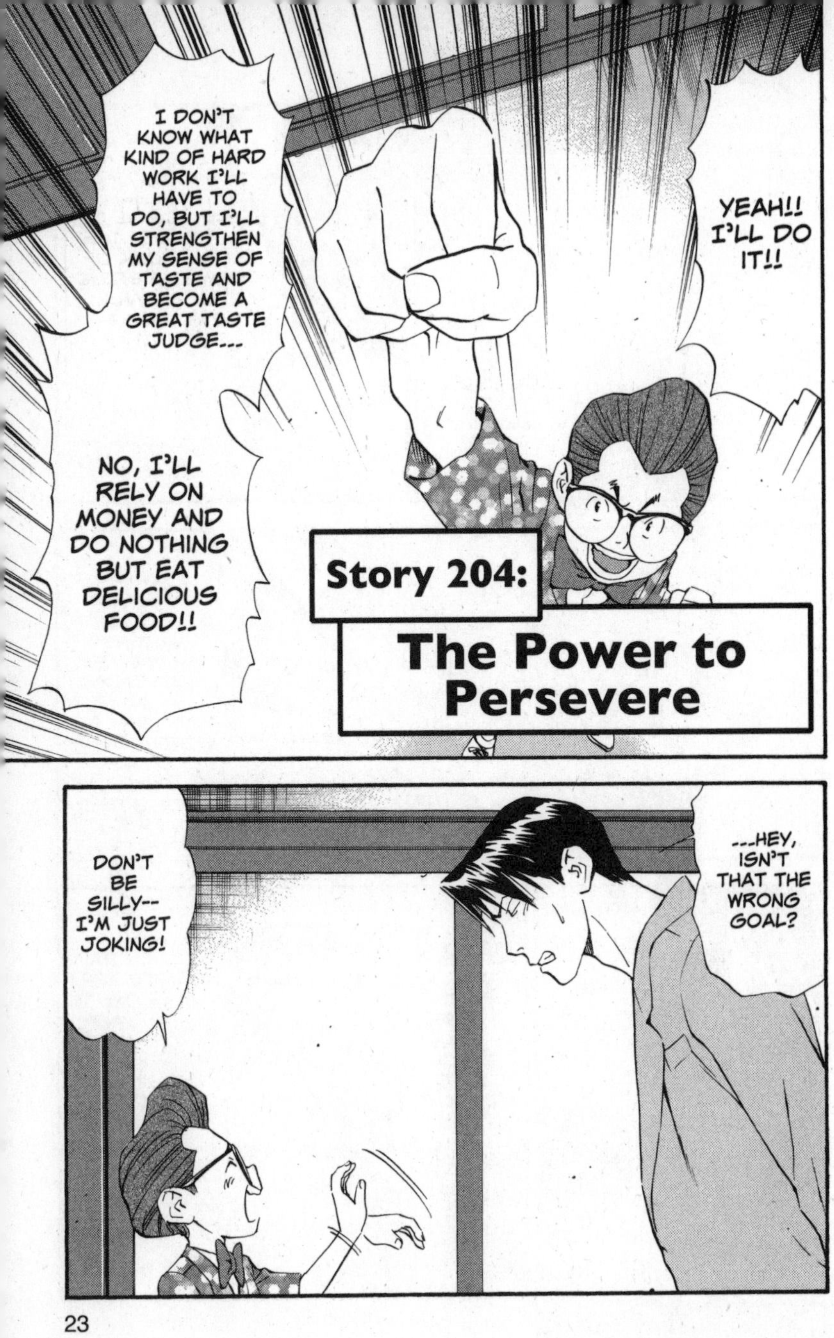
YEAH!! I'LL DO IT!!
I DON'T KNOW WHAT KIND OF HARD WORK I'LL HAVE TO DO, BUT I'LL STRENGTHEN MY SENSE OF TASTE AND BECOME A GREAT TASTE JUDGE...
NO, I'LL RELY ON MONEY AND DO NOTHING BUT EAT DELICIOUS FOOD!!
Story 204:
The Power to Persevere
---HEY, ISN'T THAT THE WRONG GOAL?
DON'T BE SILLY-- I'M JUST JOKING!

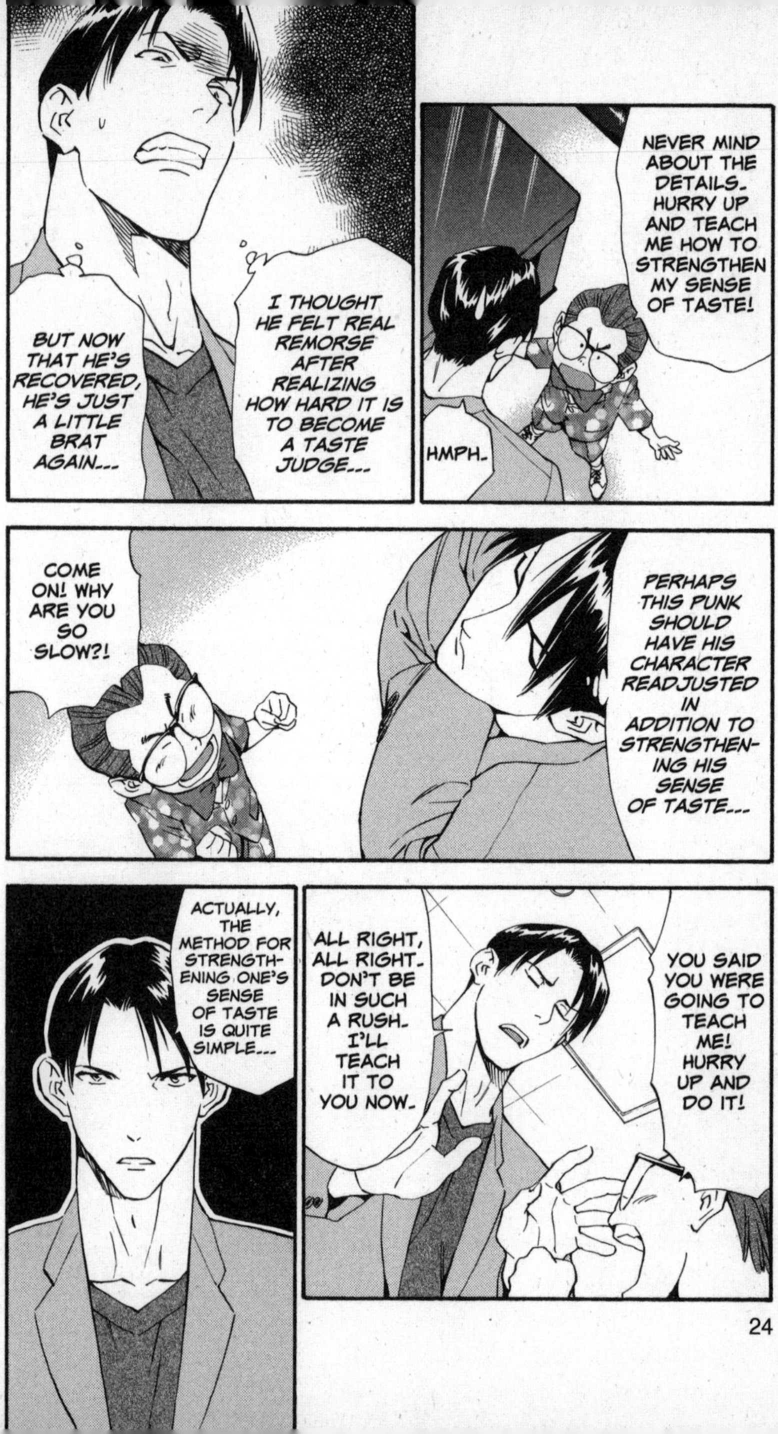
NEVER MIND ABOUT THE DETAILS. HURRY UP AND TEACH ME HOW TO STRENGTHEN MY SENSE OF TASTE!
HMPH.
I THOUGHT HE FELT REAL REMORSE AFTER REALIZING HOW HARD IT IS TO BECOME A TASTE JUDGE...
BUT NOW THAT HE'S RECOVERED, HE'S JUST A LITTLE BRAT AGAIN...
PERHAPS THIS PUNK SHOULD HAVE HIS CHARACTER READJUSTED IN ADDITION TO STRENGTHENING HIS SENSE OF TASTE...
COME ON! WHY ARE YOU SO SLOW?!
YOU SAID YOU WERE GOING TO TEACH ME! HURRY UP AND DO IT!
ALL RIGHT, ALL RIGHT. DON'T BE IN SUCH A RUSH. I'LL TEACH IT TO YOU NOW.
ACTUALLY, THE METHOD FOR STRENGTHENING ONE'S SENSE OF TASTE IS QUITE SIMPLE...

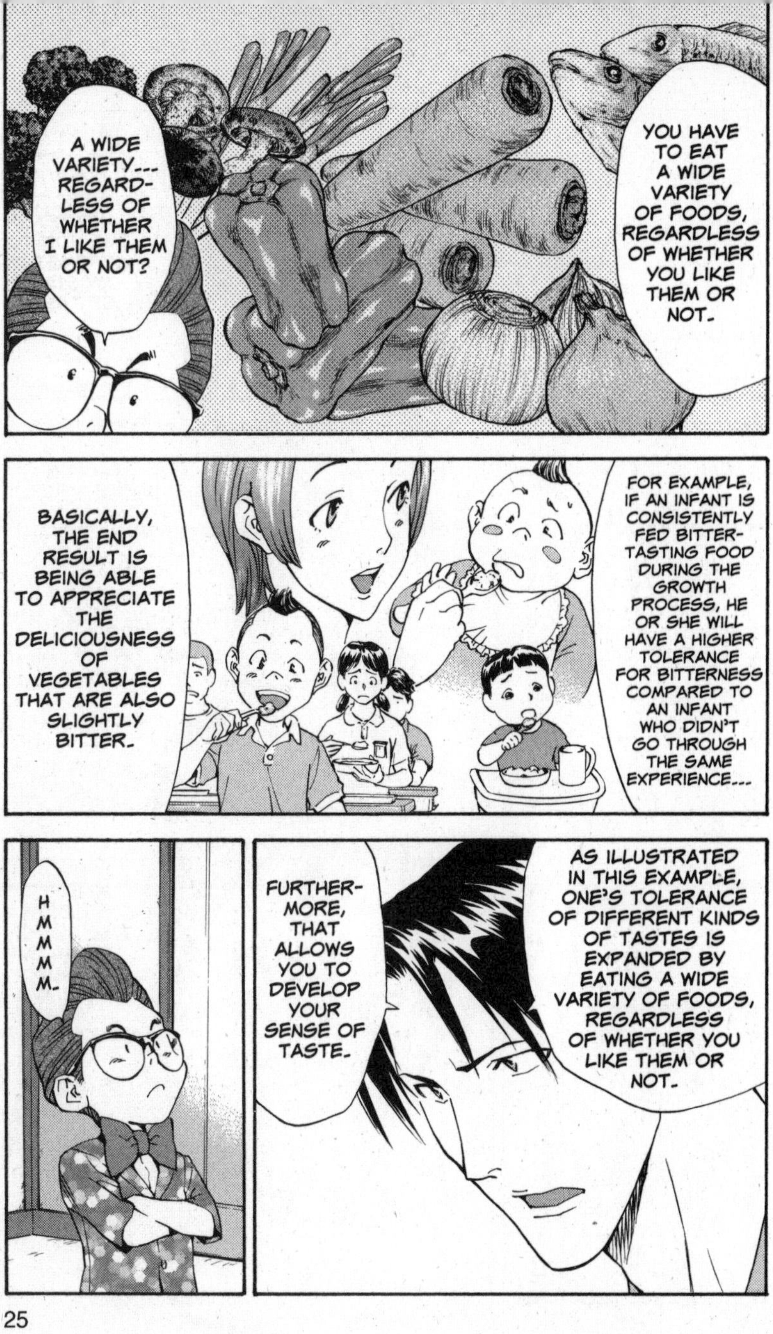
YOU HAVE TO EAT A WIDE VARIETY OF FOODS, REGARDLESS OF WHETHER YOU LIKE THEM OR NOT.
A WIDE VARIETY... REGARDLESS OF WHETHER I LIKE THEM OR NOT?
FOR EXAMPLE, IF AN INFANT IS CONSISTENTLY FED BITTER-TASTING FOOD DURING THE GROWTH PROCESS, HE OR SHE WILL HAVE A HIGHER TOLERANCE FOR BITTERNESS COMPARED TO AN INFANT WHO DIDN'T GO THROUGH THE SAME EXPERIENCE...
BASICALLY, THE END RESULT IS BEING ABLE TO APPRECIATE THE DELICIOUSNESS OF VEGETABLES THAT ARE ALSO SLIGHTLY BITTER.
AS ILLUSTRATED IN THIS EXAMPLE, ONE'S TOLERANCE OF DIFFERENT KINDS OF TASTES IS EXPANDED BY EATING A WIDE VARIETY OF FOODS, REGARDLESS OF WHETHER YOU LIKE THEM OR NOT.
FURTHERMORE, THAT ALLOWS YOU TO DEVELOP YOUR SENSE OF TASTE.
HMMMM.

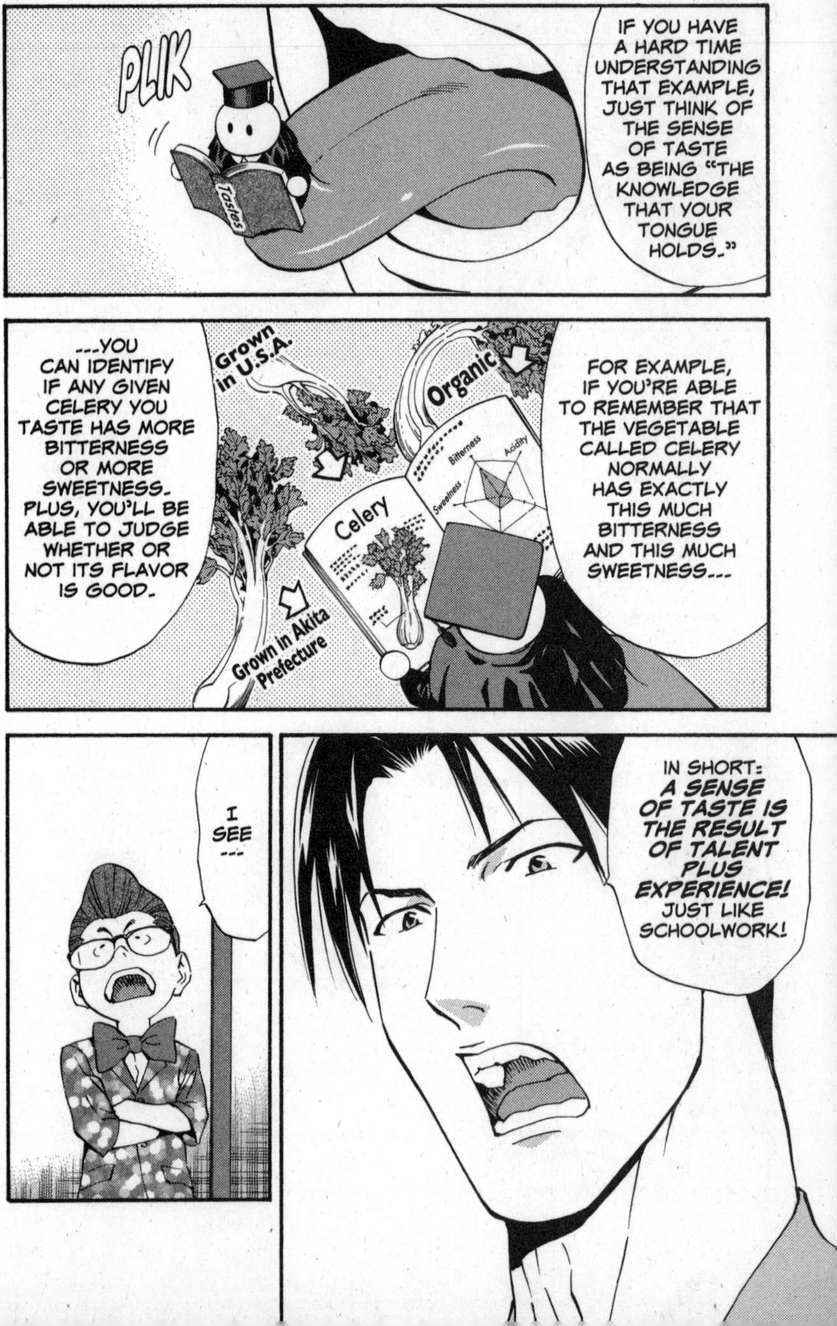
IF YOU HAVE A HARD TIME UNDERSTANDING THAT EXAMPLE, JUST THINK OF THE SENSE OF TASTE AS BEING "THE KNOWLEDGE THAT YOUR TONGUE HOLDS."
PLIK
Tastes
FOR EXAMPLE, IF YOU'RE ABLE TO REMEMBER THAT THE VEGETABLE CALLED CELERY NORMALLY HAS EXACTLY THIS MUCH BITTERNESS AND THIS MUCH SWEETNESS...
Organic
Grown in U.S.A.
Acidity
Bitterness
Sweetness
Celery
Grown in Akita Prefecture
...YOU CAN IDENTIFY IF ANY GIVEN CELERY YOU TASTE HAS MORE BITTERNESS OR MORE SWEETNESS. PLUS, YOU'LL BE ABLE TO JUDGE WHETHER OR NOT ITS FLAVOR IS GOOD.
IN SHORT: A SENSE OF TASTE IS THE RESULT OF TALENT PLUS EXPERIENCE! JUST LIKE SCHOOLWORK!
I SEE...

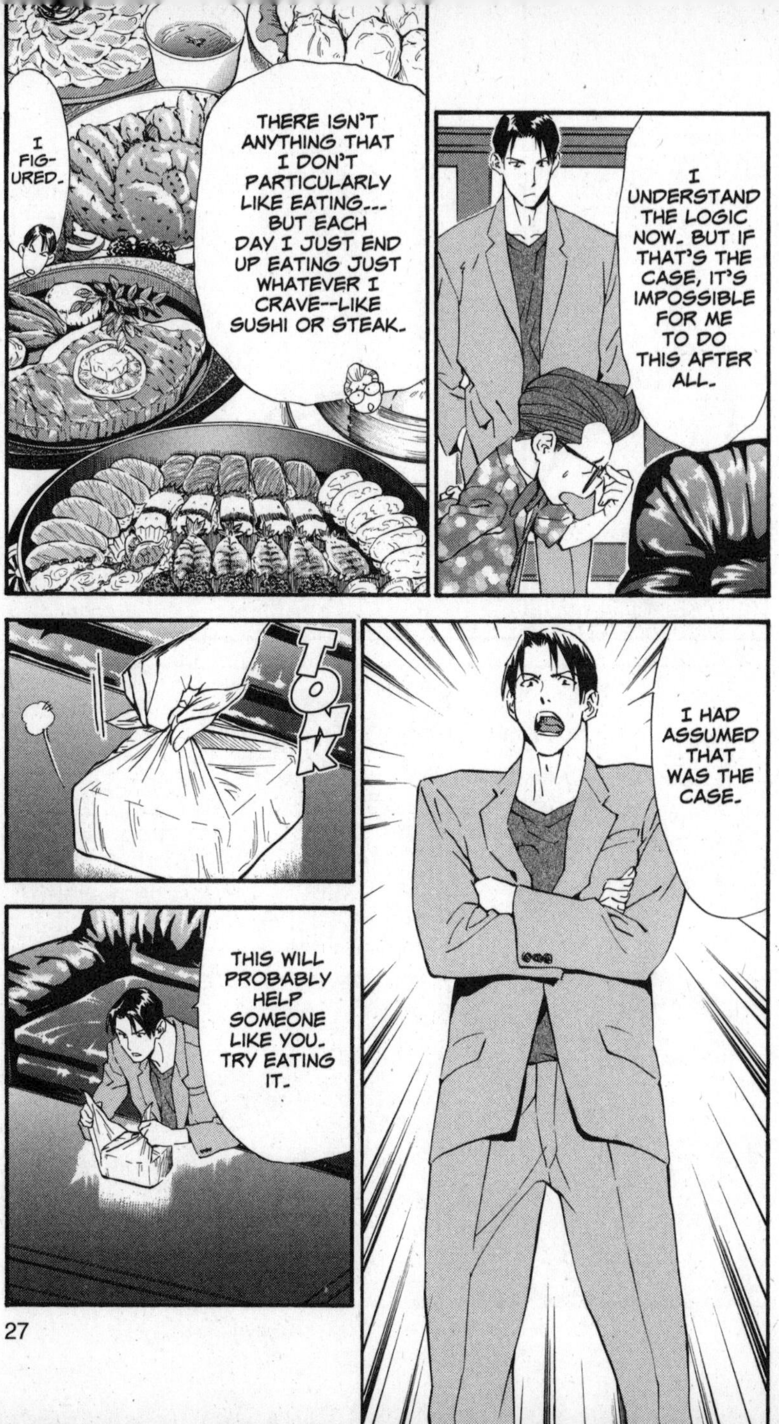
I UNDERSTAND THE LOGIC NOW. BUT IF THAT'S THE CASE, IT'S IMPOSSIBLE FOR ME TO DO THIS AFTER ALL.
THERE ISN'T ANYTHING THAT I DON'T PARTICULARLY LIKE EATING... BUT EACH DAY I JUST END UP EATING JUST WHATEVER I CRAVE--LIKE SUSHI OR STEAK.
I FIGURED.
I HAD ASSUMED THAT WAS THE CASE.
TONK
THIS WILL PROBABLY HELP SOMEONE LIKE YOU. TRY EATING IT.

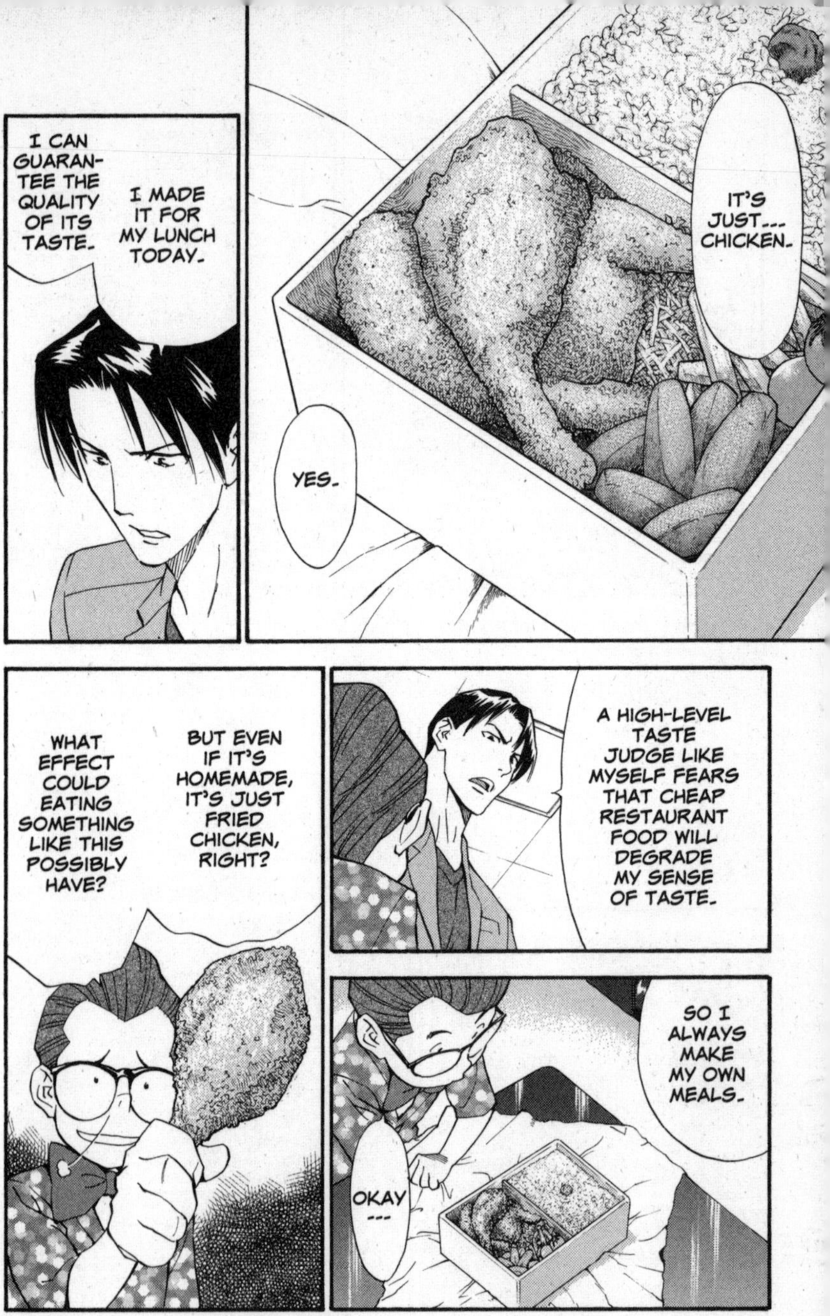
IT'S JUST... CHICKEN.
YES.
I MADE IT FOR MY LUNCH TODAY.
I CAN GUARANTEE THE QUALITY OF ITS TASTE.
A HIGH-LEVEL TASTE JUDGE LIKE MYSELF FEARS THAT CHEAP RESTAURANT FOOD WILL DEGRADE MY SENSE OF TASTE.
SO I ALWAYS MAKE MY OWN MEALS.
OKAY...
BUT EVEN IF IT'S HOMEMADE, IT'S JUST FRIED CHICKEN, RIGHT?
WHAT EFFECT COULD EATING SOMETHING LIKE THIS POSSIBLY HAVE?

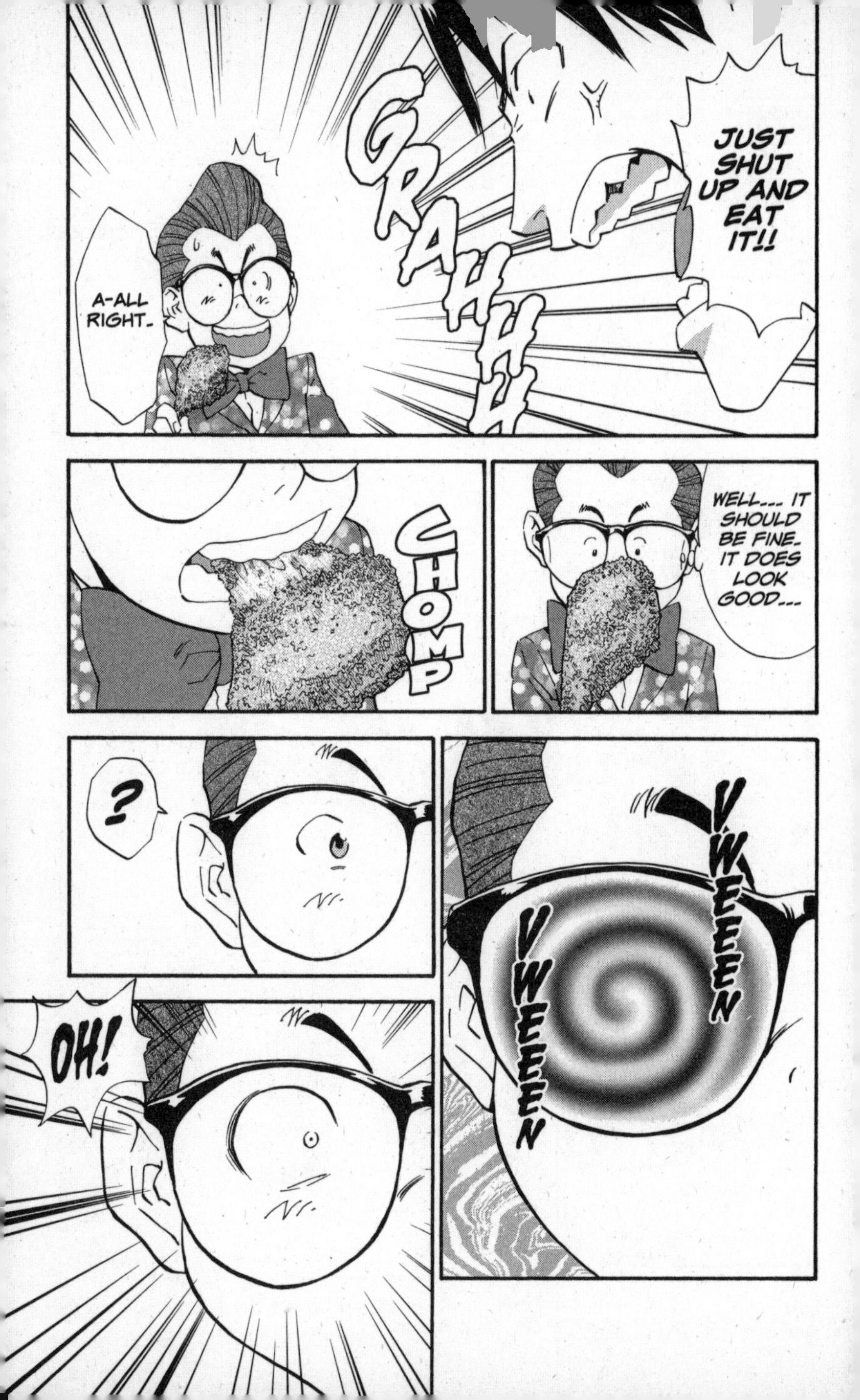
JUST SHUT UP AND EAT IT!!
GRAHHHH
A-ALL RIGHT...
WELL... IT SHOULD BE FINE. IT DOES LOOK GOOD...
CHOMP
VWEEEEN
VWEEEEN
?
OH!

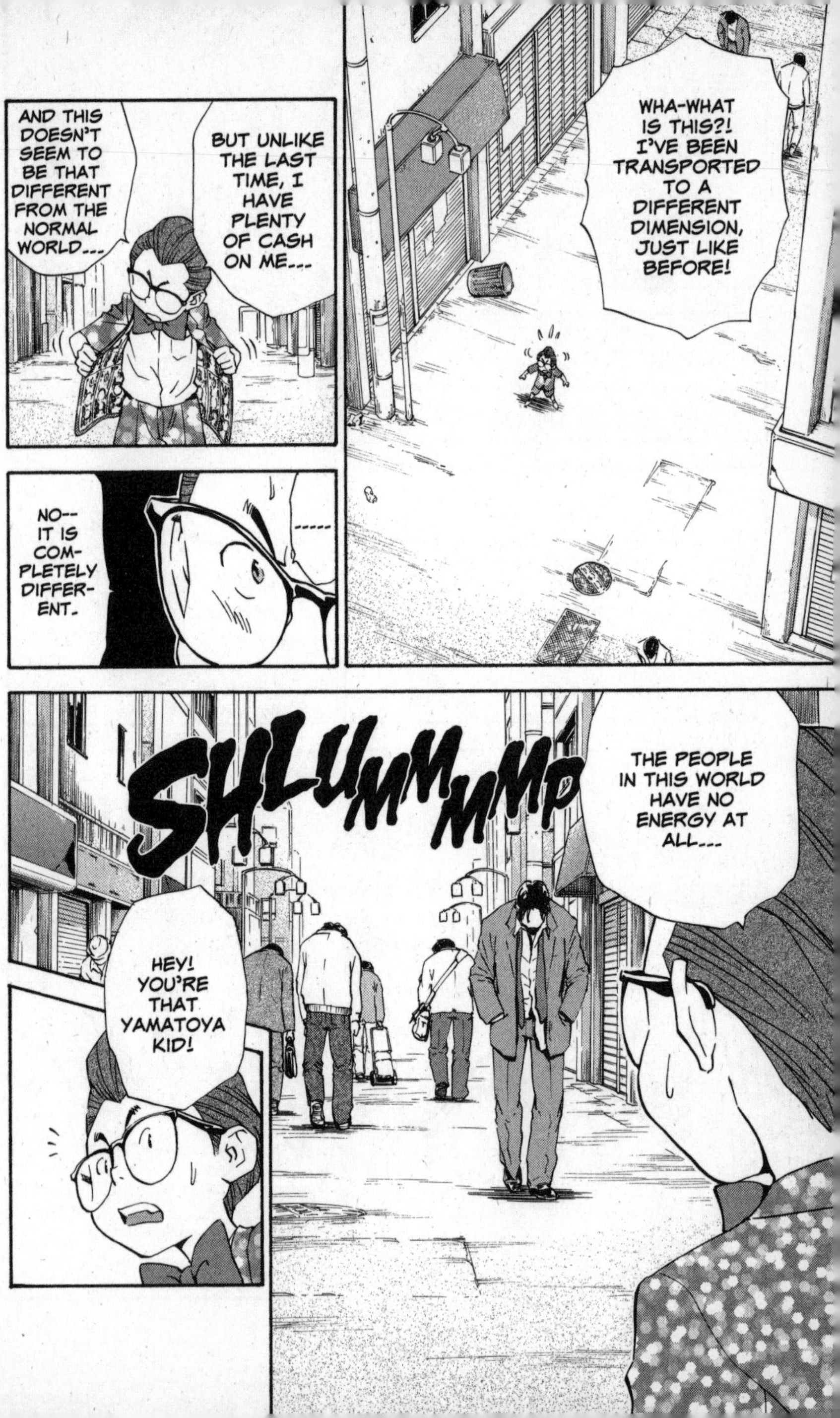
WHA-WHAT IS THIS?! I'VE BEEN TRANSPORTED TO A DIFFERENT DIMENSION, JUST LIKE BEFORE!
BUT UNLIKE THE LAST TIME, I HAVE PLENTY OF CASH ON ME...
AND THIS DOESN'T SEEM TO BE THAT DIFFERENT FROM THE NORMAL WORLD...

NO-- IT IS COM-PLETELY DIFFER-ENT.
THE PEOPLE IN THIS WORLD HAVE NO ENERGY AT ALL...
SHLUMMMMMP
HEY! YOU'RE THAT YAMATOYA KID!

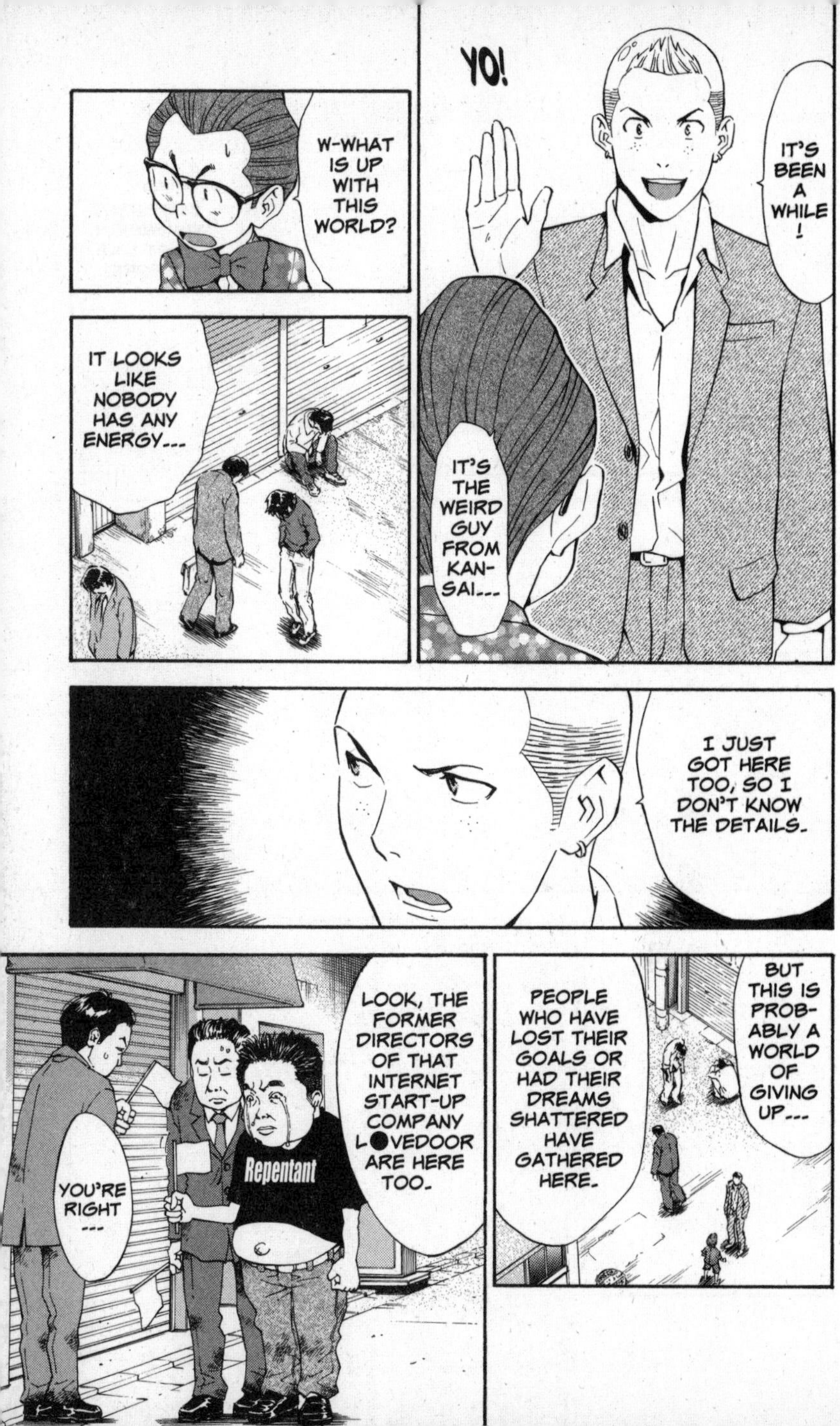
YO!
IT'S BEEN A WHILE!
IT'S THE WEIRD GUY FROM KAN-SAI...
W-WHAT IS UP WITH THIS WORLD?
IT LOOKS LIKE NOBODY HAS ANY ENERGY...
I JUST GOT HERE TOO, SO I DON'T KNOW THE DETAILS.
BUT THIS IS PROBABLY A WORLD OF GIVING UP...
PEOPLE WHO HAVE LOST THEIR GOALS OR HAD THEIR DREAMS SHATTERED HAVE GATHERED HERE.
LOOK, THE FORMER DIRECTORS OF THAT INTERNET START-UP COMPANY L●VEDOOR ARE HERE TOO.
Repentant
YOU'RE RIGHT...

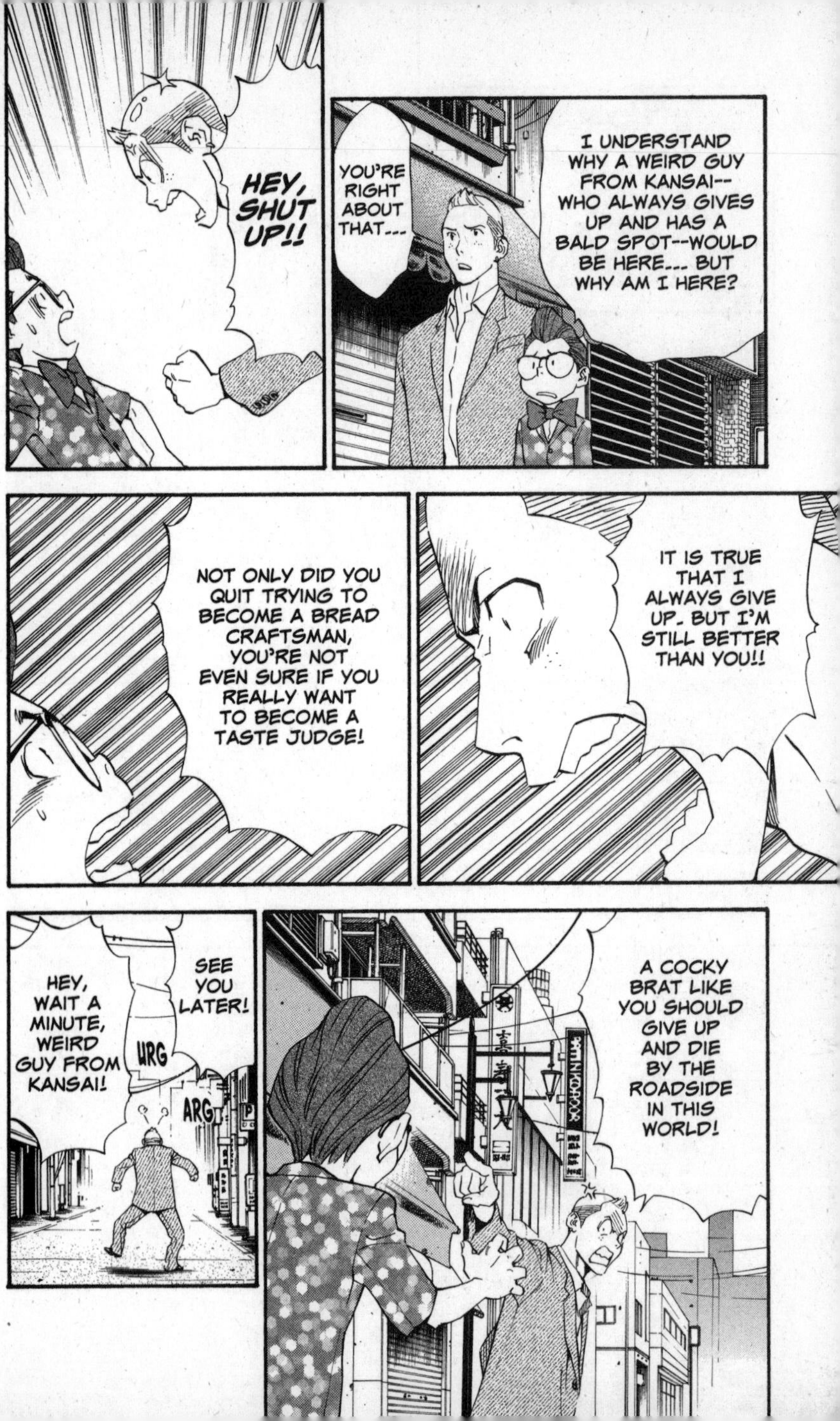
I UNDERSTAND WHY A WEIRD GUY FROM KANSAI-- WHO ALWAYS GIVES UP AND HAS A BALD SPOT--WOULD BE HERE... BUT WHY AM I HERE?
YOU'RE RIGHT ABOUT THAT...
HEY, SHUT UP!!
IT IS TRUE THAT I ALWAYS GIVE UP. BUT I'M STILL BETTER THAN YOU!!
NOT ONLY DID YOU QUIT TRYING TO BECOME A BREAD CRAFTSMAN, YOU'RE NOT EVEN SURE IF YOU REALLY WANT TO BECOME A TASTE JUDGE!
A COCKY BRAT LIKE YOU SHOULD GIVE UP AND DIE BY THE ROADSIDE IN THIS WORLD!
SEE YOU LATER!
HEY, WAIT A MINUTE, WEIRD GUY FROM KANSAI!
URG
ARG

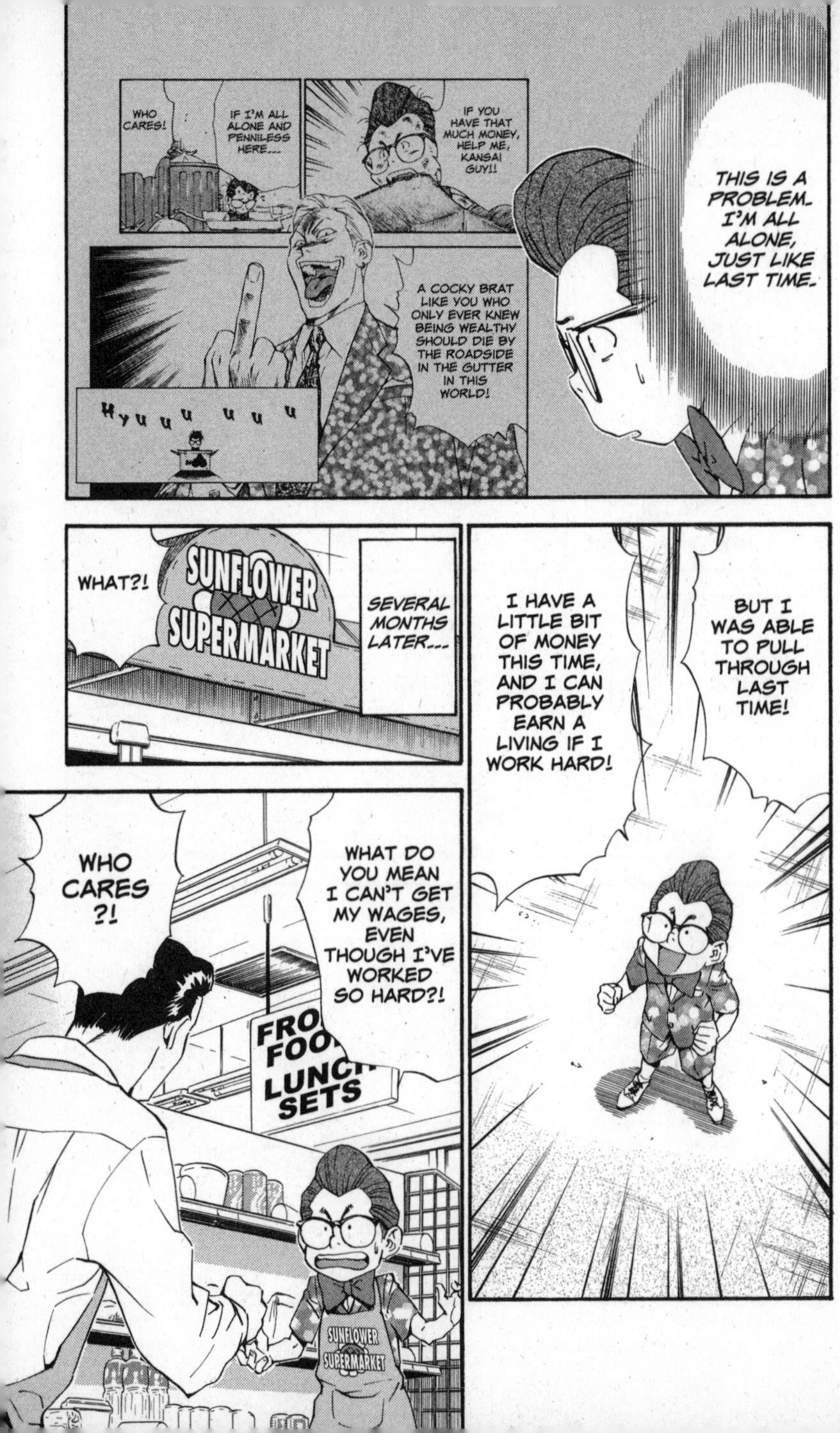
THIS IS A PROBLEM... I'M ALL ALONE, JUST LIKE LAST TIME...
IF YOU HAVE THAT MUCH MONEY, HELP ME, KANSAI GUY!!
IF I'M ALL ALONE AND PENNILESS HERE...
WHO CARES!
A COCKY BRAT LIKE YOU WHO ONLY EVER KNEW BEING WEALTHY SHOULD DIE BY THE ROADSIDE IN THE GUTTER IN THIS WORLD!
Hyuuu uuu
BUT I WAS ABLE TO PULL THROUGH LAST TIME!
I HAVE A LITTLE BIT OF MONEY THIS TIME, AND I CAN PROBABLY EARN A LIVING IF I WORK HARD!
SEVERAL MONTHS LATER...
SUNFLOWER SUPERMARKET
WHAT?!
WHAT DO YOU MEAN I CAN'T GET MY WAGES, EVEN THOUGH I'VE WORKED SO HARD?!
WHO CARES?!
LUNCH SETS
SUNFLOWER SUPERMARKET

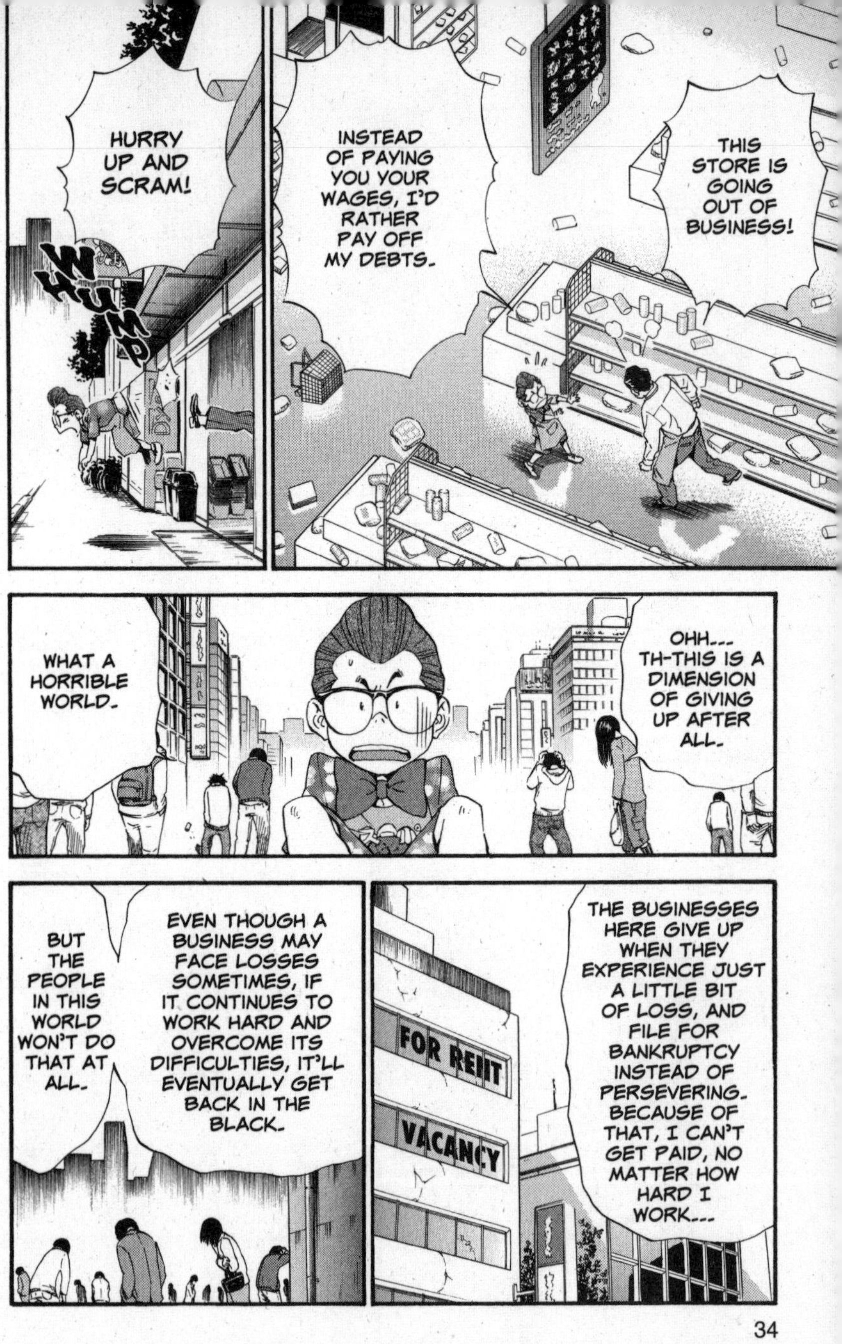
THIS STORE IS GOING OUT OF BUSINESS!
INSTEAD OF PAYING YOU YOUR WAGES, I'D RATHER PAY OFF MY DEBTS.
HURRY UP AND SCRAM!
WHUMP
OHH... TH-THIS IS A DIMENSION OF GIVING UP AFTER ALL.
WHAT A HORRIBLE WORLD.
THE BUSINESSES HERE GIVE UP WHEN THEY EXPERIENCE JUST A LITTLE BIT OF LOSS, AND FILE FOR BANKRUPTCY INSTEAD OF PERSEVERING. BECAUSE OF THAT, I CAN'T GET PAID, NO MATTER HOW HARD I WORK...
FOR RENT
VACANCY
EVEN THOUGH A BUSINESS MAY FACE LOSSES SOMETIMES, IF IT CONTINUES TO WORK HARD AND OVERCOME ITS DIFFICULTIES, IT'LL EVENTUALLY GET BACK IN THE BLACK.
BUT THE PEOPLE IN THIS WORLD WON'T DO THAT AT ALL.

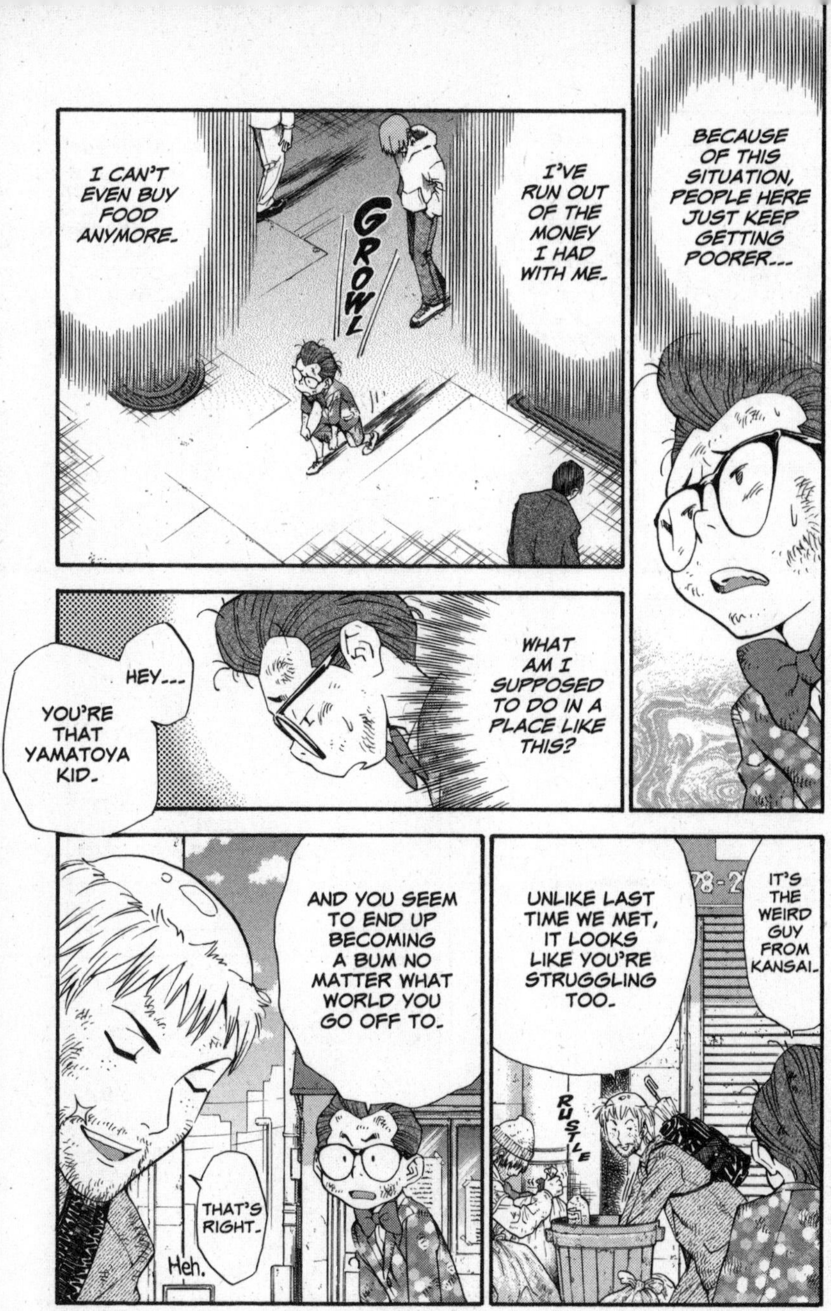
BECAUSE OF THIS SITUATION, PEOPLE HERE JUST KEEP GETTING POORER...
I'VE RUN OUT OF THE MONEY I HAD WITH ME.
GROWL
I CAN'T EVEN BUY FOOD ANYMORE.
WHAT AM I SUPPOSED TO DO IN A PLACE LIKE THIS?
HEY... YOU'RE THAT YAMATOYA KID.
IT'S THE WEIRD GUY FROM KANSAI.
UNLIKE LAST TIME WE MET, IT LOOKS LIKE YOU'RE STRUGGLING TOO.
RUSTLE
AND YOU SEEM TO END UP BECOMING A BUM NO MATTER WHAT WORLD YOU GO OFF TO.
THAT'S RIGHT.
Heh.

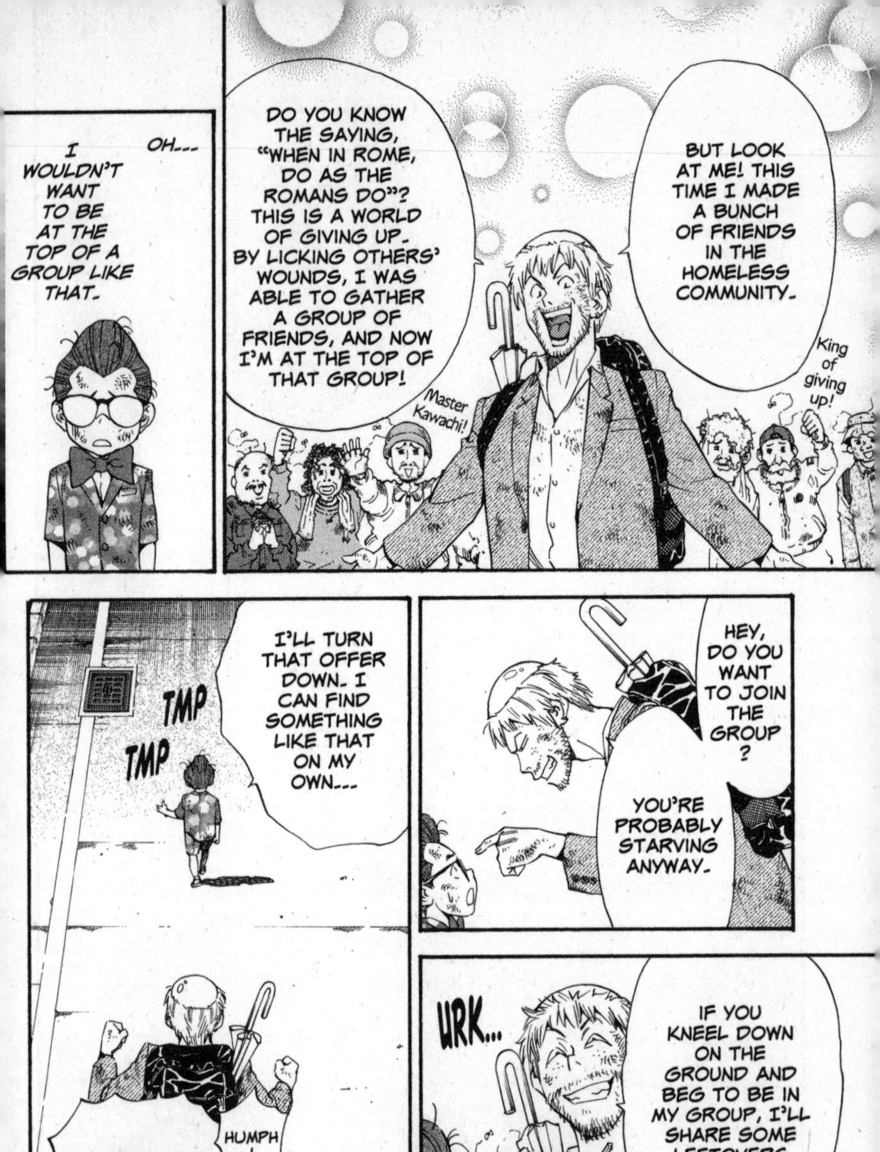
BUT LOOK AT ME! THIS TIME I MADE A BUNCH OF FRIENDS IN THE HOMELESS COMMUNITY.
King of giving up!
DO YOU KNOW THE SAYING, "WHEN IN ROME, DO AS THE ROMANS DO"? THIS IS A WORLD OF GIVING UP. BY LICKING OTHERS' WOUNDS, I WAS ABLE TO GATHER A GROUP OF FRIENDS, AND NOW I'M AT THE TOP OF THAT GROUP!
Master Kawachi!
OH...
I WOULDN'T WANT TO BE AT THE TOP OF A GROUP LIKE THAT.
HEY, DO YOU WANT TO JOIN THE GROUP?
YOU'RE PROBABLY STARVING ANYWAY.
IF YOU KNEEL DOWN ON THE GROUND AND BEG TO BE IN MY GROUP, I'LL SHARE SOME LEFTOVERS WITH YOU.
URK...
I'LL TURN THAT OFFER DOWN. I CAN FIND SOMETHING LIKE THAT ON MY OWN...
TMP
TMP
HUMPH!
YOU'RE SUCH A RUDE LITTLE BRAT! HOW CAN YOU IGNORE MY KINDNESS?!

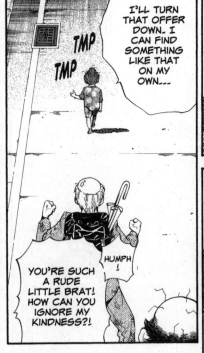

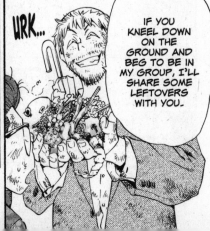

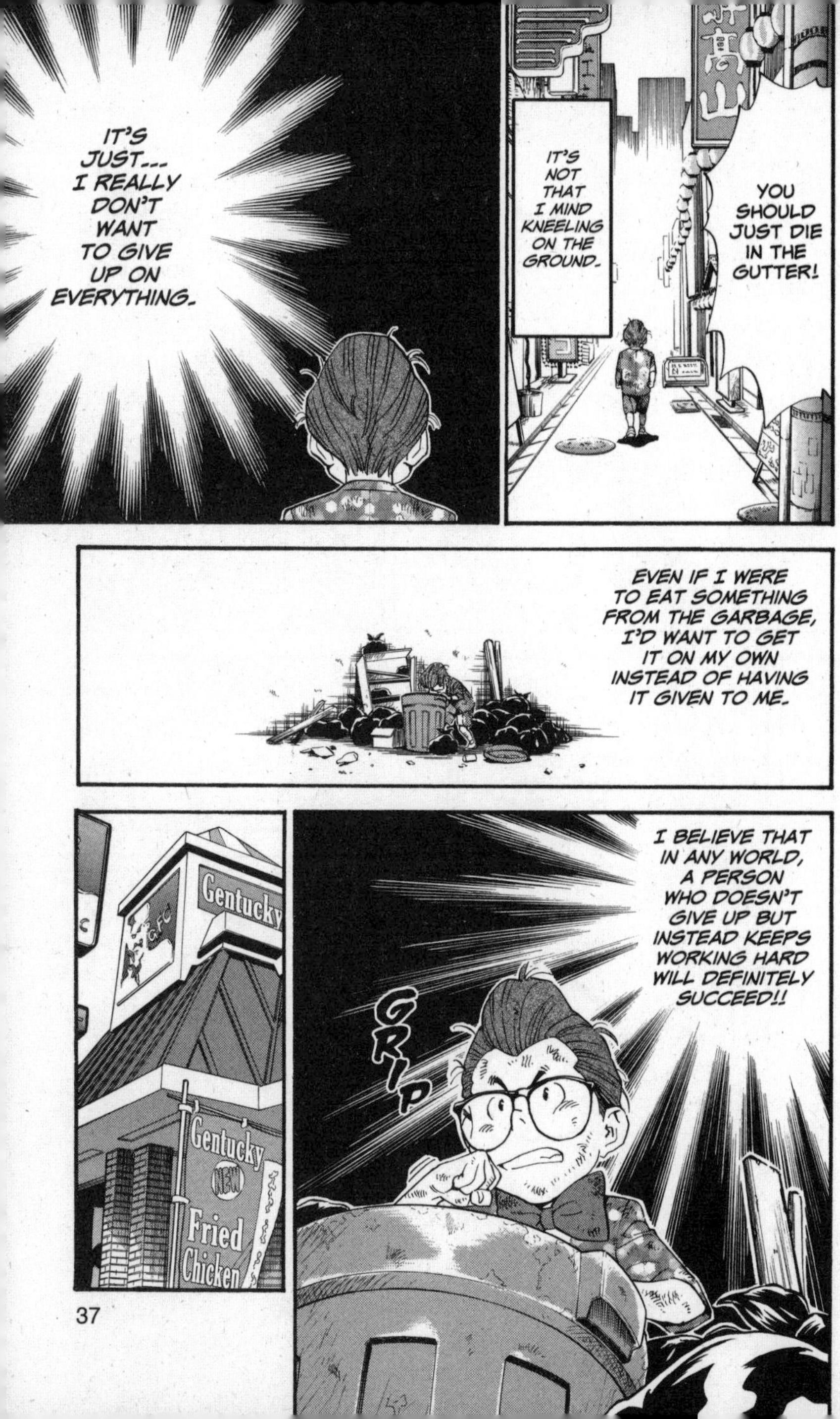
YOU SHOULD JUST DIE IN THE GUTTER!
IT'S NOT THAT I MIND KNEELING ON THE GROUND.
IT'S JUST... I REALLY DON'T WANT TO GIVE UP ON EVERYTHING.
EVEN IF I WERE TO EAT SOMETHING FROM THE GARBAGE, I'D WANT TO GET IT ON MY OWN INSTEAD OF HAVING IT GIVEN TO ME.
I BELIEVE THAT IN ANY WORLD, A PERSON WHO DOESN'T GIVE UP BUT INSTEAD KEEPS WORKING HARD WILL DEFINITELY SUCCEED!!
GRIP
Gentucky
Gentucky
NEW
Fried
Chicken

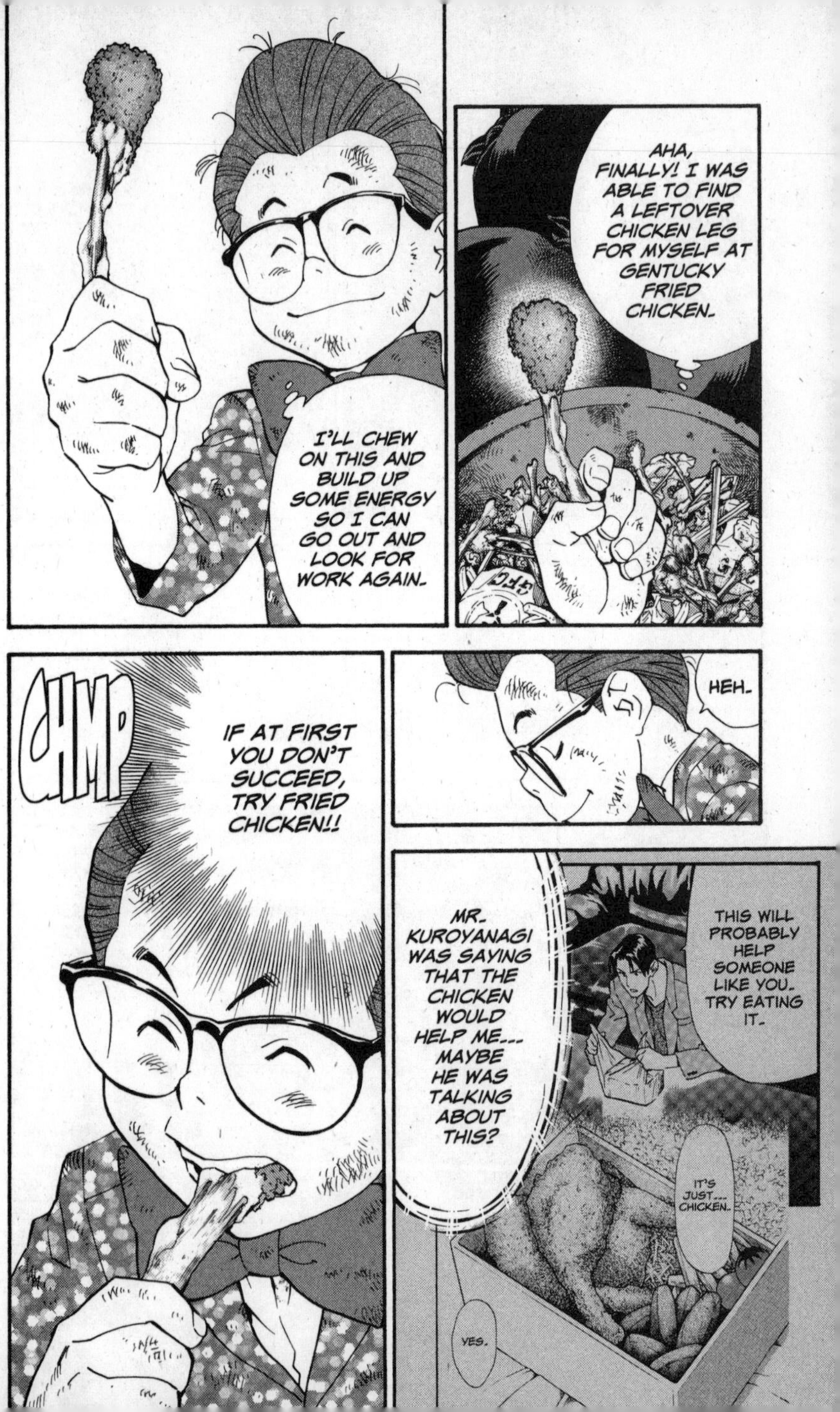
AHA, FINALLY! I WAS ABLE TO FIND A LEFTOVER CHICKEN LEG FOR MYSELF AT GENTUCKY FRIED CHICKEN.
I'LL CHEW ON THIS AND BUILD UP SOME ENERGY SO I CAN GO OUT AND LOOK FOR WORK AGAIN.
HEH.
THIS WILL PROBABLY HELP SOMEONE LIKE YOU. TRY EATING IT.
MR. KUROYANAGI WAS SAYING THAT THE CHICKEN WOULD HELP ME... MAYBE HE WAS TALKING ABOUT THIS?
IT'S JUST... CHICKEN.
YES.
CHMP
IF AT FIRST YOU DON'T SUCCEED, TRY FRIED CHICKEN!!

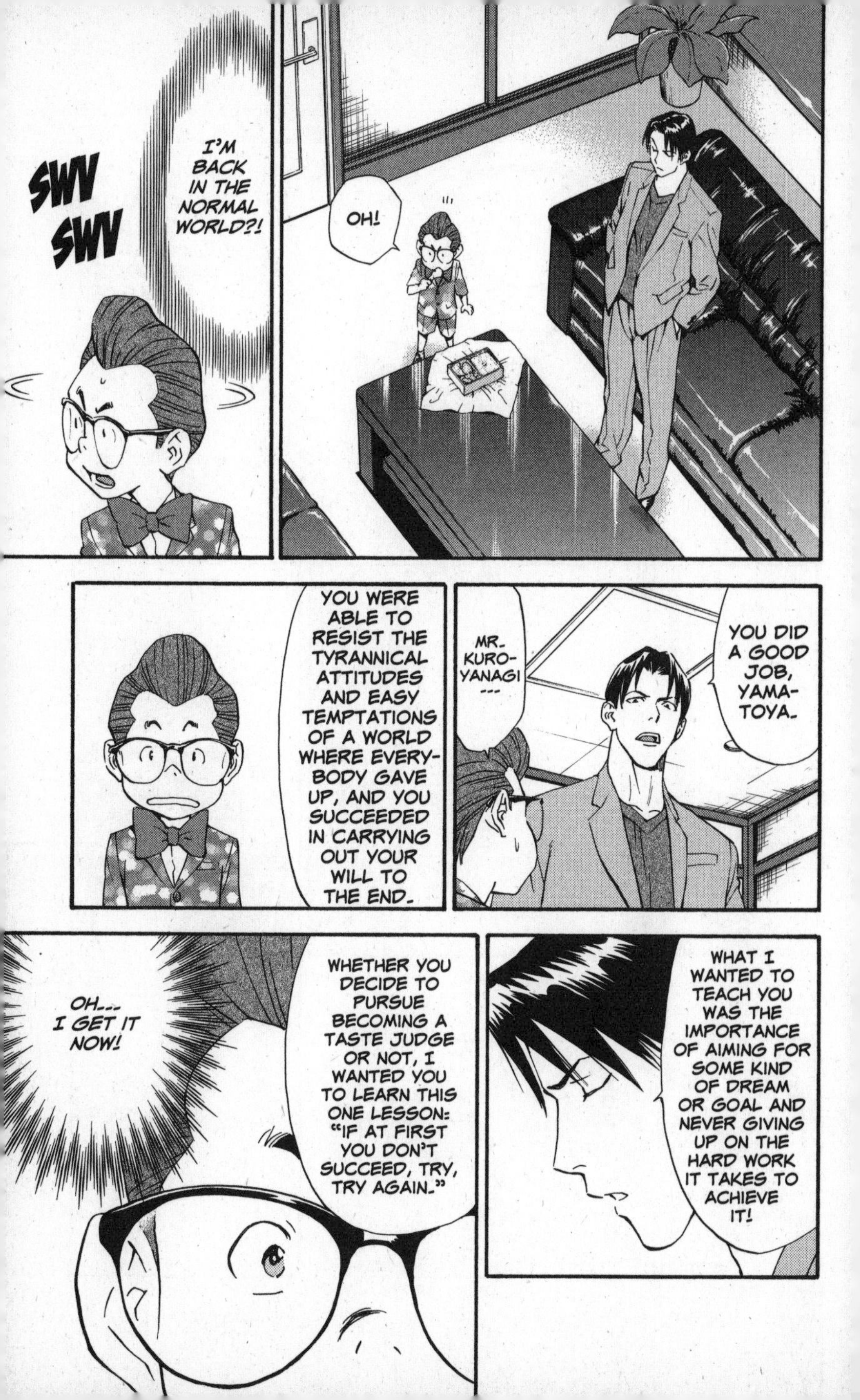
OH!
I'M BACK IN THE NORMAL WORLD?!
SWV SWV
YOU DID A GOOD JOB, YAMATOYA.
MR. KUROYANAGI...
YOU WERE ABLE TO RESIST THE TYRANNICAL ATTITUDES AND EASY TEMPTATIONS OF A WORLD WHERE EVERYBODY GAVE UP, AND YOU SUCCEEDED IN CARRYING OUT YOUR WILL TO THE END.
WHAT I WANTED TO TEACH YOU WAS THE IMPORTANCE OF AIMING FOR SOME KIND OF DREAM OR GOAL AND NEVER GIVING UP ON THE HARD WORK IT TAKES TO ACHIEVE IT!
WHETHER YOU DECIDE TO PURSUE BECOMING A TASTE JUDGE OR NOT, I WANTED YOU TO LEARN THIS ONE LESSON: "IF AT FIRST YOU DON'T SUCCEED, TRY, TRY AGAIN."
OH... I GET IT NOW!

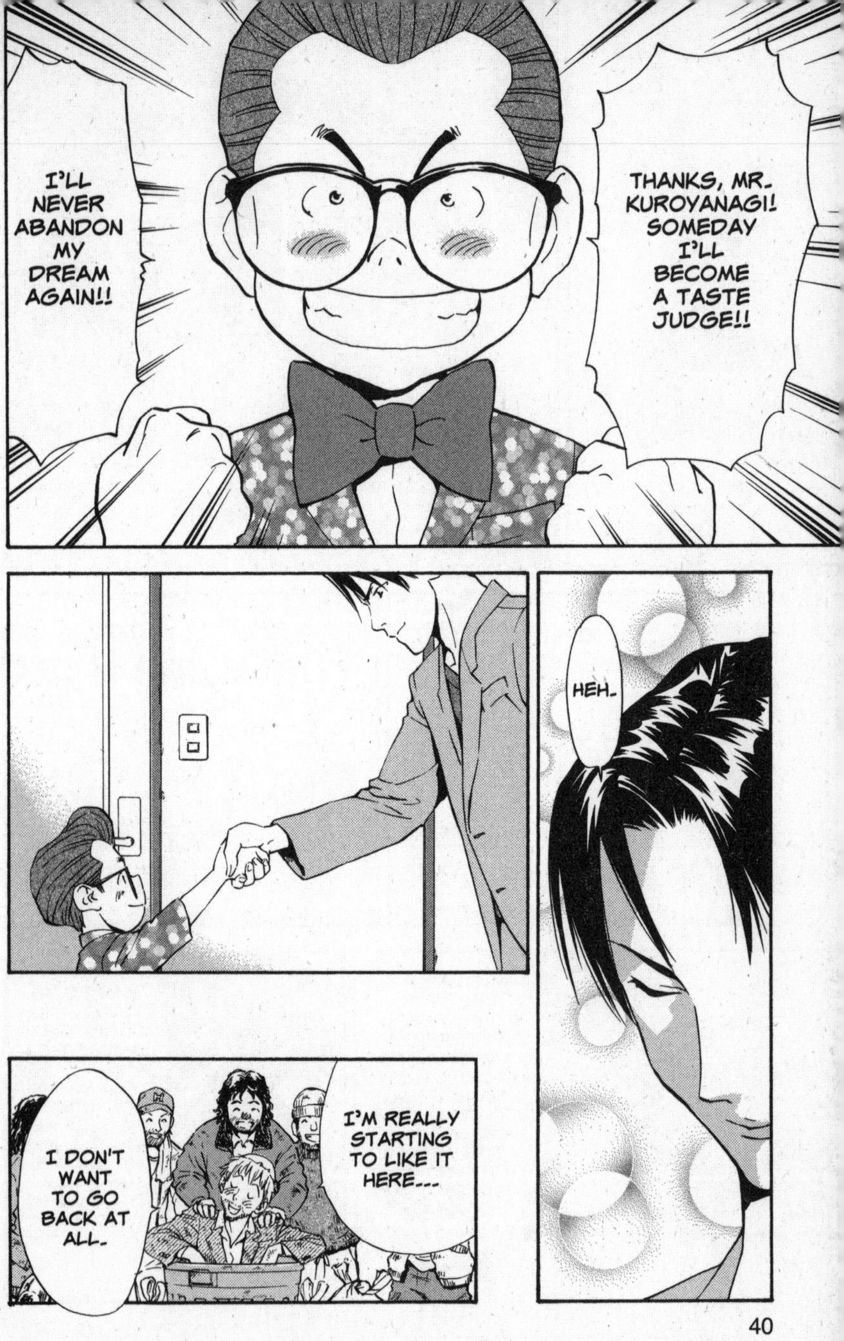
THANKS, MR. KUROYANAGI! SOMEDAY I'LL BECOME A TASTE JUDGE!!
I'LL NEVER ABANDON MY DREAM AGAIN!!
HEH.
I'M REALLY STARTING TO LIKE IT HERE...
I DON'T WANT TO GO BACK AT ALL.

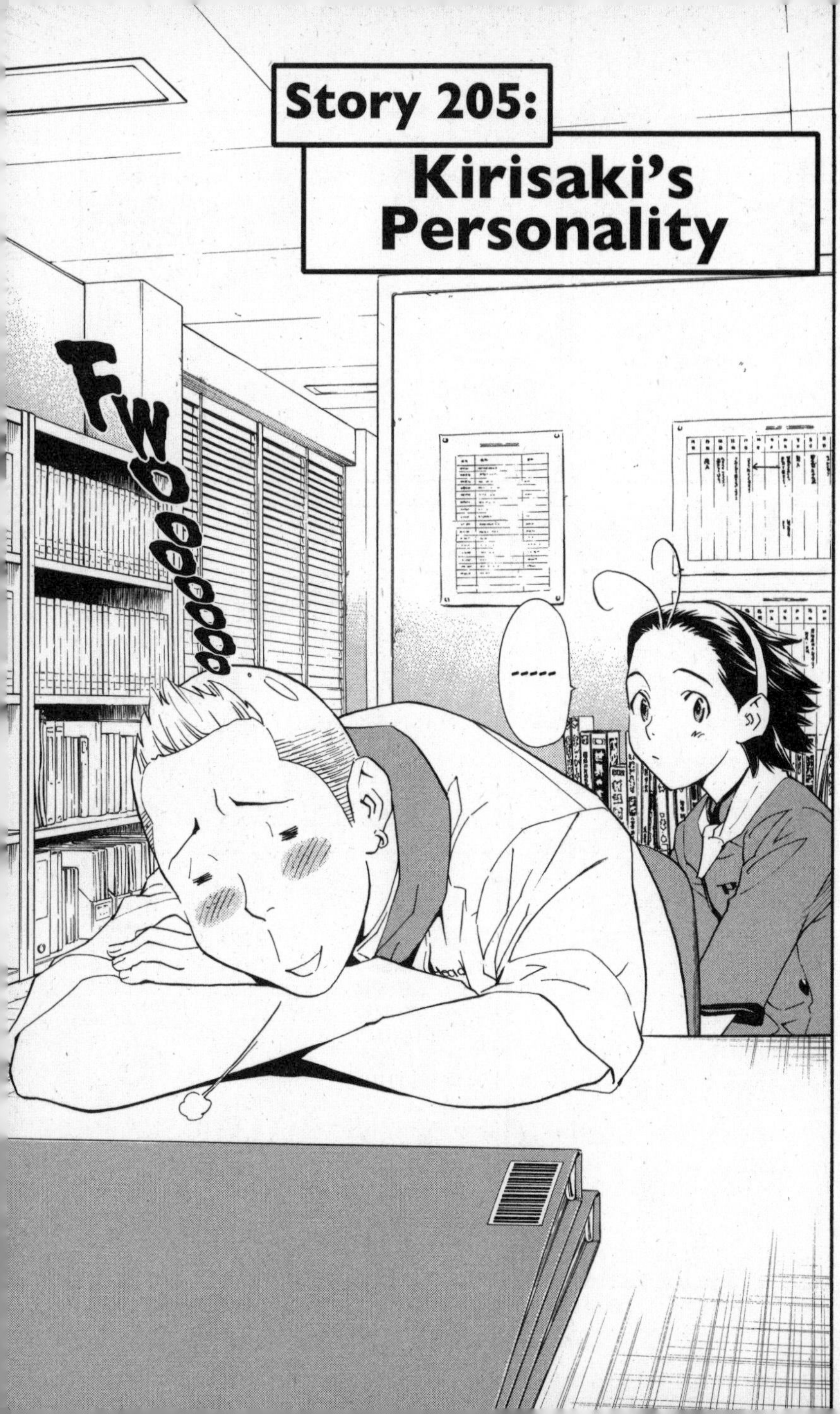
Story 205:
Kirisaki's Personality
FWOOOOOOOOO

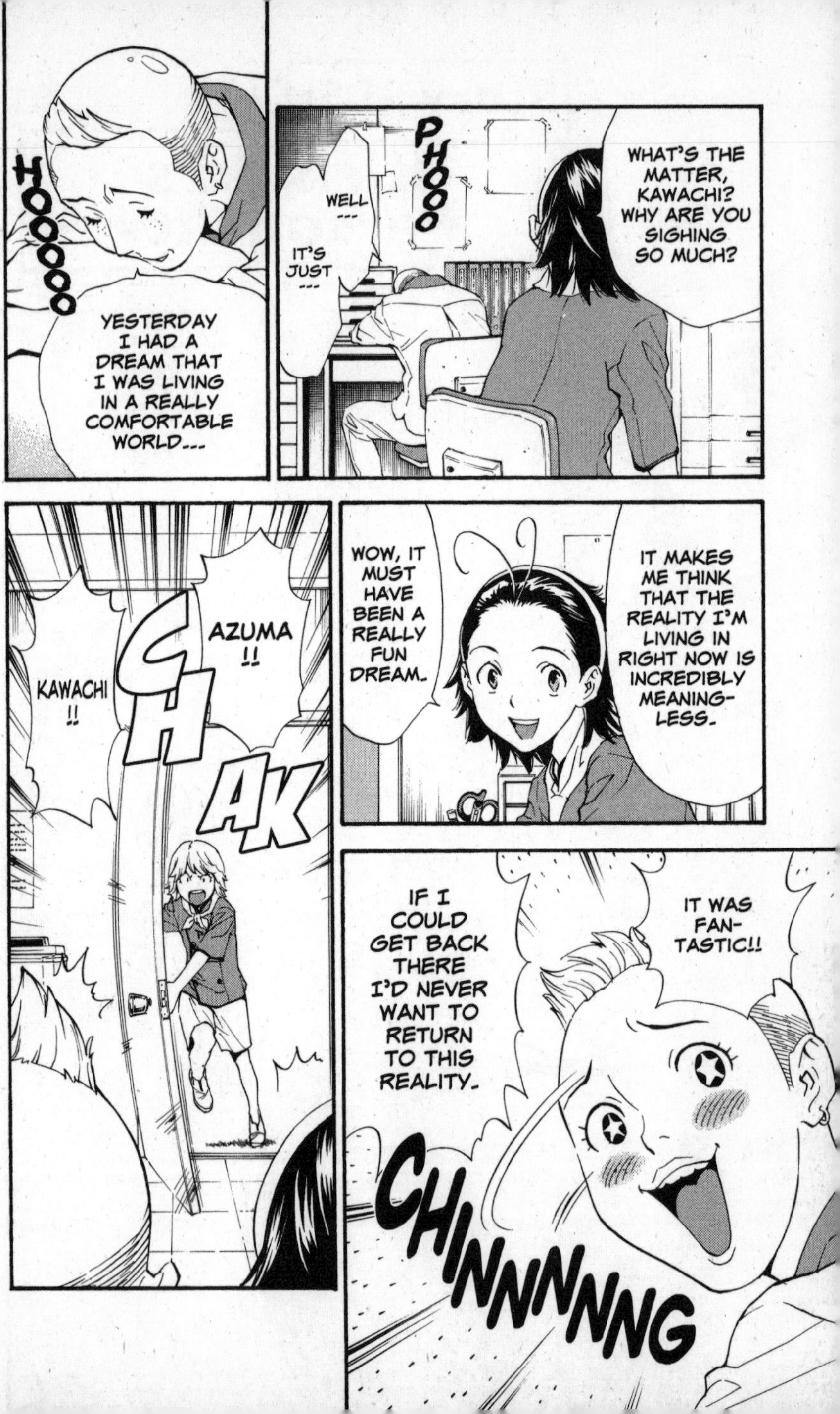
WHAT'S THE MATTER, KAWACHI? WHY ARE YOU SIGHING SO MUCH?
PHOOOO
WELL---
IT'S JUST---
HOOOOOO
YESTERDAY I HAD A DREAM THAT I WAS LIVING IN A REALLY COMFORTABLE WORLD...
IT MAKES ME THINK THAT THE REALITY I'M LIVING IN RIGHT NOW IS INCREDIBLY MEANING-LESS.
WOW, IT MUST HAVE BEEN A REALLY FUN DREAM.
IT WAS FAN-TASTIC!!
IF I COULD GET BACK THERE I'D NEVER WANT TO RETURN TO THIS REALITY.
CHINNNNNNG
AZUMA!!
CHAK
KAWACHI!!

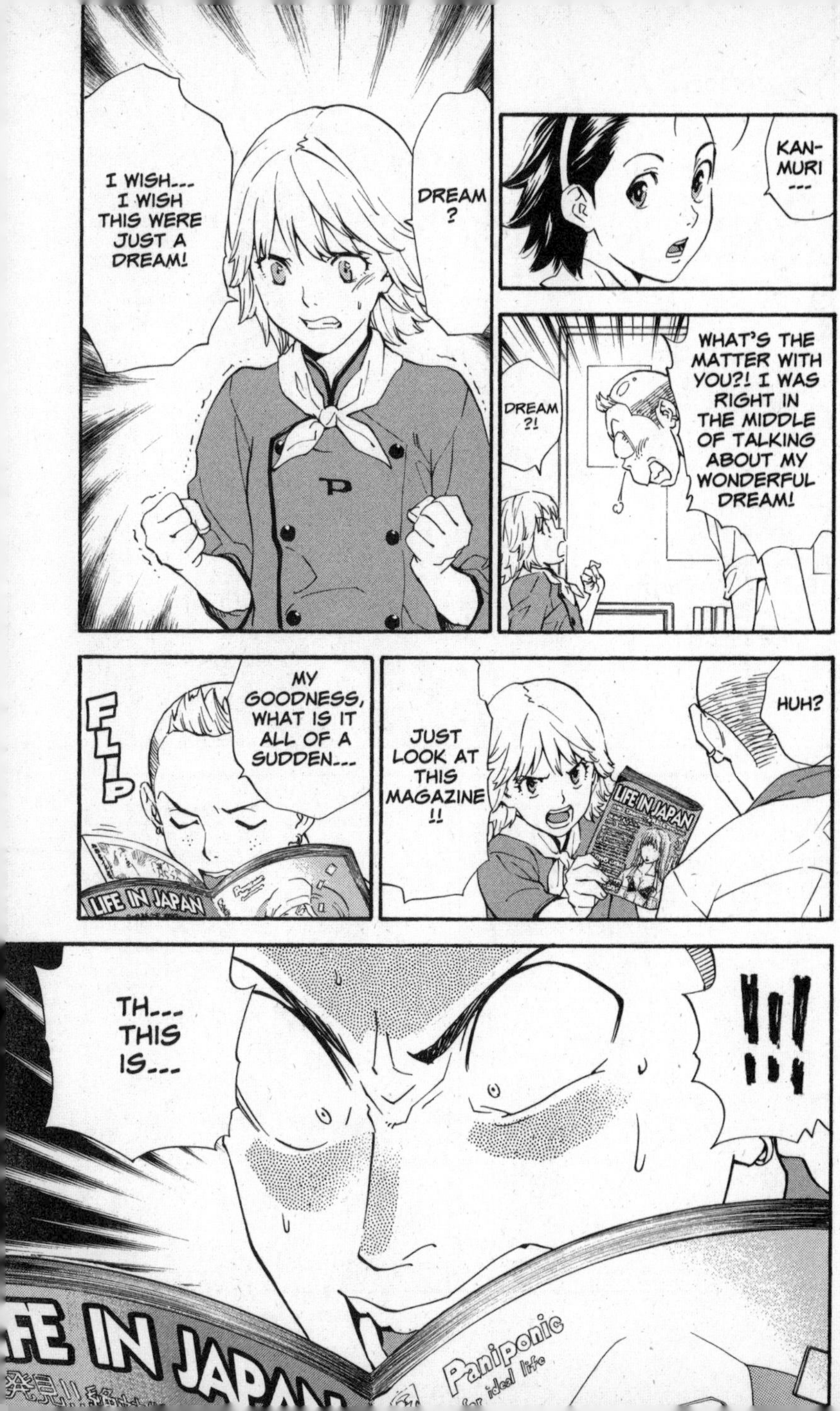
KAN-MURI...
WHAT'S THE MATTER WITH YOU?! I WAS RIGHT IN THE MIDDLE OF TALKING ABOUT MY WONDERFUL DREAM!
DREAM?!
DREAM?
I WISH... I WISH THIS WERE JUST A DREAM!
HUH?
JUST LOOK AT THIS MAGAZINE!!
LIFE IN JAPAN
MY GOODNESS, WHAT IS IT ALL OF A SUDDEN...
FLIP
LIFE IN JAPAN
!!!
TH... THIS IS...
Paniponic
for ideal life

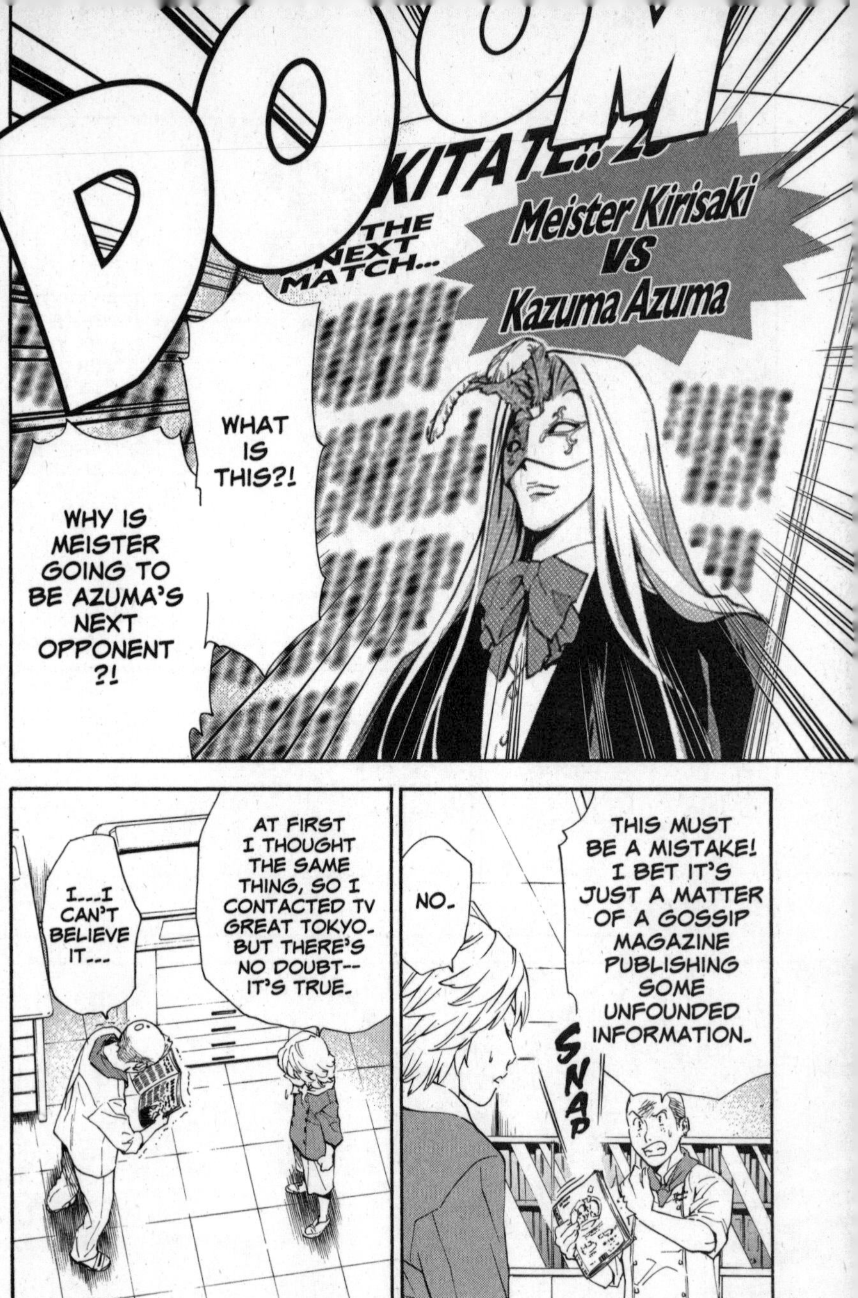
DOOM
KITATE
THE NEXT MATCH...
Meister Kirisaki VS Kazuma Azuma
WHAT IS THIS?!
WHY IS MEISTER GOING TO BE AZUMA'S NEXT OPPONENT?!
THIS MUST BE A MISTAKE! I BET IT'S JUST A MATTER OF A GOSSIP MAGAZINE PUBLISHING SOME UNFOUNDED INFORMATION.
SNAP
NO.
AT FIRST I THOUGHT THE SAME THING, SO I CONTACTED TV GREAT TOKYO. BUT THERE'S NO DOUBT-- IT'S TRUE.
I...I CAN'T BELIEVE IT...

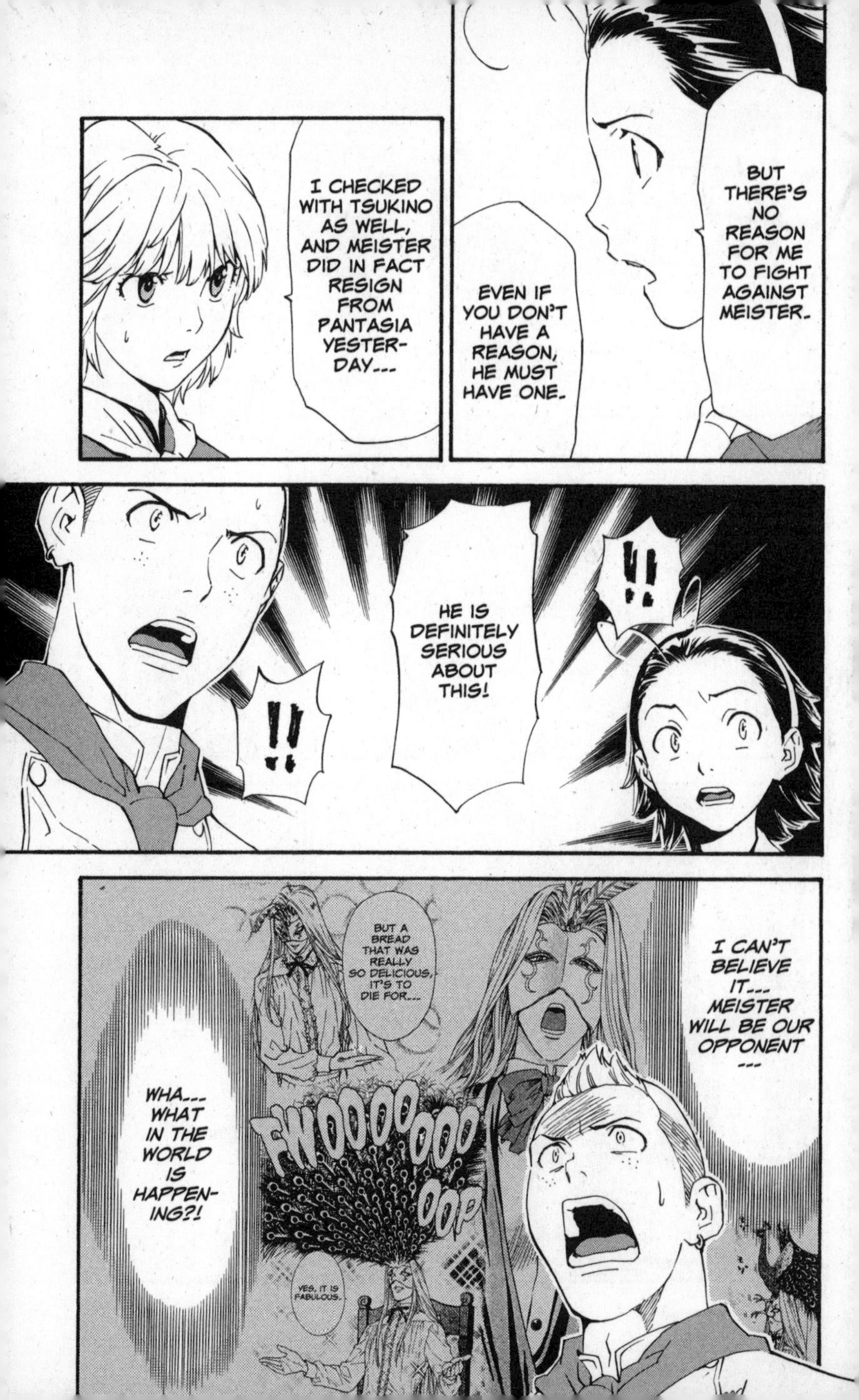

BUT THERE'S NO REASON FOR ME TO FIGHT AGAINST MEISTER.
EVEN IF YOU DON'T HAVE A REASON, HE MUST HAVE ONE.
I CHECKED WITH TSUKINO AS WELL, AND MEISTER DID IN FACT RESIGN FROM PANTASIA YESTER-DAY...
!!
HE IS DEFINITELY SERIOUS ABOUT THIS!
!!
I CAN'T BELIEVE IT... MEISTER WILL BE OUR OPPONENT...
BUT A BREAD THAT WAS REALLY SO DELICIOUS, IT'S TO DIE FOR...
FWOOOOOOOOOP
WHA... WHAT IN THE WORLD IS HAPPEN-ING?!
YES, IT IS FABULOUS.

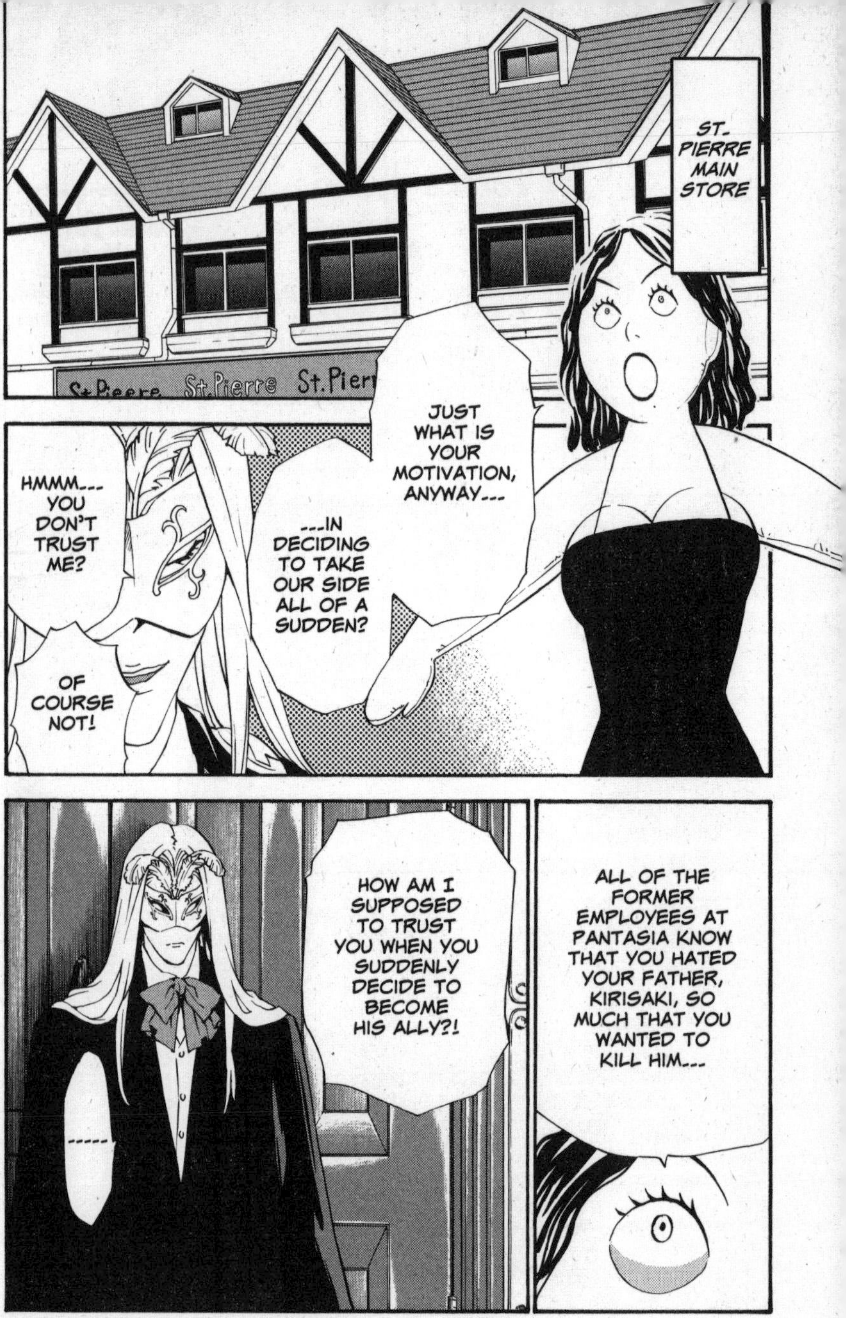
ST. PIERRE MAIN STORE
St.Pierre St.Pierre
JUST WHAT IS YOUR MOTIVATION, ANYWAY...
...IN DECIDING TO TAKE OUR SIDE ALL OF A SUDDEN?
HMMM... YOU DON'T TRUST ME?
OF COURSE NOT!
ALL OF THE FORMER EMPLOYEES AT PANTASIA KNOW THAT YOU HATED YOUR FATHER, KIRISAKI, SO MUCH THAT YOU WANTED TO KILL HIM...
HOW AM I SUPPOSED TO TRUST YOU WHEN YOU SUDDENLY DECIDE TO BECOME HIS ALLY?!
.....

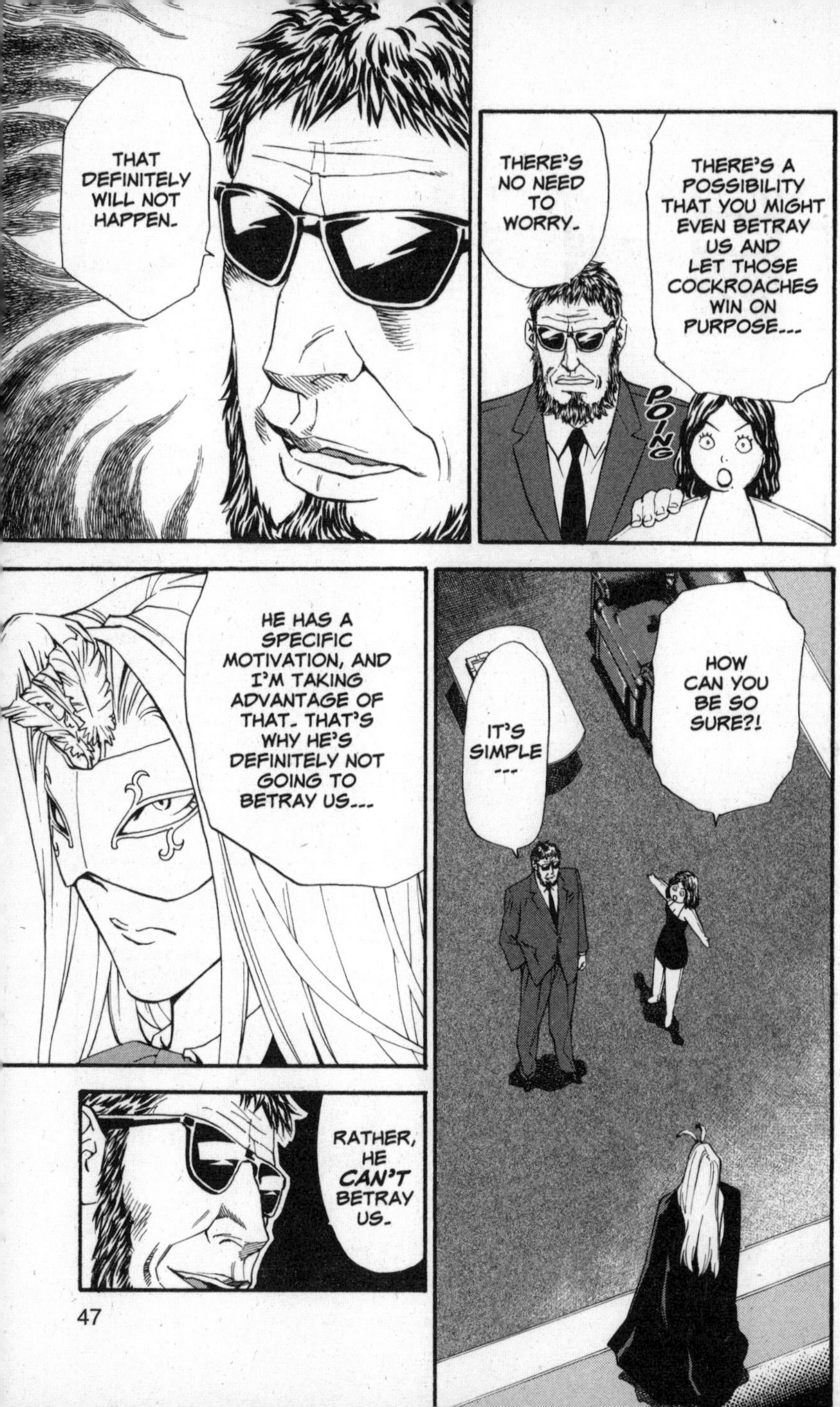
THERE'S A POSSIBILITY THAT YOU MIGHT EVEN BETRAY US AND LET THOSE COCKROACHES WIN ON PURPOSE...
THERE'S NO NEED TO WORRY.
POING
THAT DEFINITELY WILL NOT HAPPEN.
HOW CAN YOU BE SO SURE?!
IT'S SIMPLE ...
HE HAS A SPECIFIC MOTIVATION, AND I'M TAKING ADVANTAGE OF THAT. THAT'S WHY HE'S DEFINITELY NOT GOING TO BETRAY US...
RATHER, HE *CAN'T* BETRAY US.

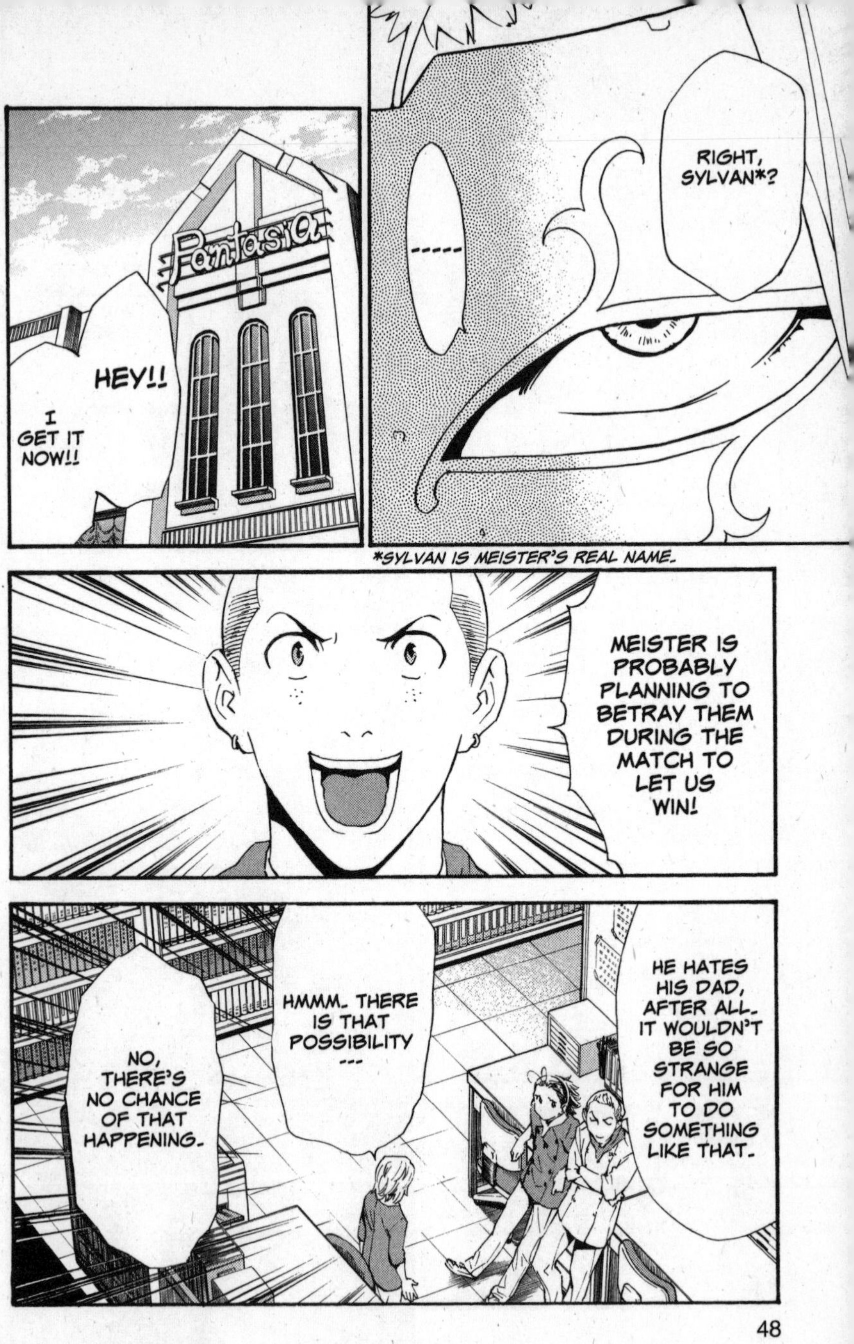
RIGHT, SYLVAN*?

HEY!!
I GET IT NOW!!
*SYLVAN IS MEISTER'S REAL NAME.
MEISTER IS PROBABLY PLANNING TO BETRAY THEM DURING THE MATCH TO LET US WIN!
HE HATES HIS DAD, AFTER ALL. IT WOULDN'T BE SO STRANGE FOR HIM TO DO SOMETHING LIKE THAT.
HMMM. THERE IS THAT POSSIBILITY...
NO, THERE'S NO CHANCE OF THAT HAPPENING.

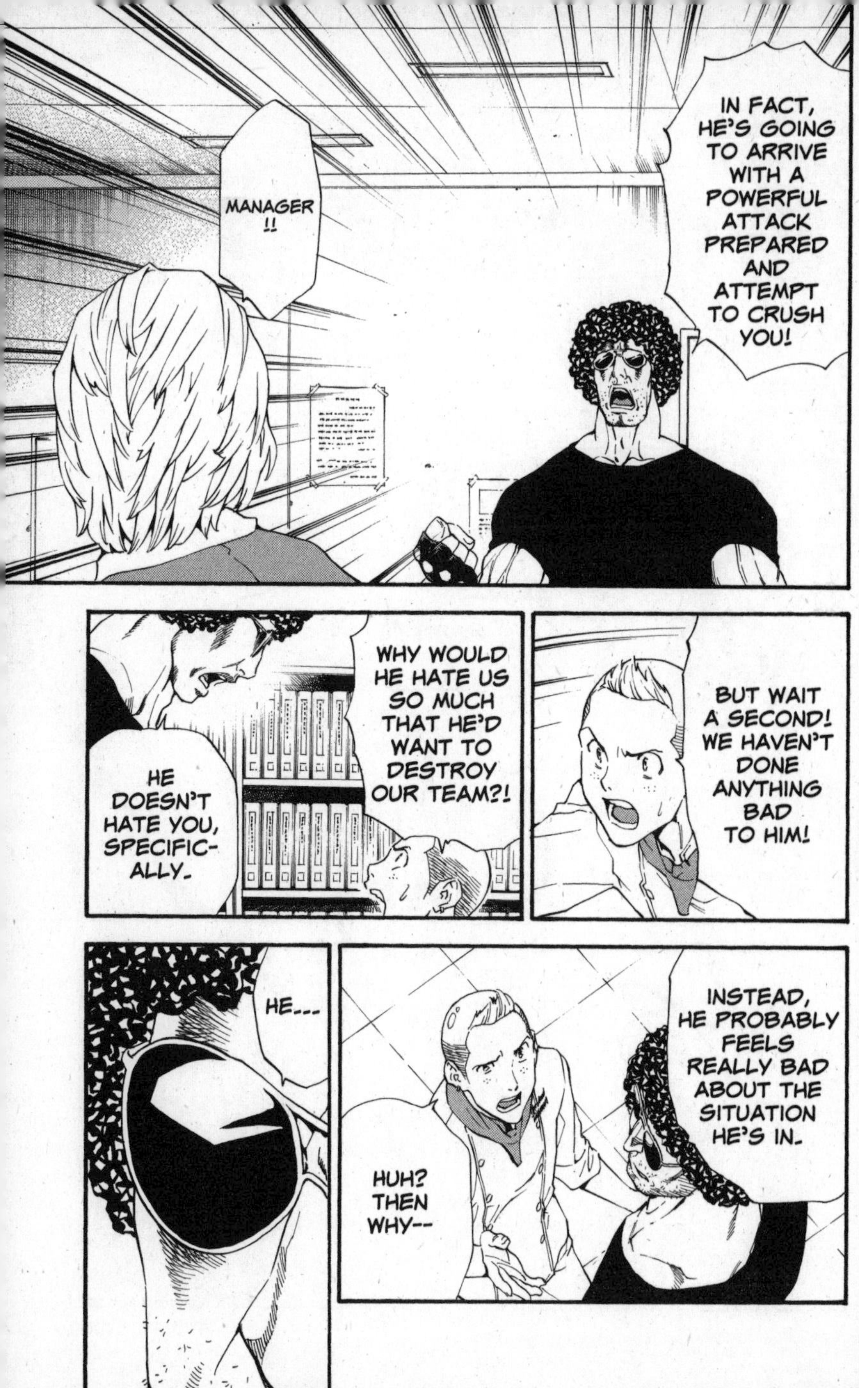
IN FACT, HE'S GOING TO ARRIVE WITH A POWERFUL ATTACK PREPARED AND ATTEMPT TO CRUSH YOU!
MANAGER!!
BUT WAIT A SECOND! WE HAVEN'T DONE ANYTHING BAD TO HIM!
WHY WOULD HE HATE US SO MUCH THAT HE'D WANT TO DESTROY OUR TEAM?!
HE DOESN'T HATE YOU, SPECIFIC-ALLY.
INSTEAD, HE PROBABLY FEELS REALLY BAD ABOUT THE SITUATION HE'S IN.
HUH? THEN WHY--
HE...

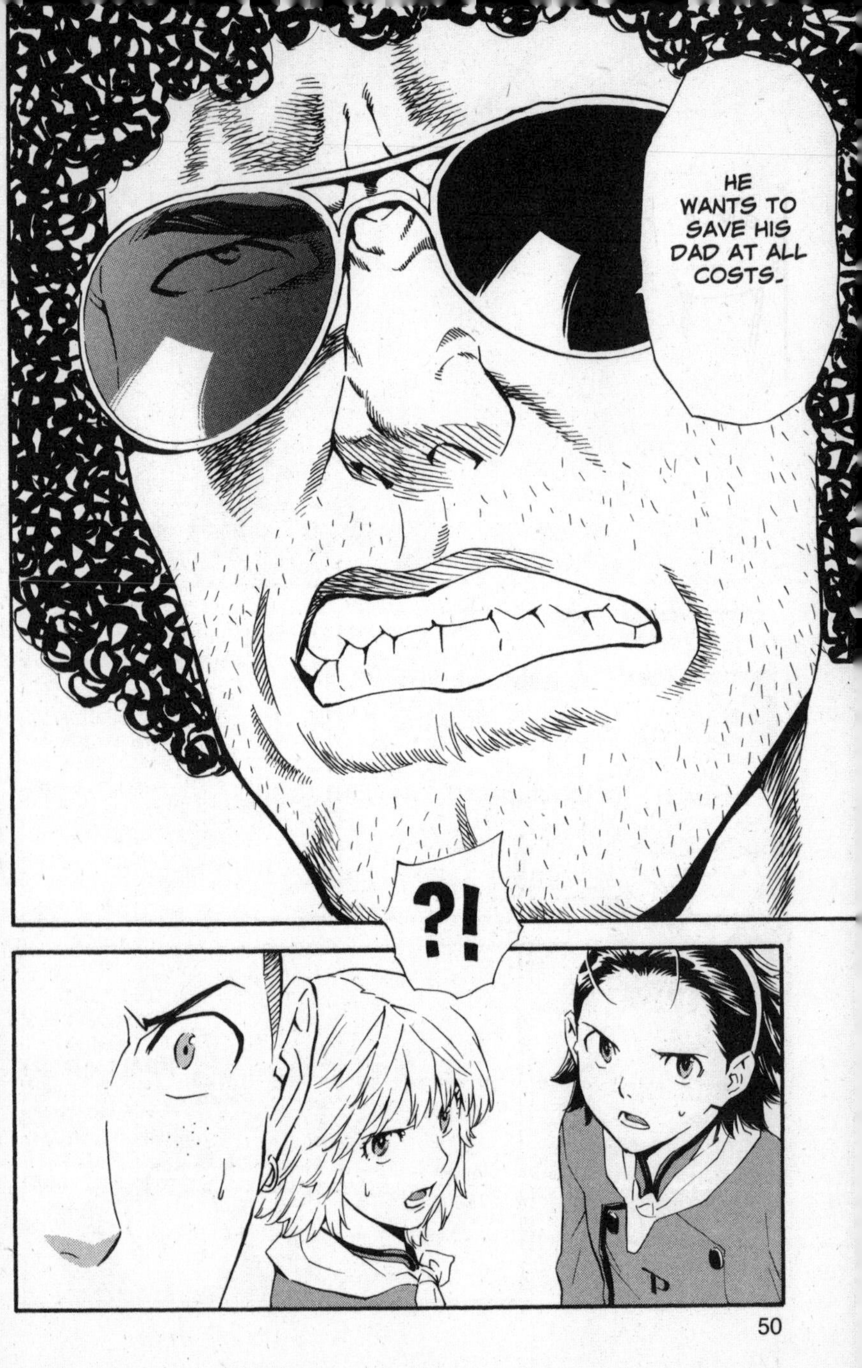
HE WANTS TO SAVE HIS DAD AT ALL COSTS.
?!

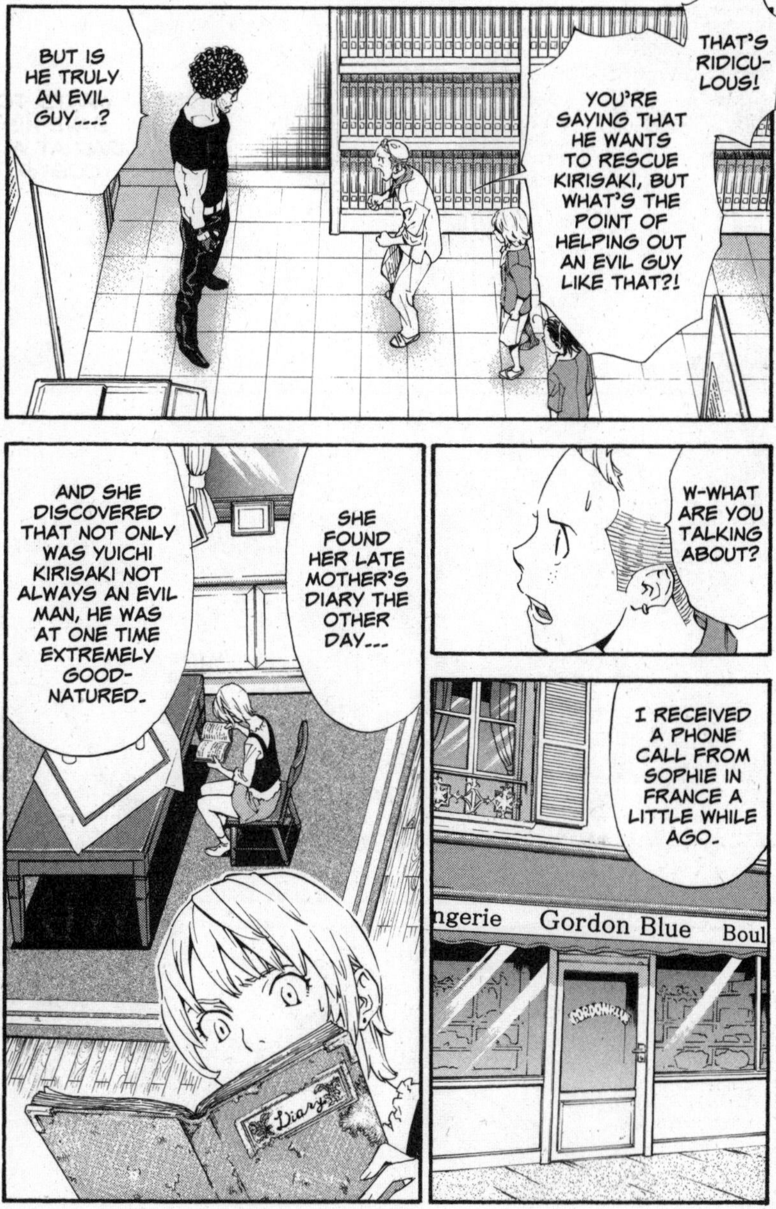
THAT'S RIDICULOUS!
YOU'RE SAYING THAT HE WANTS TO RESCUE KIRISAKI, BUT WHAT'S THE POINT OF HELPING OUT AN EVIL GUY LIKE THAT?!
BUT IS HE TRULY AN EVIL GUY...?
W-WHAT ARE YOU TALKING ABOUT?
I RECEIVED A PHONE CALL FROM SOPHIE IN FRANCE A LITTLE WHILE AGO.
ngerie Gordon Blue Boul
SHE FOUND HER LATE MOTHER'S DIARY THE OTHER DAY...
AND SHE DISCOVERED THAT NOT ONLY WAS YUICHI KIRISAKI NOT ALWAYS AN EVIL MAN, HE WAS AT ONE TIME EXTREMELY GOOD-NATURED.
Diary

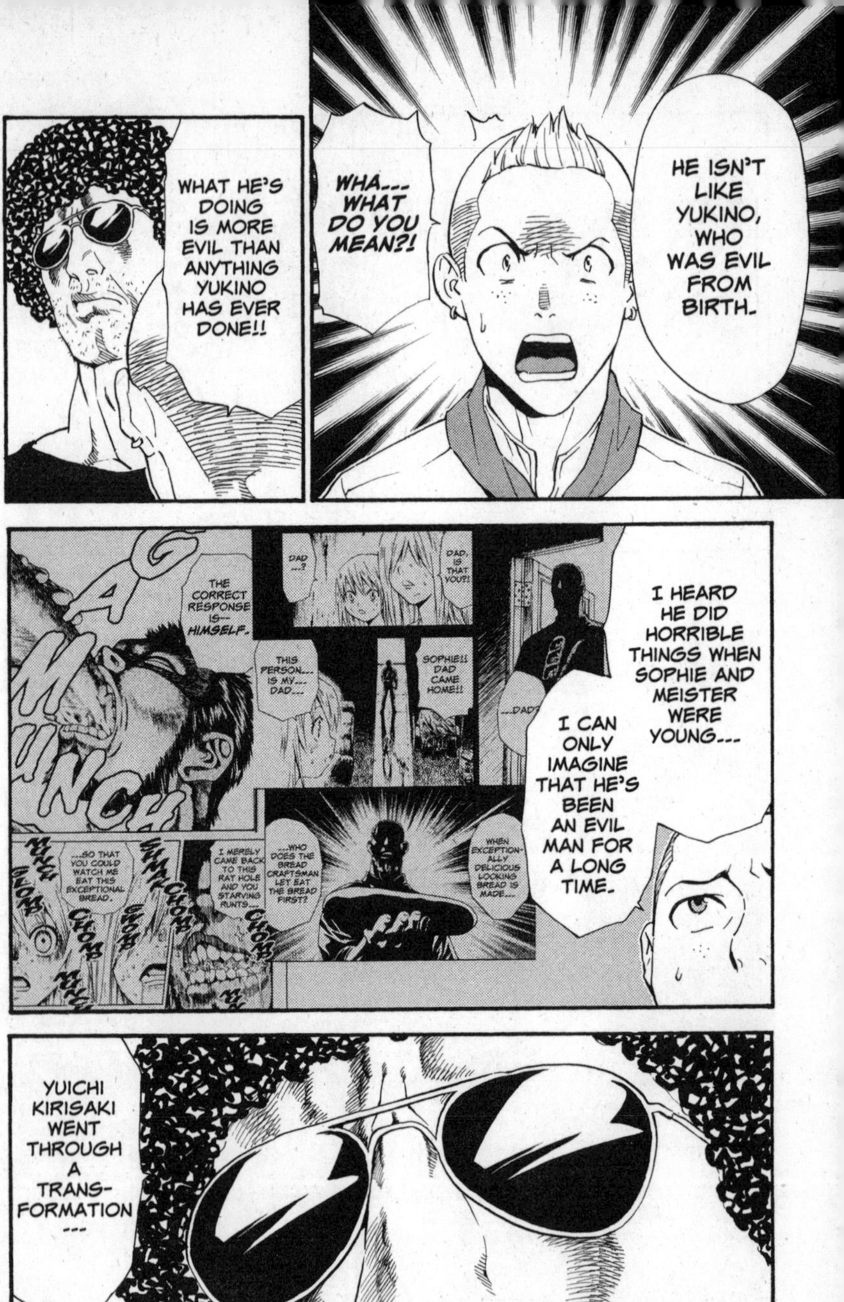
HE ISN'T LIKE YUKINO, WHO WAS EVIL FROM BIRTH.
WHA... WHAT DO YOU MEAN?!
WHAT HE'S DOING IS MORE EVIL THAN ANYTHING YUKINO HAS EVER DONE!!
I HEARD HE DID HORRIBLE THINGS WHEN SOPHIE AND MEISTER WERE YOUNG...
I CAN ONLY IMAGINE THAT HE'S BEEN AN EVIL MAN FOR A LONG TIME.
DAD, IS THAT YOU?!
DAD...?
THE CORRECT RESPONSE IS— HIMSELF.
SOPHIE!! DAD CAME HOME!!
...DAD?
THIS PERSON... IS MY... DAD...
WHEN EXCEPTIONALLY DELICIOUS LOOKING BREAD IS MADE...
...WHO DOES THE BREAD CRAFTSMAN LET EAT THE BREAD FIRST?
I MERELY CAME BACK TO THIS RAT HOLE AND YOU STARVING RUNTS...
...SO THAT YOU COULD WATCH ME EAT THIS EXCEPTIONAL BREAD.
YUICHI KIRISAKI WENT THROUGH A TRANS-FORMATION ---

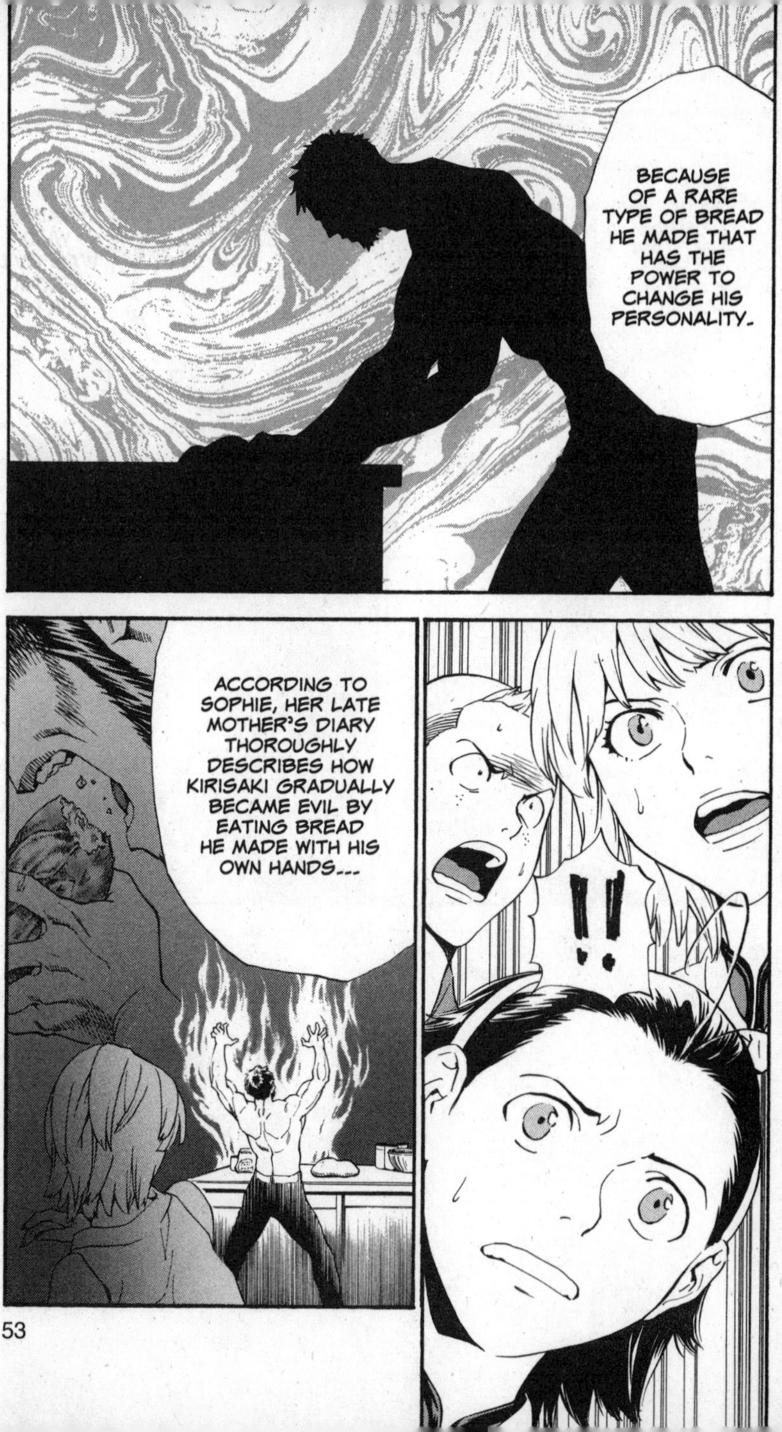
BECAUSE OF A RARE TYPE OF BREAD HE MADE THAT HAS THE POWER TO CHANGE HIS PERSONALITY.
!!
ACCORDING TO SOPHIE, HER LATE MOTHER'S DIARY THOROUGHLY DESCRIBES HOW KIRISAKI GRADUALLY BECAME EVIL BY EATING BREAD HE MADE WITH HIS OWN HANDS...

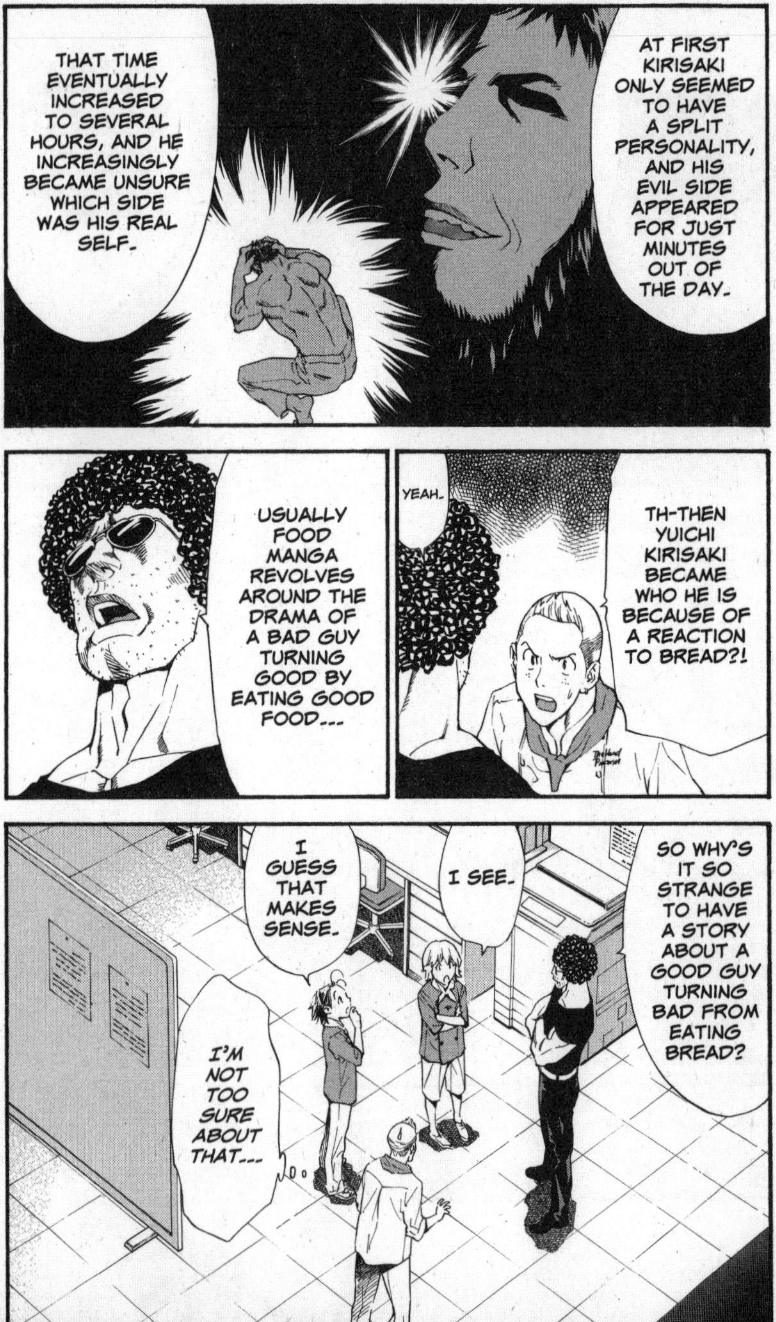
AT FIRST KIRISAKI ONLY SEEMED TO HAVE A SPLIT PERSONALITY, AND HIS EVIL SIDE APPEARED FOR JUST MINUTES OUT OF THE DAY.
THAT TIME EVENTUALLY INCREASED TO SEVERAL HOURS, AND HE INCREASINGLY BECAME UNSURE WHICH SIDE WAS HIS REAL SELF.
TH-THEN YUICHI KIRISAKI BECAME WHO HE IS BECAUSE OF A REACTION TO BREAD?!
YEAH.
USUALLY FOOD MANGA REVOLVES AROUND THE DRAMA OF A BAD GUY TURNING GOOD BY EATING GOOD FOOD...
SO WHY'S IT SO STRANGE TO HAVE A STORY ABOUT A GOOD GUY TURNING BAD FROM EATING BREAD?
I SEE.
I GUESS THAT MAKES SENSE.
I'M NOT TOO SURE ABOUT THAT...

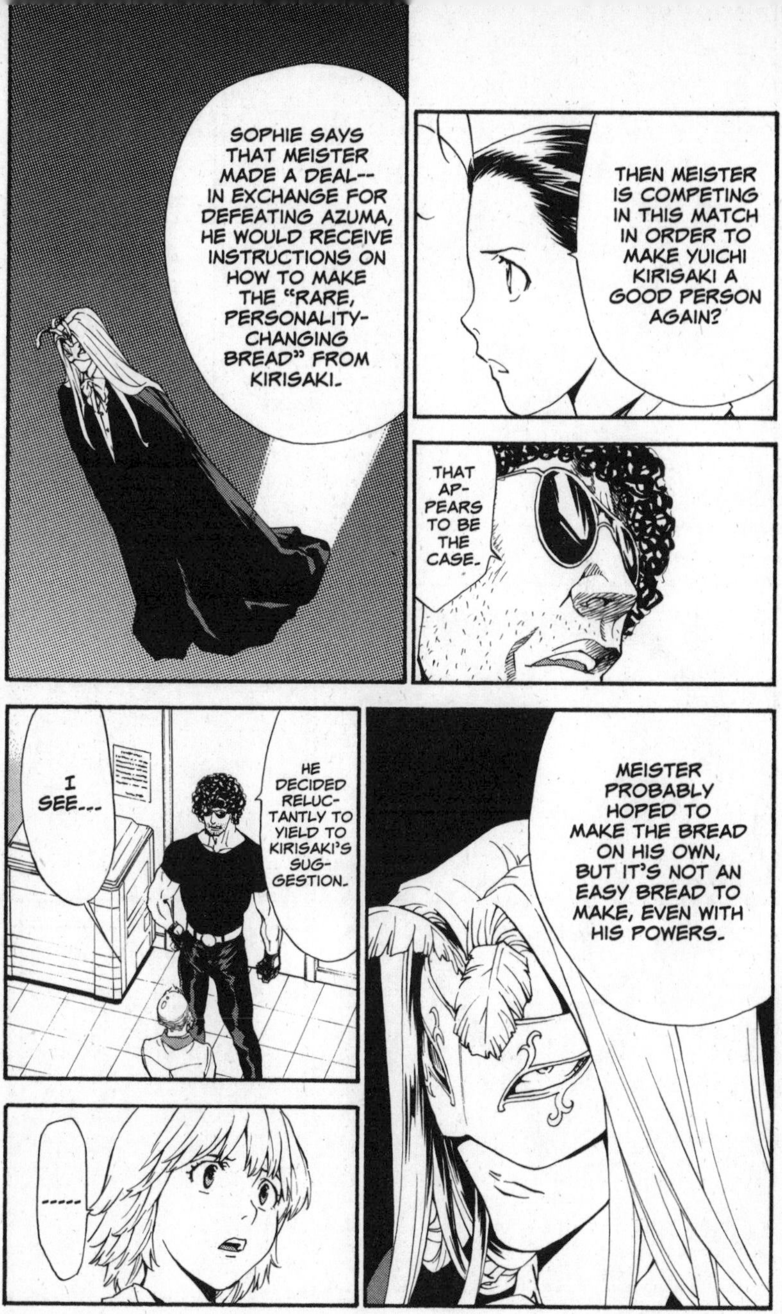
THEN MEISTER IS COMPETING IN THIS MATCH IN ORDER TO MAKE YUICHI KIRISAKI A GOOD PERSON AGAIN?
THAT AP-PEARS TO BE THE CASE.
SOPHIE SAYS THAT MEISTER MADE A DEAL-- IN EXCHANGE FOR DEFEATING AZUMA, HE WOULD RECEIVE INSTRUCTIONS ON HOW TO MAKE THE "RARE, PERSONALITY-CHANGING BREAD" FROM KIRISAKI.
MEISTER PROBABLY HOPED TO MAKE THE BREAD ON HIS OWN, BUT IT'S NOT AN EASY BREAD TO MAKE, EVEN WITH HIS POWERS.
HE DECIDED RELUC-TANTLY TO YIELD TO KIRISAKI'S SUG-GESTION.
I SEE...
.....

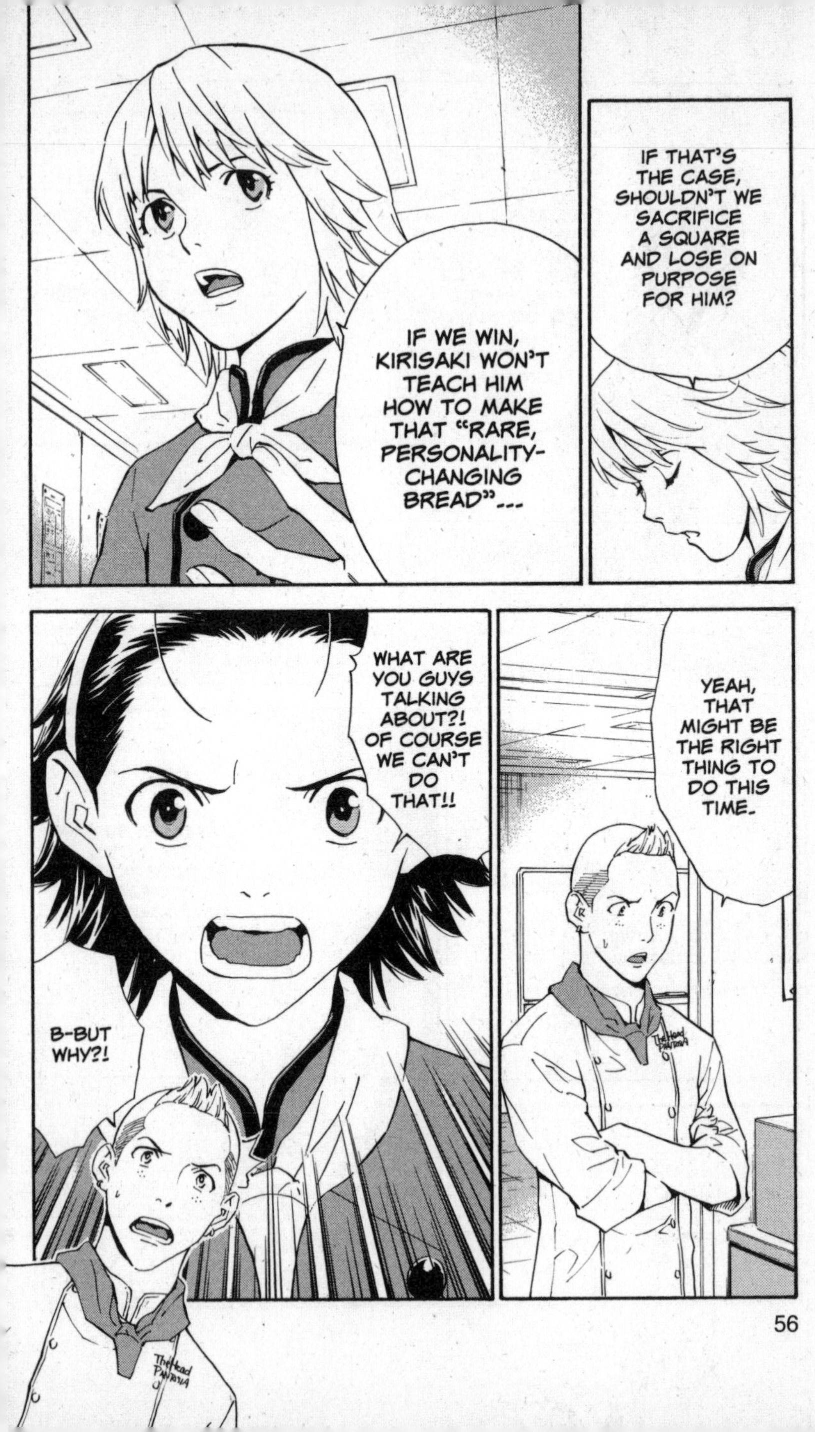
IF THAT'S THE CASE, SHOULDN'T WE SACRIFICE A SQUARE AND LOSE ON PURPOSE FOR HIM?
IF WE WIN, KIRISAKI WON'T TEACH HIM HOW TO MAKE THAT "RARE, PERSONALITY-CHANGING BREAD"...
YEAH, THAT MIGHT BE THE RIGHT THING TO DO THIS TIME.
WHAT ARE YOU GUYS TALKING ABOUT?! OF COURSE WE CAN'T DO THAT!!
B-BUT WHY?!

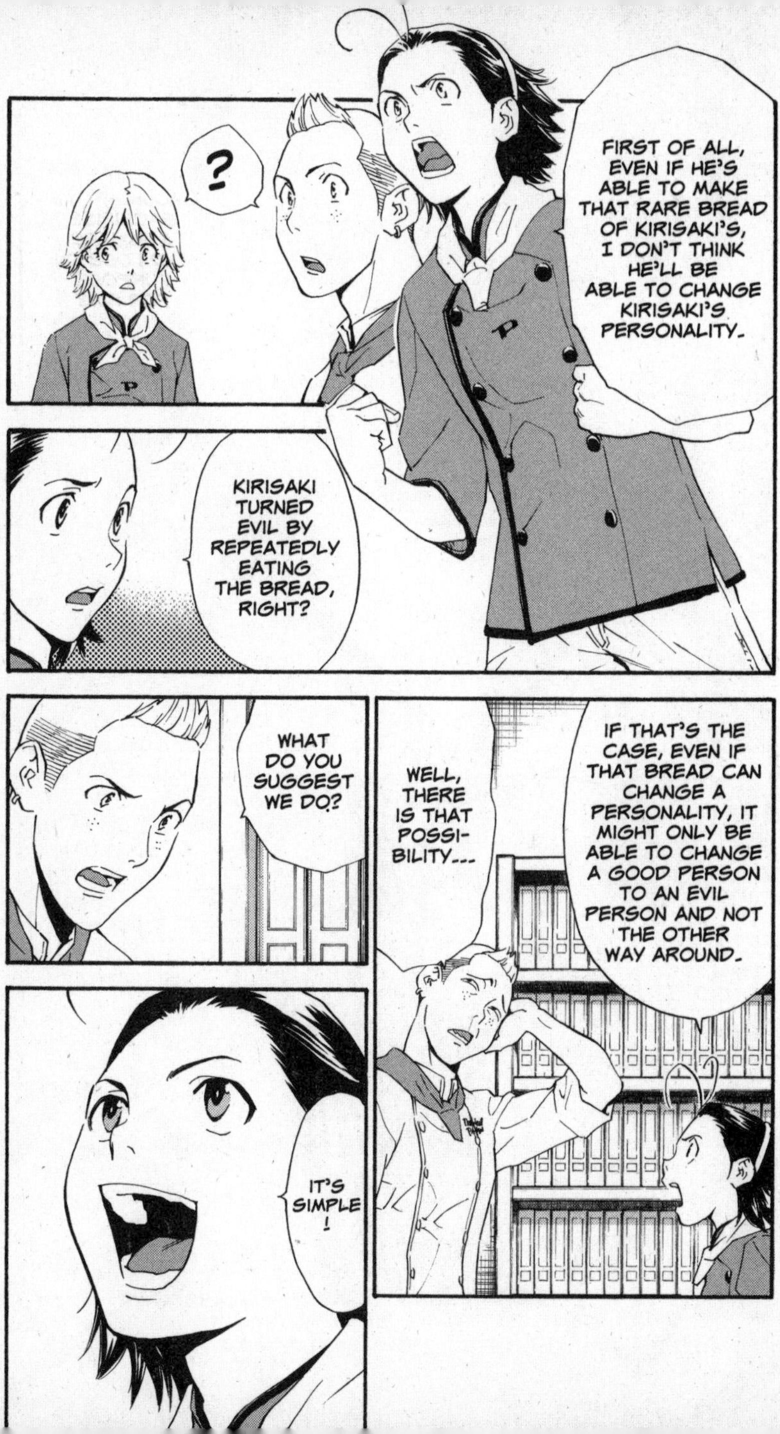
FIRST OF ALL, EVEN IF HE'S ABLE TO MAKE THAT RARE BREAD OF KIRISAKI'S, I DON'T THINK HE'LL BE ABLE TO CHANGE KIRISAKI'S PERSONALITY.
?
KIRISAKI TURNED EVIL BY REPEATEDLY EATING THE BREAD, RIGHT?
IF THAT'S THE CASE, EVEN IF THAT BREAD CAN CHANGE A PERSONALITY, IT MIGHT ONLY BE ABLE TO CHANGE A GOOD PERSON TO AN EVIL PERSON AND NOT THE OTHER WAY AROUND.
WELL, THERE IS THAT POSSIBILITY...
WHAT DO YOU SUGGEST WE DO?
IT'S SIMPLE!

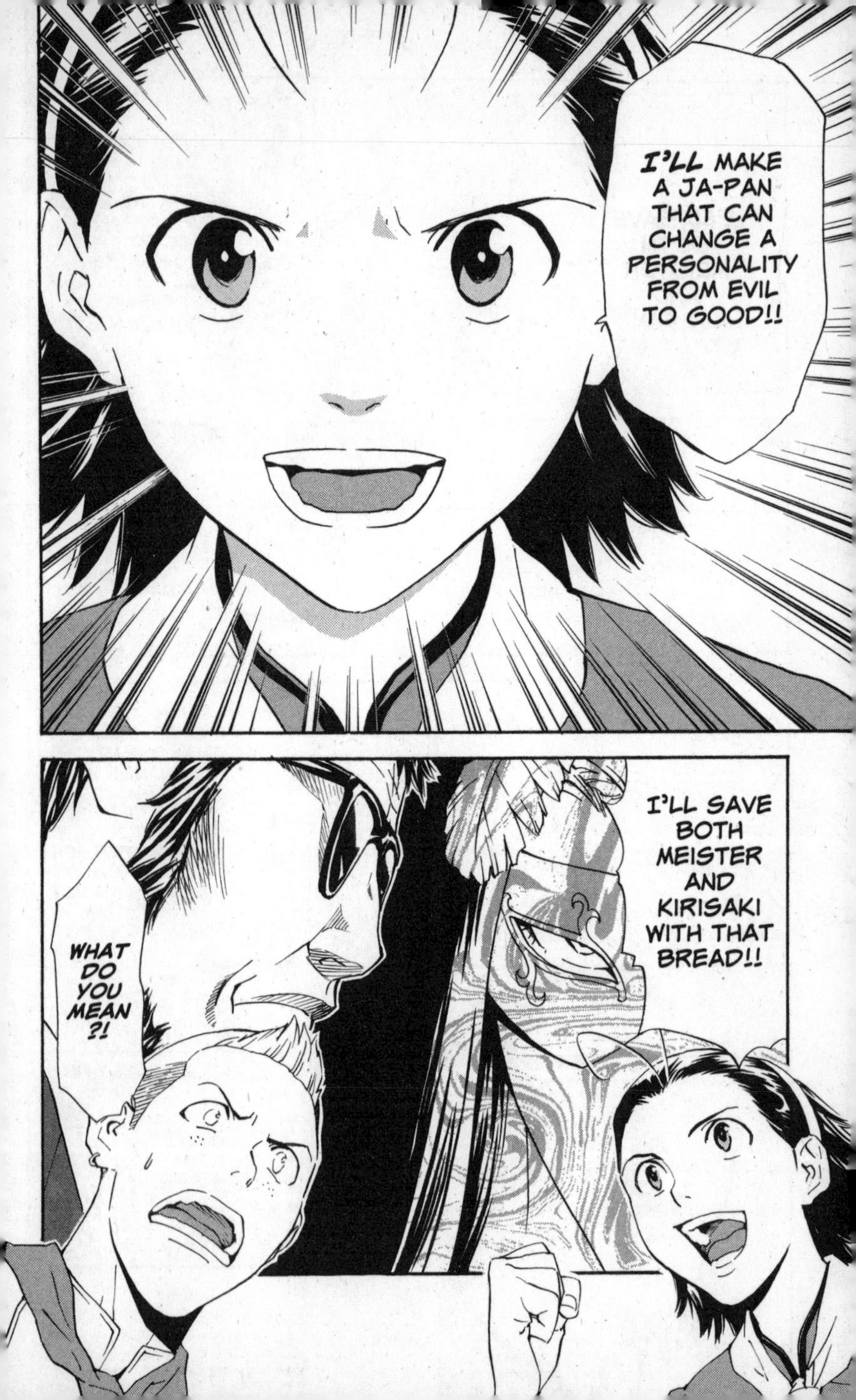
I'LL MAKE A JA-PAN THAT CAN CHANGE A PERSONALITY FROM EVIL TO GOOD!!
I'LL SAVE BOTH MEISTER AND KIRISAKI WITH THAT BREAD!!
WHAT DO YOU MEAN?!

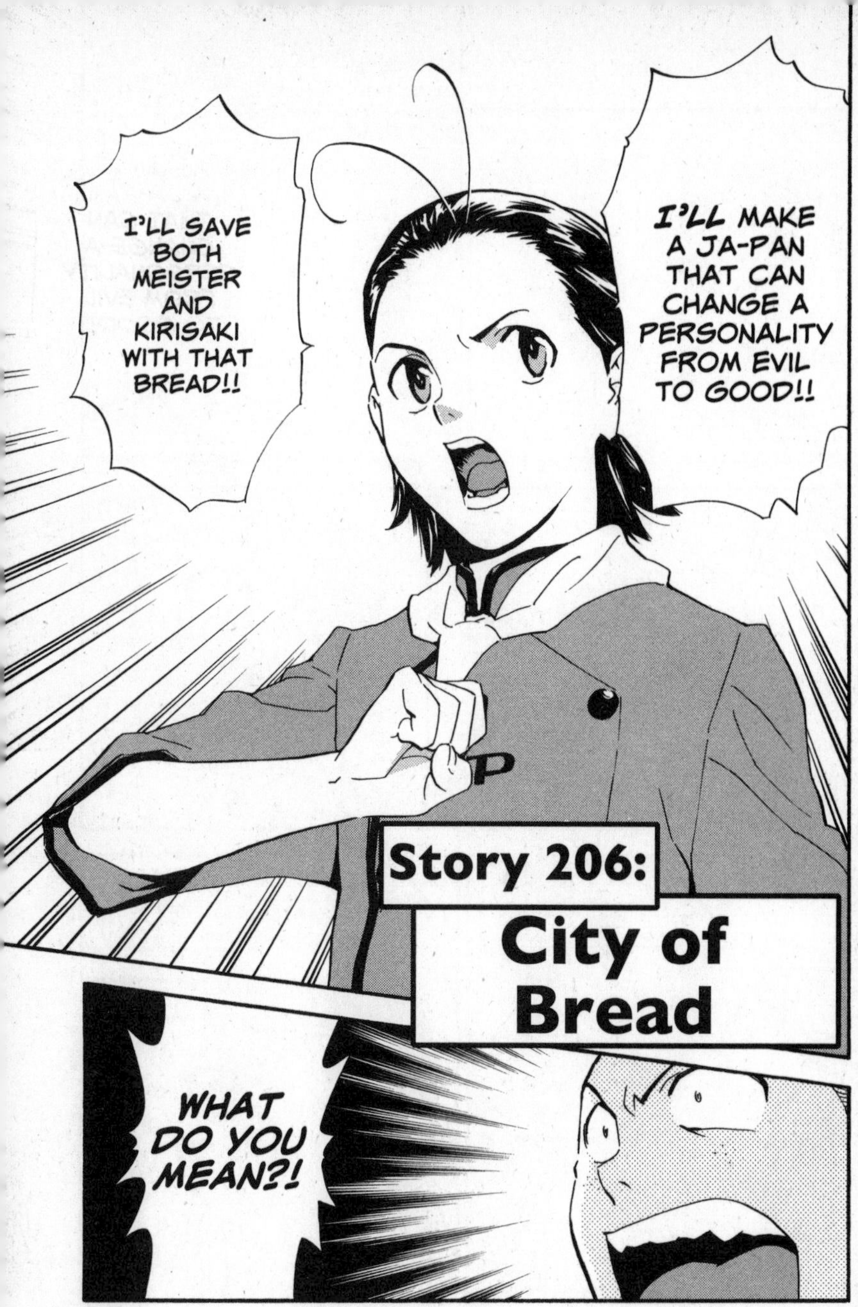
I'LL MAKE A JA-PAN THAT CAN CHANGE A PERSONALITY FROM EVIL TO GOOD!!
I'LL SAVE BOTH MEISTER AND KIRISAKI WITH THAT BREAD!!
Story 206:
City of Bread
WHAT DO YOU MEAN?!

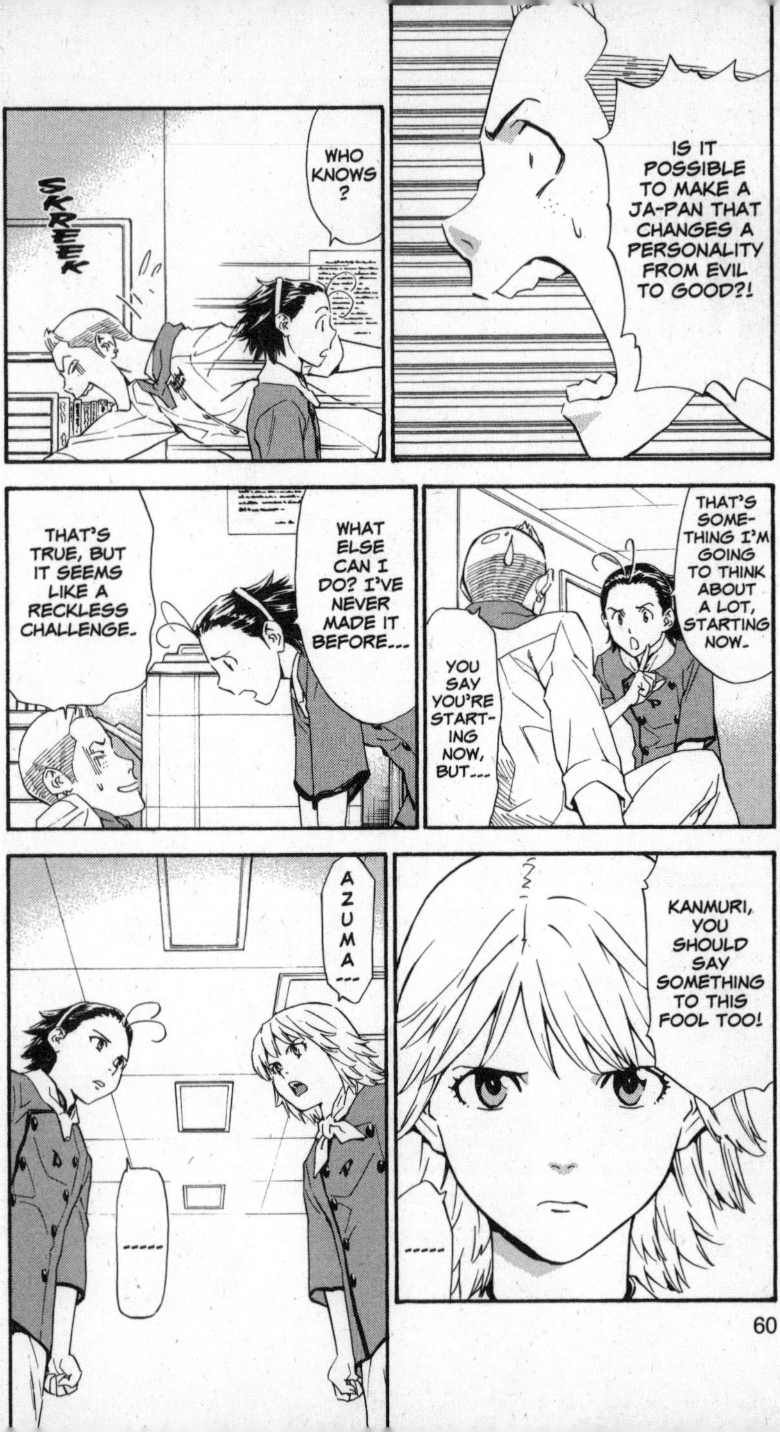
IS IT POSSIBLE TO MAKE A JA-PAN THAT CHANGES A PERSONALITY FROM EVIL TO GOOD?!
WHO KNOWS?
SKREEK
THAT'S SOMETHING I'M GOING TO THINK ABOUT A LOT, STARTING NOW.
YOU SAY YOU'RE STARTING NOW, BUT...
WHAT ELSE CAN I DO? I'VE NEVER MADE IT BEFORE...
THAT'S TRUE, BUT IT SEEMS LIKE A RECKLESS CHALLENGE.
KANMURI, YOU SHOULD SAY SOMETHING TO THIS FOOL TOO!
.....
AZUMA...
.....

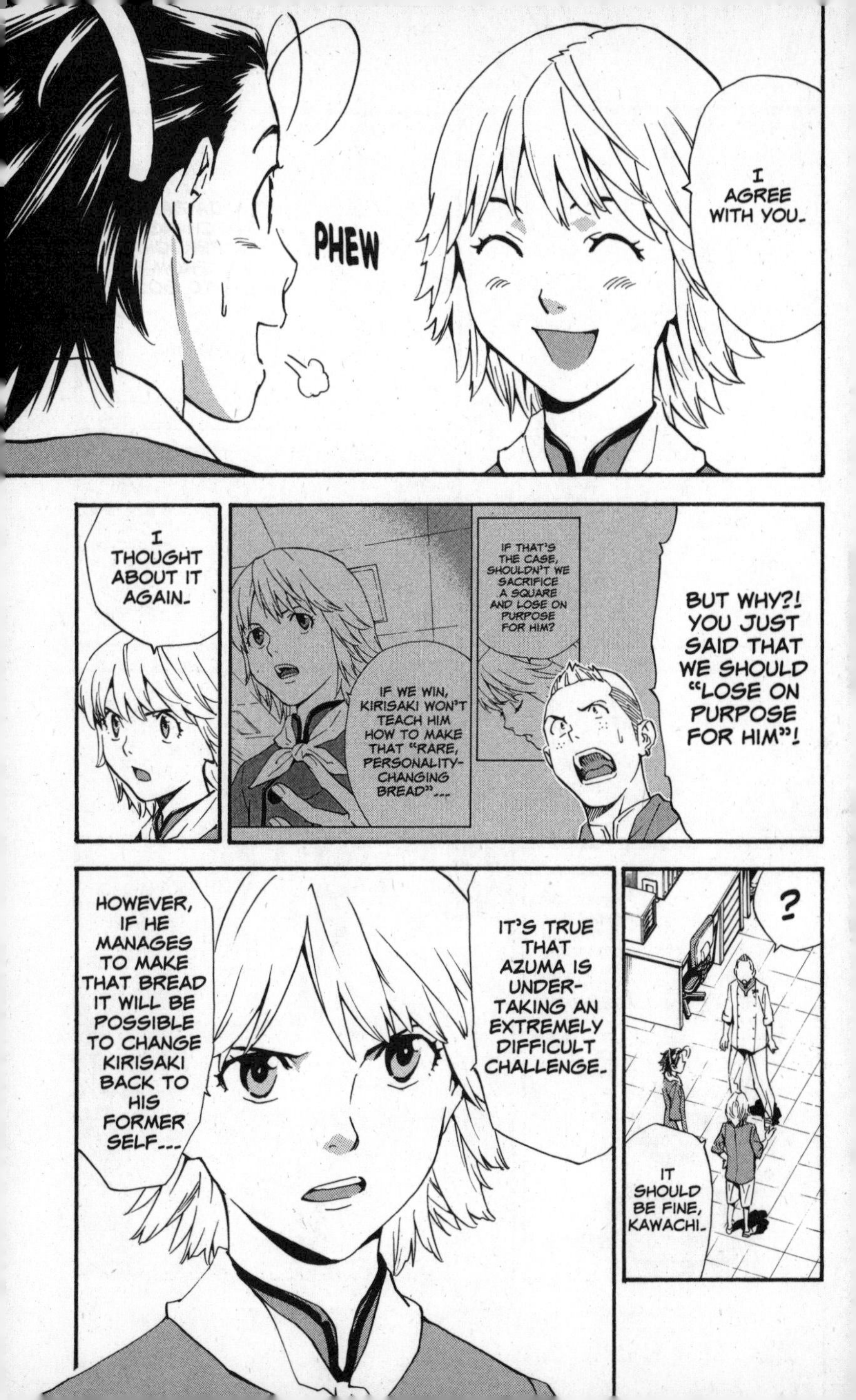
I AGREE WITH YOU.
PHEW
BUT WHY?! YOU JUST SAID THAT WE SHOULD “LOSE ON PURPOSE FOR HIM”!
IF THAT’S THE CASE, SHOULDN’T WE SACRIFICE A SQUARE AND LOSE ON PURPOSE FOR HIM?
IF WE WIN, KIRISAKI WON’T TEACH HIM HOW TO MAKE THAT “RARE, PERSONALITY-CHANGING BREAD”...
I THOUGHT ABOUT IT AGAIN.
?
IT SHOULD BE FINE, KAWACHI.
IT’S TRUE THAT AZUMA IS UNDER-TAKING AN EXTREMELY DIFFICULT CHALLENGE.
HOWEVER, IF HE MANAGES TO MAKE THAT BREAD IT WILL BE POSSIBLE TO CHANGE KIRISAKI BACK TO HIS FORMER SELF...

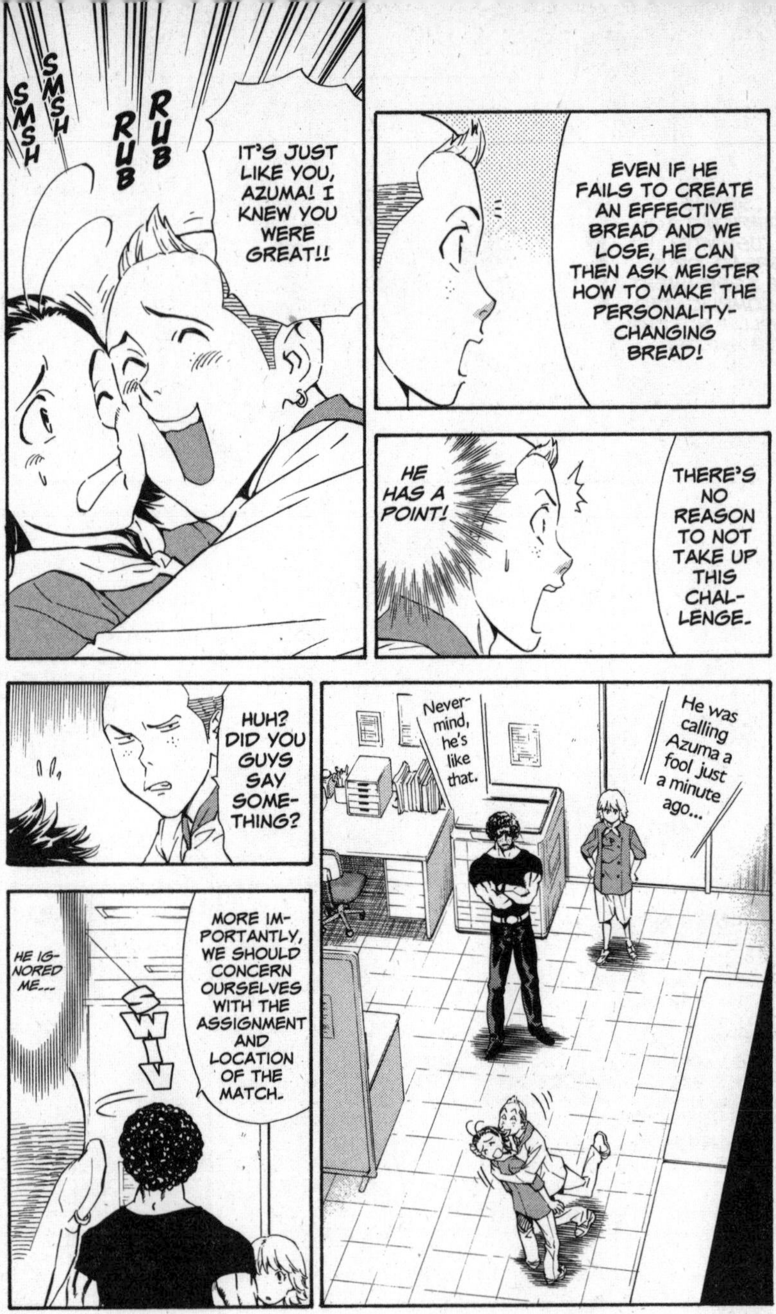
EVEN IF HE FAILS TO CREATE AN EFFECTIVE BREAD AND WE LOSE, HE CAN THEN ASK MEISTER HOW TO MAKE THE PERSONALITY-CHANGING BREAD!
THERE'S NO REASON TO NOT TAKE UP THIS CHAL-LENGE.
HE HAS A POINT!
IT'S JUST LIKE YOU, AZUMA! I KNEW YOU WERE GREAT!!
RUB RUB
SMSH SMSH
He was calling Azuma a fool just a minute ago...
Never-mind, he's like that.
HUH? DID YOU GUYS SAY SOME-THING?
MORE IM-PORTANTLY, WE SHOULD CONCERN OURSELVES WITH THE ASSIGNMENT AND LOCATION OF THE MATCH.
SWIV
HE IG-NORED ME...

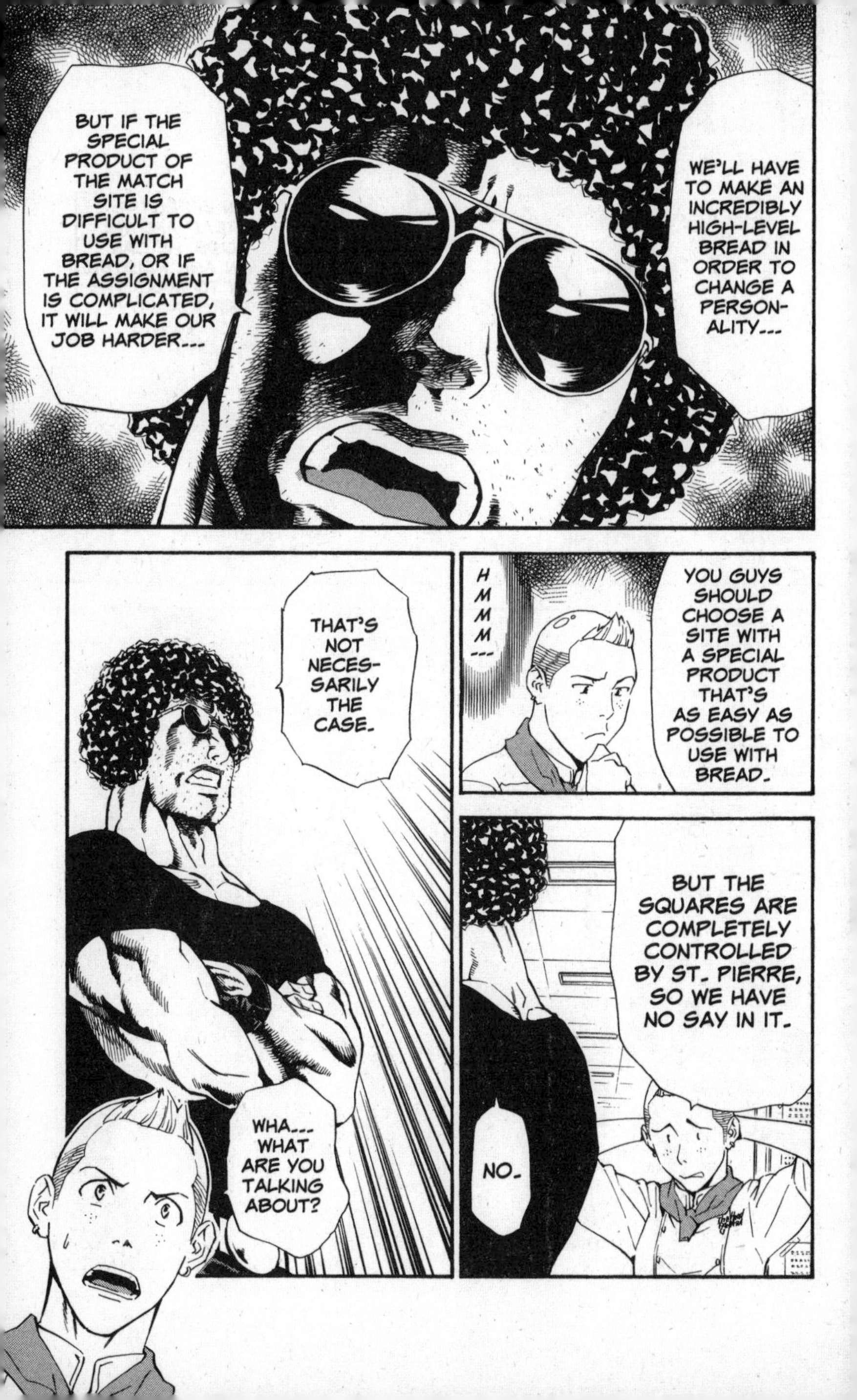
WE'LL HAVE TO MAKE AN INCREDIBLY HIGH-LEVEL BREAD IN ORDER TO CHANGE A PERSON-ALITY...
BUT IF THE SPECIAL PRODUCT OF THE MATCH SITE IS DIFFICULT TO USE WITH BREAD, OR IF THE ASSIGNMENT IS COMPLICATED, IT WILL MAKE OUR JOB HARDER...
YOU GUYS SHOULD CHOOSE A SITE WITH A SPECIAL PRODUCT THAT'S AS EASY AS POSSIBLE TO USE WITH BREAD.
HMMM...
BUT THE SQUARES ARE COMPLETELY CONTROLLED BY ST. PIERRE, SO WE HAVE NO SAY IN IT.
NO.
THAT'S NOT NECES-SARILY THE CASE.
WHA... WHAT ARE YOU TALKING ABOUT?

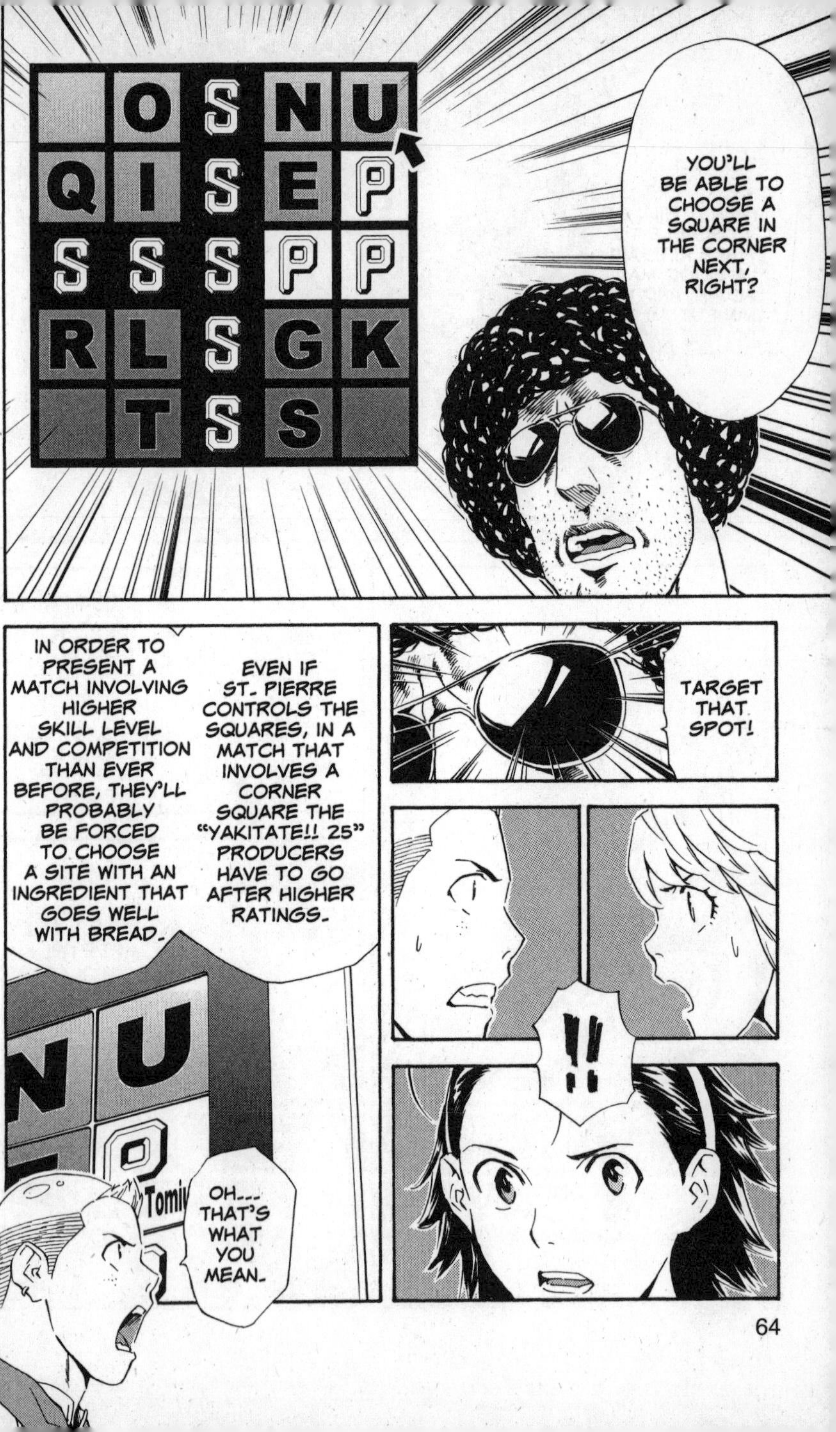
YOU'LL BE ABLE TO CHOOSE A SQUARE IN THE CORNER NEXT, RIGHT?
TARGET THAT SPOT!
!!
EVEN IF ST. PIERRE CONTROLS THE SQUARES, IN A MATCH THAT INVOLVES A CORNER SQUARE THE "YAKITATE!! 25" PRODUCERS HAVE TO GO AFTER HIGHER RATINGS.
IN ORDER TO PRESENT A MATCH INVOLVING HIGHER SKILL LEVEL AND COMPETITION THAN EVER BEFORE, THEY'LL PROBABLY BE FORCED TO CHOOSE A SITE WITH AN INGREDIENT THAT GOES WELL WITH BREAD.
OH... THAT'S WHAT YOU MEAN.

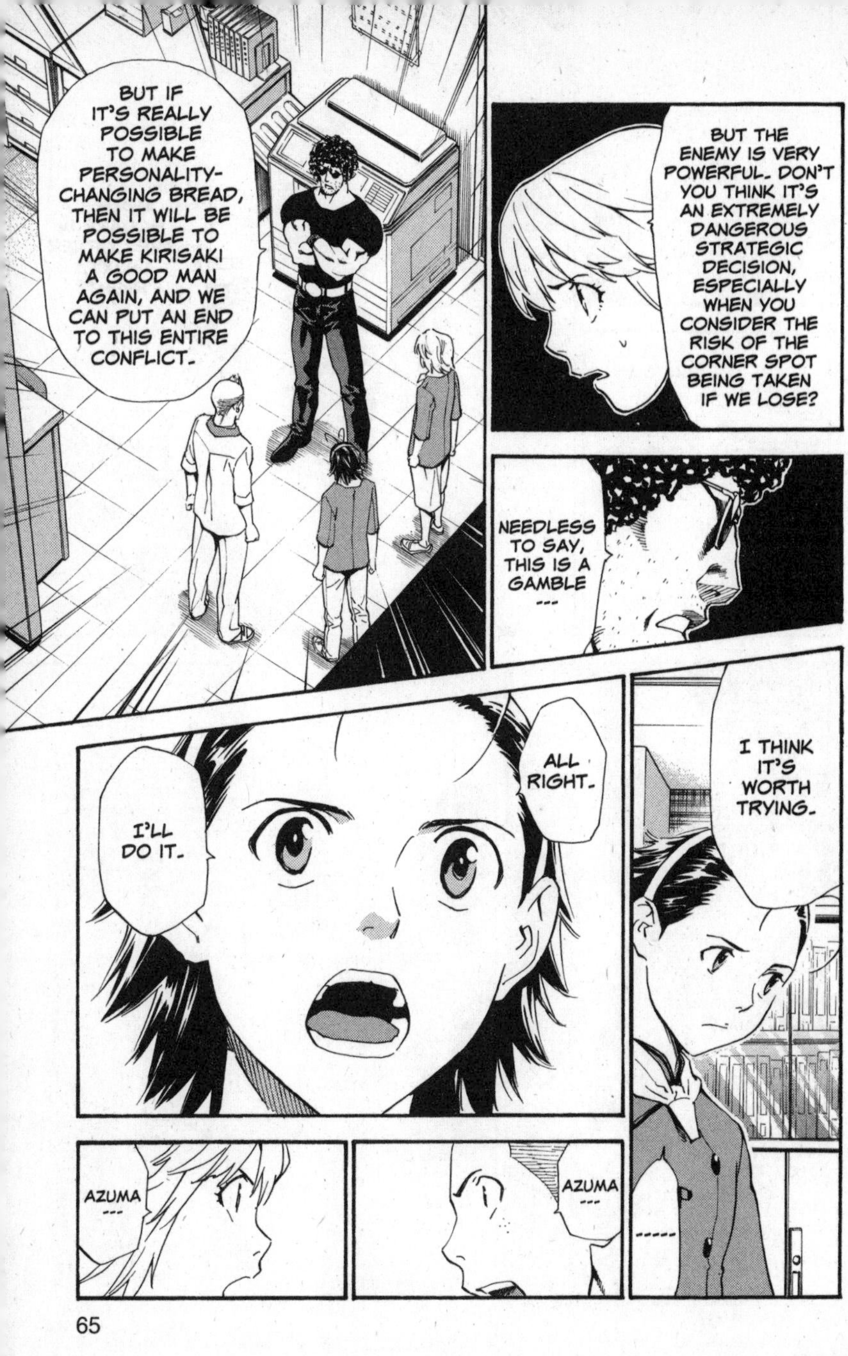
BUT IF IT'S REALLY POSSIBLE TO MAKE PERSONALITY-CHANGING BREAD, THEN IT WILL BE POSSIBLE TO MAKE KIRISAKI A GOOD MAN AGAIN, AND WE CAN PUT AN END TO THIS ENTIRE CONFLICT.
BUT THE ENEMY IS VERY POWERFUL. DON'T YOU THINK IT'S AN EXTREMELY DANGEROUS STRATEGIC DECISION, ESPECIALLY WHEN YOU CONSIDER THE RISK OF THE CORNER SPOT BEING TAKEN IF WE LOSE?
NEEDLESS TO SAY, THIS IS A GAMBLE ---
ALL RIGHT.
I'LL DO IT.
AZUMA ---
AZUMA ---
I THINK IT'S WORTH TRYING.

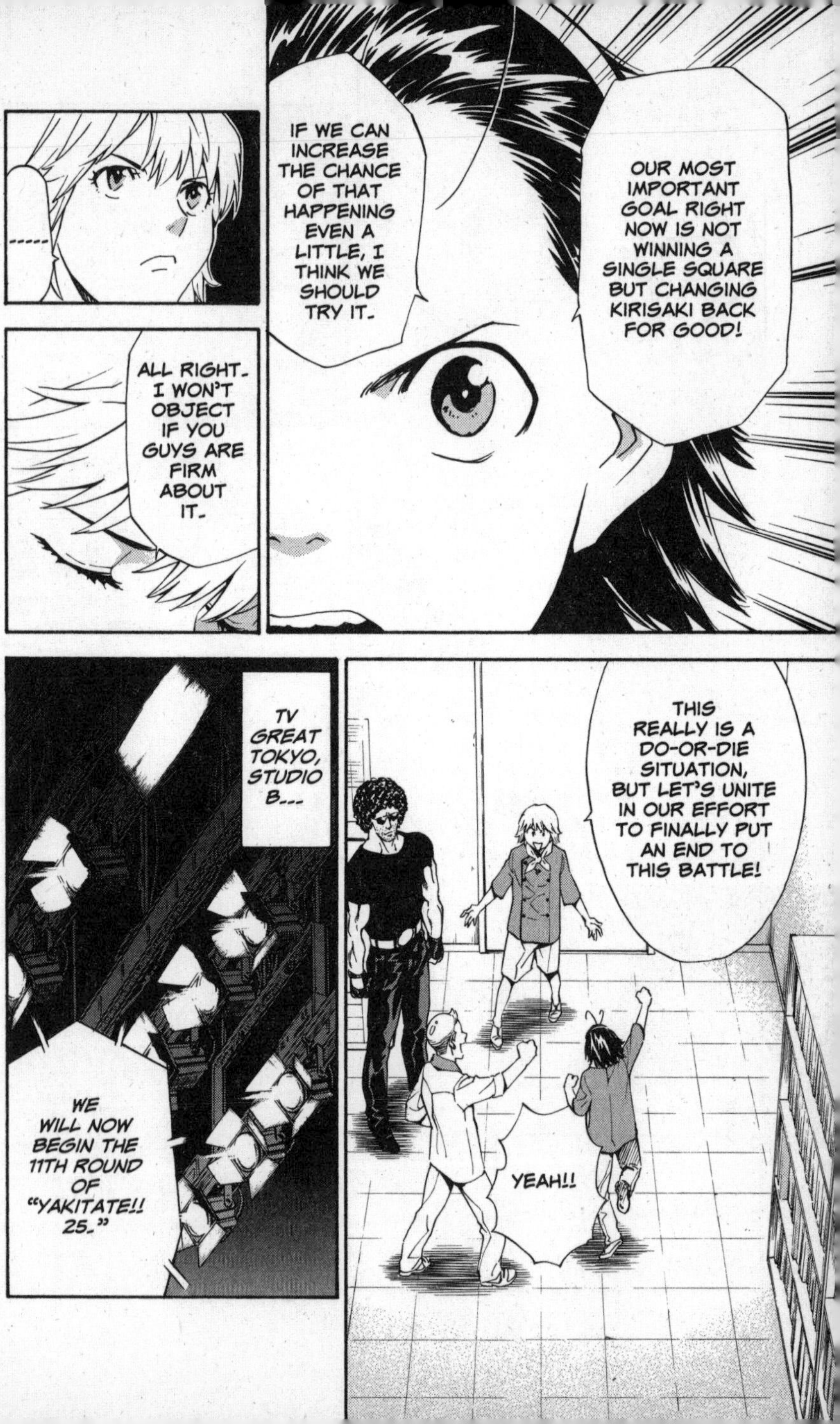
OUR MOST IMPORTANT GOAL RIGHT NOW IS NOT WINNING A SINGLE SQUARE BUT CHANGING KIRISAKI BACK FOR GOOD!
IF WE CAN INCREASE THE CHANCE OF THAT HAPPENING EVEN A LITTLE, I THINK WE SHOULD TRY IT.
.....
ALL RIGHT. I WON'T OBJECT IF YOU GUYS ARE FIRM ABOUT IT.
THIS REALLY IS A DO-OR-DIE SITUATION, BUT LET'S UNITE IN OUR EFFORT TO FINALLY PUT AN END TO THIS BATTLE!
YEAH!!
TV GREAT TOKYO, STUDIO B...
WE WILL NOW BEGIN THE 11TH ROUND OF "YAKITATE!! 25."

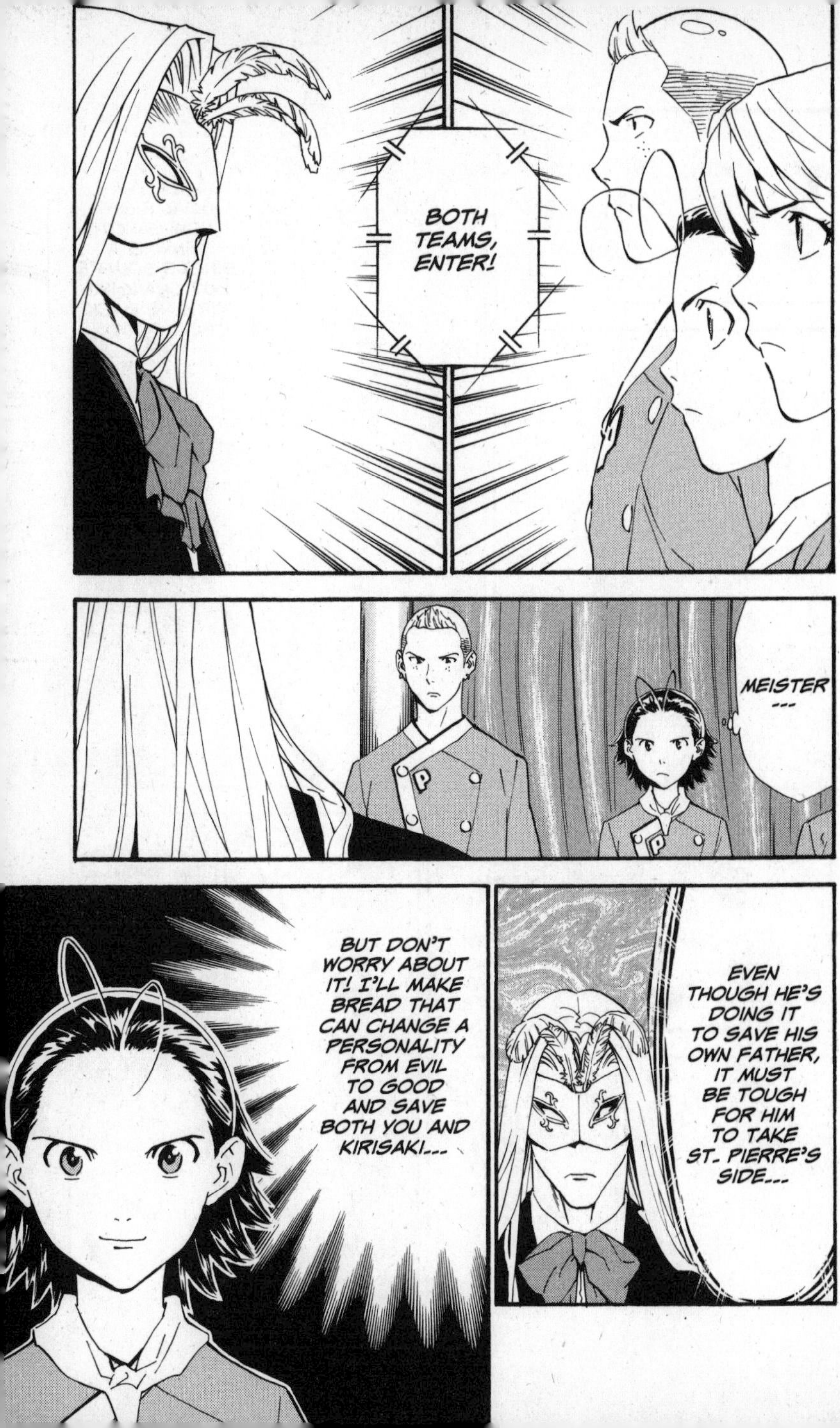
BOTH TEAMS, ENTER!
MEISTER---
EVEN THOUGH HE'S DOING IT TO SAVE HIS OWN FATHER, IT MUST BE TOUGH FOR HIM TO TAKE ST. PIERRE'S SIDE...
BUT DON'T WORRY ABOUT IT! I'LL MAKE BREAD THAT CAN CHANGE A PERSONALITY FROM EVIL TO GOOD AND SAVE BOTH YOU AND KIRISAKI...

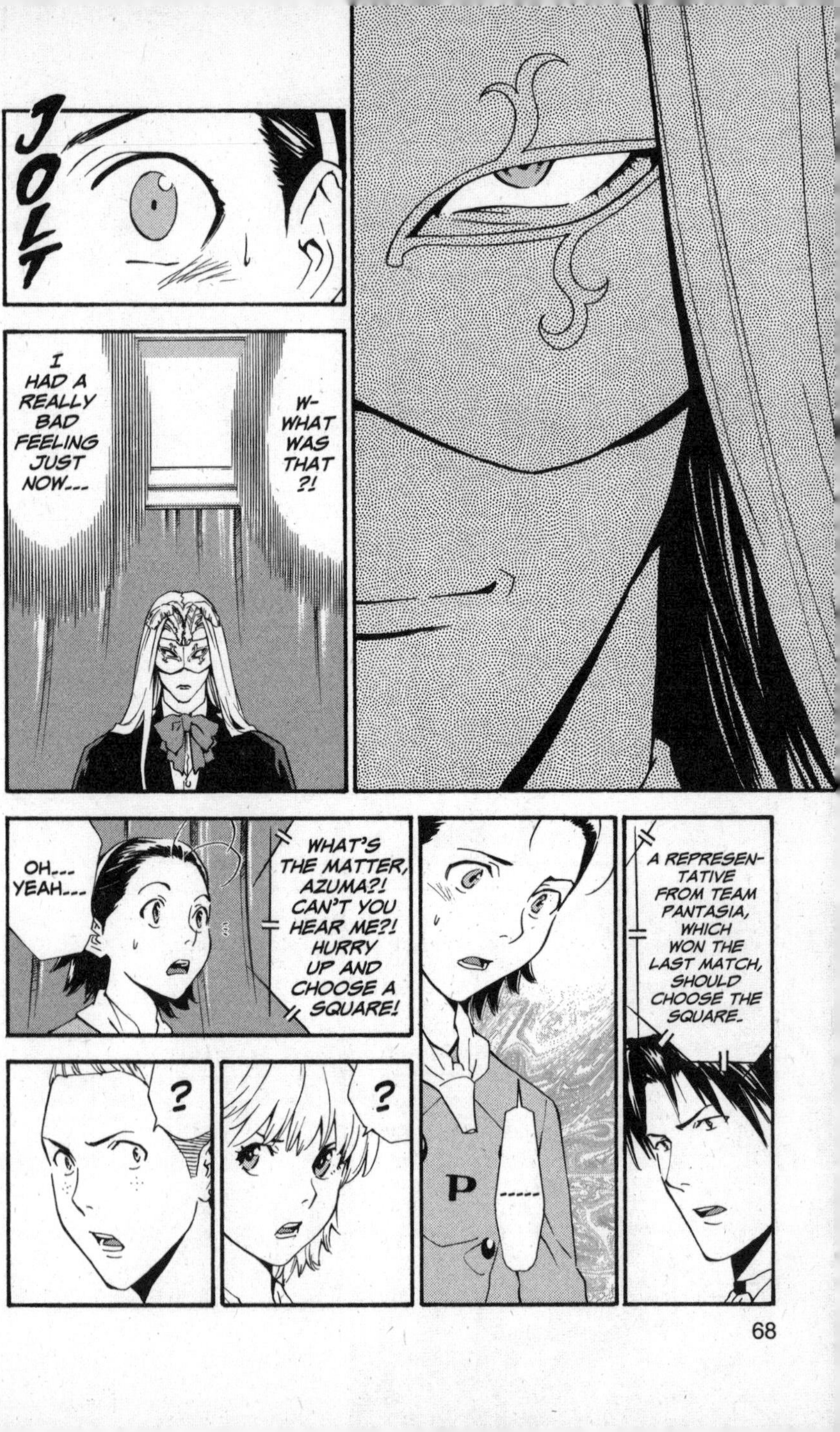
JOLT
W-WHAT WAS THAT?!
I HAD A REALLY BAD FEELING JUST NOW...
A REPRESENTATIVE FROM TEAM PANTASIA, WHICH WON THE LAST MATCH, SHOULD CHOOSE THE SQUARE.
P
......
WHAT'S THE MATTER, AZUMA?! CAN'T YOU HEAR ME?! HURRY UP AND CHOOSE A SQUARE!
OH... YEAH...
?
?

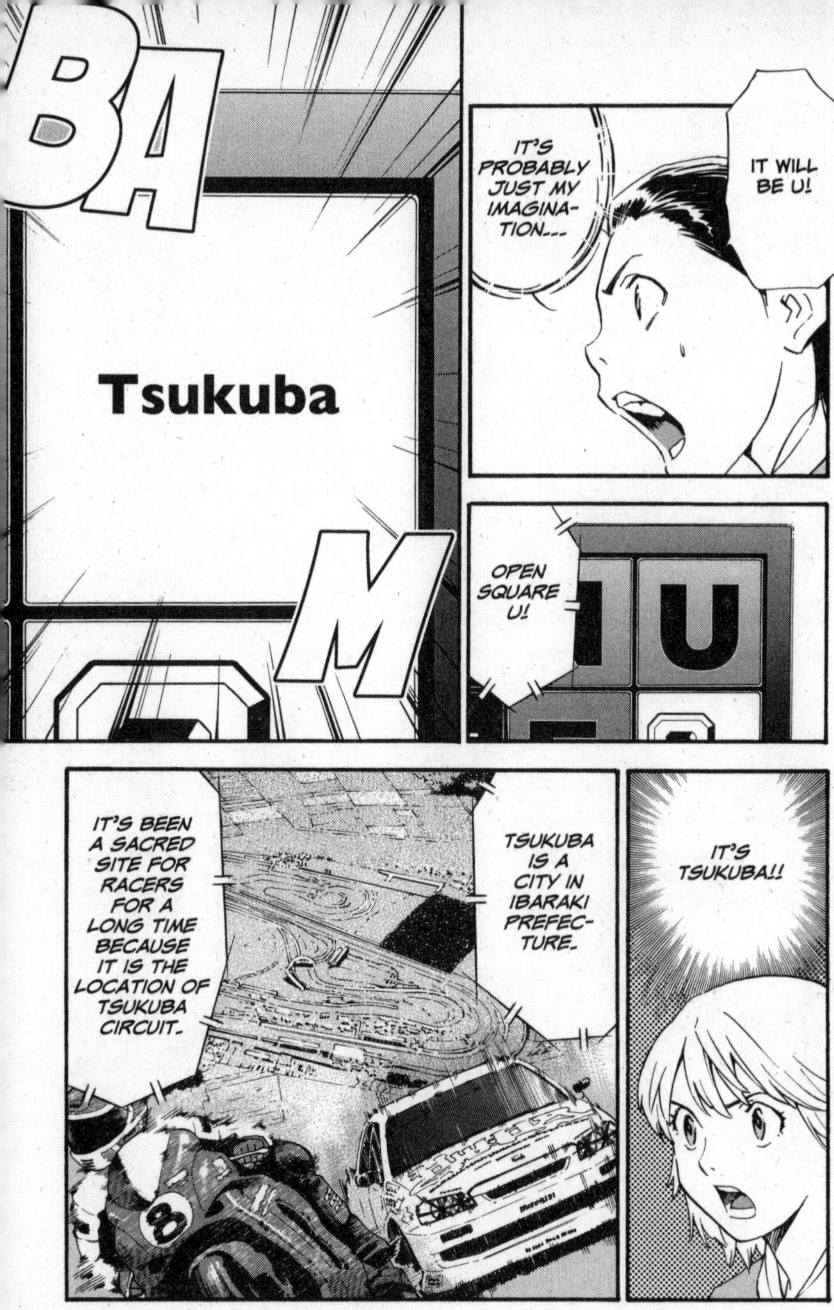
IT WILL BE U!
IT'S PROBABLY JUST MY IMAGINATION...
OPEN SQUARE U!
U
BA
Tsukuba
M
IT'S TSUKUBA!!
TSUKUBA IS A CITY IN IBARAKI PREFECTURE.
IT'S BEEN A SACRED SITE FOR RACERS FOR A LONG TIME BECAUSE IT IS THE LOCATION OF TSUKUBA CIRCUIT.

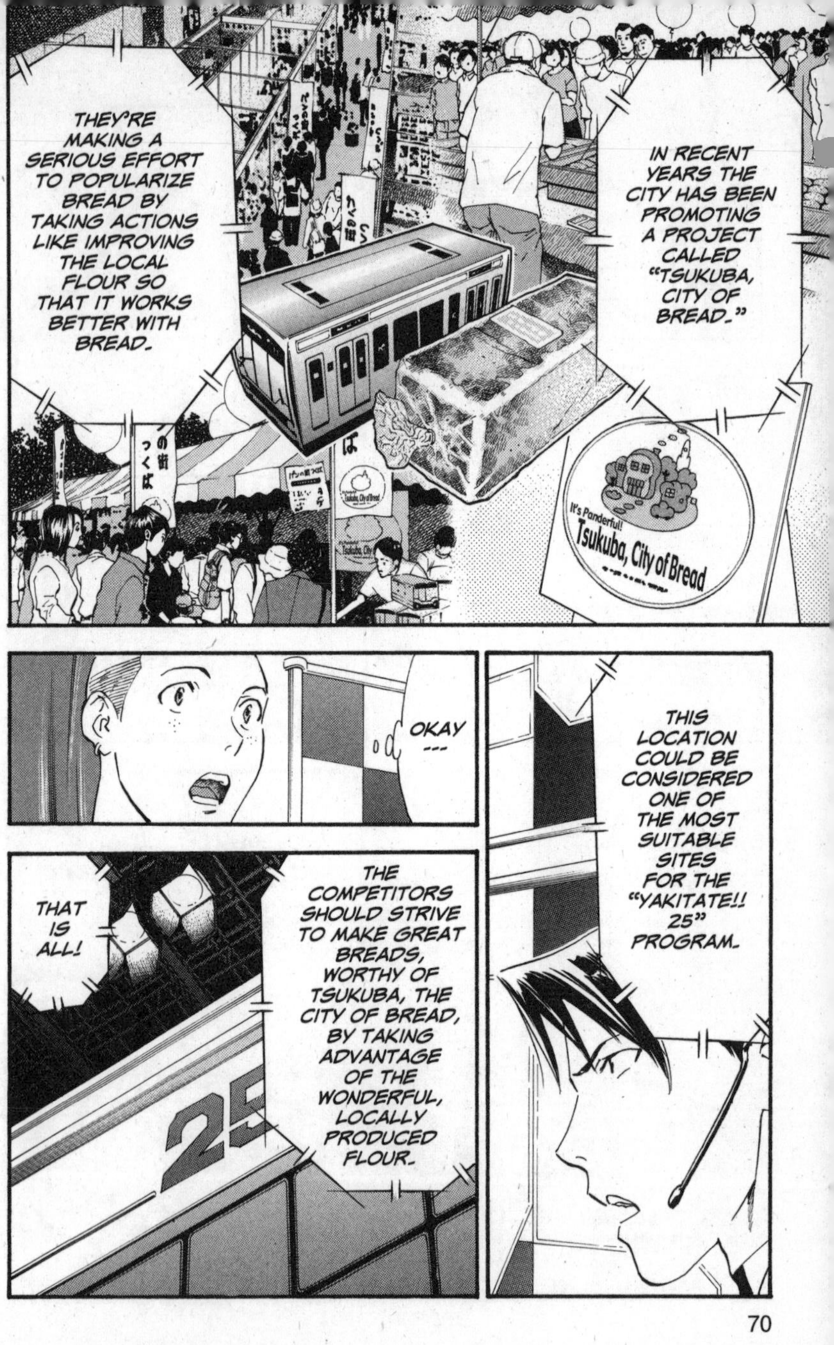
IN RECENT YEARS THE CITY HAS BEEN PROMOTING A PROJECT CALLED "TSUKUBA, CITY OF BREAD."
THEY'RE MAKING A SERIOUS EFFORT TO POPULARIZE BREAD BY TAKING ACTIONS LIKE IMPROVING THE LOCAL FLOUR SO THAT IT WORKS BETTER WITH BREAD.
It's Panderful!
Tsukuba, City of Bread
THIS LOCATION COULD BE CONSIDERED ONE OF THE MOST SUITABLE SITES FOR THE "YAKITATE!! 25" PROGRAM.
OKAY ---
THE COMPETITORS SHOULD STRIVE TO MAKE GREAT BREADS, WORTHY OF TSUKUBA, THE CITY OF BREAD, BY TAKING ADVANTAGE OF THE WONDERFUL, LOCALLY PRODUCED FLOUR.
THAT IS ALL!
25

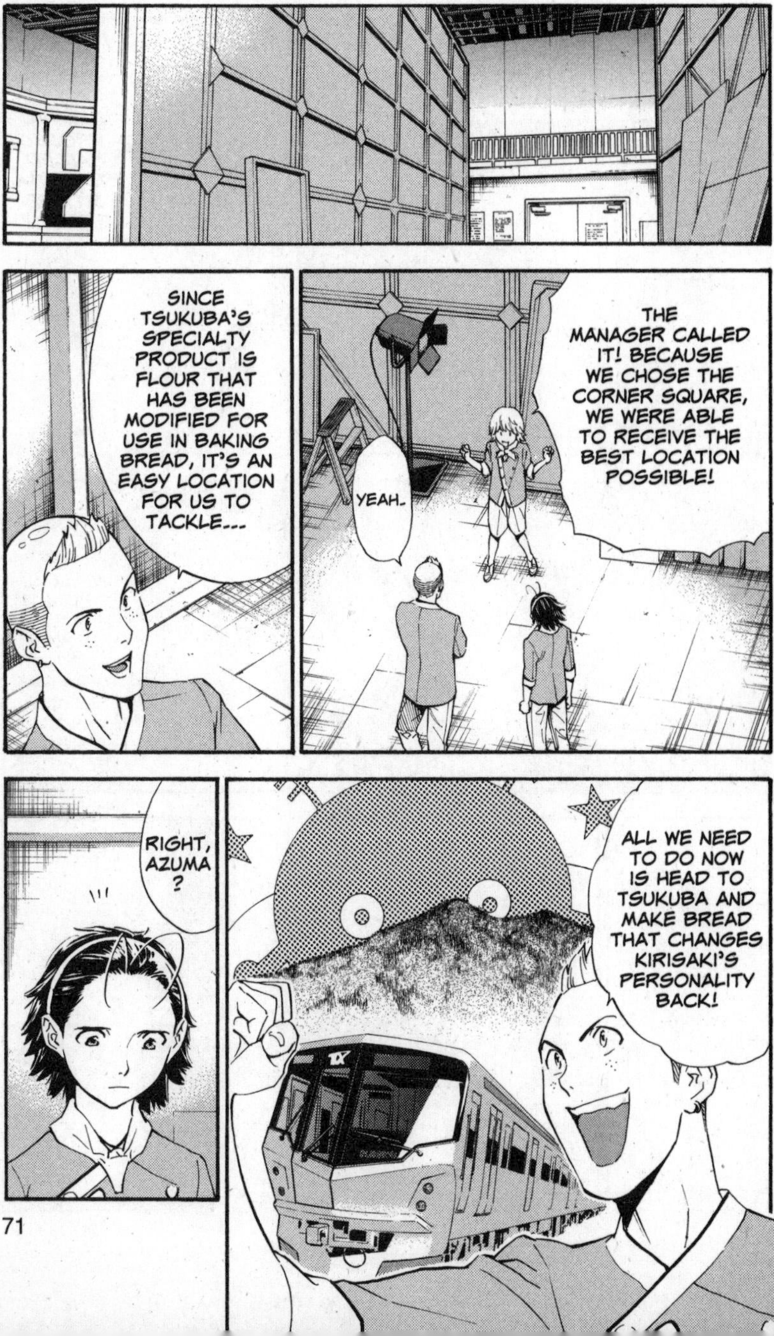
THE MANAGER CALLED IT! BECAUSE WE CHOSE THE CORNER SQUARE, WE WERE ABLE TO RECEIVE THE BEST LOCATION POSSIBLE!
YEAH.
SINCE TSUKUBA'S SPECIALTY PRODUCT IS FLOUR THAT HAS BEEN MODIFIED FOR USE IN BAKING BREAD, IT'S AN EASY LOCATION FOR US TO TACKLE...
ALL WE NEED TO DO NOW IS HEAD TO TSUKUBA AND MAKE BREAD THAT CHANGES KIRISAKI'S PERSONALITY BACK!
RIGHT, AZUMA?

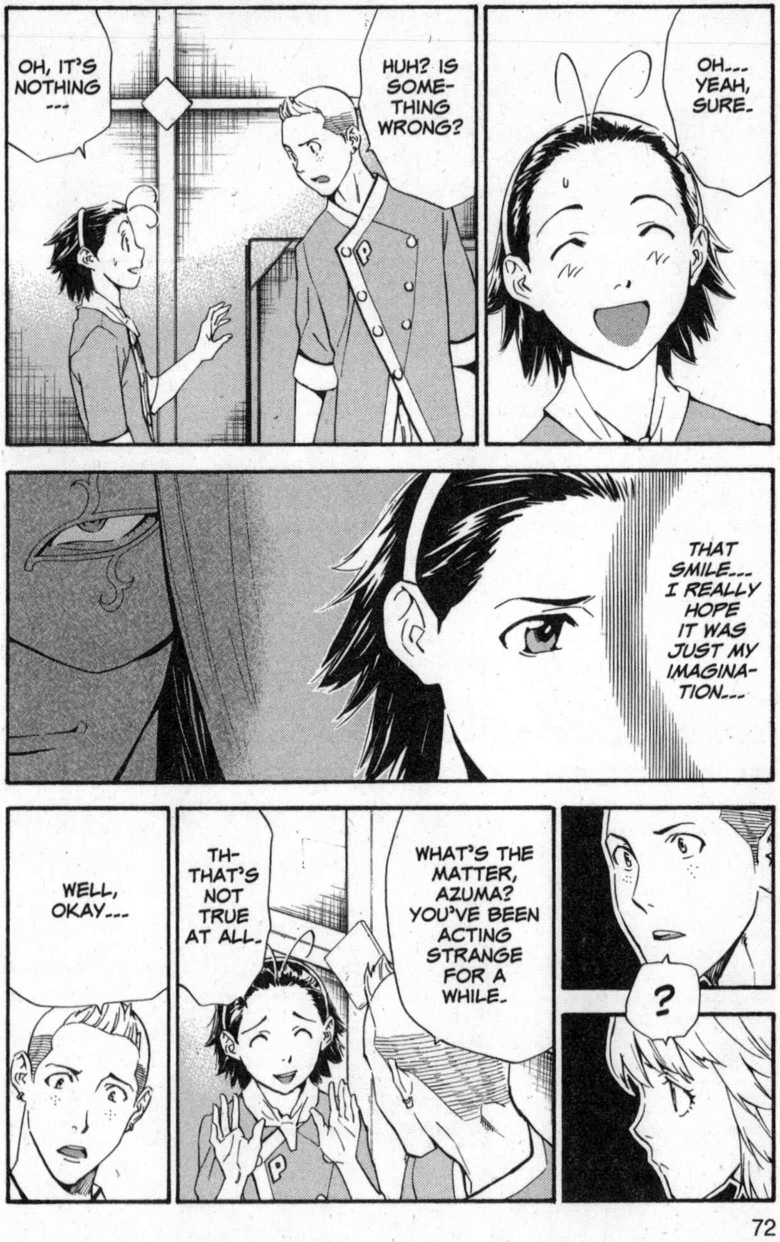
OH... YEAH, SURE.
HUH? IS SOME-THING WRONG?
OH, IT'S NOTHING ---
THAT SMILE... I REALLY HOPE IT WAS JUST MY IMAGINA-TION...
?
WHAT'S THE MATTER, AZUMA? YOU'VE BEEN ACTING STRANGE FOR A WHILE.
TH- THAT'S NOT TRUE AT ALL.
WELL, OKAY...

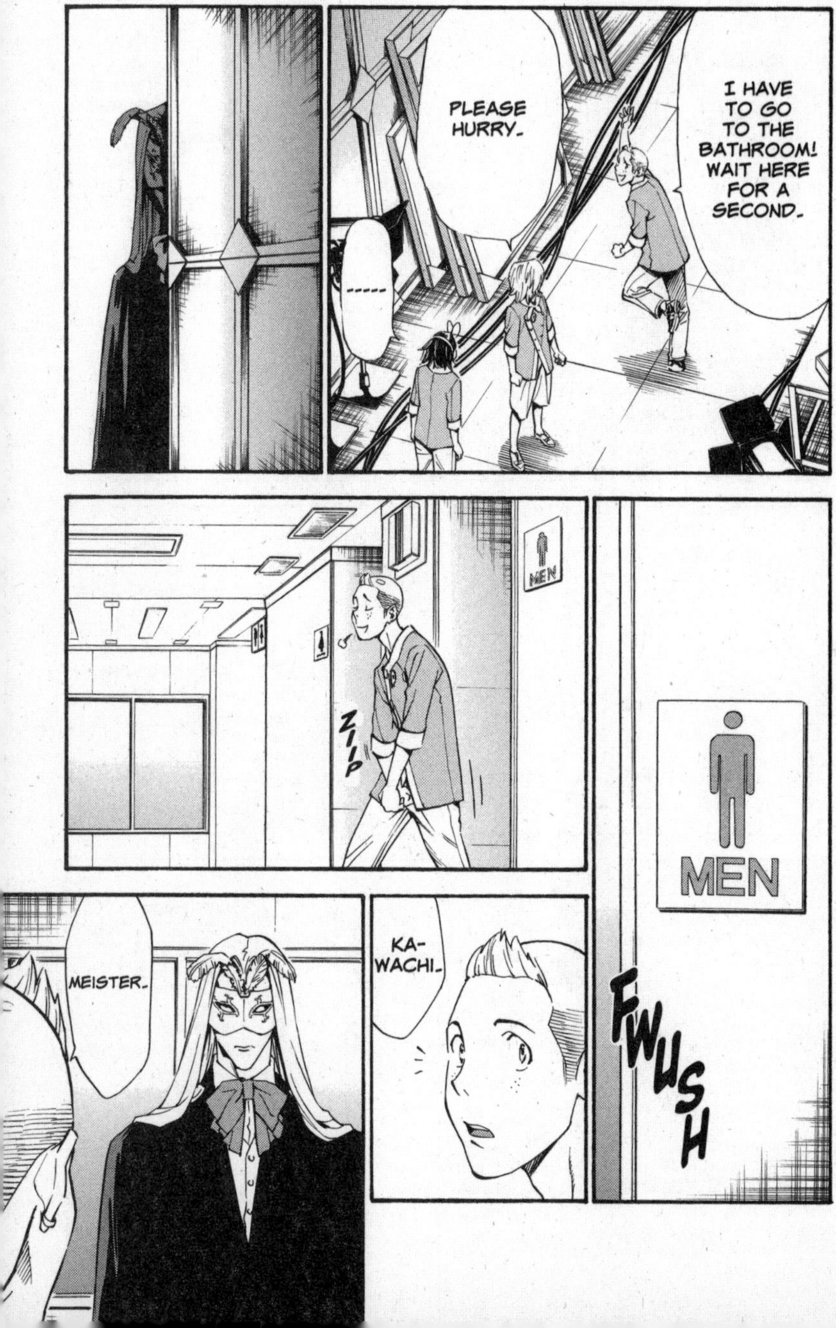
I HAVE TO GO TO THE BATHROOM! WAIT HERE FOR A SECOND..
PLEASE HURRY..
......
MEN
FWUSH
MEN
ZIIP
KA-WACHI..
MEISTER..

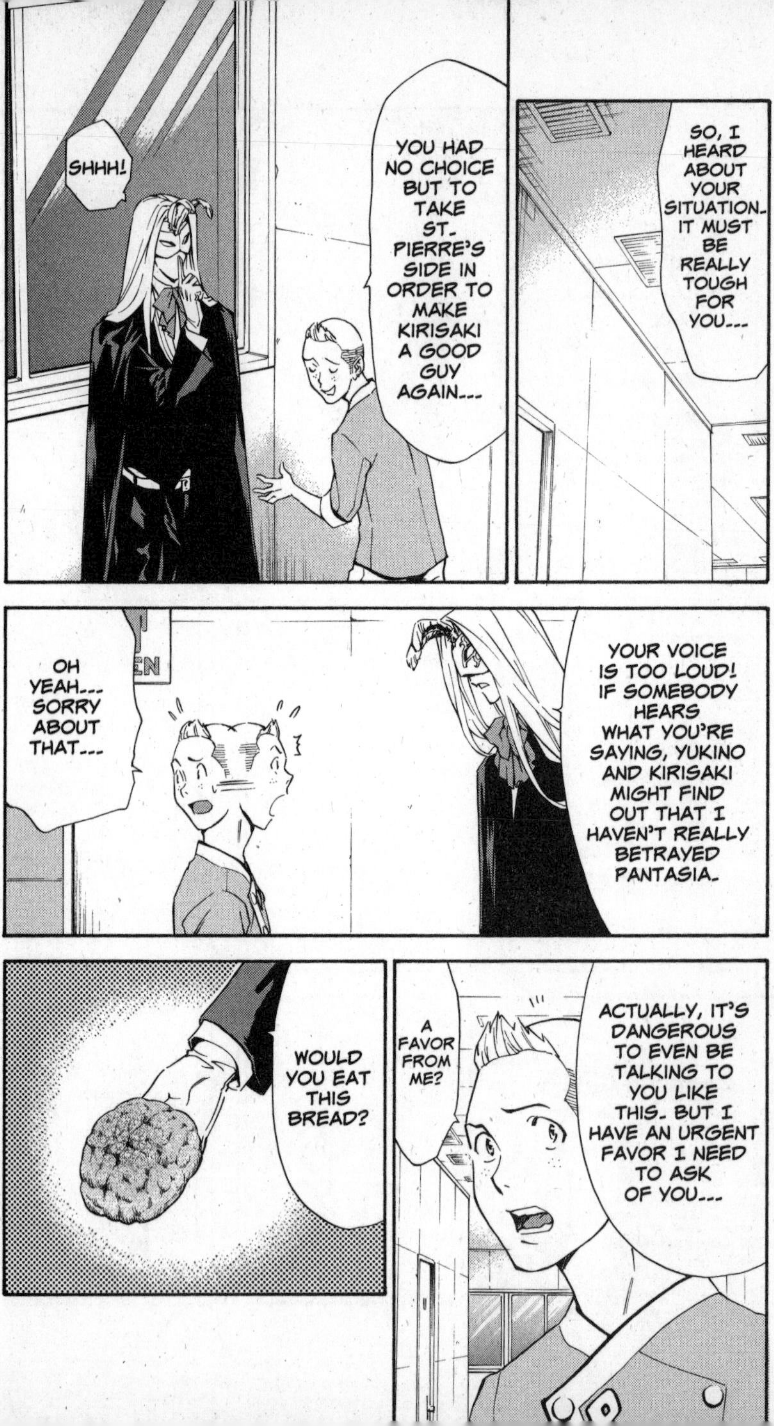
SO, I HEARD ABOUT YOUR SITUATION. IT MUST BE REALLY TOUGH FOR YOU...
YOU HAD NO CHOICE BUT TO TAKE ST. PIERRE'S SIDE IN ORDER TO MAKE KIRISAKI A GOOD GUY AGAIN...
SHHH!
YOUR VOICE IS TOO LOUD! IF SOMEBODY HEARS WHAT YOU'RE SAYING, YUKINO AND KIRISAKI MIGHT FIND OUT THAT I HAVEN'T REALLY BETRAYED PANTASIA.
OH YEAH... SORRY ABOUT THAT...
ACTUALLY, IT'S DANGEROUS TO EVEN BE TALKING TO YOU LIKE THIS. BUT I HAVE AN URGENT FAVOR I NEED TO ASK OF YOU...
A FAVOR FROM ME?
WOULD YOU EAT THIS BREAD?

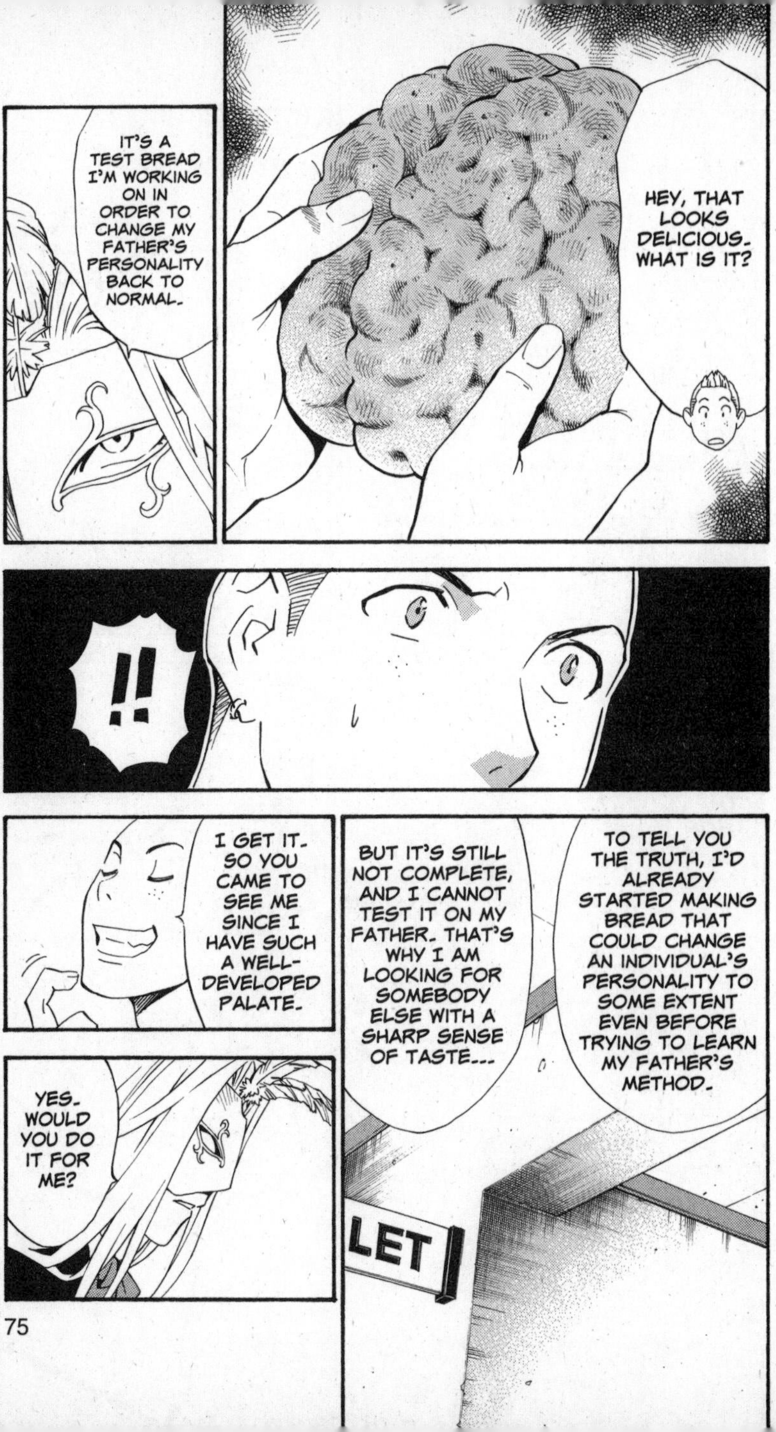
HEY, THAT LOOKS DELICIOUS. WHAT IS IT?
IT'S A TEST BREAD I'M WORKING ON IN ORDER TO CHANGE MY FATHER'S PERSONALITY BACK TO NORMAL.
!!
TO TELL YOU THE TRUTH, I'D ALREADY STARTED MAKING BREAD THAT COULD CHANGE AN INDIVIDUAL'S PERSONALITY TO SOME EXTENT EVEN BEFORE TRYING TO LEARN MY FATHER'S METHOD.
BUT IT'S STILL NOT COMPLETE, AND I CANNOT TEST IT ON MY FATHER. THAT'S WHY I AM LOOKING FOR SOMEBODY ELSE WITH A SHARP SENSE OF TASTE...
LET
I GET IT. SO YOU CAME TO SEE ME SINCE I HAVE SUCH A WELL-DEVELOPED PALATE.
YES. WOULD YOU DO IT FOR ME?

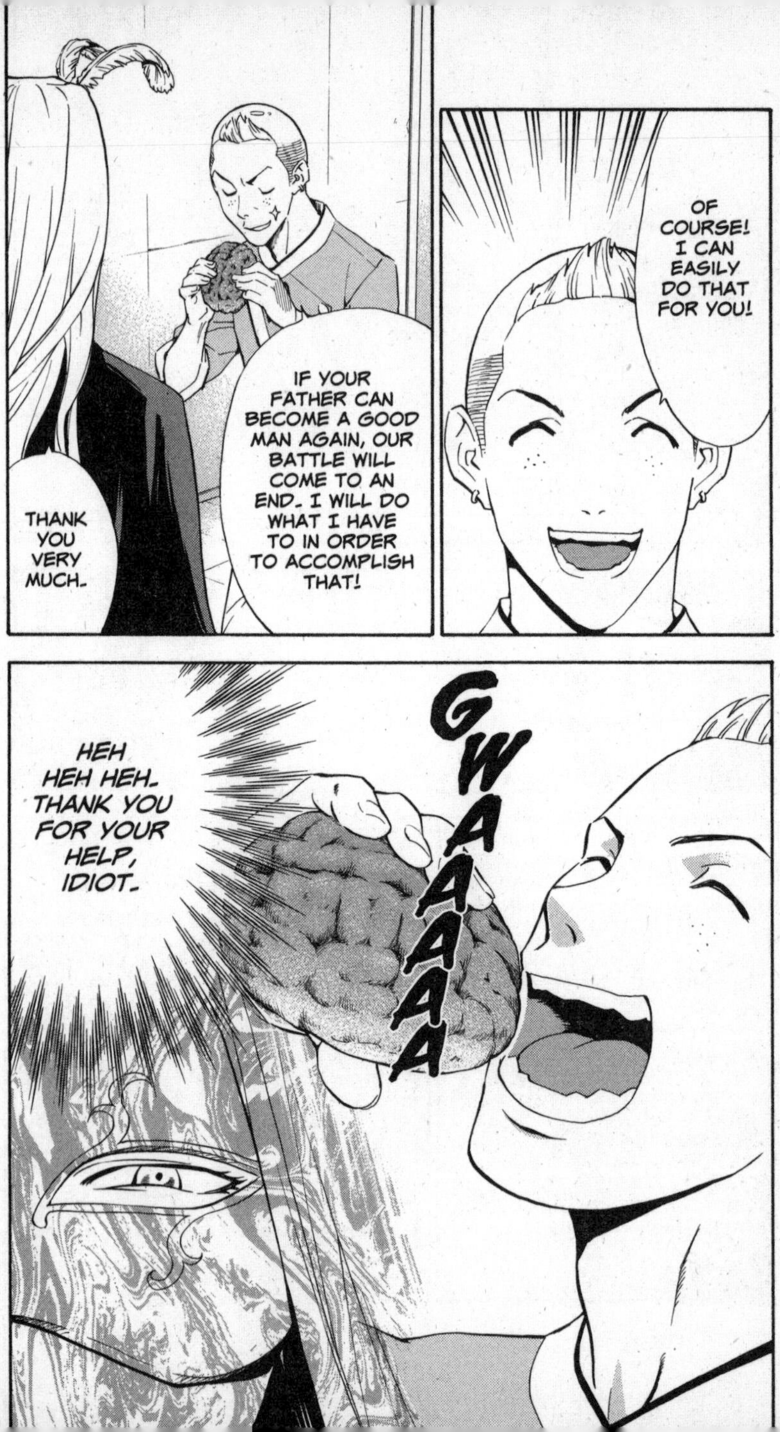
OF COURSE! I CAN EASILY DO THAT FOR YOU!
IF YOUR FATHER CAN BECOME A GOOD MAN AGAIN, OUR BATTLE WILL COME TO AN END. I WILL DO WHAT I HAVE TO IN ORDER TO ACCOMPLISH THAT!
THANK YOU VERY MUCH.
GWAAAAAAA
HEH HEH HEH. THANK YOU FOR YOUR HELP, IDIOT.

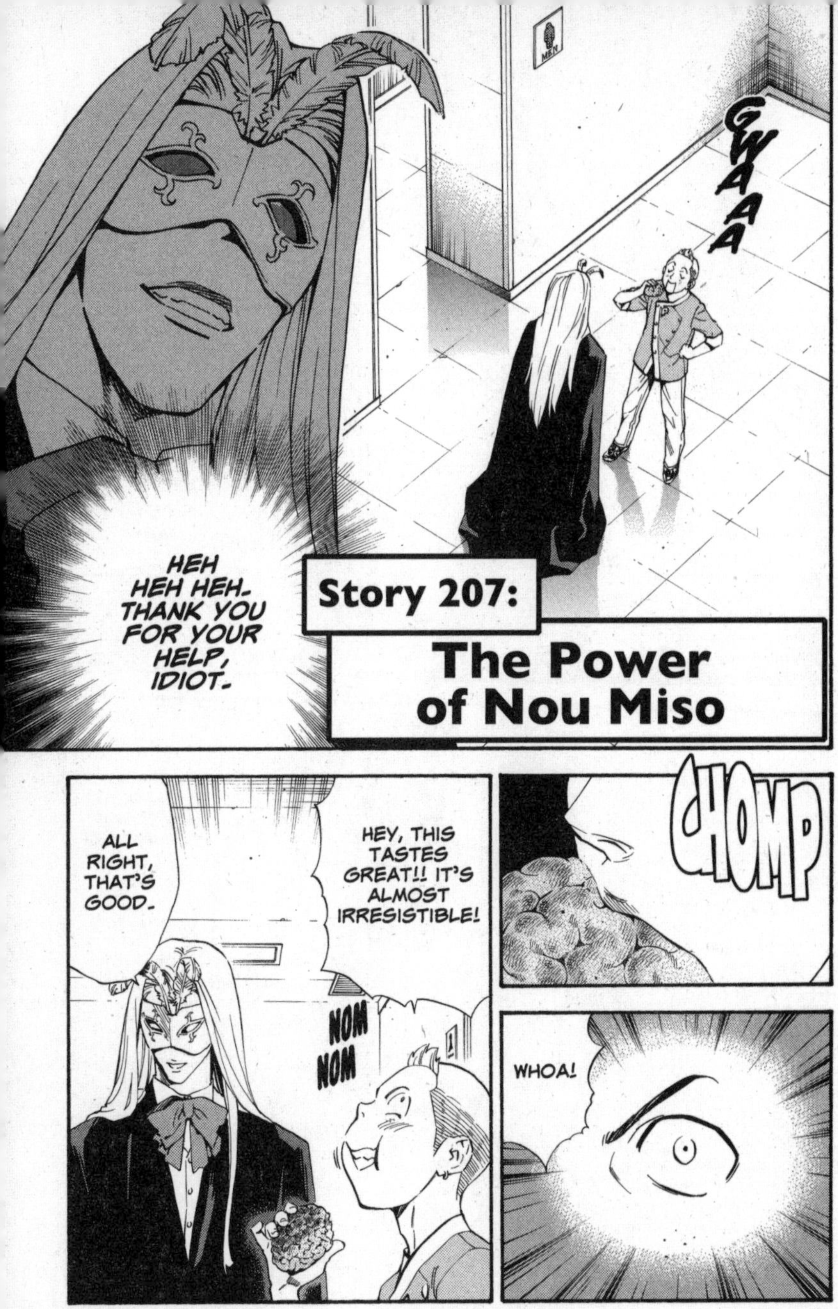
GWAAAA
HEH HEH HEH. THANK YOU FOR YOUR HELP, IDIOT.
Story 207:
The Power of Nou Miso
CHOMP
WHOA!
HEY, THIS TASTES GREAT!! IT'S ALMOST IRRESISTIBLE!
ALL RIGHT, THAT'S GOOD.
NOM NOM

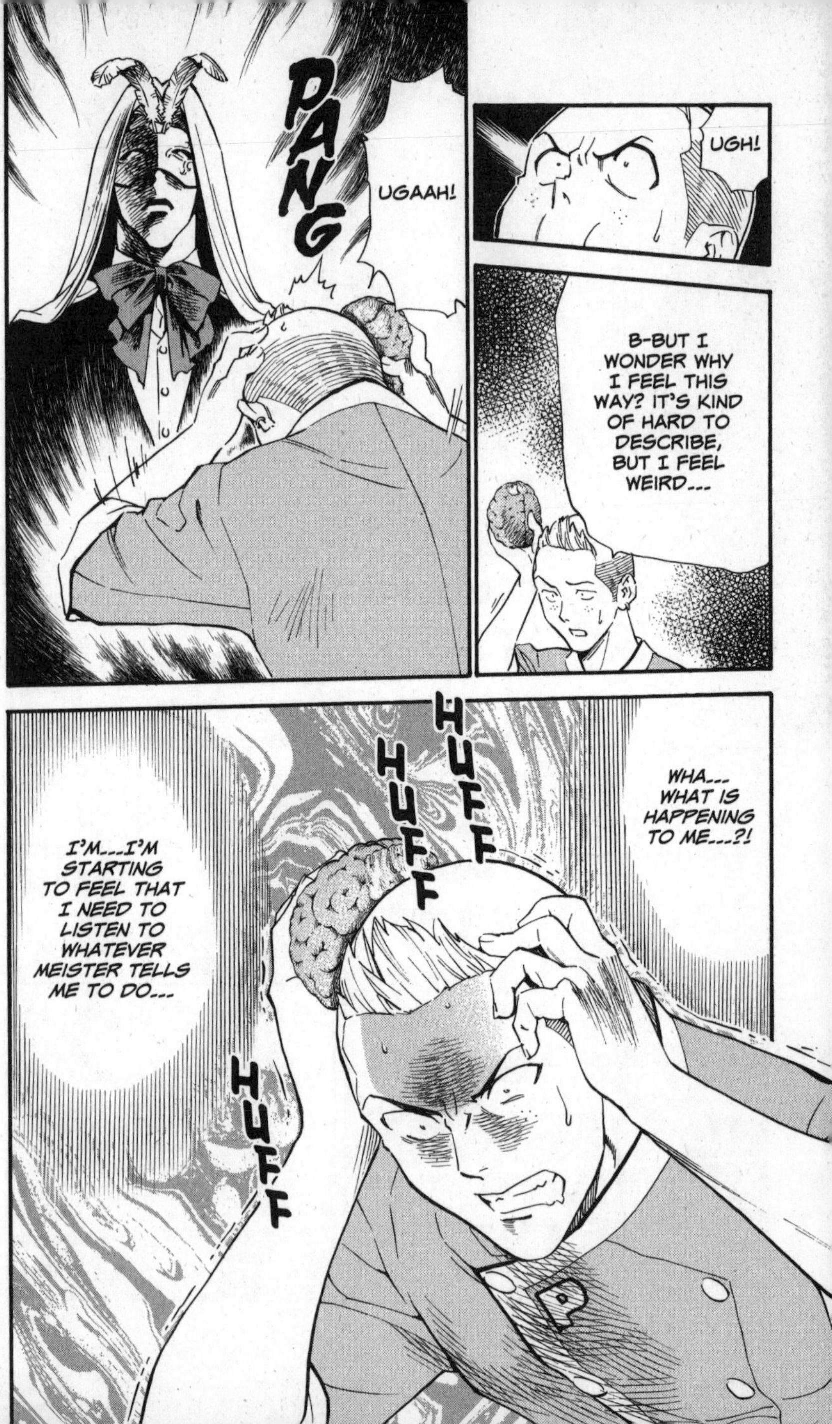
UGH!
B-BUT I WONDER WHY I FEEL THIS WAY? IT'S KIND OF HARD TO DESCRIBE, BUT I FEEL WEIRD...
PANG
UGAAH!
HUFF HUFF
WHA... WHAT IS HAPPENING TO ME...?!
I'M...I'M STARTING TO FEEL THAT I NEED TO LISTEN TO WHATEVER MEISTER TELLS ME TO DO...
HUFF HUFF

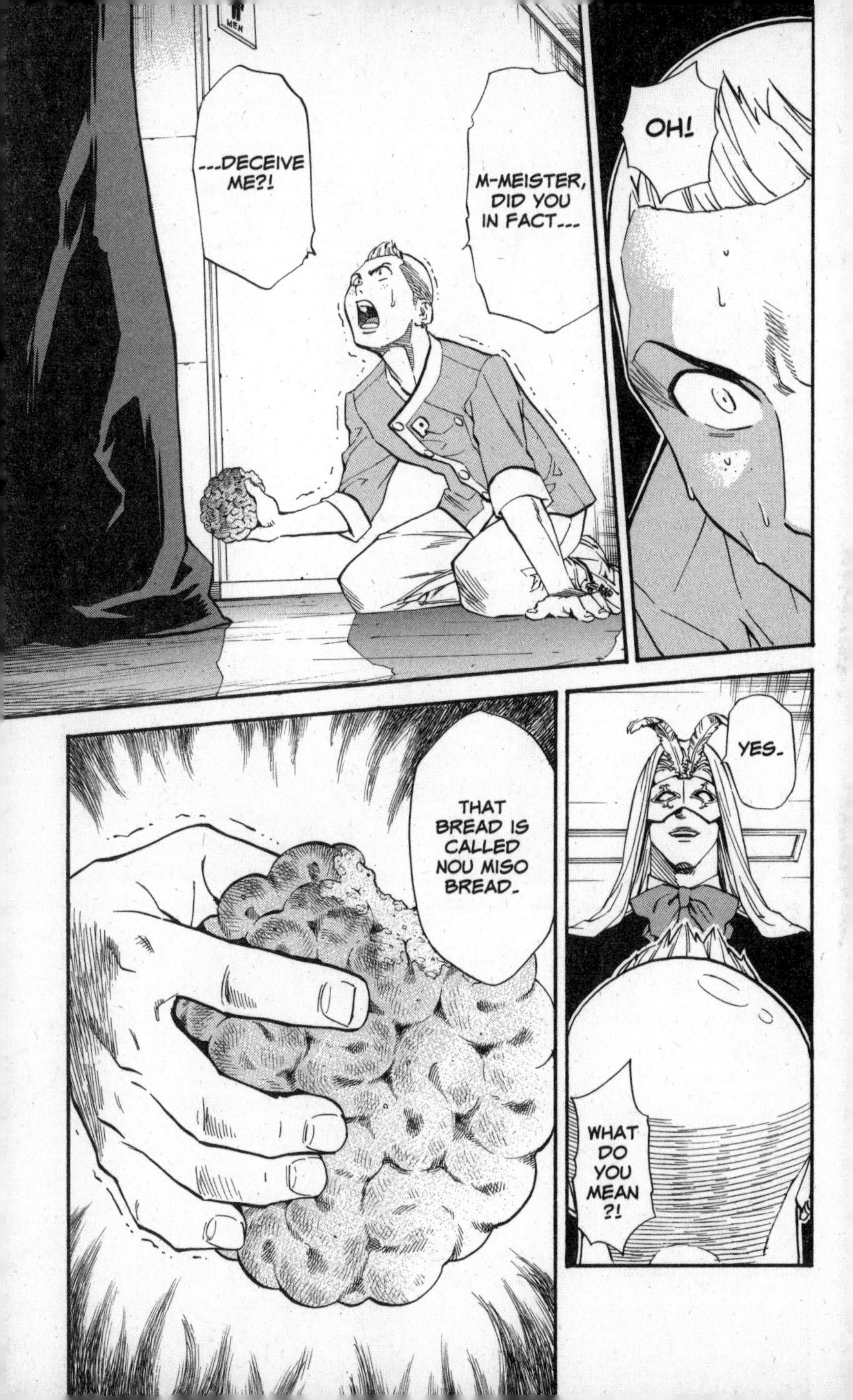
OH!
MEN
M-MEISTER, DID YOU IN FACT...
...DECEIVE ME?!
YES.
WHAT DO YOU MEAN?!
THAT BREAD IS CALLED NOU MISO BREAD.

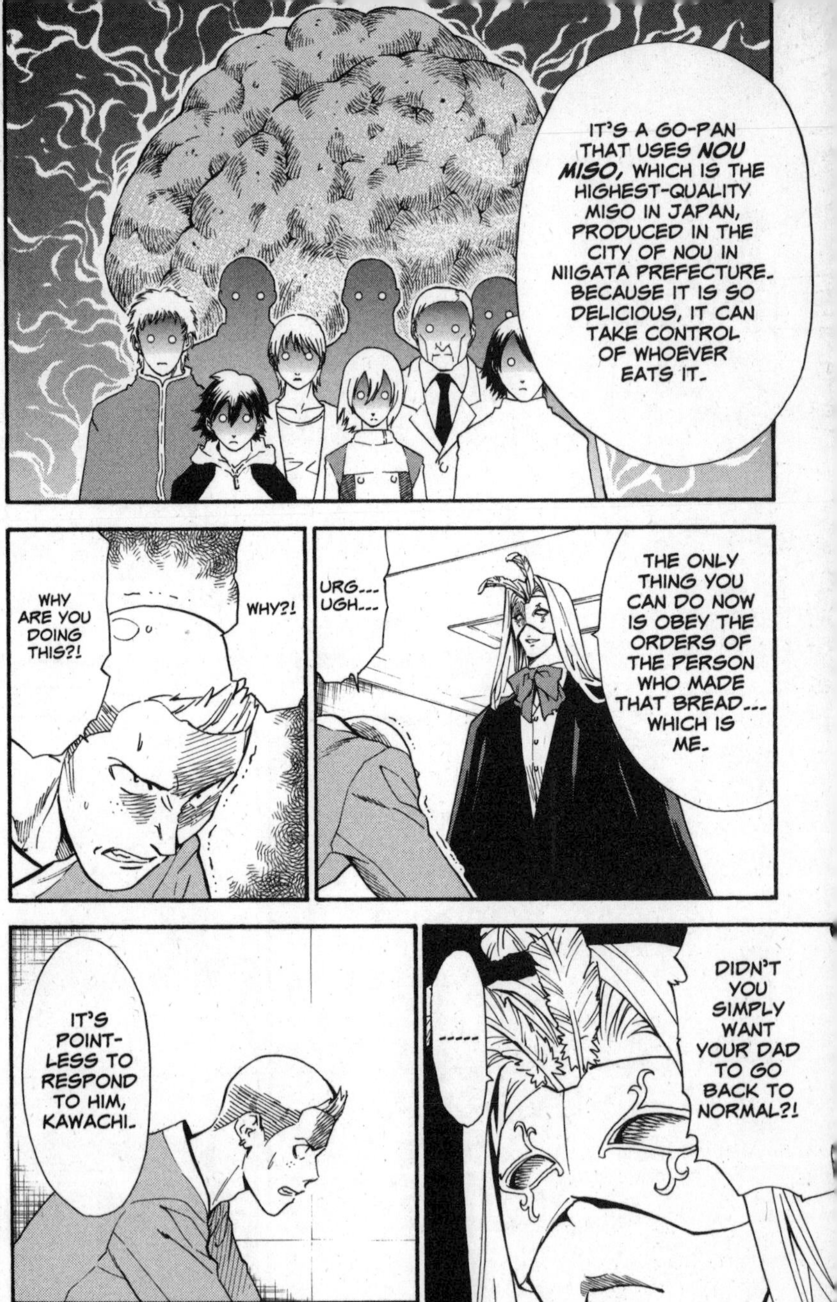
IT'S A GO-PAN THAT USES NOU MISO, WHICH IS THE HIGHEST-QUALITY MISO IN JAPAN, PRODUCED IN THE CITY OF NOU IN NIIGATA PREFECTURE. BECAUSE IT IS SO DELICIOUS, IT CAN TAKE CONTROL OF WHOEVER EATS IT.
THE ONLY THING YOU CAN DO NOW IS OBEY THE ORDERS OF THE PERSON WHO MADE THAT BREAD... WHICH IS ME.
URG... UGH...
WHY?!
WHY ARE YOU DOING THIS?!
DIDN'T YOU SIMPLY WANT YOUR DAD TO GO BACK TO NORMAL?!
.....
IT'S POINT-LESS TO RESPOND TO HIM, KAWACHI.

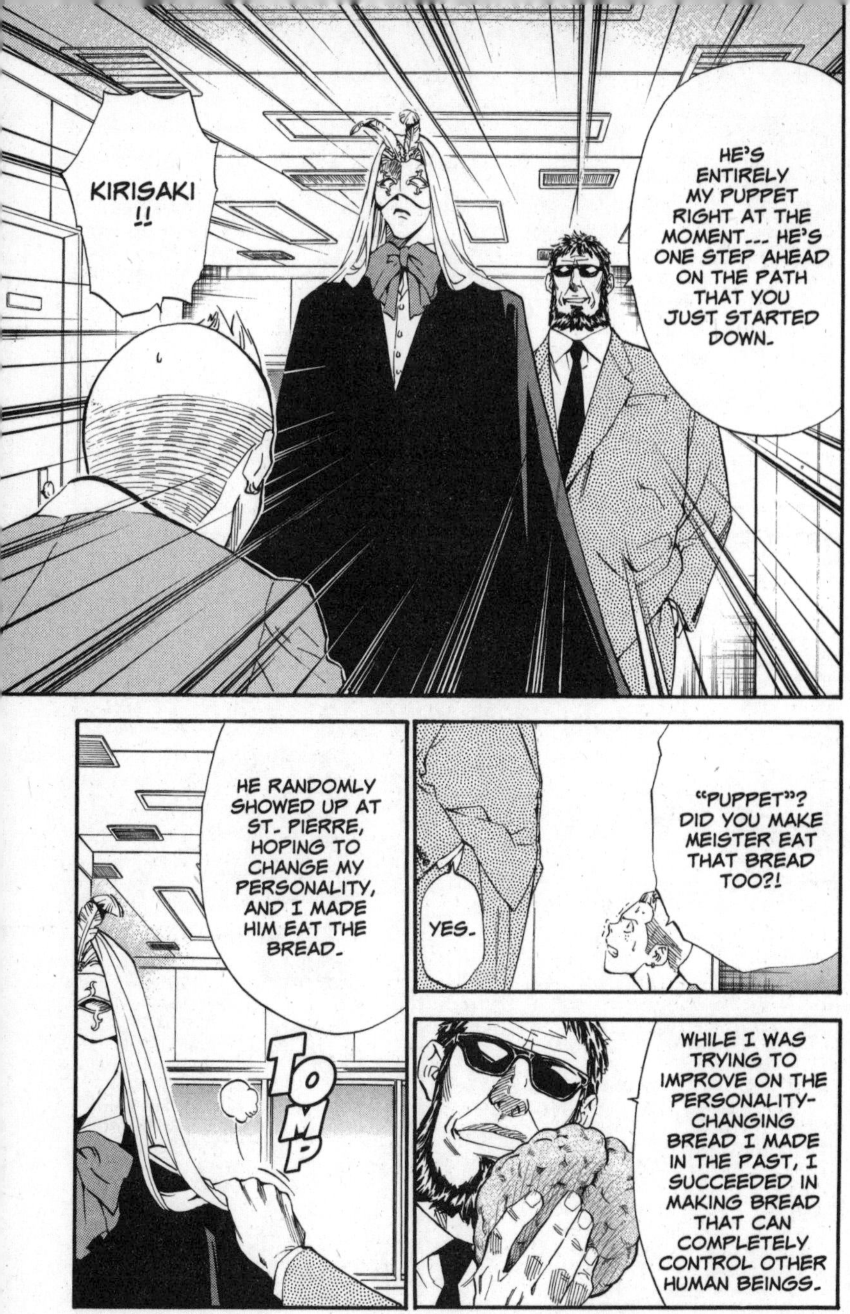
HE'S ENTIRELY MY PUPPET RIGHT AT THE MOMENT... HE'S ONE STEP AHEAD ON THE PATH THAT YOU JUST STARTED DOWN.
KIRISAKI !!
"PUPPET"? DID YOU MAKE MEISTER EAT THAT BREAD TOO?!
YES.
WHILE I WAS TRYING TO IMPROVE ON THE PERSONALITY-CHANGING BREAD I MADE IN THE PAST, I SUCCEEDED IN MAKING BREAD THAT CAN COMPLETELY CONTROL OTHER HUMAN BEINGS.
HE RANDOMLY SHOWED UP AT ST. PIERRE, HOPING TO CHANGE MY PERSONALITY, AND I MADE HIM EAT THE BREAD.
TOMP

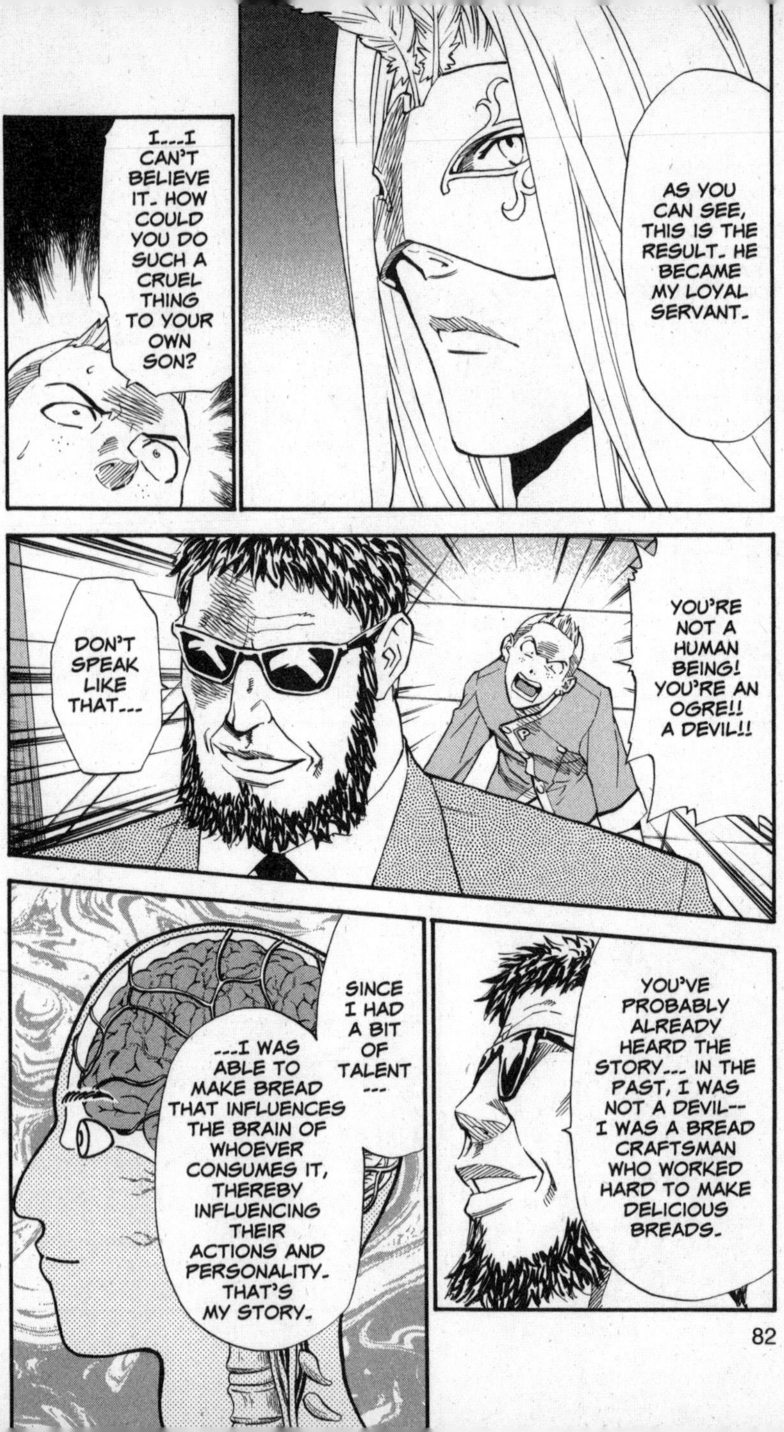
AS YOU CAN SEE, THIS IS THE RESULT. HE BECAME MY LOYAL SERVANT.
I...I CAN'T BELIEVE IT. HOW COULD YOU DO SUCH A CRUEL THING TO YOUR OWN SON?
YOU'RE NOT A HUMAN BEING! YOU'RE AN OGRE!! A DEVIL!!
DON'T SPEAK LIKE THAT...
YOU'VE PROBABLY ALREADY HEARD THE STORY... IN THE PAST, I WAS NOT A DEVIL-- I WAS A BREAD CRAFTSMAN WHO WORKED HARD TO MAKE DELICIOUS BREADS.
SINCE I HAD A BIT OF TALENT ---
---I WAS ABLE TO MAKE BREAD THAT INFLUENCES THE BRAIN OF WHOEVER CONSUMES IT, THEREBY INFLUENCING THEIR ACTIONS AND PERSONALITY. THAT'S MY STORY.

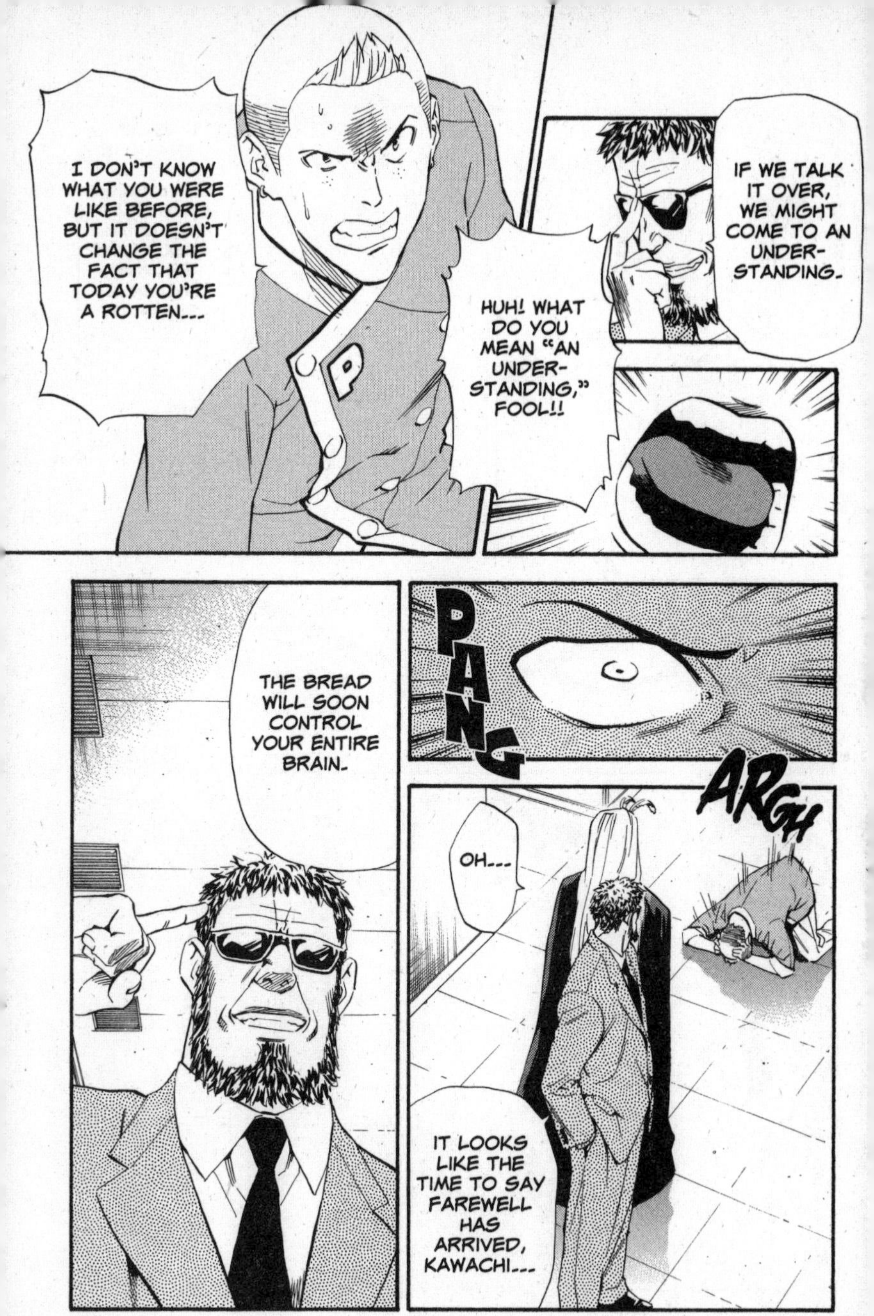
IF WE TALK IT OVER, WE MIGHT COME TO AN UNDER-STANDING.
HUH! WHAT DO YOU MEAN "AN UNDER-STANDING," FOOL!!
I DON'T KNOW WHAT YOU WERE LIKE BEFORE, BUT IT DOESN'T CHANGE THE FACT THAT TODAY YOU'RE A ROTTEN...
PANG
ARGH
OH...
IT LOOKS LIKE THE TIME TO SAY FAREWELL HAS ARRIVED, KAWACHI...
THE BREAD WILL SOON CONTROL YOUR ENTIRE BRAIN.

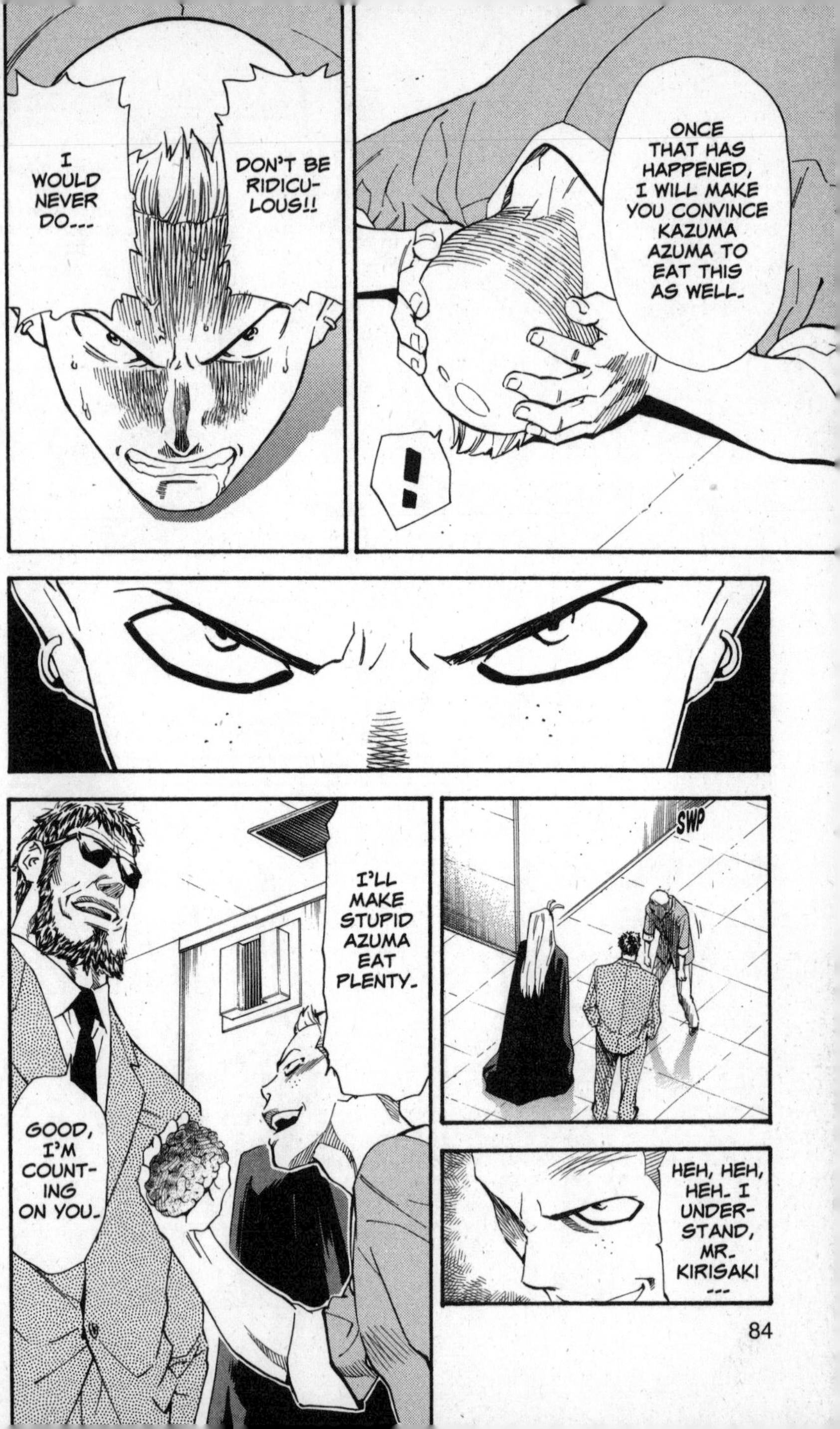
ONCE THAT HAS HAPPENED, I WILL MAKE YOU CONVINCE KAZUMA AZUMA TO EAT THIS AS WELL.
!
DON'T BE RIDICULOUS!!
I WOULD NEVER DO...
SWP
HEH, HEH, HEH. I UNDERSTAND, MR. KIRISAKI...
I'LL MAKE STUPID AZUMA EAT PLENTY.
GOOD, I'M COUNTING ON YOU.

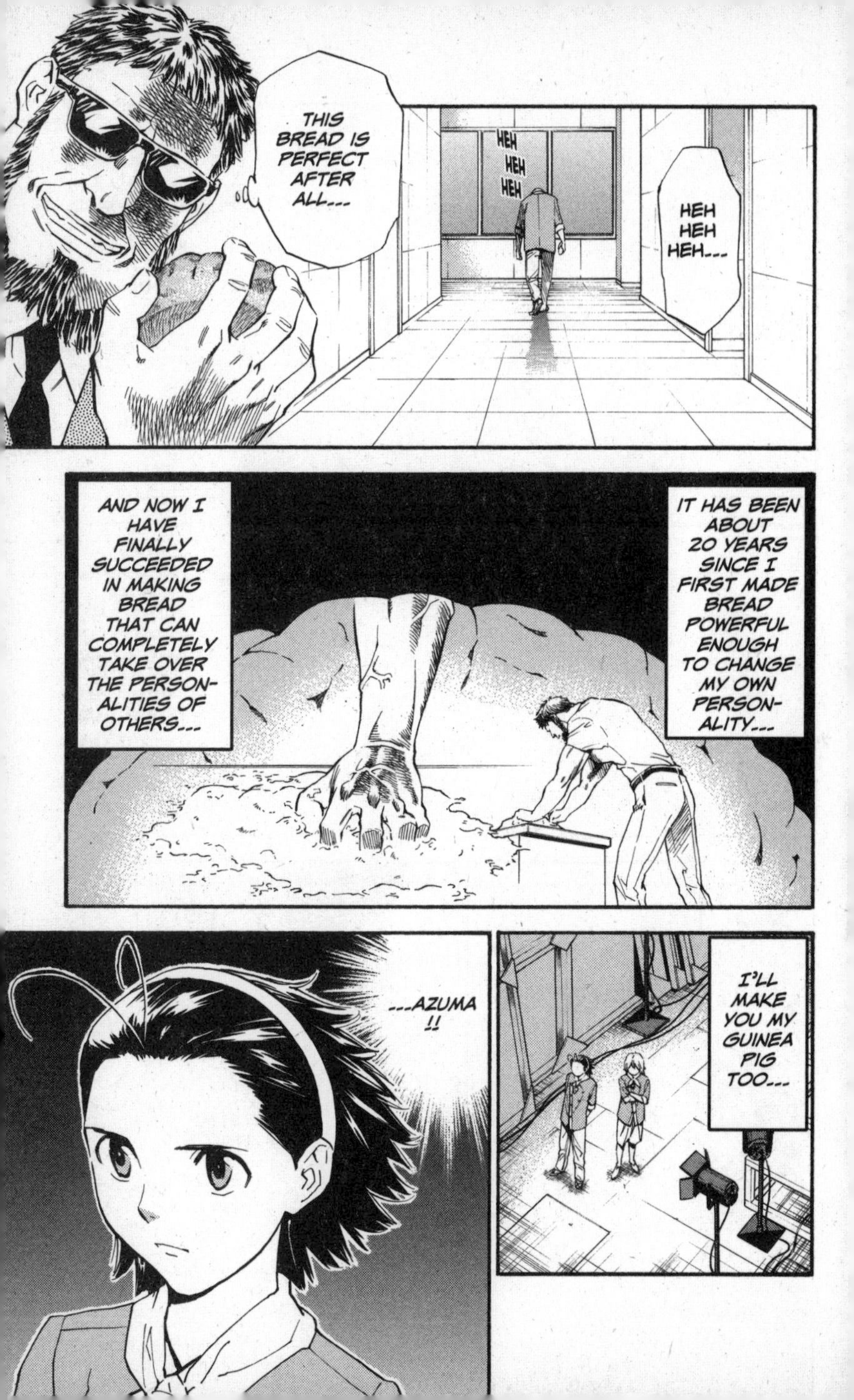
HEH HEH HEH...
HEH HEH HEH
THIS BREAD IS PERFECT AFTER ALL...
IT HAS BEEN ABOUT 20 YEARS SINCE I FIRST MADE BREAD POWERFUL ENOUGH TO CHANGE MY OWN PERSON-ALITY...
AND NOW I HAVE FINALLY SUCCEEDED IN MAKING BREAD THAT CAN COMPLETELY TAKE OVER THE PERSON-ALITIES OF OTHERS...
I'LL MAKE YOU MY GUINEA PIG TOO...
...AZUMA!!

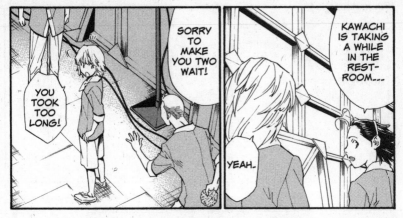

KAWACHI IS TAKING A WHILE IN THE REST-ROOM...
YEAH.
SORRY TO MAKE YOU TWO WAIT!
YOU TOOK TOO LONG!
I WAS WORRIED YOU FELL INTO THE TOILET AGAIN, LIKE THAT TIME WITH THE RICE-FLOUR DUMP-LINGS.
Ha ha!
SORRY ABOUT THAT...
MY CRAP WAS JUST SO LONG...
Wa ha ha!
?
OH MY, THAT'S DIS-GUSTING.
.....
THERE'S SOME-THING STRANGE ABOUT KAWACHI...

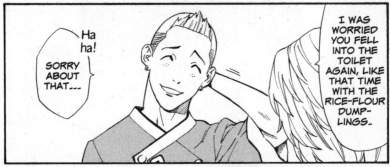

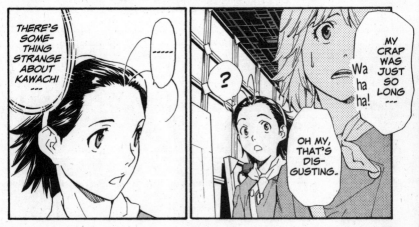

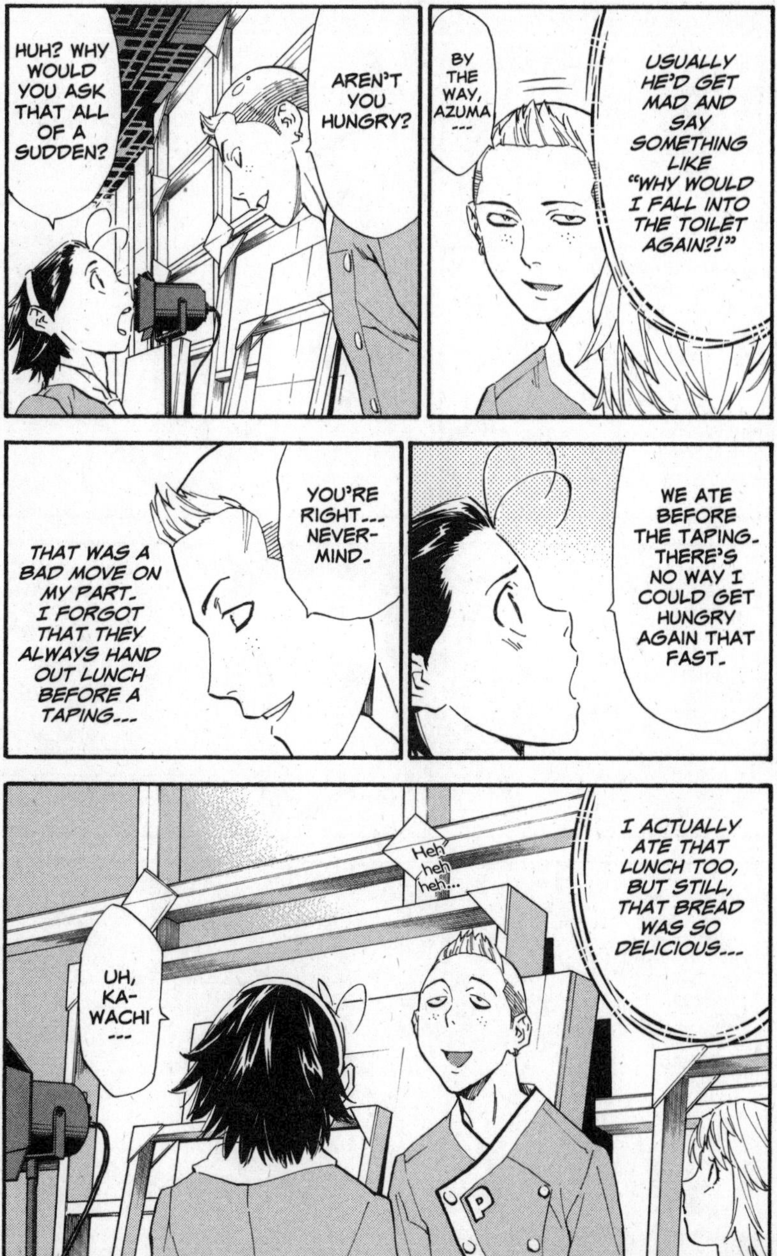
USUALLY HE'D GET MAD AND SAY SOMETHING LIKE "WHY WOULD I FALL INTO THE TOILET AGAIN?!"
BY THE WAY, AZUMA---
AREN'T YOU HUNGRY?
HUH? WHY WOULD YOU ASK THAT ALL OF A SUDDEN?
WE ATE BEFORE THE TAPING. THERE'S NO WAY I COULD GET HUNGRY AGAIN THAT FAST.
YOU'RE RIGHT... NEVER-MIND.
THAT WAS A BAD MOVE ON MY PART. I FORGOT THAT THEY ALWAYS HAND OUT LUNCH BEFORE A TAPING...
I ACTUALLY ATE THAT LUNCH TOO, BUT STILL, THAT BREAD WAS SO DELICIOUS...
Heh heh heh...
UH, KA-WACHI---

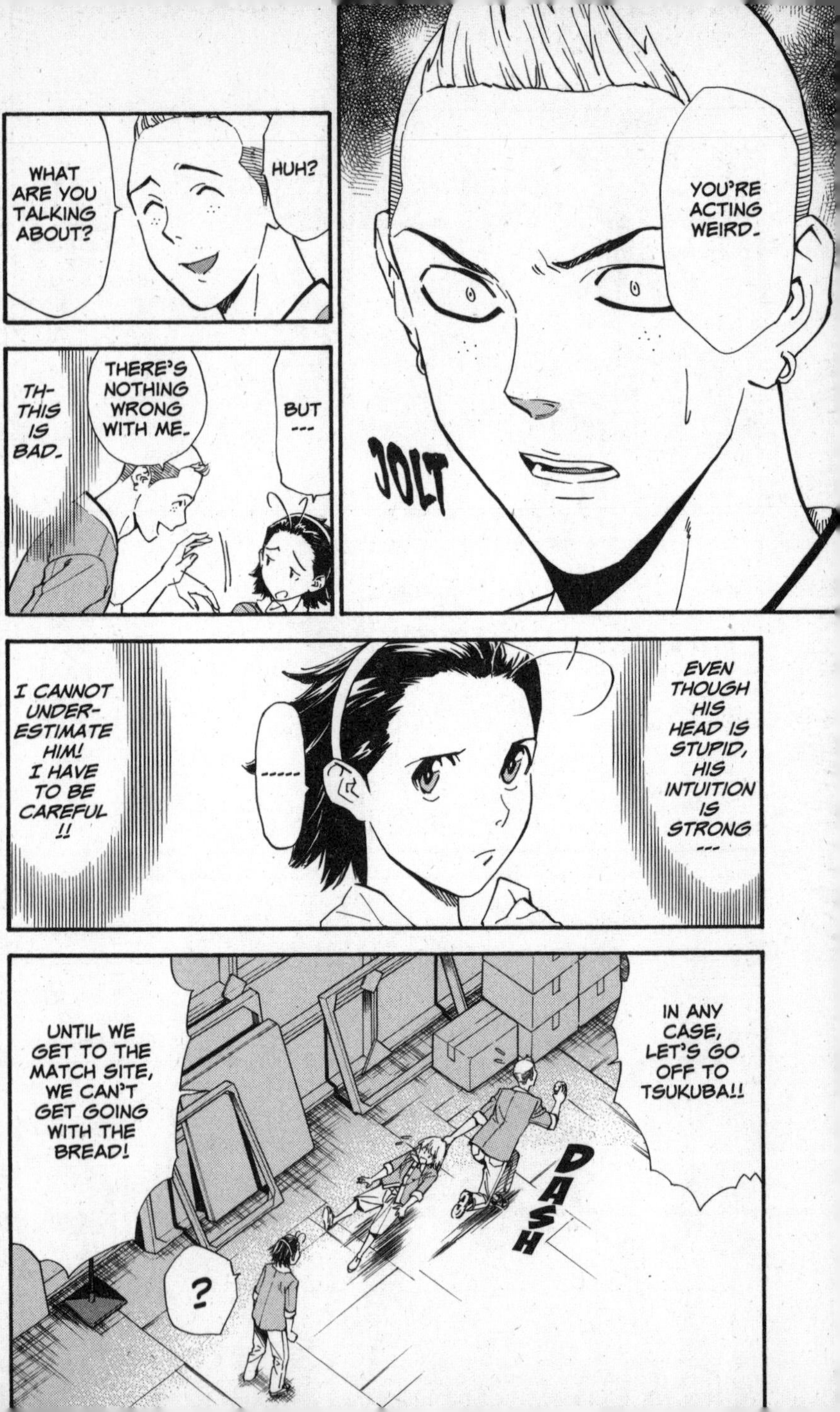
YOU'RE ACTING WEIRD.
JOLT
HUH?
WHAT ARE YOU TALKING ABOUT?
BUT ---
THERE'S NOTHING WRONG WITH ME.
TH-THIS IS BAD.
EVEN THOUGH HIS HEAD IS STUPID, HIS INTUITION IS STRONG ---

I CANNOT UNDER-ESTIMATE HIM! I HAVE TO BE CAREFUL!!
IN ANY CASE, LET'S GO OFF TO TSUKUBA!!
DASH
UNTIL WE GET TO THE MATCH SITE, WE CAN'T GET GOING WITH THE BREAD!
?

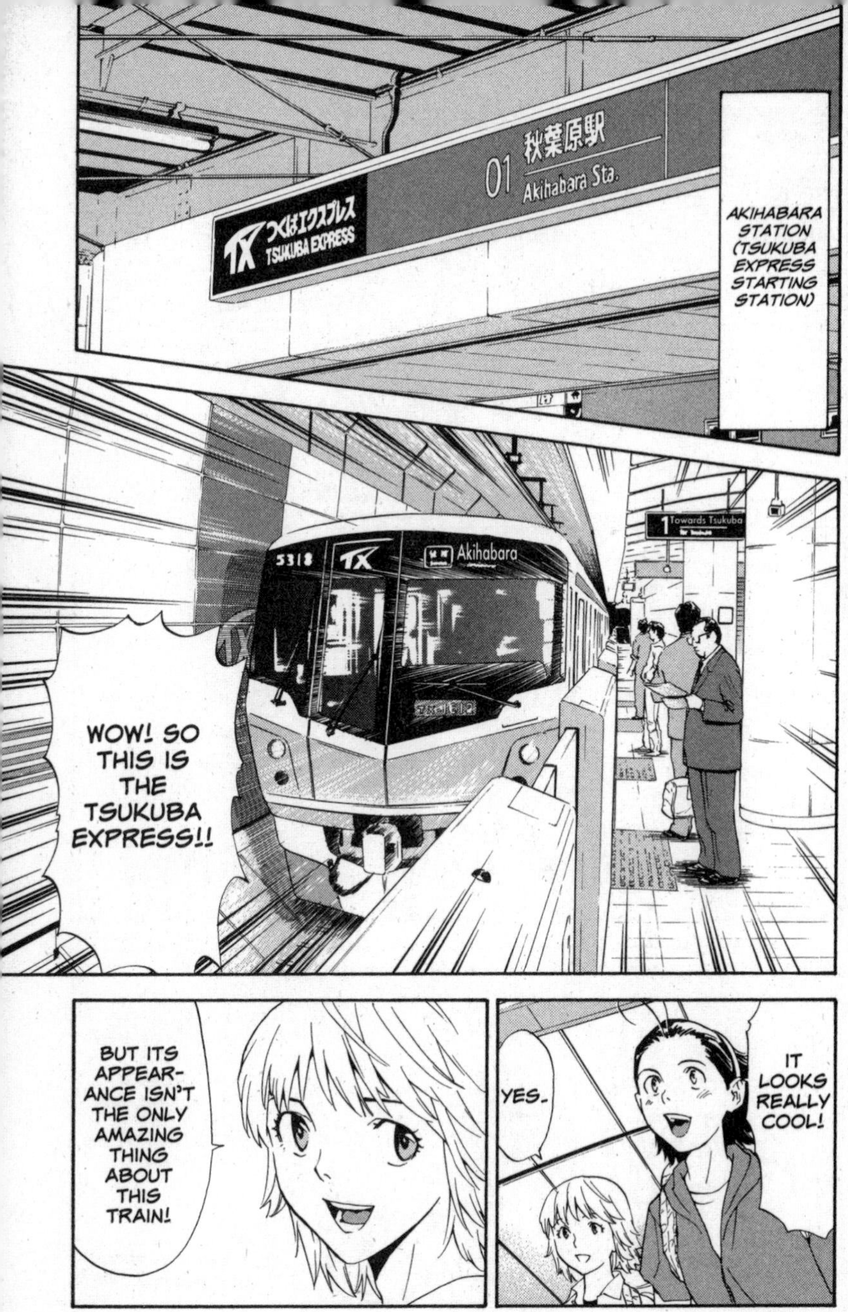
AKIHABARA STATION (TSUKUBA EXPRESS STARTING STATION)
秋葉原駅
01
Akihabara Sta.
TX
つくばエクスプレス
TSUKUBA EXPRESS
1 Towards Tsukuba
5318
TX
Akihabara
WOW! SO THIS IS THE TSUKUBA EXPRESS!!
IT LOOKS REALLY COOL!
YES.
BUT ITS APPEARANCE ISN'T THE ONLY AMAZING THING ABOUT THIS TRAIN!

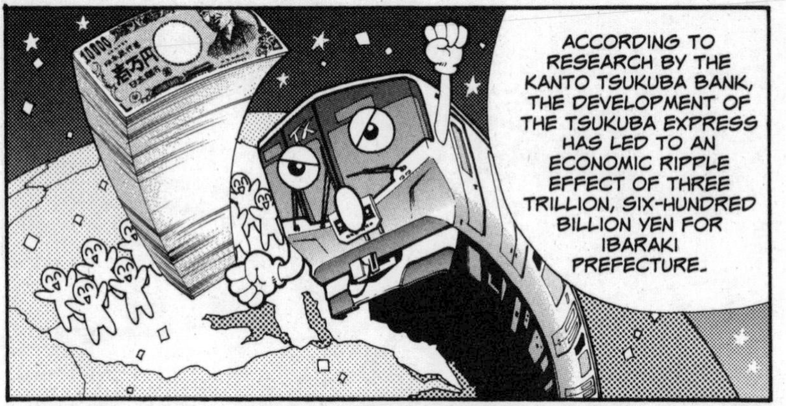
ACCORDING TO RESEARCH BY THE KANTO TSUKUBA BANK, THE DEVELOPMENT OF THE TSUKUBA EXPRESS HAS LED TO AN ECONOMIC RIPPLE EFFECT OF THREE TRILLION, SIX-HUNDRED BILLION YEN FOR IBARAKI PREFECTURE.

A CALCULATION OF PUBLIC INVESTMENTS + PRIVATE INVESTMENTS + RESIDENTIAL CONSTRUCTIONS.

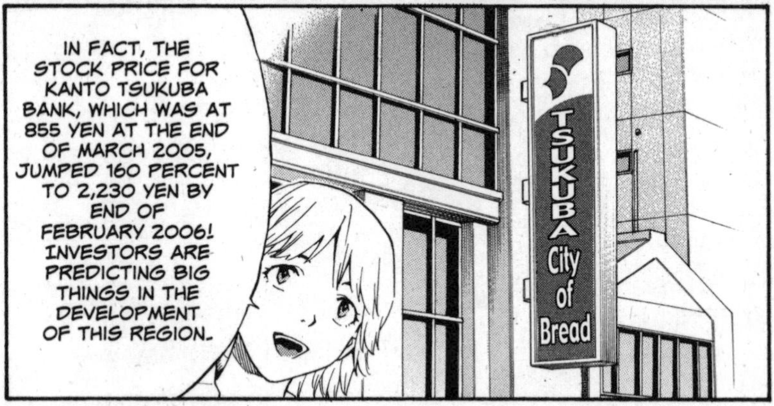
TSUKUBA City of Bread
IN FACT, THE STOCK PRICE FOR KANTO TSUKUBA BANK, WHICH WAS AT 855 YEN AT THE END OF MARCH 2005, JUMPED 160 PERCENT TO 2,230 YEN BY END OF FEBRUARY 2006! INVESTORS ARE PREDICTING BIG THINGS IN THE DEVELOPMENT OF THIS REGION.

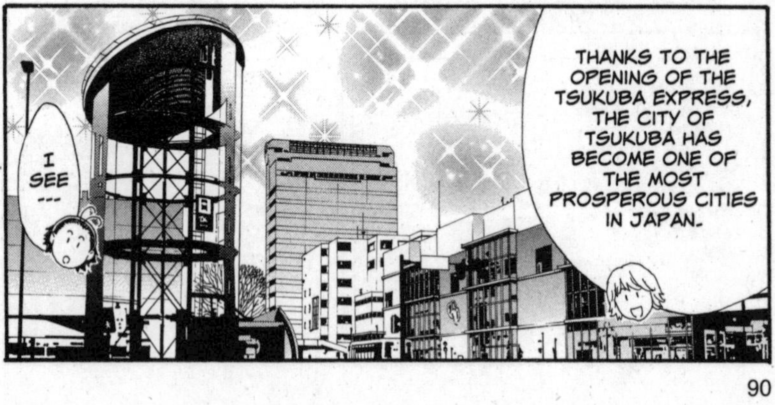
THANKS TO THE OPENING OF THE TSUKUBA EXPRESS, THE CITY OF TSUKUBA HAS BECOME ONE OF THE MOST PROSPEROUS CITIES IN JAPAN.
I SEE ---

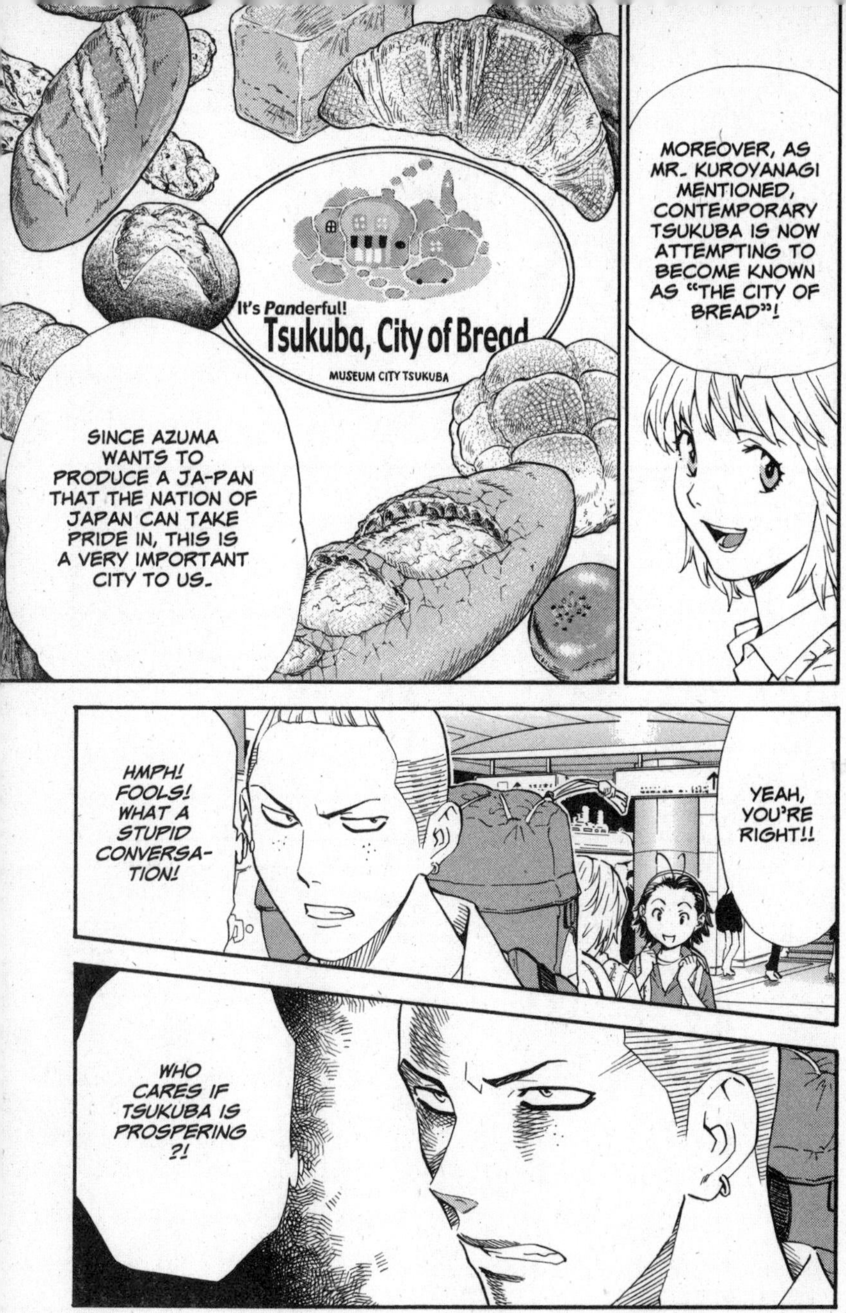
MOREOVER, AS MR. KUROYANAGI MENTIONED, CONTEMPORARY TSUKUBA IS NOW ATTEMPTING TO BECOME KNOWN AS "THE CITY OF BREAD"!
It's Panderful!
Tsukuba, City of Bread
MUSEUM CITY TSUKUBA
SINCE AZUMA WANTS TO PRODUCE A JA-PAN THAT THE NATION OF JAPAN CAN TAKE PRIDE IN, THIS IS A VERY IMPORTANT CITY TO US.
YEAH, YOU'RE RIGHT!!
HMPH! FOOLS! WHAT A STUPID CONVERSA-TION!
WHO CARES IF TSUKUBA IS PROSPERING ?!

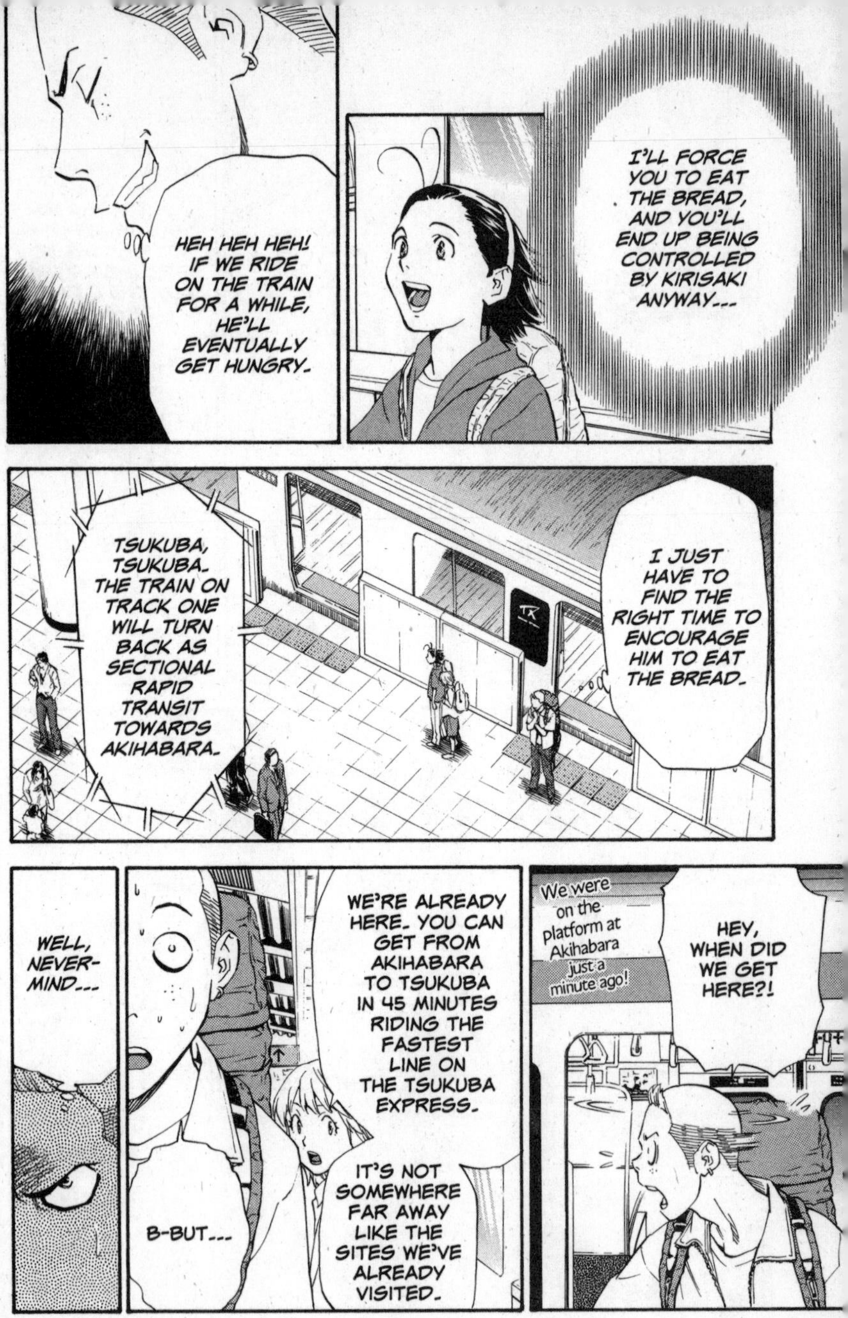
I'LL FORCE YOU TO EAT THE BREAD, AND YOU'LL END UP BEING CONTROLLED BY KIRISAKI ANYWAY...
HEH HEH HEH! IF WE RIDE ON THE TRAIN FOR A WHILE, HE'LL EVENTUALLY GET HUNGRY.
I JUST HAVE TO FIND THE RIGHT TIME TO ENCOURAGE HIM TO EAT THE BREAD.
TSUKUBA, TSUKUBA. THE TRAIN ON TRACK ONE WILL TURN BACK AS SECTIONAL RAPID TRANSIT TOWARDS AKIHABARA.
HEY, WHEN DID WE GET HERE?!
We were on the platform at Akihabara just a minute ago!
WE'RE ALREADY HERE. YOU CAN GET FROM AKIHABARA TO TSUKUBA IN 45 MINUTES RIDING THE FASTEST LINE ON THE TSUKUBA EXPRESS.
IT'S NOT SOMEWHERE FAR AWAY LIKE THE SITES WE'VE ALREADY VISITED.
B-BUT...
WELL, NEVER-MIND...

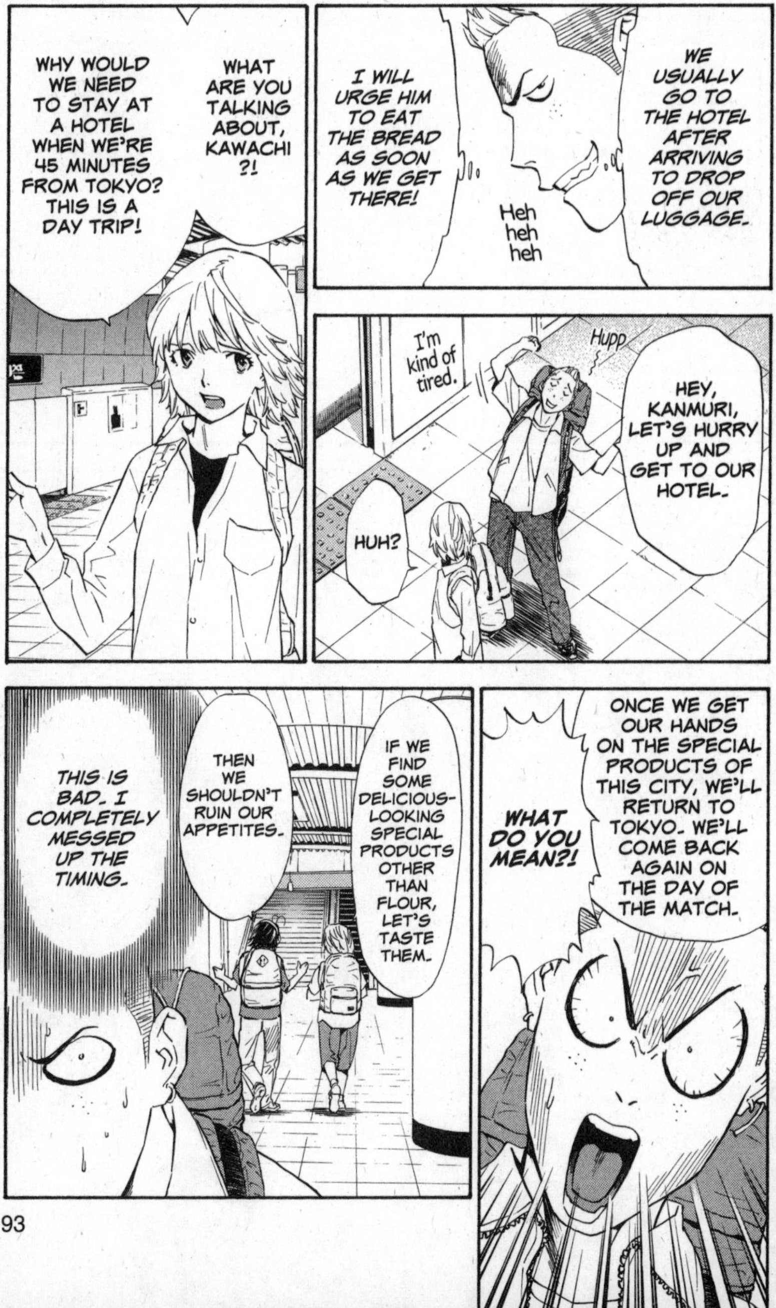
WE USUALLY GO TO THE HOTEL AFTER ARRIVING TO DROP OFF OUR LUGGAGE.
Heh heh heh
I WILL URGE HIM TO EAT THE BREAD AS SOON AS WE GET THERE!
HEY, KANMURI, LET'S HURRY UP AND GET TO OUR HOTEL.
Hupp
I'm kind of tired.
HUH?
WHAT ARE YOU TALKING ABOUT, KAWACHI?!
WHY WOULD WE NEED TO STAY AT A HOTEL WHEN WE'RE 45 MINUTES FROM TOKYO? THIS IS A DAY TRIP!
ONCE WE GET OUR HANDS ON THE SPECIAL PRODUCTS OF THIS CITY, WE'LL RETURN TO TOKYO. WE'LL COME BACK AGAIN ON THE DAY OF THE MATCH.
WHAT DO YOU MEAN?!
IF WE FIND SOME DELICIOUS-LOOKING SPECIAL PRODUCTS OTHER THAN FLOUR, LET'S TASTE THEM.
THEN WE SHOULDN'T RUIN OUR APPETITES.
THIS IS BAD. I COMPLETELY MESSED UP THE TIMING.

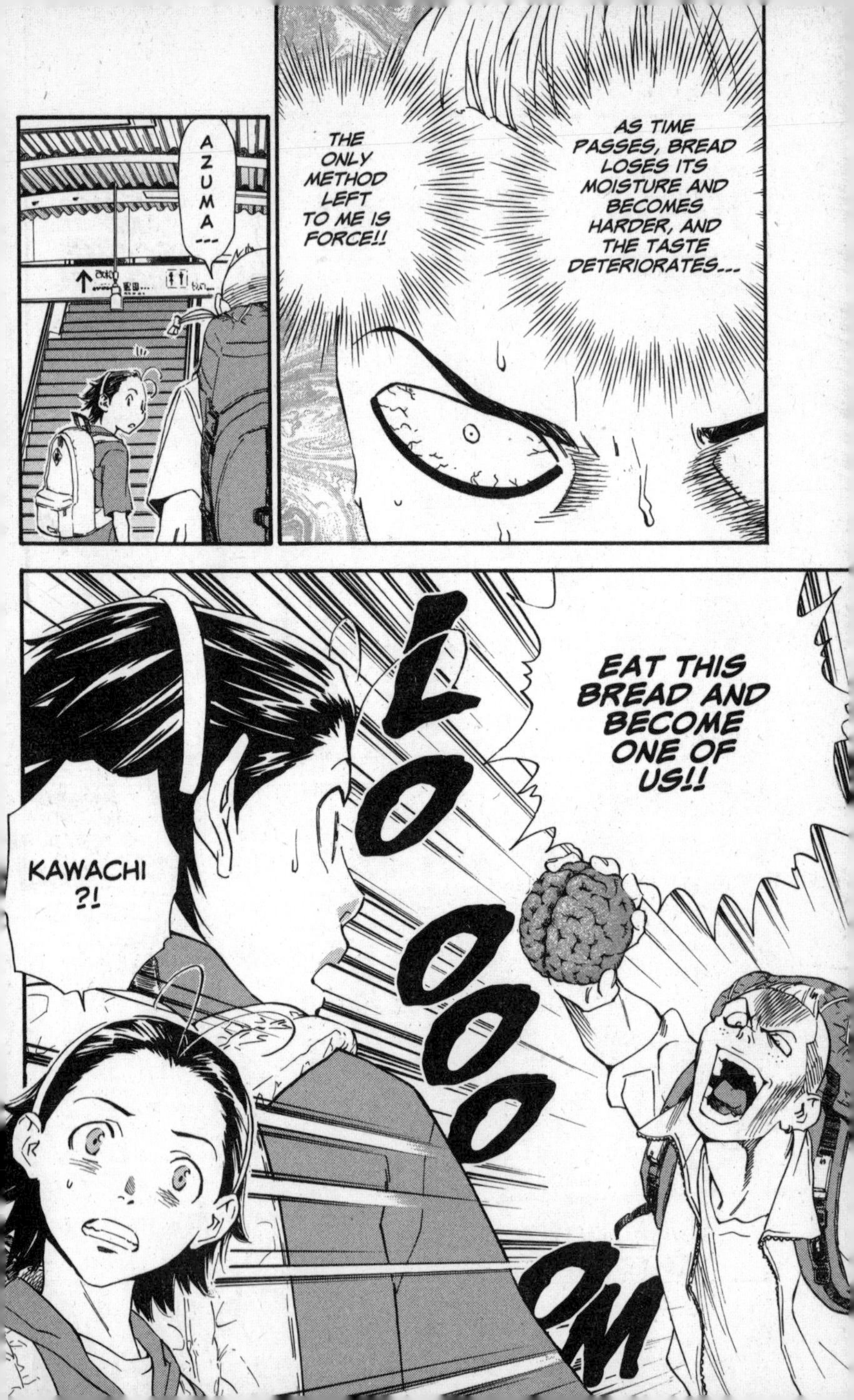
AS TIME PASSES, BREAD LOSES ITS MOISTURE AND BECOMES HARDER, AND THE TASTE DETERIORATES...
THE ONLY METHOD LEFT TO ME IS FORCE!!
AZUMA---
EAT THIS BREAD AND BECOME ONE OF US!!
KAWACHI ?!

Story 208: Ja-pan of Justice

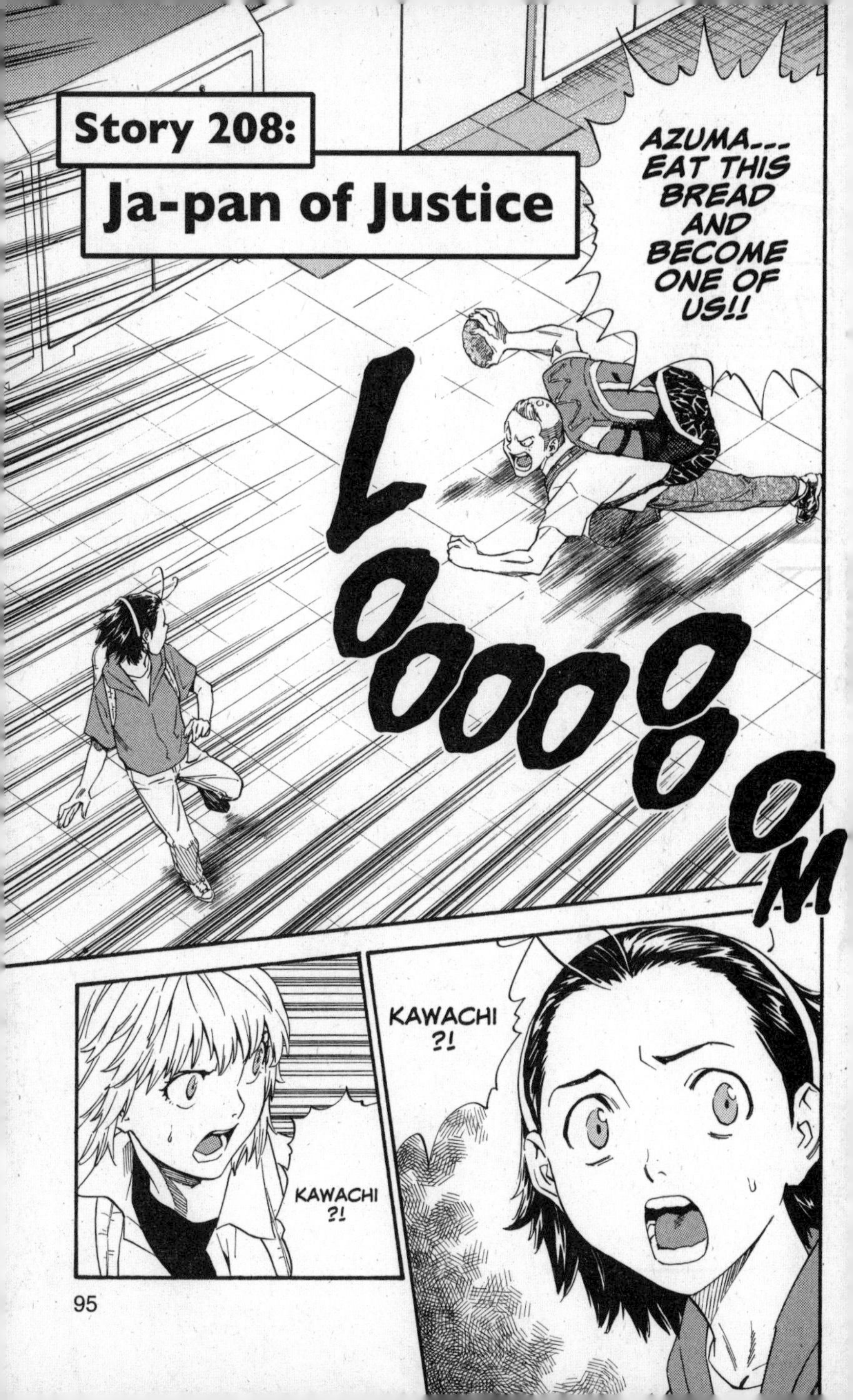
AZUMA... EAT THIS BREAD AND BECOME ONE OF US!!
LOOOOOOOM
KAWACHI ?!
KAWACHI ?!

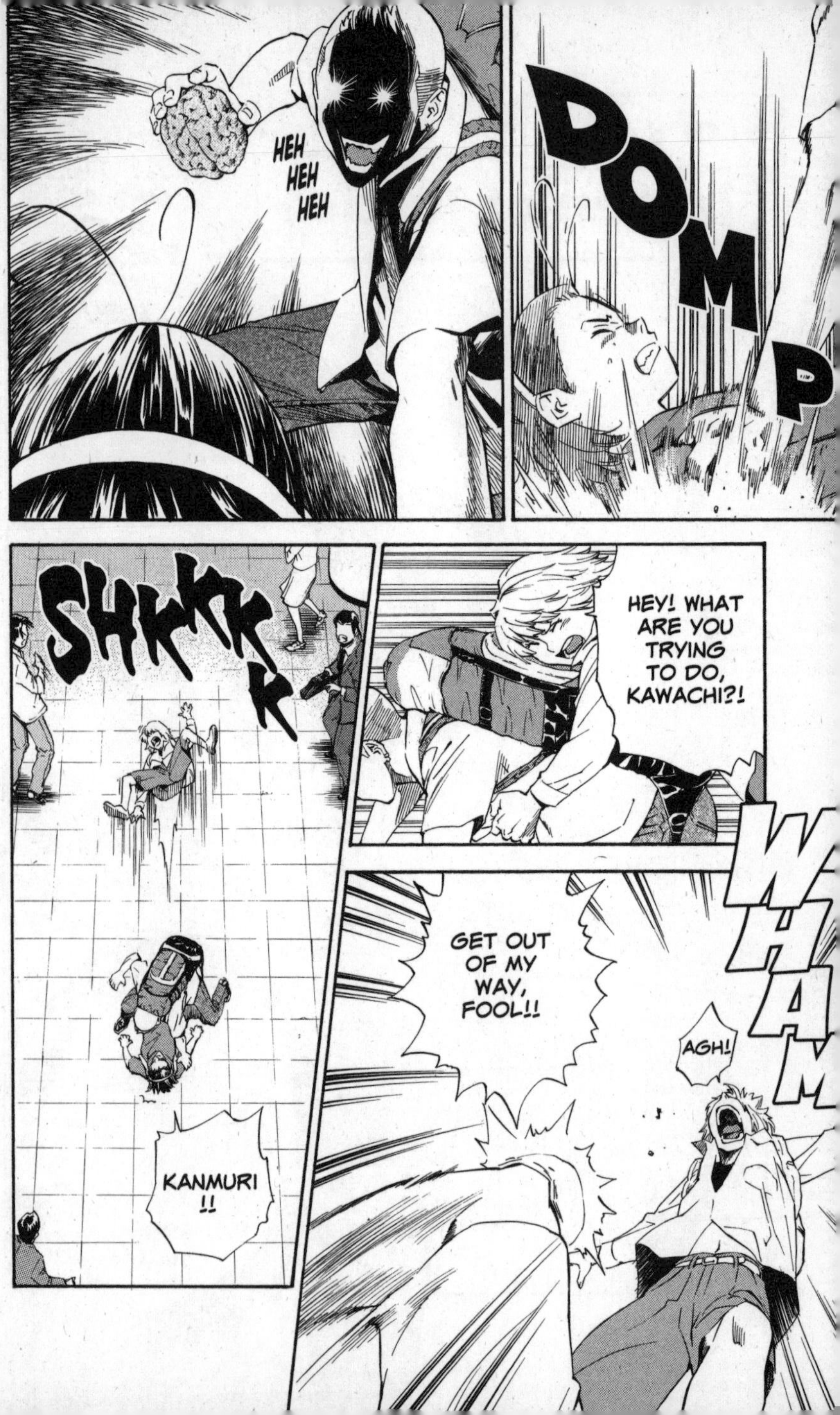
DOMP
HEH HEH HEH
HEY! WHAT ARE YOU TRYING TO DO, KAWACHI?!
WHAM
GET OUT OF MY WAY, FOOL!!
AGH!
SHKKK
KANMURI!!

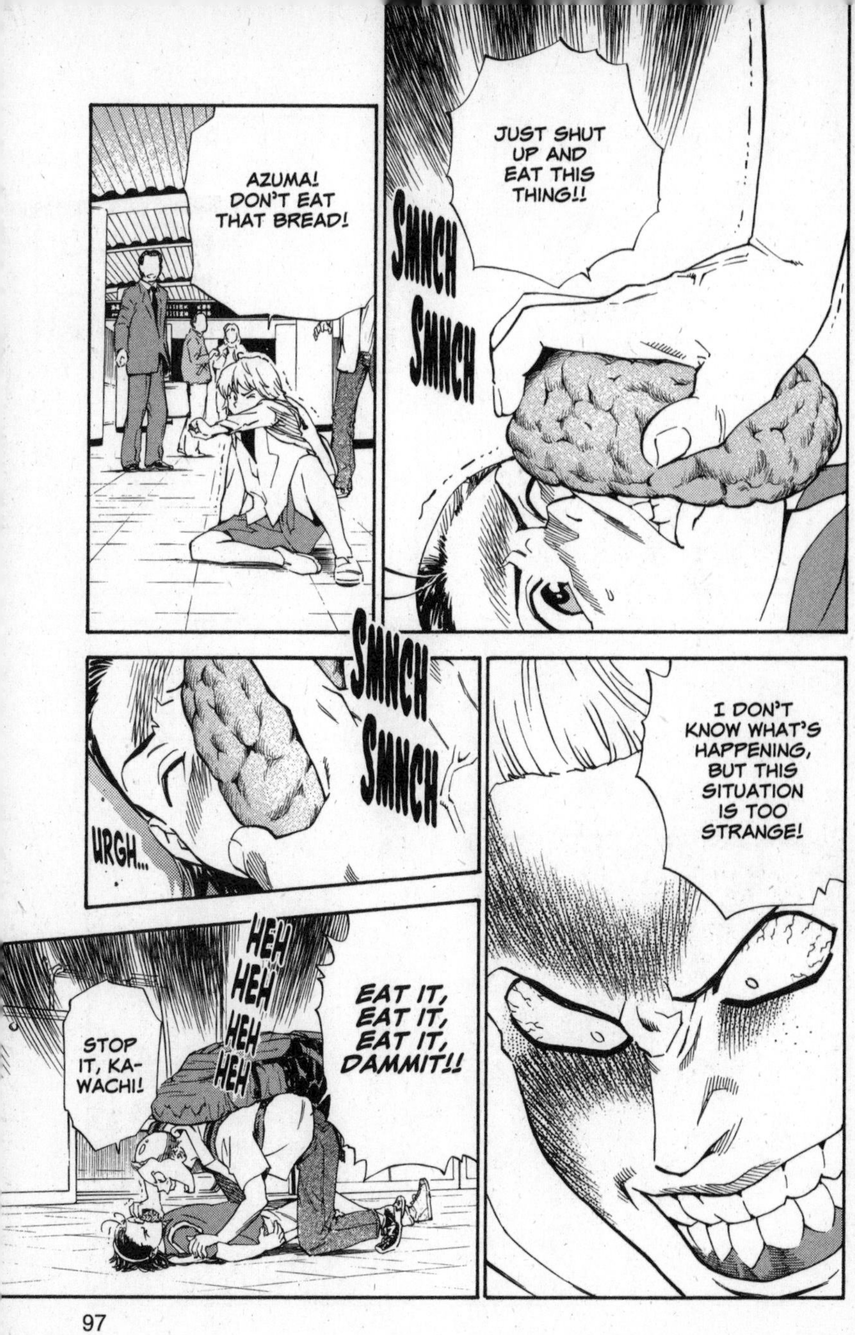

JUST SHUT UP AND EAT THIS THING!!
SMNCH SMNCH
AZUMA! DON'T EAT THAT BREAD!
I DON'T KNOW WHAT'S HAPPENING, BUT THIS SITUATION IS TOO STRANGE!
SMNCH SMNCH
URGH...
EAT IT, EAT IT, EAT IT, DAMMIT!!
HEH HEH HEH HEH
STOP IT, KA-WACHI!

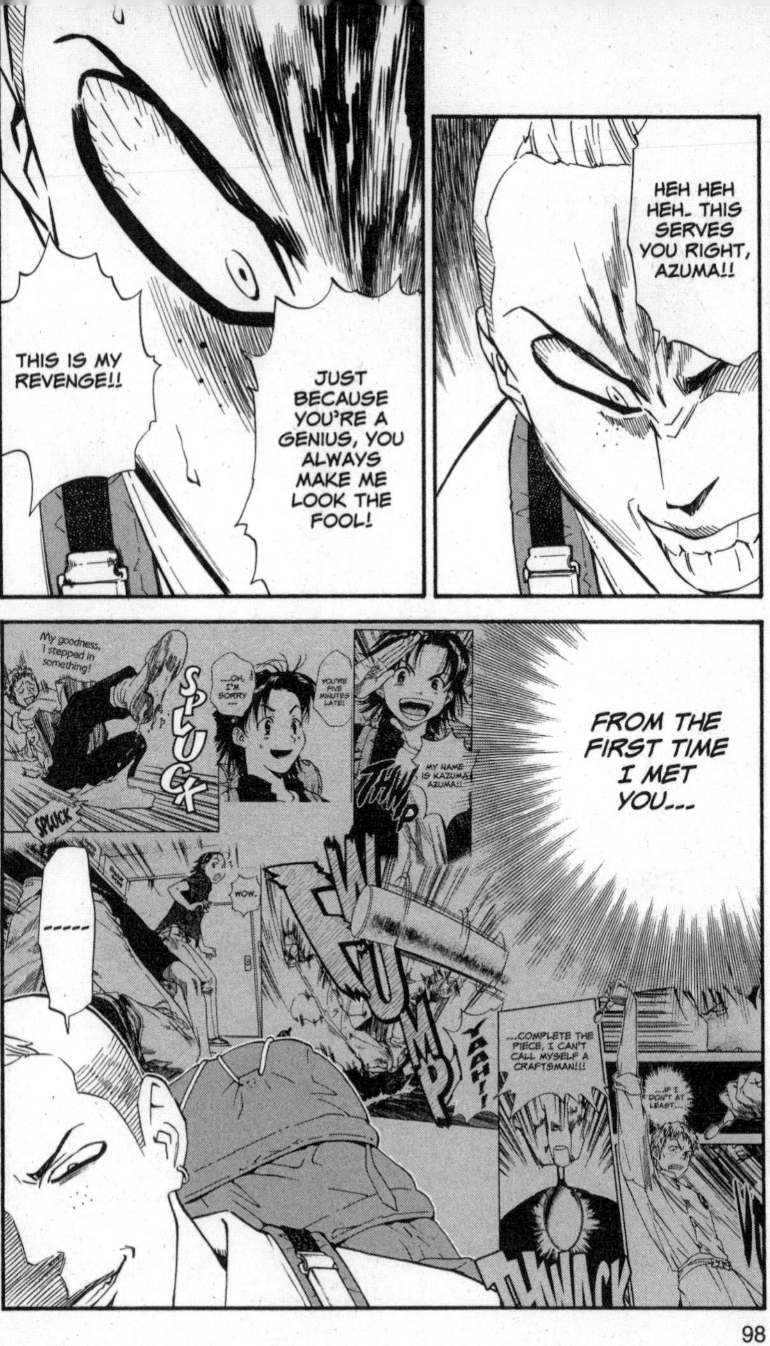
HEH HEH HEH... THIS SERVES YOU RIGHT, AZUMA!!
JUST BECAUSE YOU'RE A GENIUS, YOU ALWAYS MAKE ME LOOK THE FOOL!
THIS IS MY REVENGE!!
FROM THE FIRST TIME I MET YOU...
YOU'RE FIVE MINUTES LATE!
MY NAME IS KAZUMA AZUMA!!
THUMP
...OH, I'M SORRY...
SPLUCK
My goodness, I stepped in something!
SPLUCK
WOW...
YAAAH!!
...IF I DON'T AT LEAST...
...COMPLETE THE PIECE, I CAN'T CALL MYSELF A CRAFTSMAN!!!
THWACK
.....

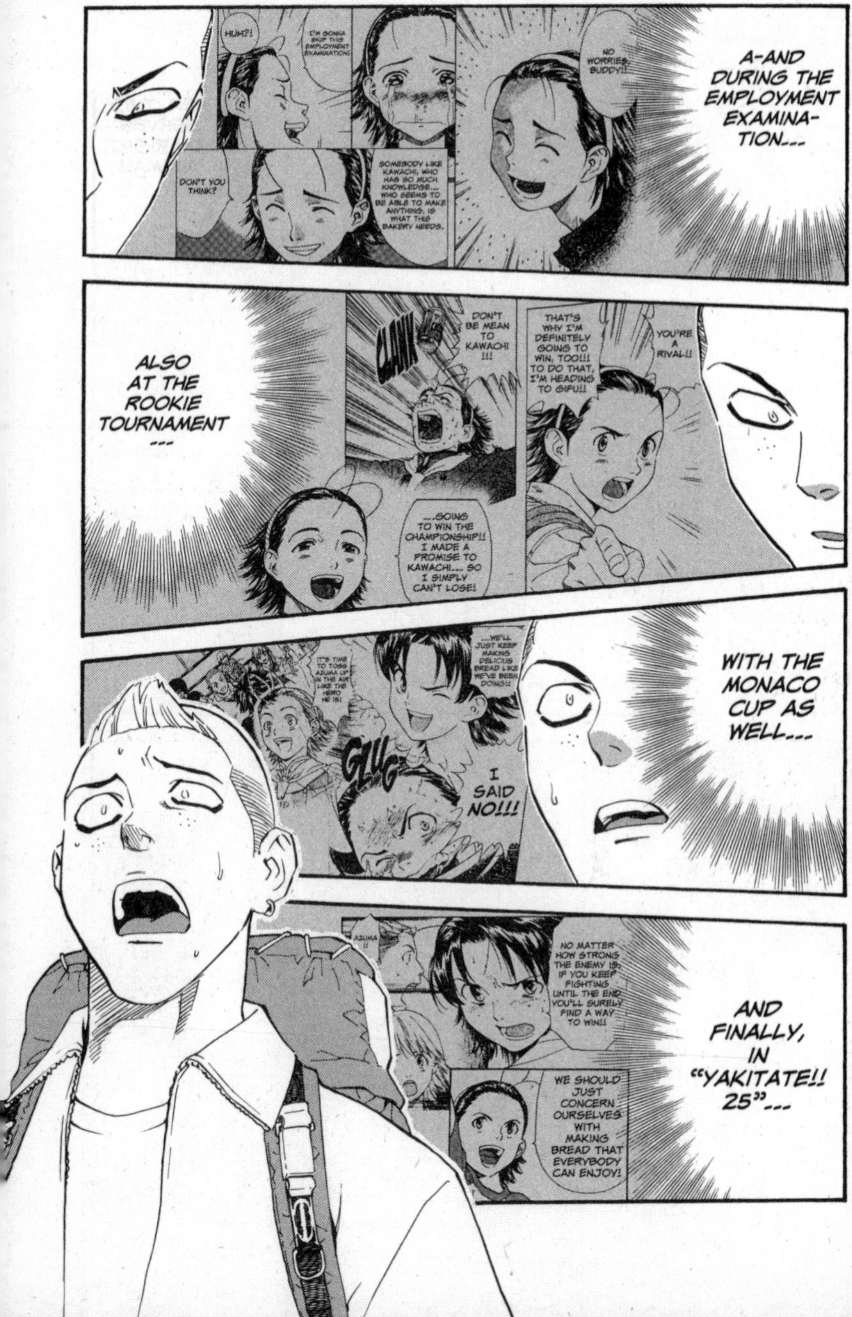
A-AND DURING THE EMPLOYMENT EXAMINATION---
NO WORRIES, BUDDY!!
I'M GONNA SKIP THIS EMPLOYMENT EXAMINATION!
HUH?!
SOMEBODY LIKE KAWACHI, WHO HAS SO MUCH KNOWLEDGE... WHO SEEMS TO BE ABLE TO MAKE ANYTHING, IS WHAT THIS BAKERY NEEDS.
DON'T YOU THINK?
YOU'RE A RIVAL!!
THAT'S WHY I'M DEFINITELY GOING TO WIN, TOO!!! TO DO THAT, I'M HEADING TO GIFU!!
DON'T BE MEAN TO KAWACHI!!!
CLANK
...GOING TO WIN THE CHAMPIONSHIP!! I MADE A PROMISE TO KAWACHI... SO I SIMPLY CAN'T LOSE!
ALSO AT THE ROOKIE TOURNAMENT---
WITH THE MONACO CUP AS WELL---
...WE'LL JUST KEEP MAKING DELICIUS BREAD LIKE WE'VE BEEN DOING!!
I SAID NO!!!
GLUG
IT'S TIME TO TOSS AZUMA UP IN THE AIR LIKE THE HERO HE IS!
AND FINALLY, IN "YAKITATE!! 25"---
NO MATTER HOW STRONG THE ENEMY IS, IF YOU KEEP FIGHTING UNTIL THE END YOU'LL SURELY FIND A WAY TO WIN!!
AZUMA!!
WE SHOULD JUST CONCERN OURSELVES WITH MAKING BREAD THAT EVERYBODY CAN ENJOY!

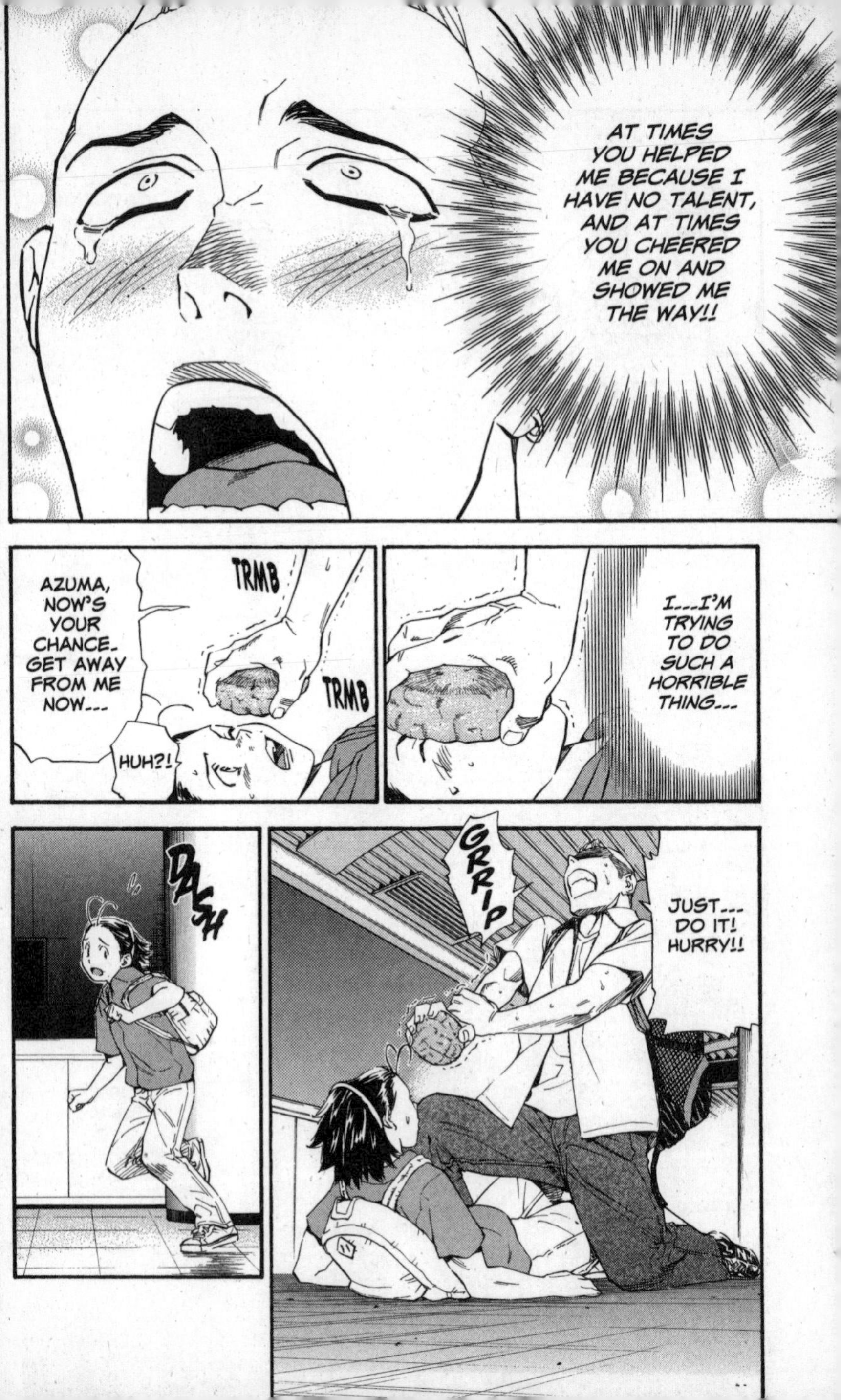
AT TIMES YOU HELPED ME BECAUSE I HAVE NO TALENT, AND AT TIMES YOU CHEERED ME ON AND SHOWED ME THE WAY!!
I...I'M TRYING TO DO SUCH A HORRIBLE THING...
TRMB
AZUMA, NOW'S YOUR CHANCE. GET AWAY FROM ME NOW...
TRMB
HUH?!
GRRIP
JUST... DO IT! HURRY!!
DASH

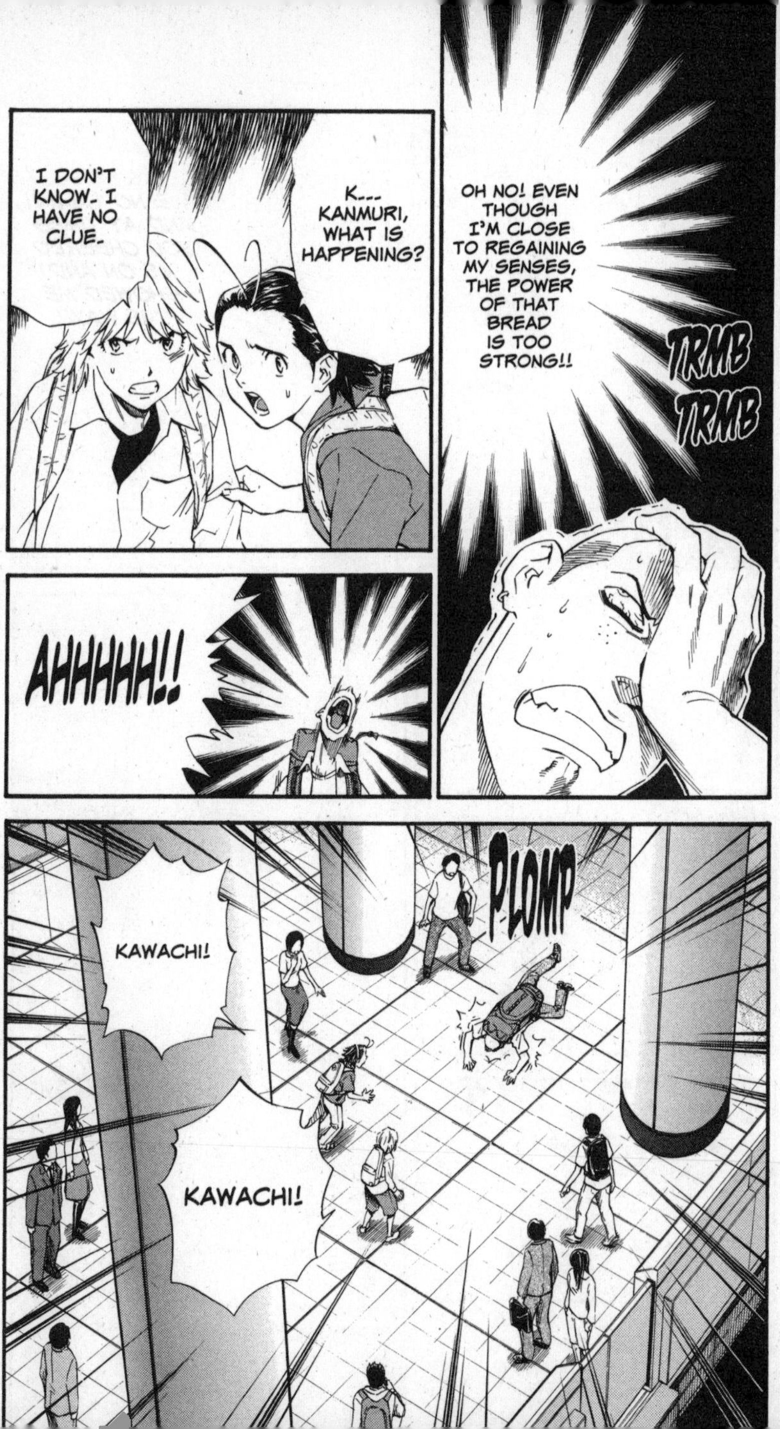

OH NO! EVEN THOUGH I'M CLOSE TO REGAINING MY SENSES, THE POWER OF THAT BREAD IS TOO STRONG!!
TRMB TRMB
K... KANMURI, WHAT IS HAPPENING?
I DON'T KNOW. I HAVE NO CLUE.
AHHHHH!!
PLOMP
KAWACHI!
KAWACHI!

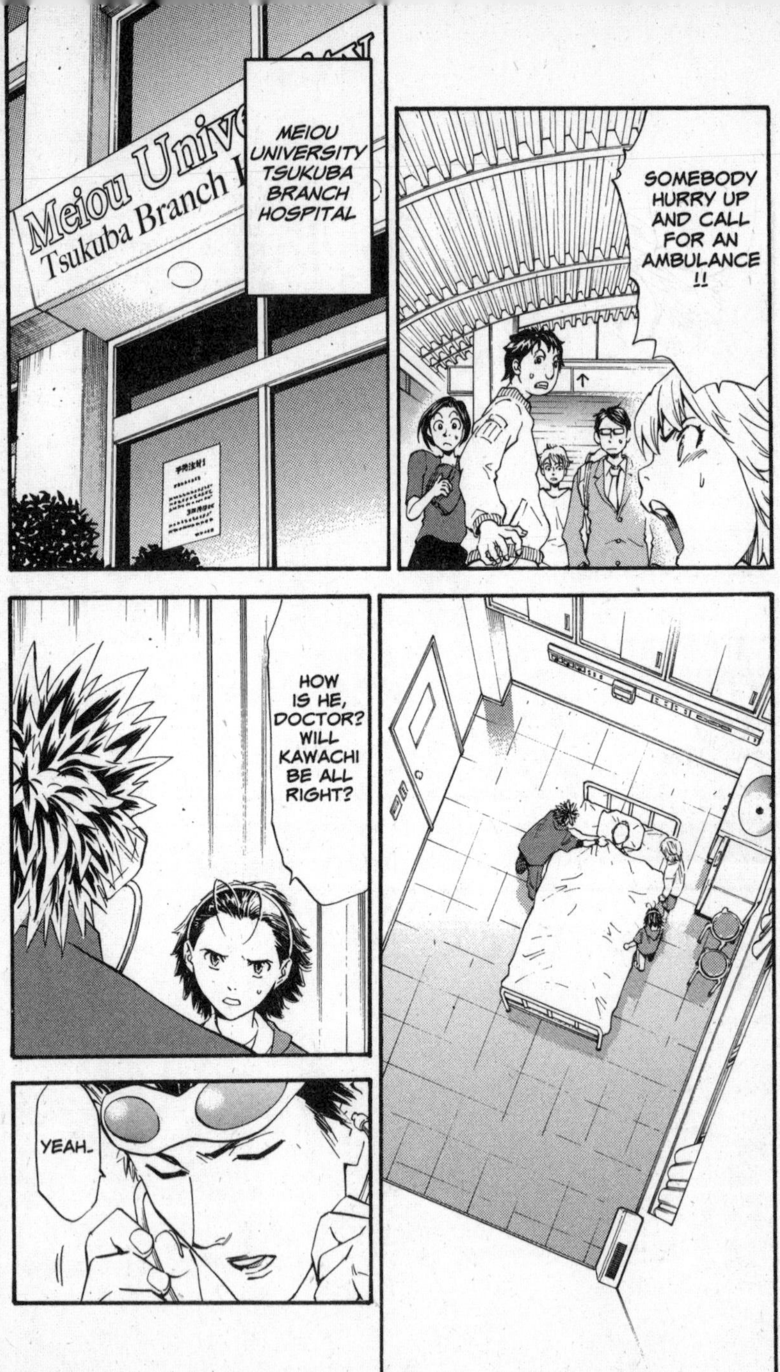
SOMEBODY HURRY UP AND CALL FOR AN AMBULANCE!!
MEIOU UNIVERSITY TSUKUBA BRANCH HOSPITAL
HOW IS HE, DOCTOR? WILL KAWACHI BE ALL RIGHT?
YEAH.

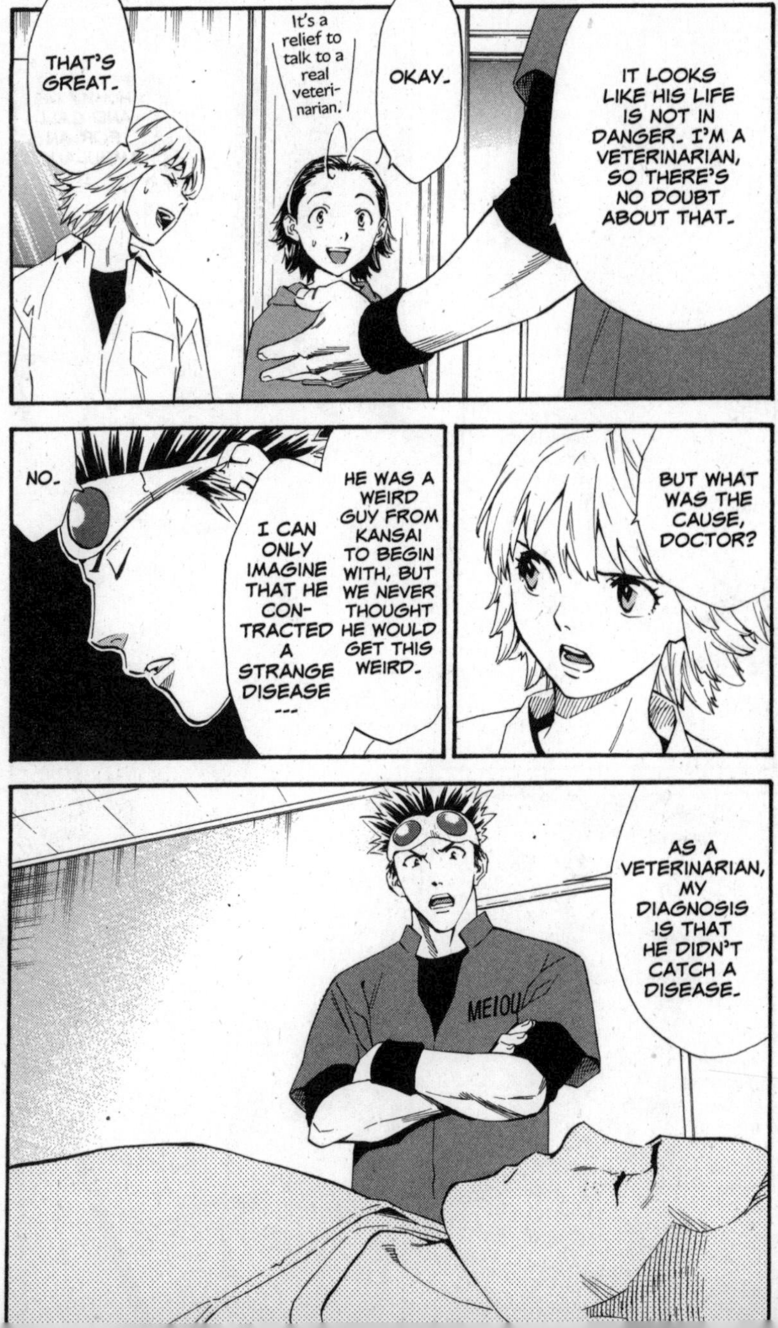
IT LOOKS LIKE HIS LIFE IS NOT IN DANGER. I'M A VETERINARIAN, SO THERE'S NO DOUBT ABOUT THAT.
OKAY.
It's a relief to talk to a real veterinarian.
THAT'S GREAT.
BUT WHAT WAS THE CAUSE, DOCTOR?
HE WAS A WEIRD GUY FROM KANSAI TO BEGIN WITH, BUT WE NEVER THOUGHT HE WOULD GET THIS WEIRD.
I CAN ONLY IMAGINE THAT HE CONTRACTED A STRANGE DISEASE...
NO.
AS A VETERINARIAN, MY DIAGNOSIS IS THAT HE DIDN'T CATCH A DISEASE.
MEIOU

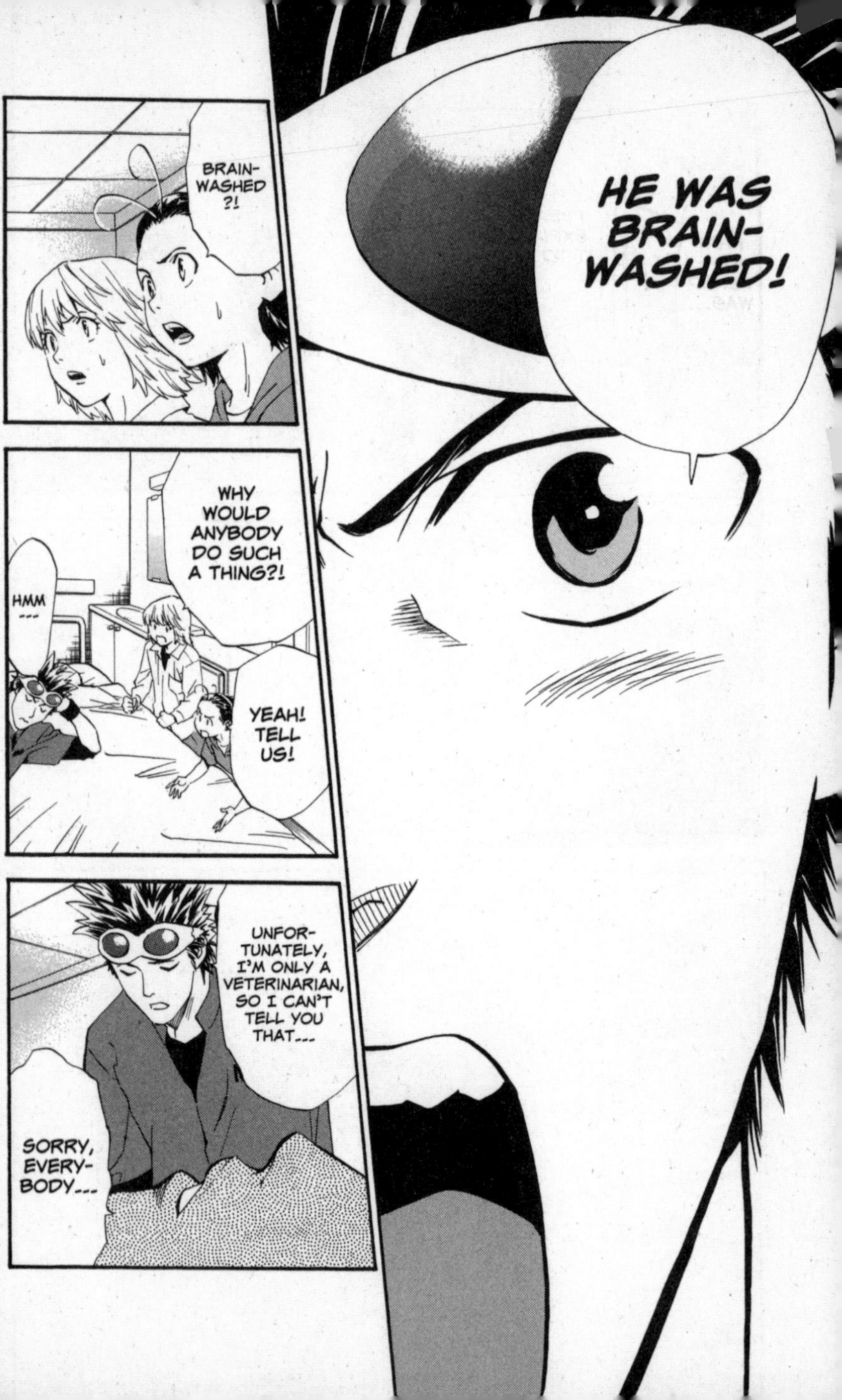
HE WAS BRAIN-WASHED!
BRAIN-WASHED?!
WHY WOULD ANYBODY DO SUCH A THING?!
YEAH! TELL US!
HMM...
UNFORTUNATELY, I'M ONLY A VETERINARIAN, SO I CAN'T TELL YOU THAT...
SORRY, EVERYBODY...

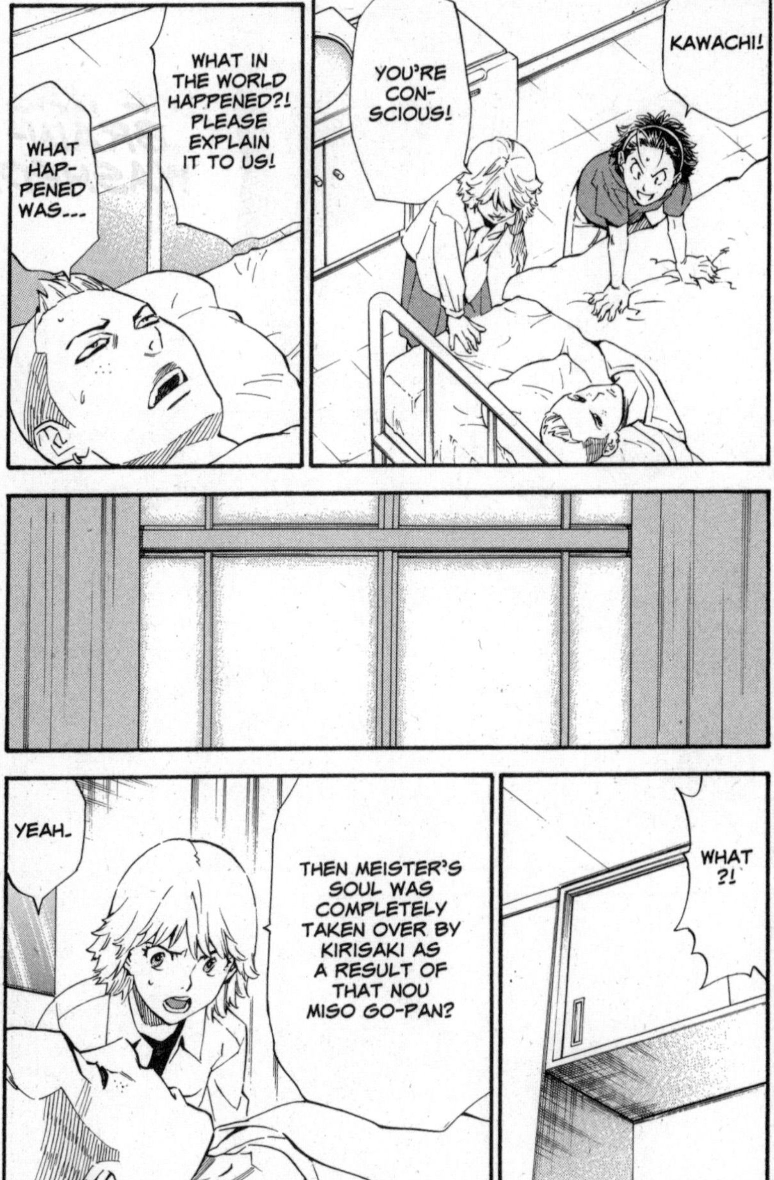
KAWACHI!
YOU'RE CON-SCIOUS!
WHAT IN THE WORLD HAPPENED?! PLEASE EXPLAIN IT TO US!
WHAT HAP-PENED WAS...
WHAT?!
THEN MEISTER'S SOUL WAS COMPLETELY TAKEN OVER BY KIRISAKI AS A RESULT OF THAT NOU MISO GO-PAN?
YEAH.

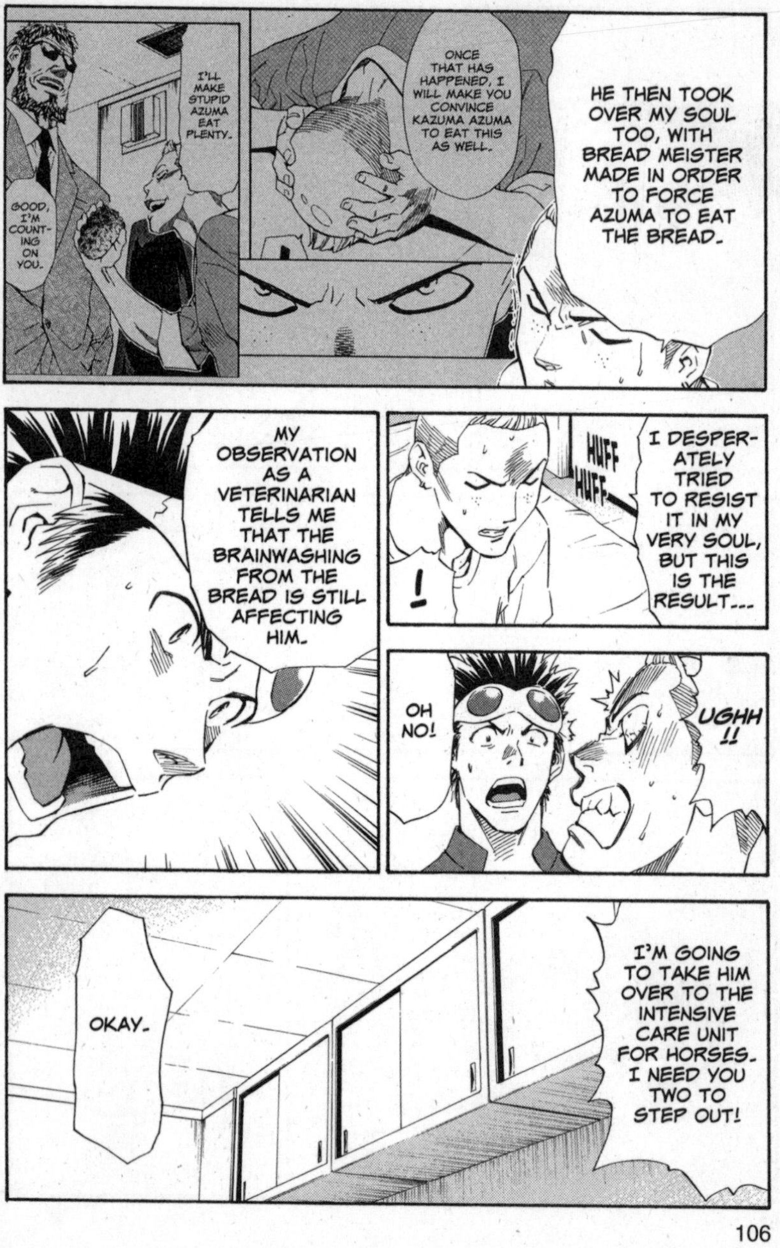
HE THEN TOOK OVER MY SOUL TOO, WITH BREAD MEISTER MADE IN ORDER TO FORCE AZUMA TO EAT THE BREAD.
ONCE THAT HAS HAPPENED, I WILL MAKE YOU CONVINCE KAZUMA AZUMA TO EAT THIS AS WELL.
I'LL MAKE STUPID AZUMA EAT PLENTY.
GOOD, I'M COUNTING ON YOU.
I DESPERATELY TRIED TO RESIST IT IN MY VERY SOUL, BUT THIS IS THE RESULT...
HUFF HUFF
!
UGHH !!
OH NO!
MY OBSERVATION AS A VETERINARIAN TELLS ME THAT THE BRAINWASHING FROM THE BREAD IS STILL AFFECTING HIM.
I'M GOING TO TAKE HIM OVER TO THE INTENSIVE CARE UNIT FOR HORSES. I NEED YOU TWO TO STEP OUT!
OKAY.

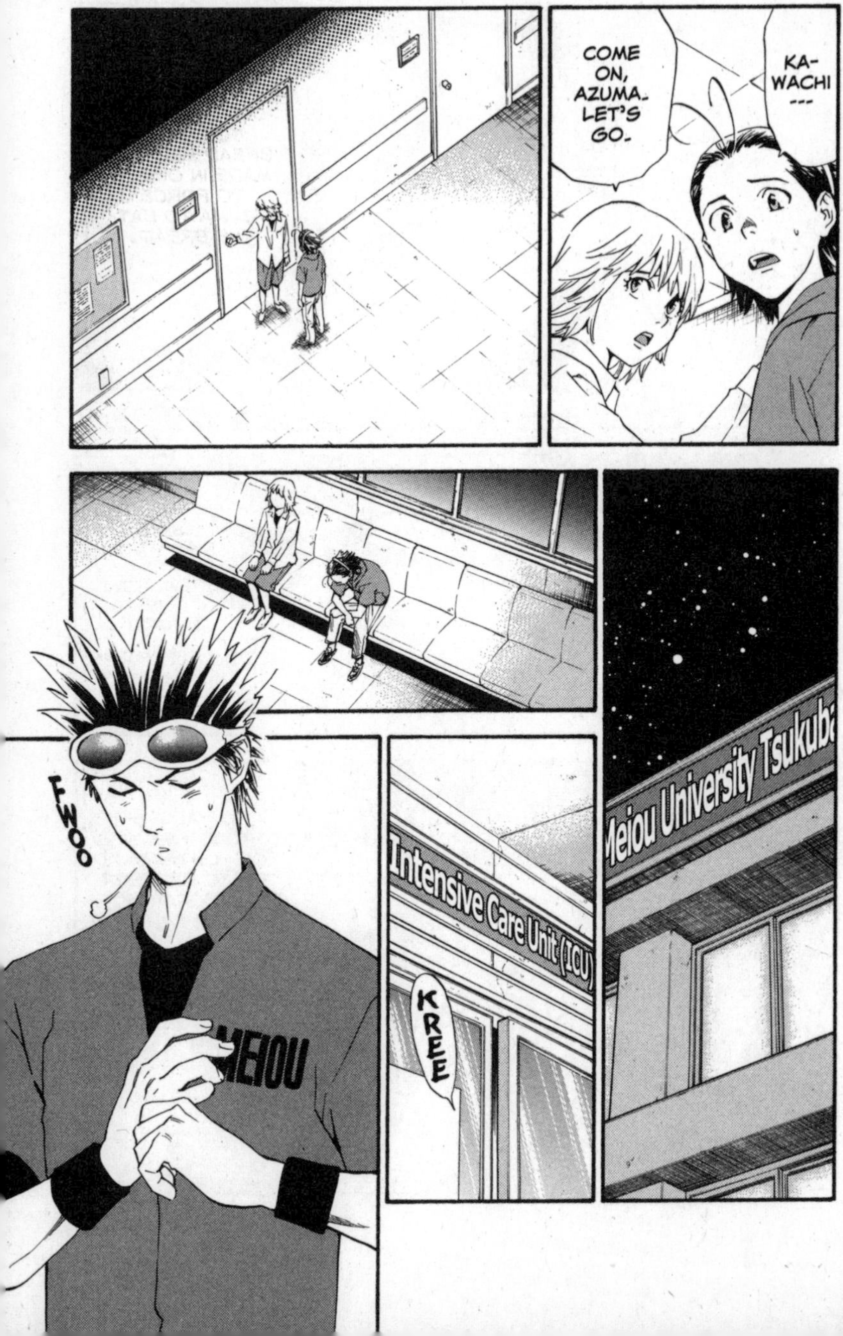
KA-WACHI...
COME ON, AZUMA. LET'S GO.
Meiou University Tsukuba
Intensive Care Unit (ICU)
KREE
FWOO
MEIOU

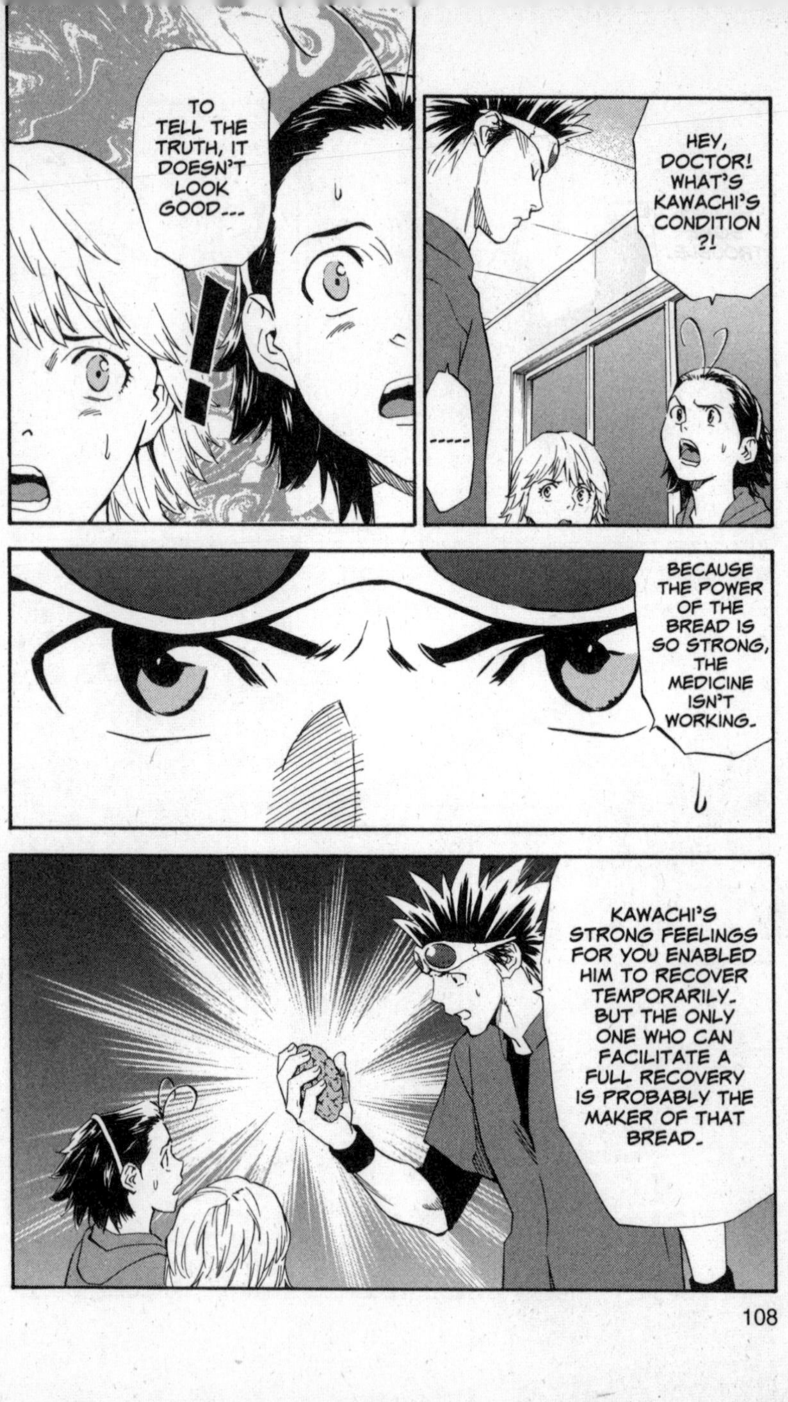
HEY, DOCTOR! WHAT'S KAWACHI'S CONDITION ?!
.....
TO TELL THE TRUTH, IT DOESN'T LOOK GOOD...
!
BECAUSE THE POWER OF THE BREAD IS SO STRONG, THE MEDICINE ISN'T WORKING.
KAWACHI'S STRONG FEELINGS FOR YOU ENABLED HIM TO RECOVER TEMPORARILY. BUT THE ONLY ONE WHO CAN FACILITATE A FULL RECOVERY IS PROBABLY THE MAKER OF THAT BREAD.

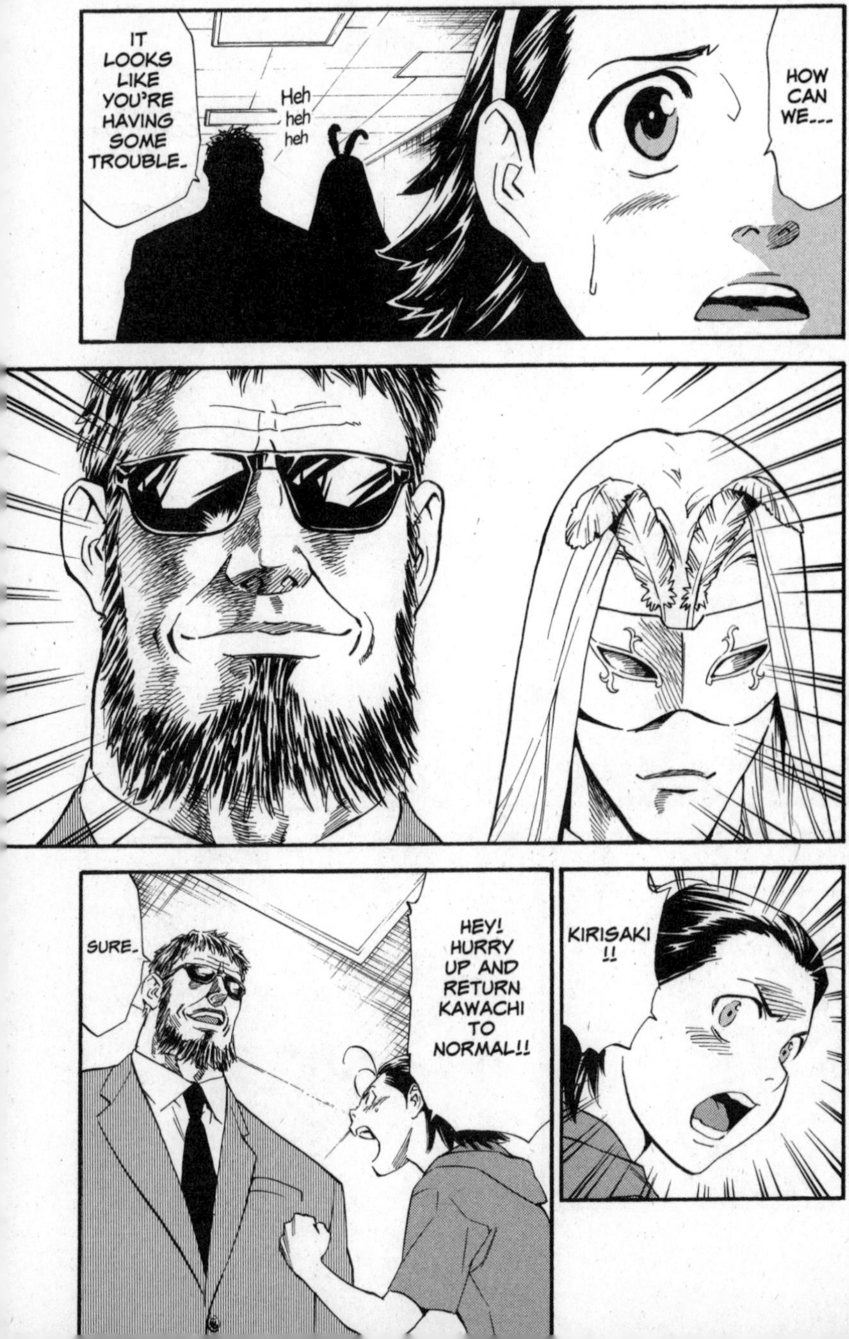
HOW CAN WE...
Heh heh heh
IT LOOKS LIKE YOU'RE HAVING SOME TROUBLE.
KIRISAKI!!
HEY! HURRY UP AND RETURN KAWACHI TO NORMAL!!
SURE.

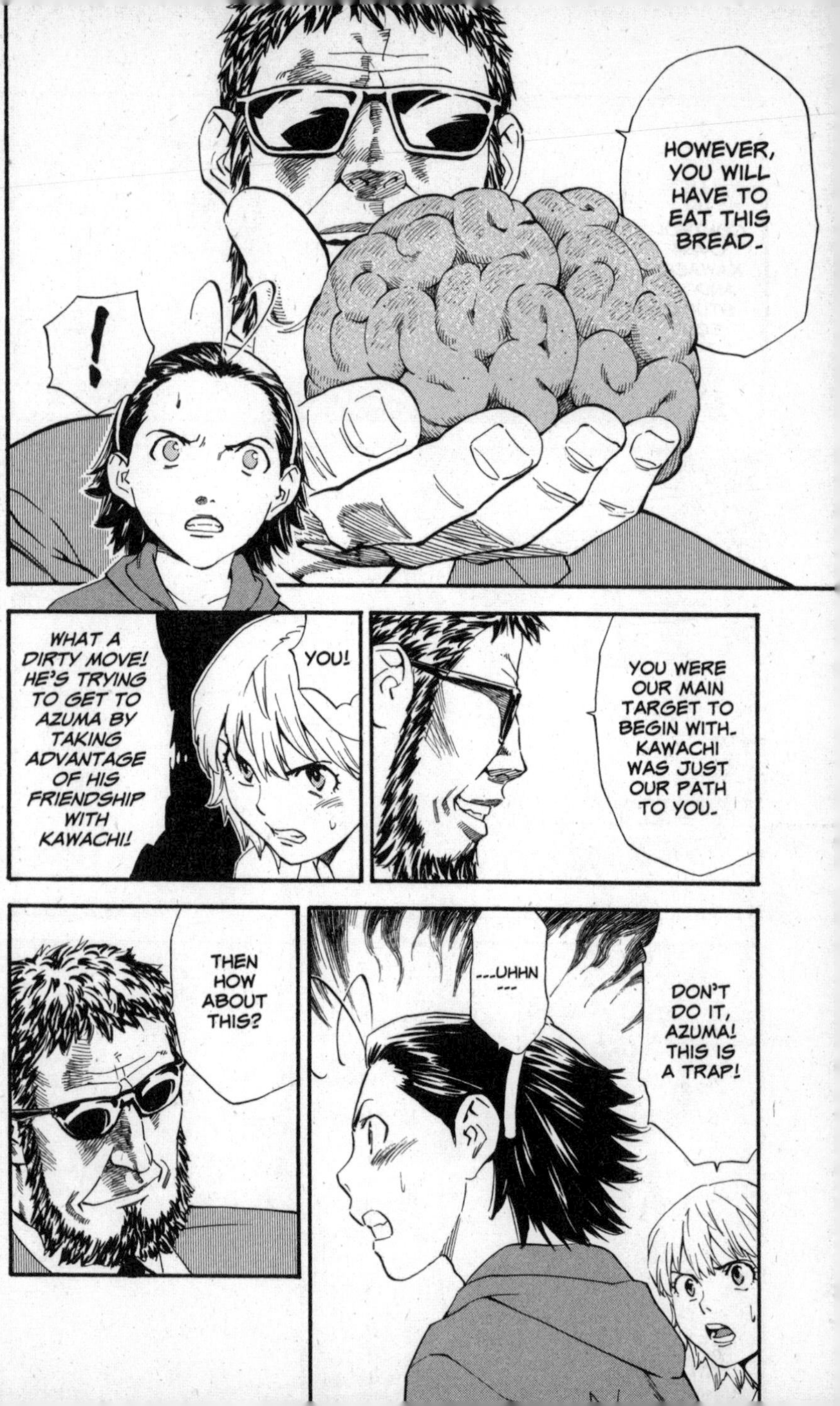
HOWEVER, YOU WILL HAVE TO EAT THIS BREAD.
!
YOU WERE OUR MAIN TARGET TO BEGIN WITH. KAWACHI WAS JUST OUR PATH TO YOU.
YOU!
WHAT A DIRTY MOVE! HE'S TRYING TO GET TO AZUMA BY TAKING ADVANTAGE OF HIS FRIENDSHIP WITH KAWACHI!
DON'T DO IT, AZUMA! THIS IS A TRAP!
...UHHN...
THEN HOW ABOUT THIS?

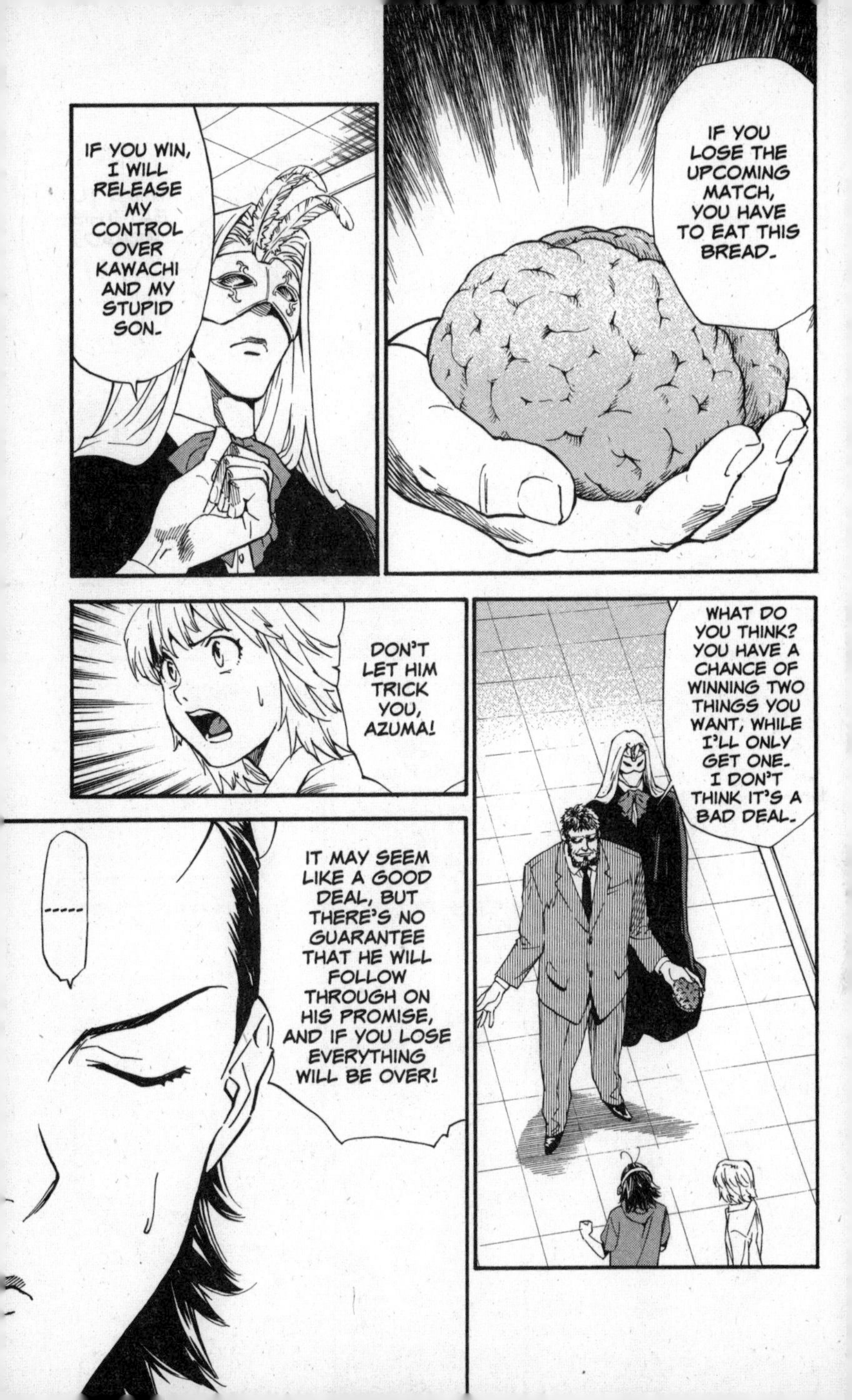
IF YOU LOSE THE UPCOMING MATCH, YOU HAVE TO EAT THIS BREAD.
IF YOU WIN, I WILL RELEASE MY CONTROL OVER KAWACHI AND MY STUPID SON.
WHAT DO YOU THINK? YOU HAVE A CHANCE OF WINNING TWO THINGS YOU WANT, WHILE I'LL ONLY GET ONE. I DON'T THINK IT'S A BAD DEAL.
DON'T LET HIM TRICK YOU, AZUMA!
IT MAY SEEM LIKE A GOOD DEAL, BUT THERE'S NO GUARANTEE THAT HE WILL FOLLOW THROUGH ON HIS PROMISE, AND IF YOU LOSE EVERYTHING WILL BE OVER!

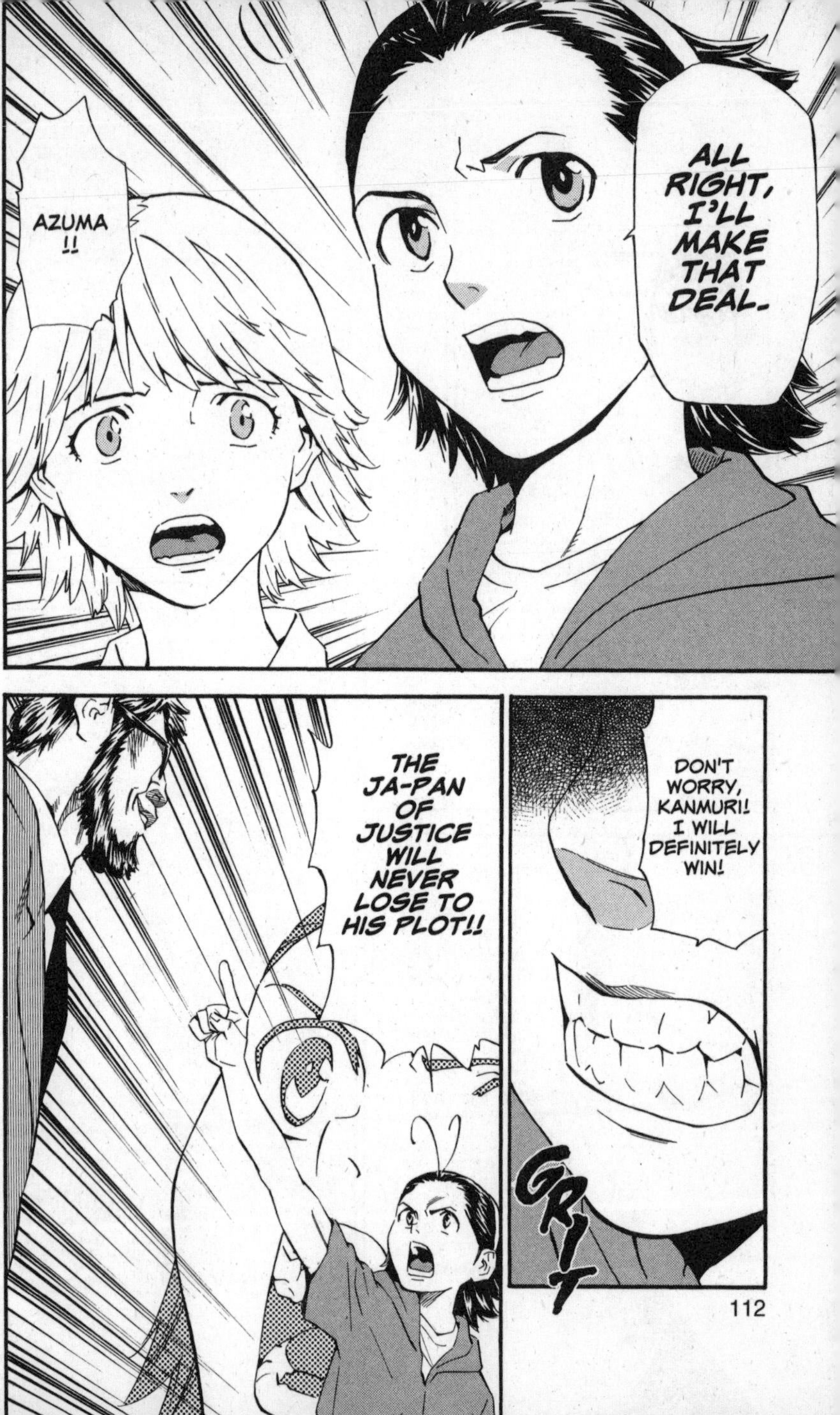
ALL RIGHT, I'LL MAKE THAT DEAL.
AZUMA !!
DON'T WORRY, KANMURI! I WILL DEFINITELY WIN!
GRIT
THE JA-PAN OF JUSTICE WILL NEVER LOSE TO HIS PLOT!!

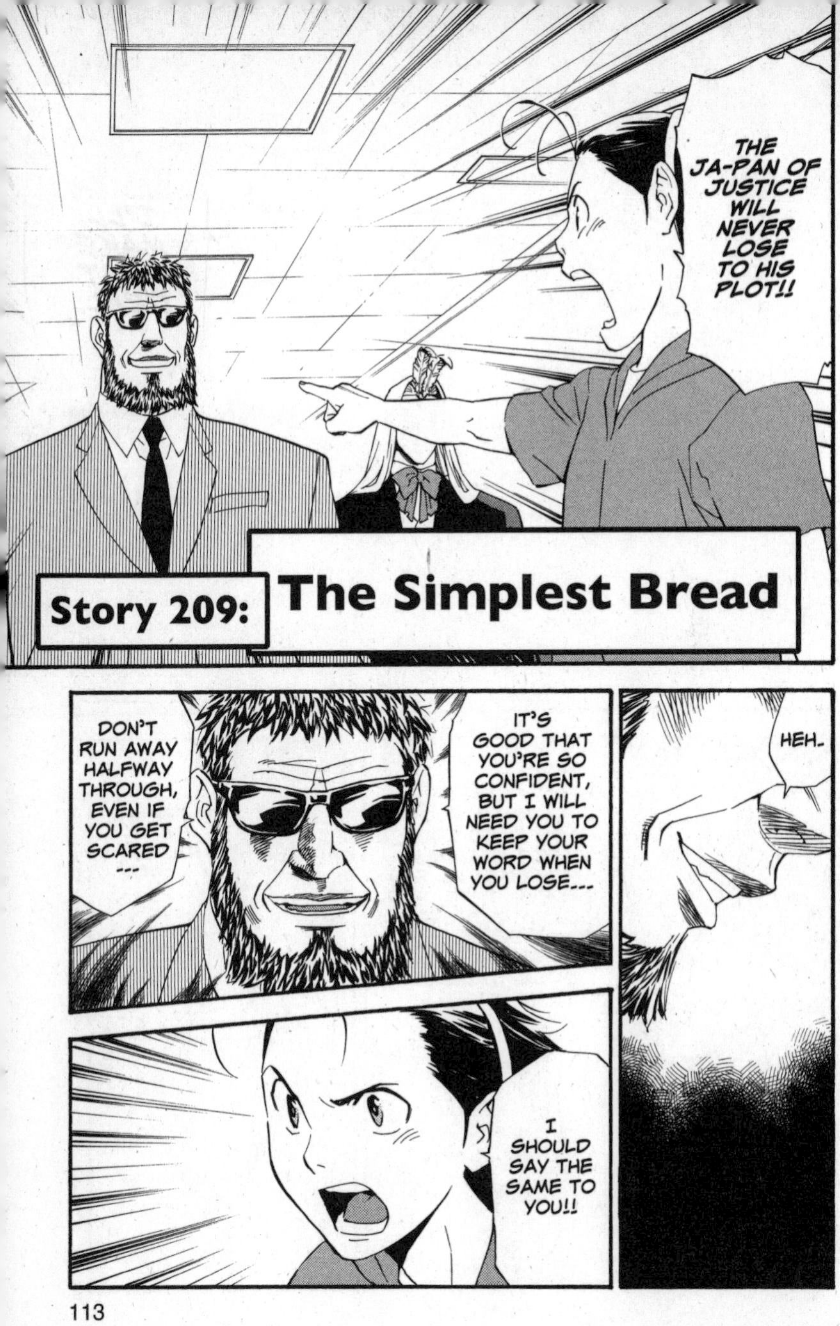
THE JA-PAN OF JUSTICE WILL NEVER LOSE TO HIS PLOT!!
Story 209: The Simplest Bread
HEH...
IT'S GOOD THAT YOU'RE SO CONFIDENT, BUT I WILL NEED YOU TO KEEP YOUR WORD WHEN YOU LOSE...
DON'T RUN AWAY HALFWAY THROUGH, EVEN IF YOU GET SCARED...
I SHOULD SAY THE SAME TO YOU!!

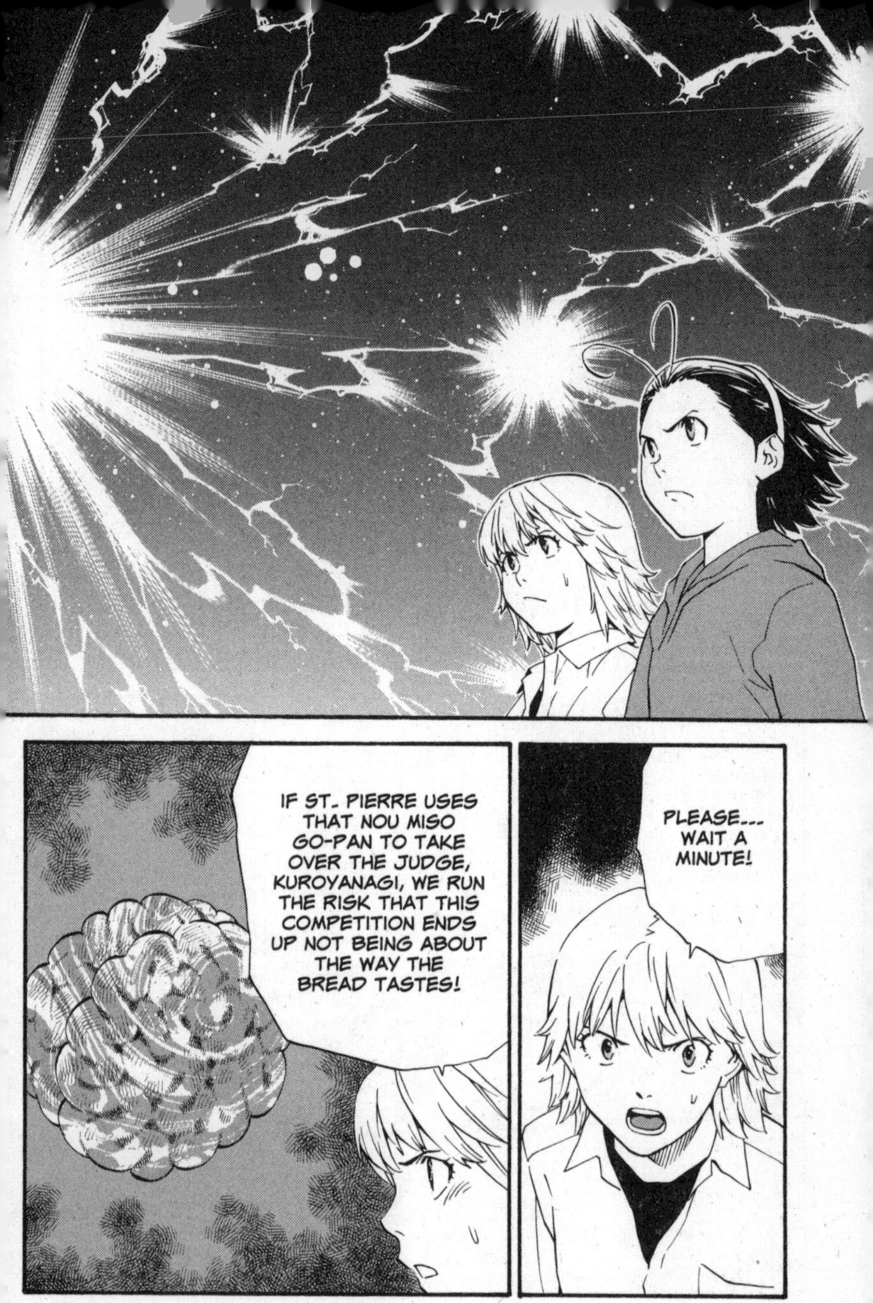
PLEASE... WAIT A MINUTE!
IF ST. PIERRE USES THAT NOU MISO GO-PAN TO TAKE OVER THE JUDGE, KUROYANAGI, WE RUN THE RISK THAT THIS COMPETITION ENDS UP NOT BEING ABOUT THE WAY THE BREAD TASTES!

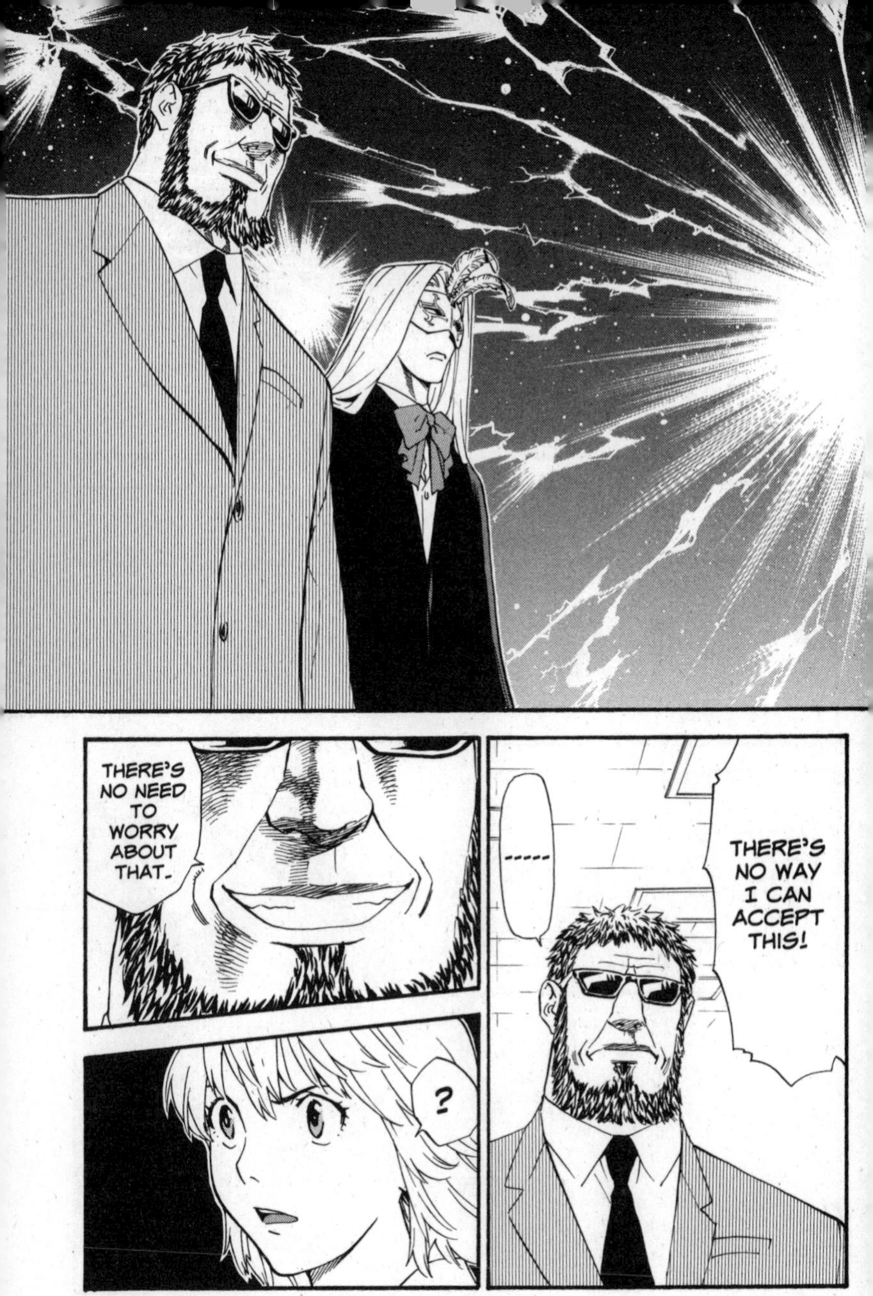
THERE'S NO WAY I CAN ACCEPT THIS!

THERE'S NO NEED TO WORRY ABOUT THAT.
?

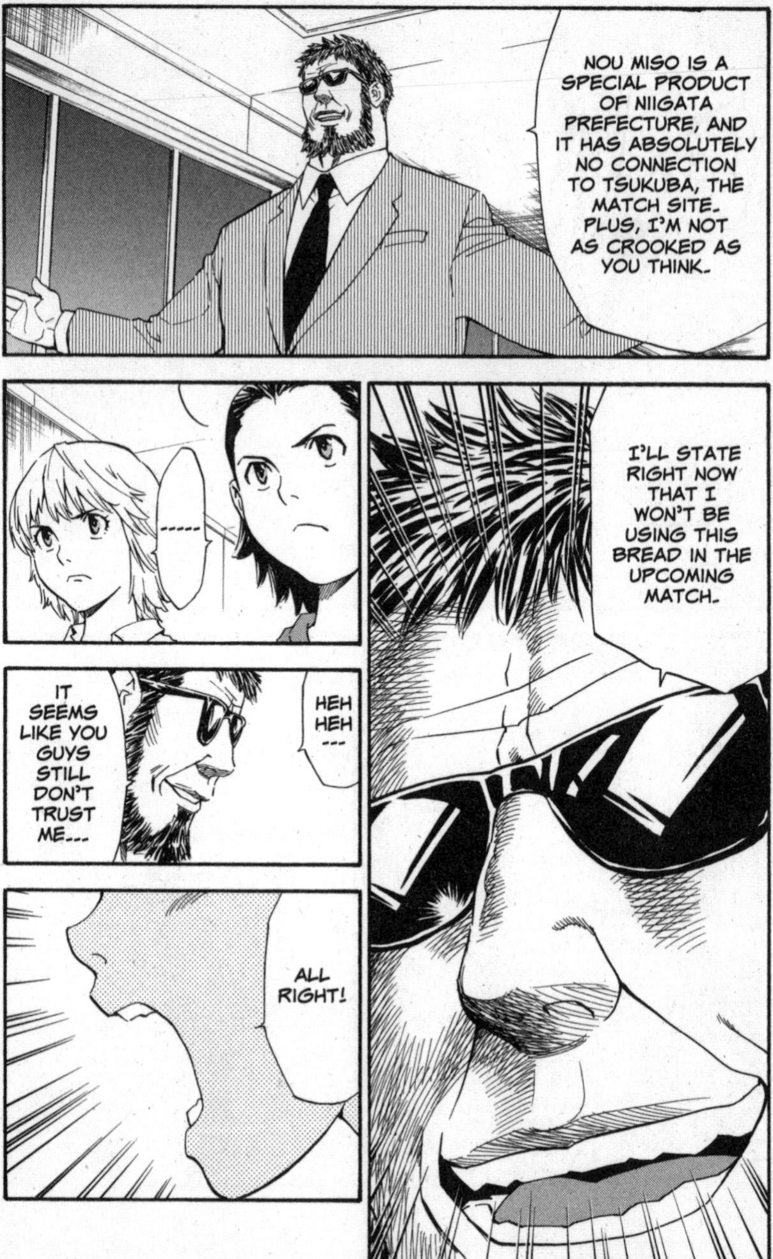
NOU MISO IS A SPECIAL PRODUCT OF NIIGATA PREFECTURE, AND IT HAS ABSOLUTELY NO CONNECTION TO TSUKUBA, THE MATCH SITE. PLUS, I'M NOT AS CROOKED AS YOU THINK.
I'LL STATE RIGHT NOW THAT I WON'T BE USING THIS BREAD IN THE UPCOMING MATCH.
.....
HEH HEH...
IT SEEMS LIKE YOU GUYS STILL DON'T TRUST ME...
ALL RIGHT!

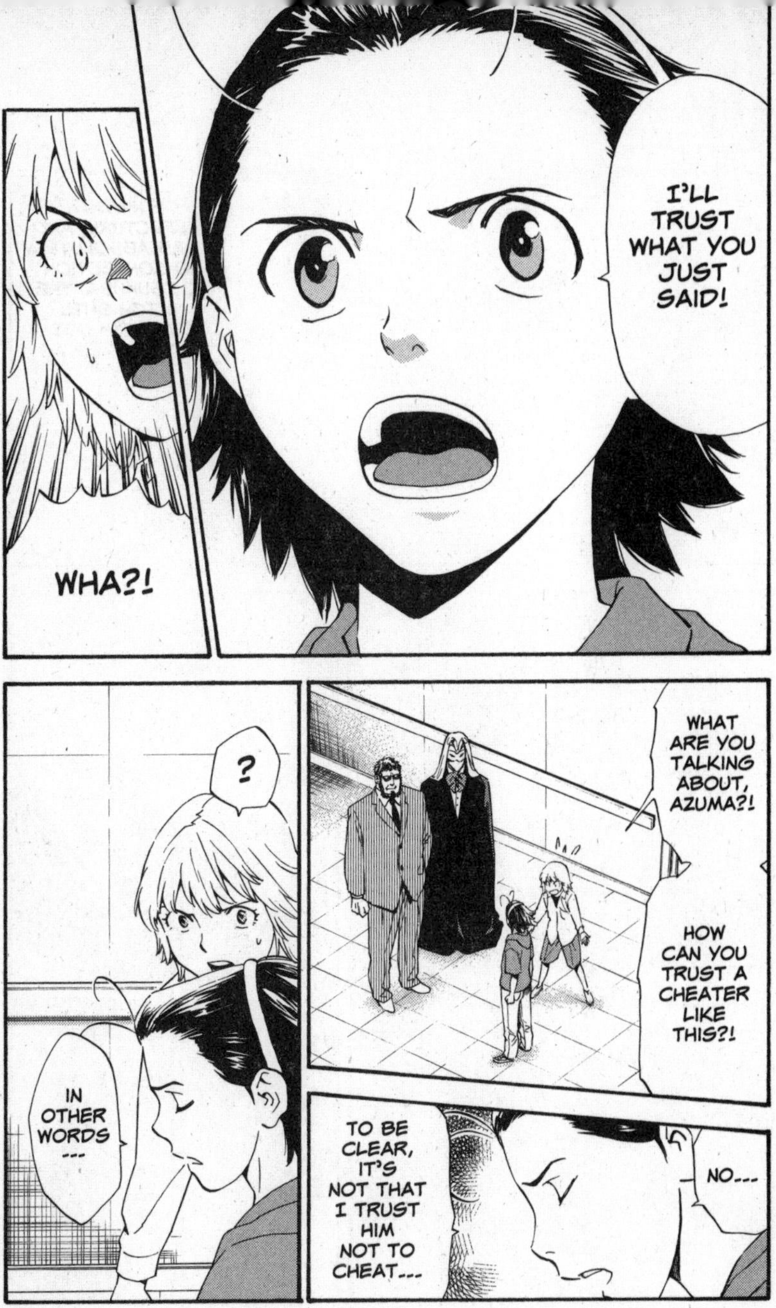
I'LL TRUST WHAT YOU JUST SAID!
WHA?!
WHAT ARE YOU TALKING ABOUT, AZUMA?!
HOW CAN YOU TRUST A CHEATER LIKE THIS?!
NO---
TO BE CLEAR, IT'S NOT THAT I TRUST HIM NOT TO CHEAT---
?
IN OTHER WORDS---

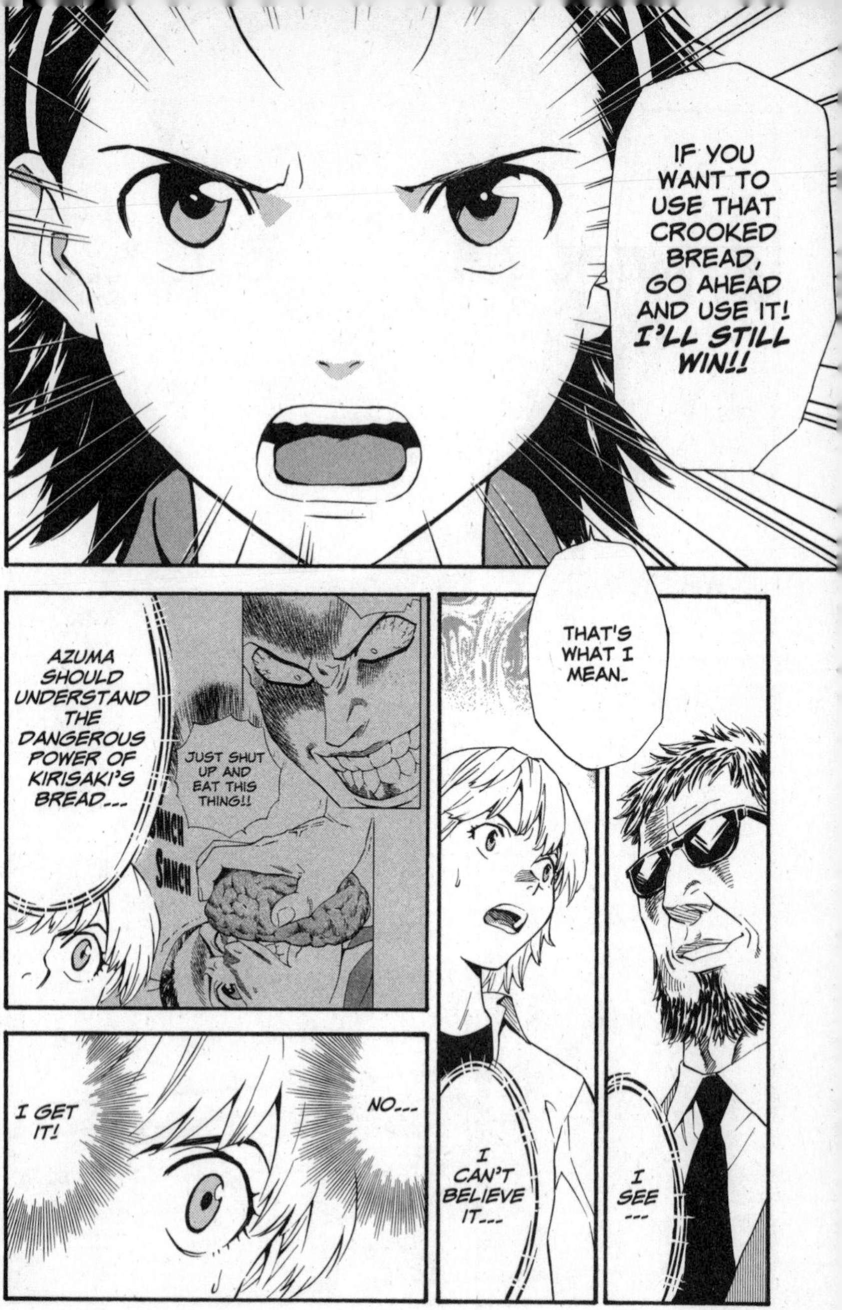
IF YOU WANT TO USE THAT CROOKED BREAD, GO AHEAD AND USE IT! I'LL STILL WIN!!
THAT'S WHAT I MEAN.
I SEE...
I CAN'T BELIEVE IT...
AZUMA SHOULD UNDERSTAND THE DANGEROUS POWER OF KIRISAKI'S BREAD...
JUST SHUT UP AND EAT THIS THING!!
SMNCH
SMNCH
NO...
I GET IT!

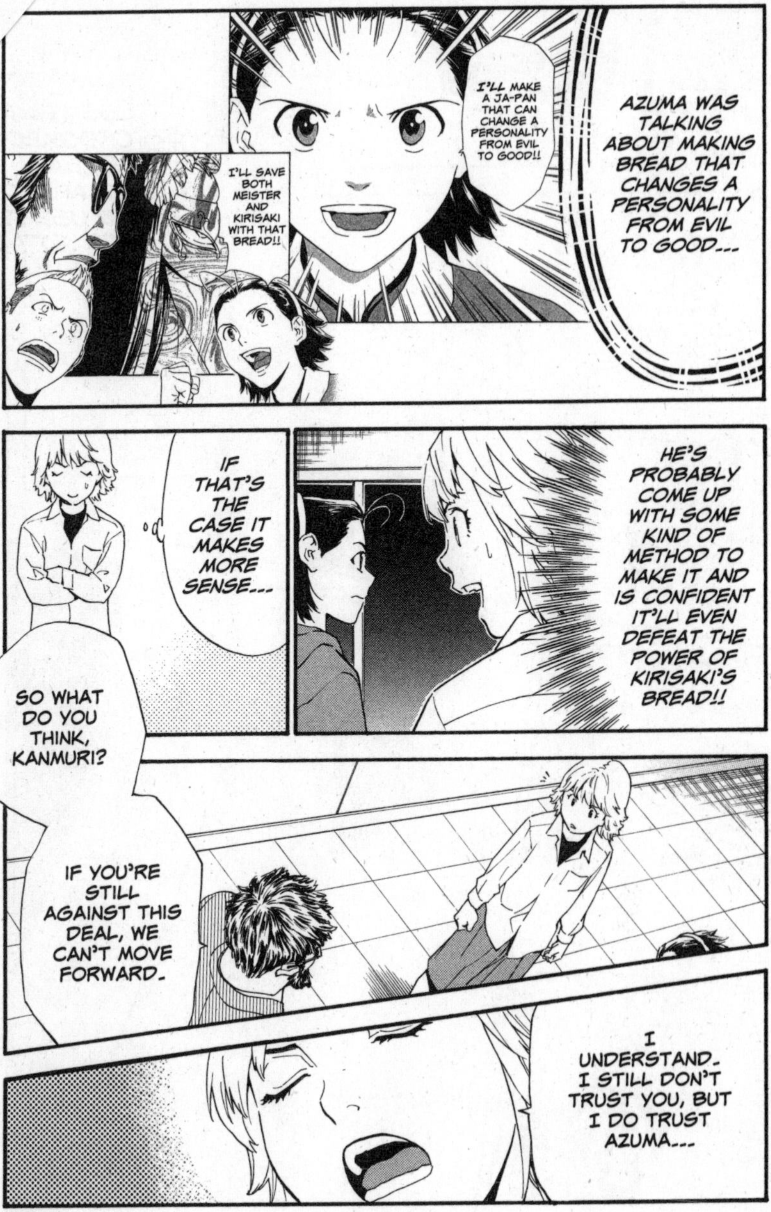
AZUMA WAS TALKING ABOUT MAKING BREAD THAT CHANGES A PERSONALITY FROM EVIL TO GOOD...
I'LL MAKE A JA-PAN THAT CAN CHANGE A PERSONALITY FROM EVIL TO GOOD!!
I'LL SAVE BOTH MEISTER AND KIRISAKI WITH THAT BREAD!!
HE'S PROBABLY COME UP WITH SOME KIND OF METHOD TO MAKE IT AND IS CONFIDENT IT'LL EVEN DEFEAT THE POWER OF KIRISAKI'S BREAD!!
IF THAT'S THE CASE IT MAKES MORE SENSE...
SO WHAT DO YOU THINK, KANMURI?
IF YOU'RE STILL AGAINST THIS DEAL, WE CAN'T MOVE FORWARD.
I UNDERSTAND. I STILL DON'T TRUST YOU, BUT I DO TRUST AZUMA...

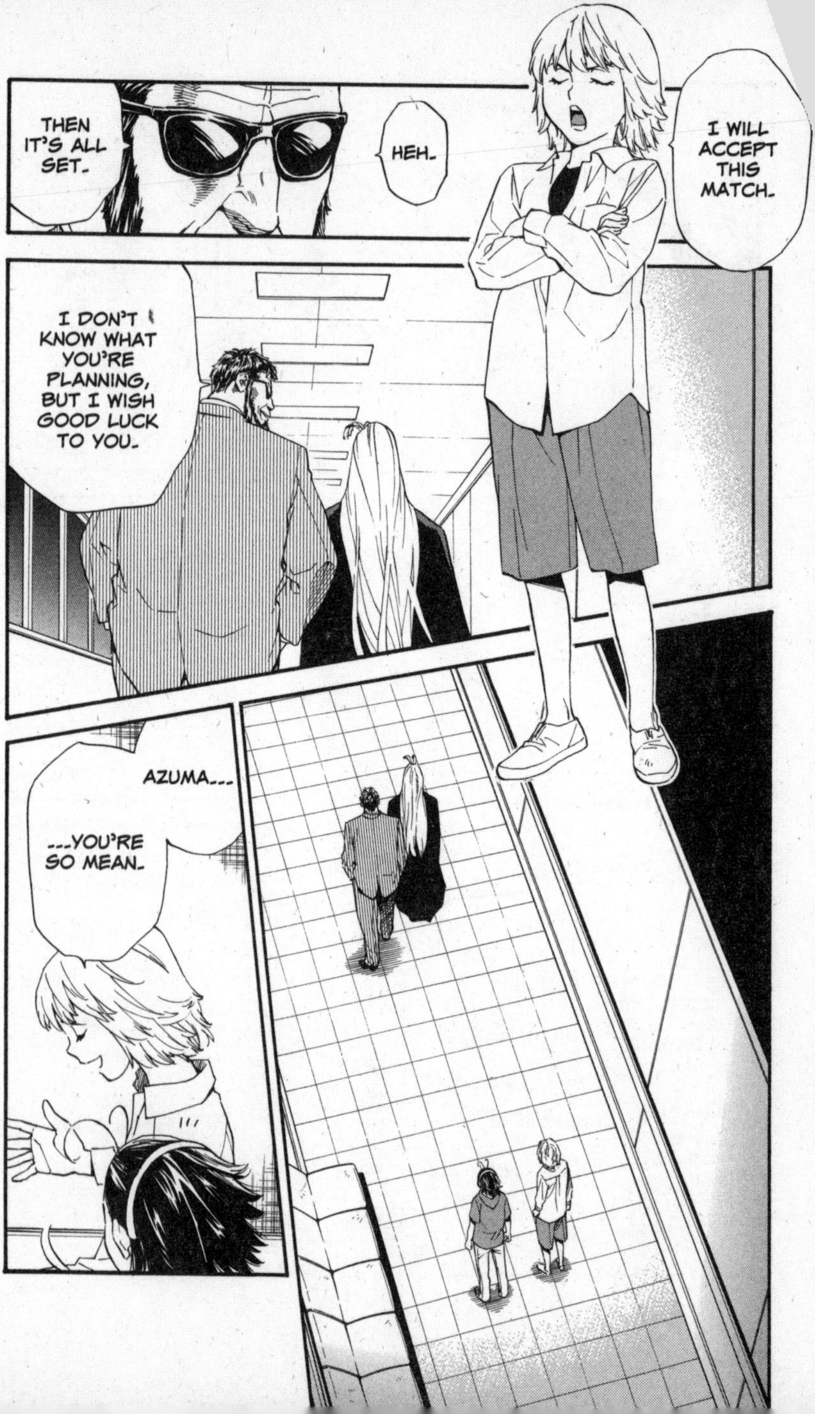
I WILL ACCEPT THIS MATCH.
HEH.
THEN IT'S ALL SET.
I DON'T KNOW WHAT YOU'RE PLANNING, BUT I WISH GOOD LUCK TO YOU.
AZUMA...
...YOU'RE SO MEAN.

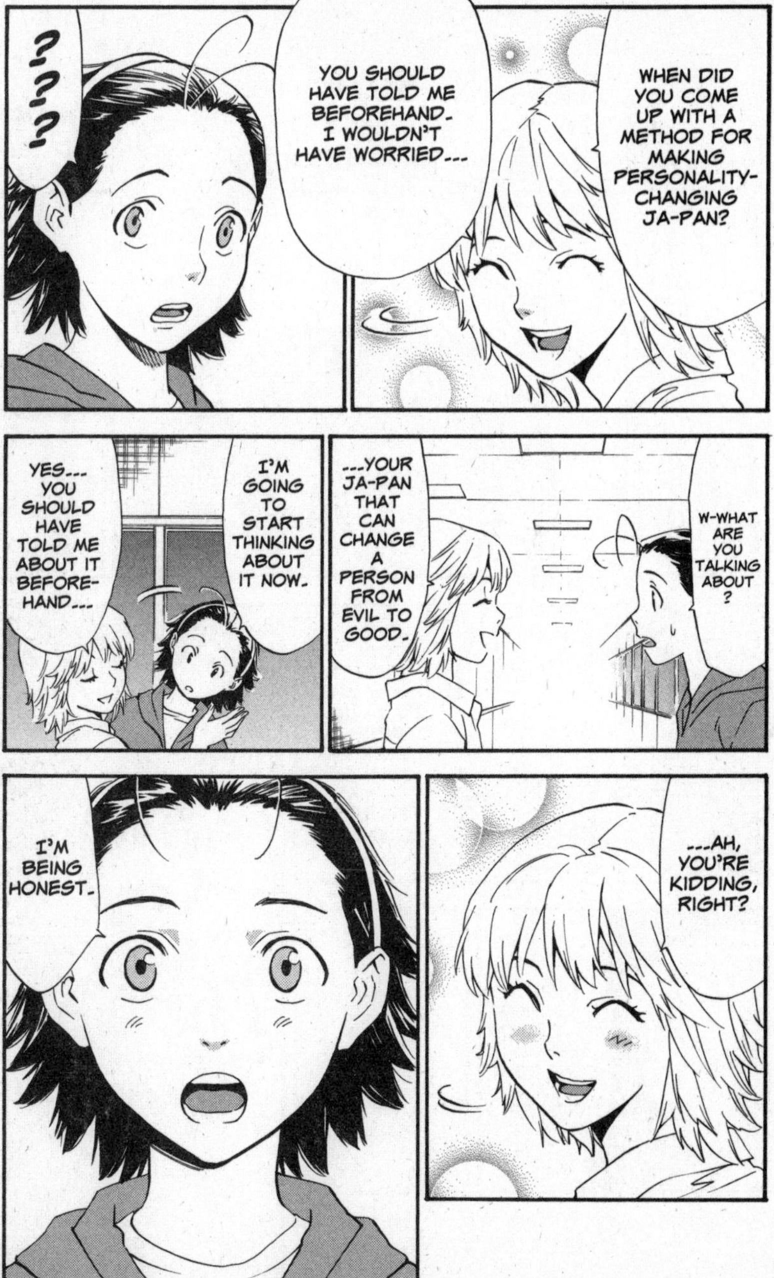
WHEN DID YOU COME UP WITH A METHOD FOR MAKING PERSONALITY-CHANGING JA-PAN?
YOU SHOULD HAVE TOLD ME BEFOREHAND. I WOULDN'T HAVE WORRIED...
???
W-WHAT ARE YOU TALKING ABOUT?
...YOUR JA-PAN THAT CAN CHANGE A PERSON FROM EVIL TO GOOD.
I'M GOING TO START THINKING ABOUT IT NOW.
YES... YOU SHOULD HAVE TOLD ME ABOUT IT BEFOREHAND...
...AH, YOU'RE KIDDING, RIGHT?
I'M BEING HONEST.

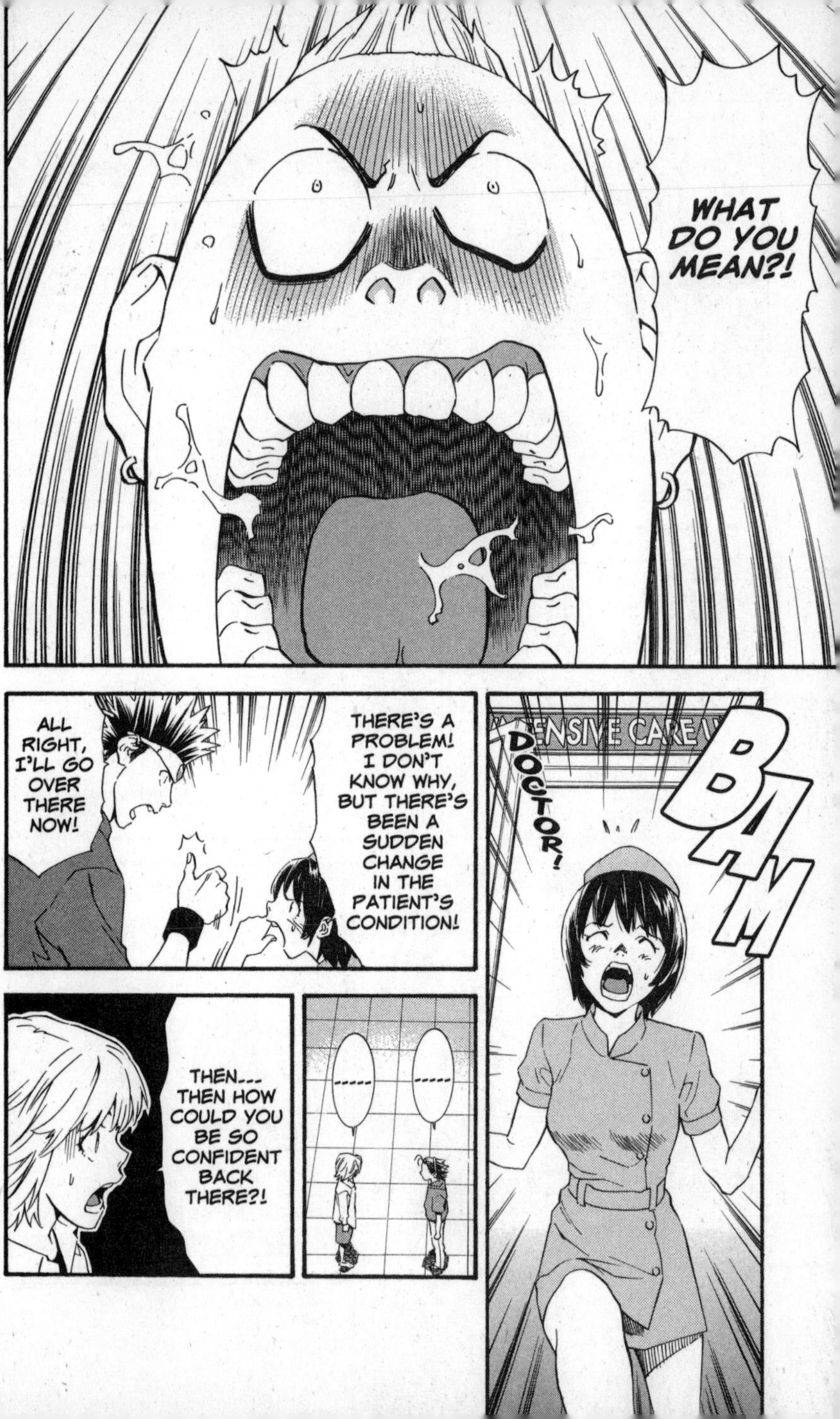
WHAT DO YOU MEAN?!
DOCTOR!
BAM
THERE'S A PROBLEM! I DON'T KNOW WHY, BUT THERE'S BEEN A SUDDEN CHANGE IN THE PATIENT'S CONDITION!
ALL RIGHT, I'LL GO OVER THERE NOW!

THEN... THEN HOW COULD YOU BE SO CONFIDENT BACK THERE?!

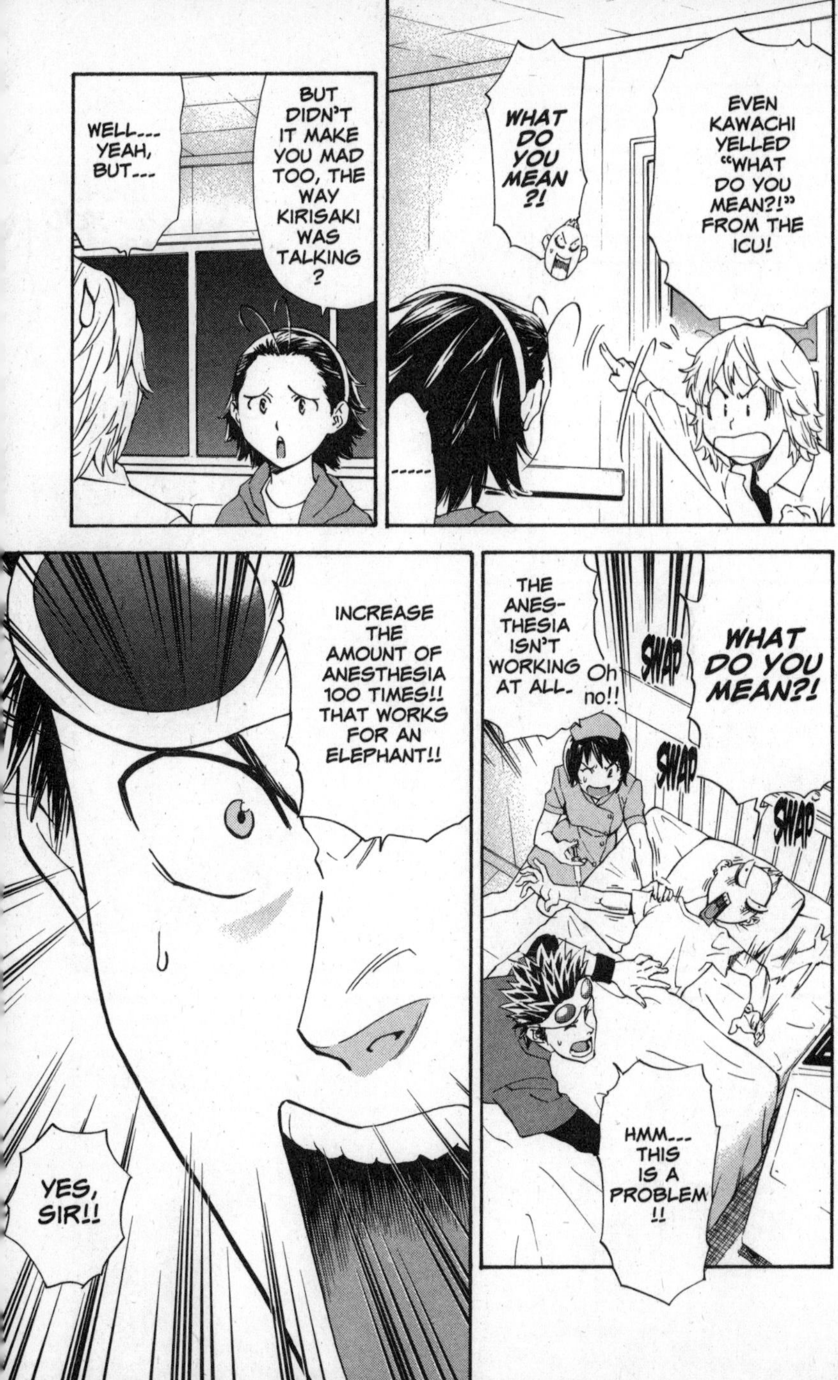
EVEN KAWACHI YELLED "WHAT DO YOU MEAN?!" FROM THE ICU!
WHAT DO YOU MEAN?!
.....
BUT DIDN'T IT MAKE YOU MAD TOO, THE WAY KIRISAKI WAS TALKING?
WELL... YEAH, BUT...
WHAT DO YOU MEAN?!
SWAP
THE ANES-THESIA ISN'T WORKING AT ALL.
Oh no!!
SWAP
SWAP
HMM... THIS IS A PROBLEM!!
INCREASE THE AMOUNT OF ANESTHESIA 100 TIMES!! THAT WORKS FOR AN ELEPHANT!!
YES, SIR!!

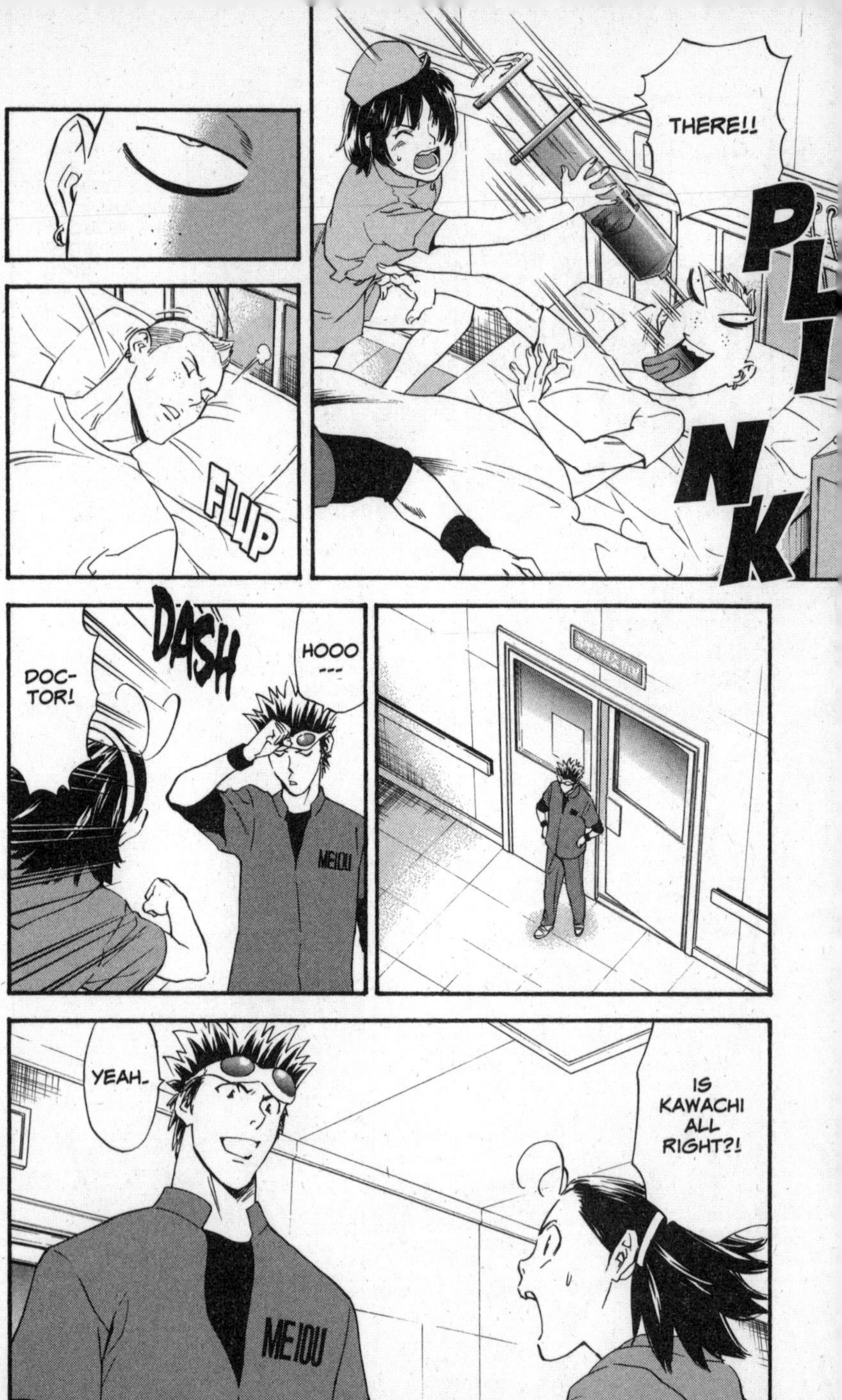

THERE!!
PLINK
FLUP
HOOO---
DASH
DOC-TOR!
IS KAWACHI ALL RIGHT?!
YEAH_

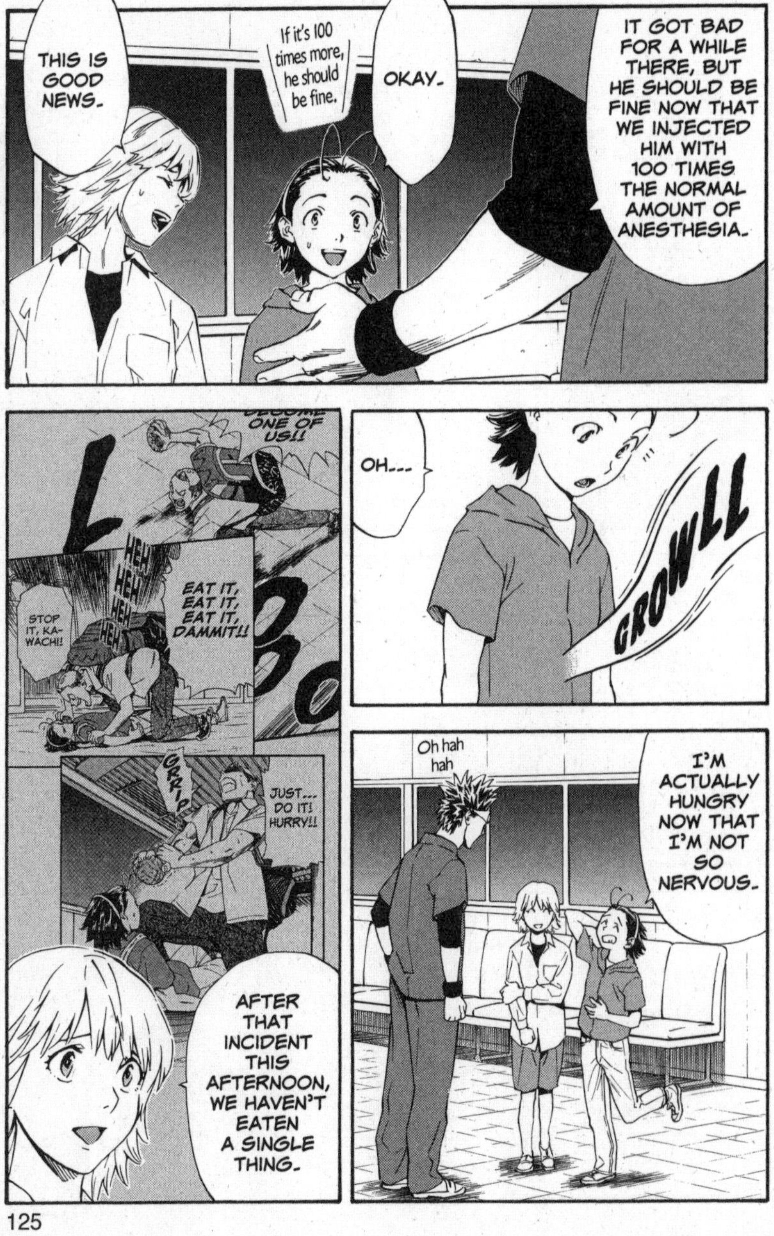

IT GOT BAD FOR A WHILE THERE, BUT HE SHOULD BE FINE NOW THAT WE INJECTED HIM WITH 100 TIMES THE NORMAL AMOUNT OF ANESTHESIA.
OKAY.
If it's 100 times more, he should be fine.
THIS IS GOOD NEWS.
OH...
GROWLL
Oh hah hah
I'M ACTUALLY HUNGRY NOW THAT I'M NOT SO NERVOUS.
ONE OF US!!
HEH HEH HEH HEH HEH
EAT IT, EAT IT, EAT IT, DAMMIT!!
STOP IT, KA-WACHI!!
GRRIP
JUST... DO IT! HURRY!!
AFTER THAT INCIDENT THIS AFTERNOON, WE HAVEN'T EATEN A SINGLE THING.

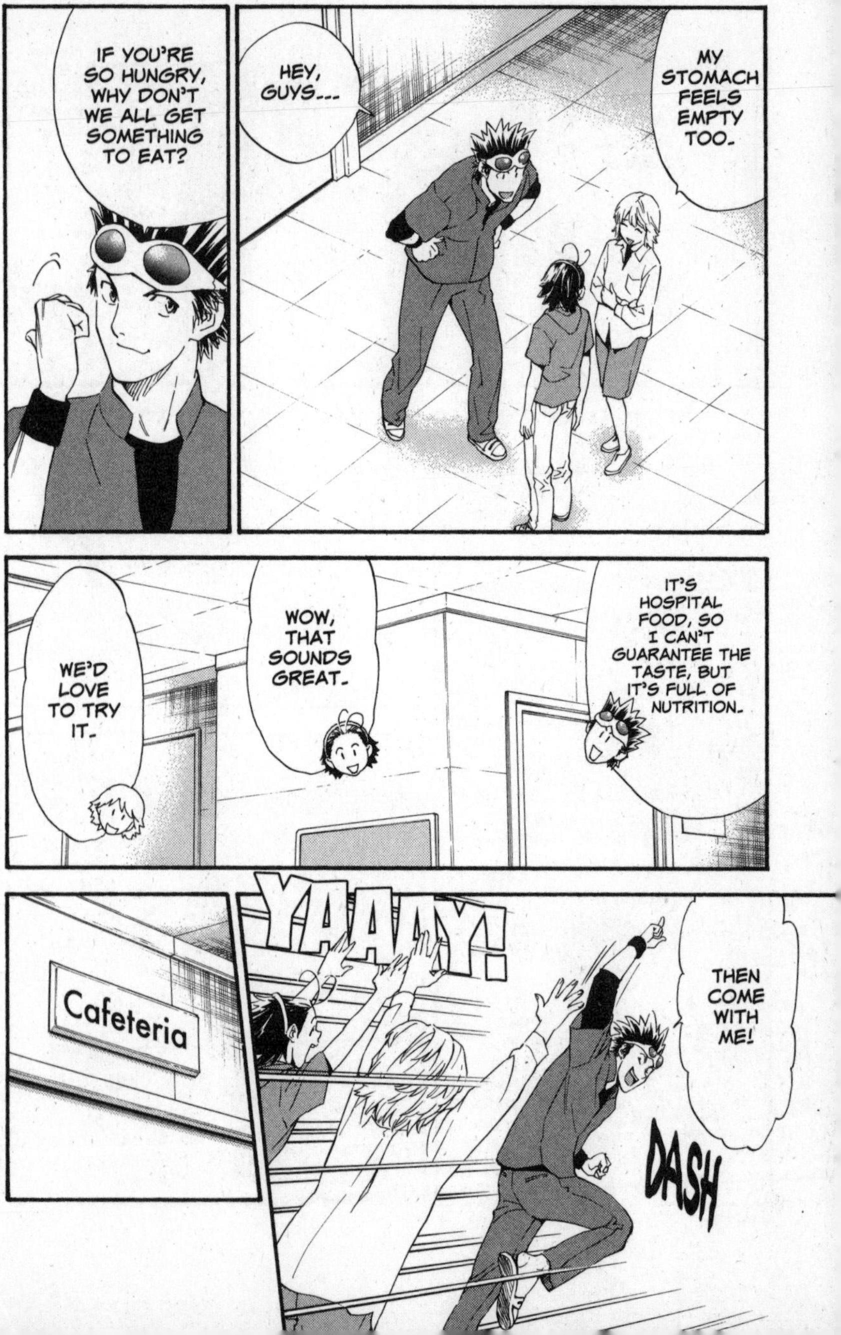
MY STOMACH FEELS EMPTY TOO.
HEY, GUYS...
IF YOU'RE SO HUNGRY, WHY DON'T WE ALL GET SOMETHING TO EAT?
IT'S HOSPITAL FOOD, SO I CAN'T GUARANTEE THE TASTE, BUT IT'S FULL OF NUTRITION.
WOW, THAT SOUNDS GREAT.
WE'D LOVE TO TRY IT.
THEN COME WITH ME!
YAAAY!
DASH
Cafeteria

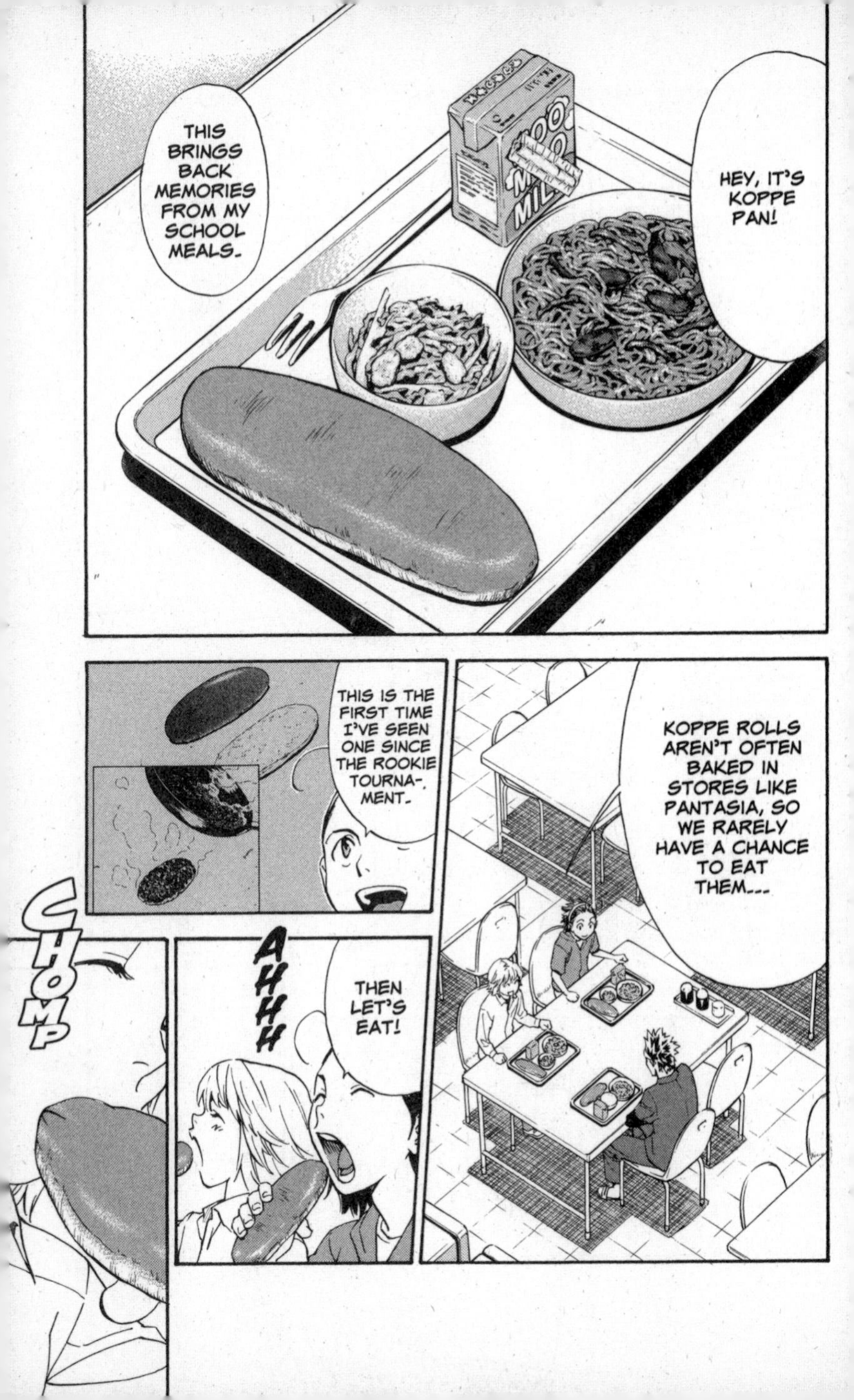
HEY, IT'S KOPPE PAN!
THIS BRINGS BACK MEMORIES FROM MY SCHOOL MEALS...
KOPPE ROLLS AREN'T OFTEN BAKED IN STORES LIKE PANTASIA, SO WE RARELY HAVE A CHANCE TO EAT THEM...
THIS IS THE FIRST TIME I'VE SEEN ONE SINCE THE ROOKIE TOURNA-MENT.
THEN LET'S EAT!
AHHH
CHOMP

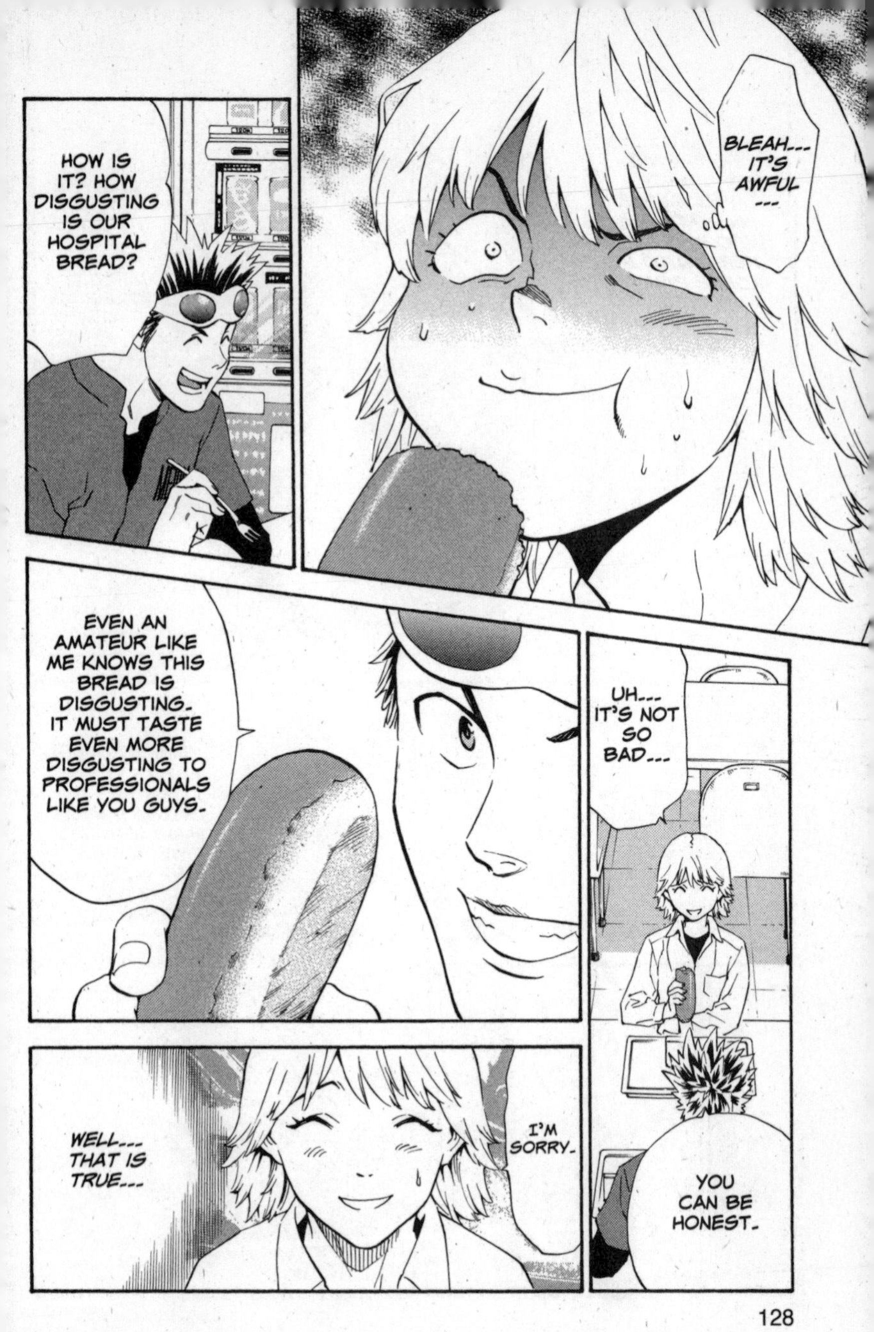
BLEAH... IT'S AWFUL ...
HOW IS IT? HOW DISGUSTING IS OUR HOSPITAL BREAD?
UH... IT'S NOT SO BAD...
YOU CAN BE HONEST.
EVEN AN AMATEUR LIKE ME KNOWS THIS BREAD IS DISGUSTING. IT MUST TASTE EVEN MORE DISGUSTING TO PROFESSIONALS LIKE YOU GUYS.
I'M SORRY.
WELL... THAT IS TRUE...

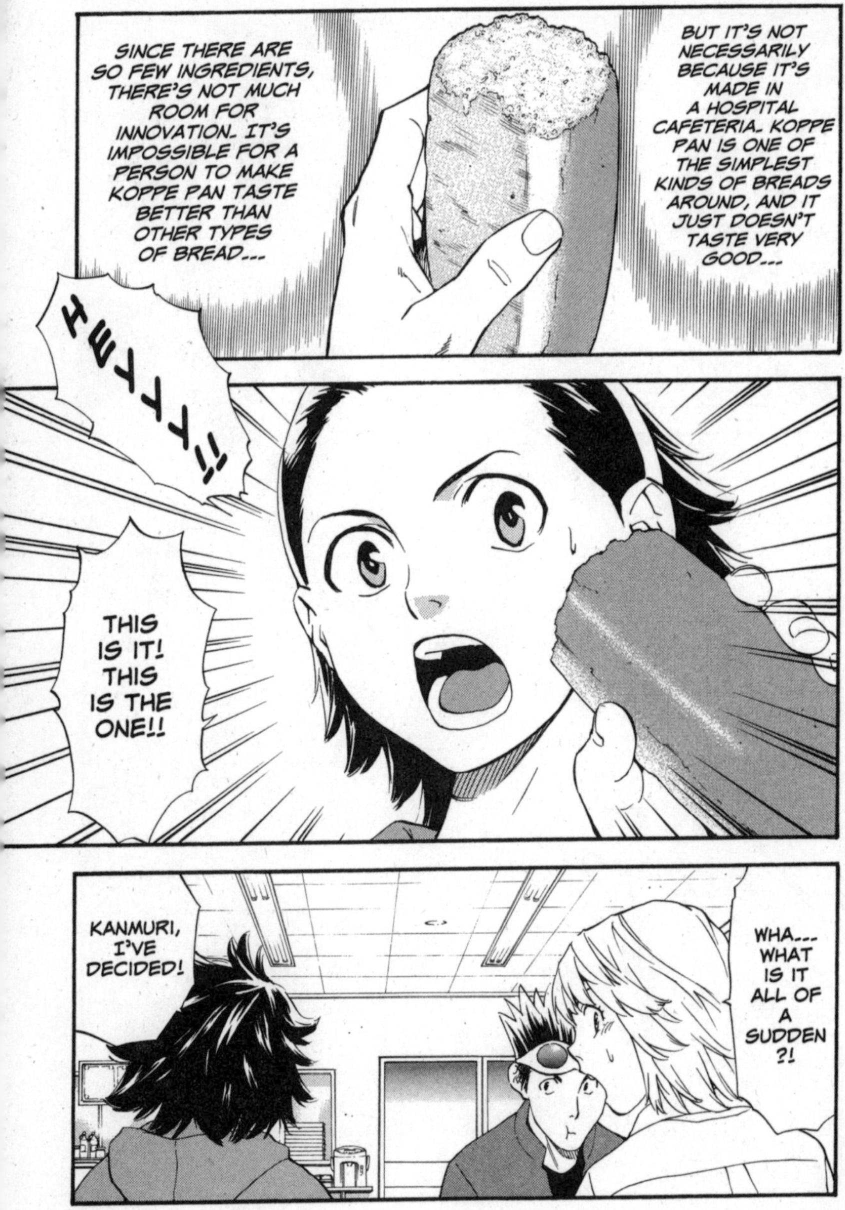
BUT IT'S NOT NECESSARILY BECAUSE IT'S MADE IN A HOSPITAL CAFETERIA. KOPPE PAN IS ONE OF THE SIMPLEST KINDS OF BREADS AROUND, AND IT JUST DOESN'T TASTE VERY GOOD...
SINCE THERE ARE SO FEW INGREDIENTS, THERE'S NOT MUCH ROOM FOR INNOVATION. IT'S IMPOSSIBLE FOR A PERSON TO MAKE KOPPE PAN TASTE BETTER THAN OTHER TYPES OF BREAD...
THIS IS IT! THIS IS THE ONE!!
KANMURI, I'VE DECIDED!
WHA... WHAT IS IT ALL OF A SUDDEN?!

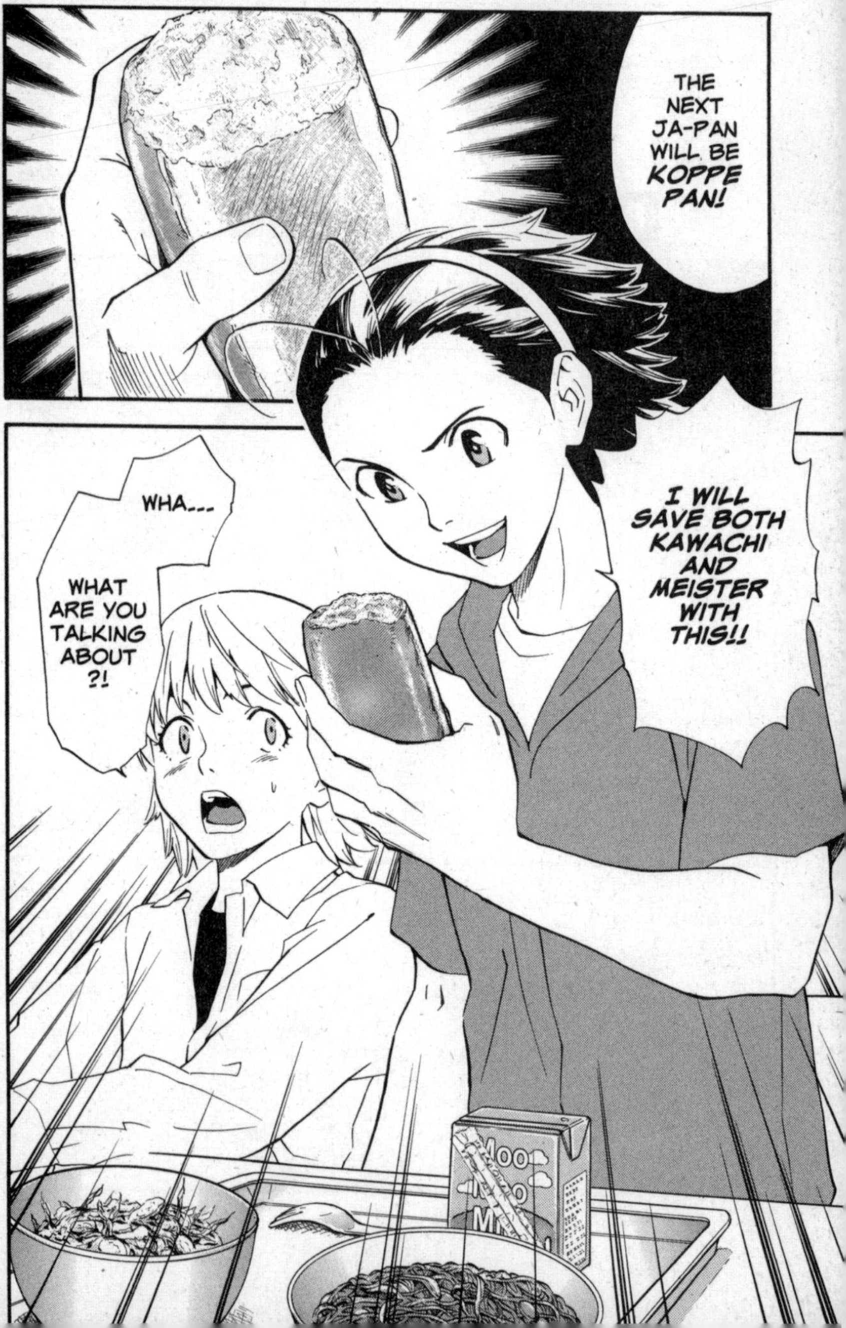
THE NEXT JA-PAN WILL BE KOPPE PAN!
I WILL SAVE BOTH KAWACHI AND MEISTER WITH THIS!!
WHA...
WHAT ARE YOU TALKING ABOUT ?!

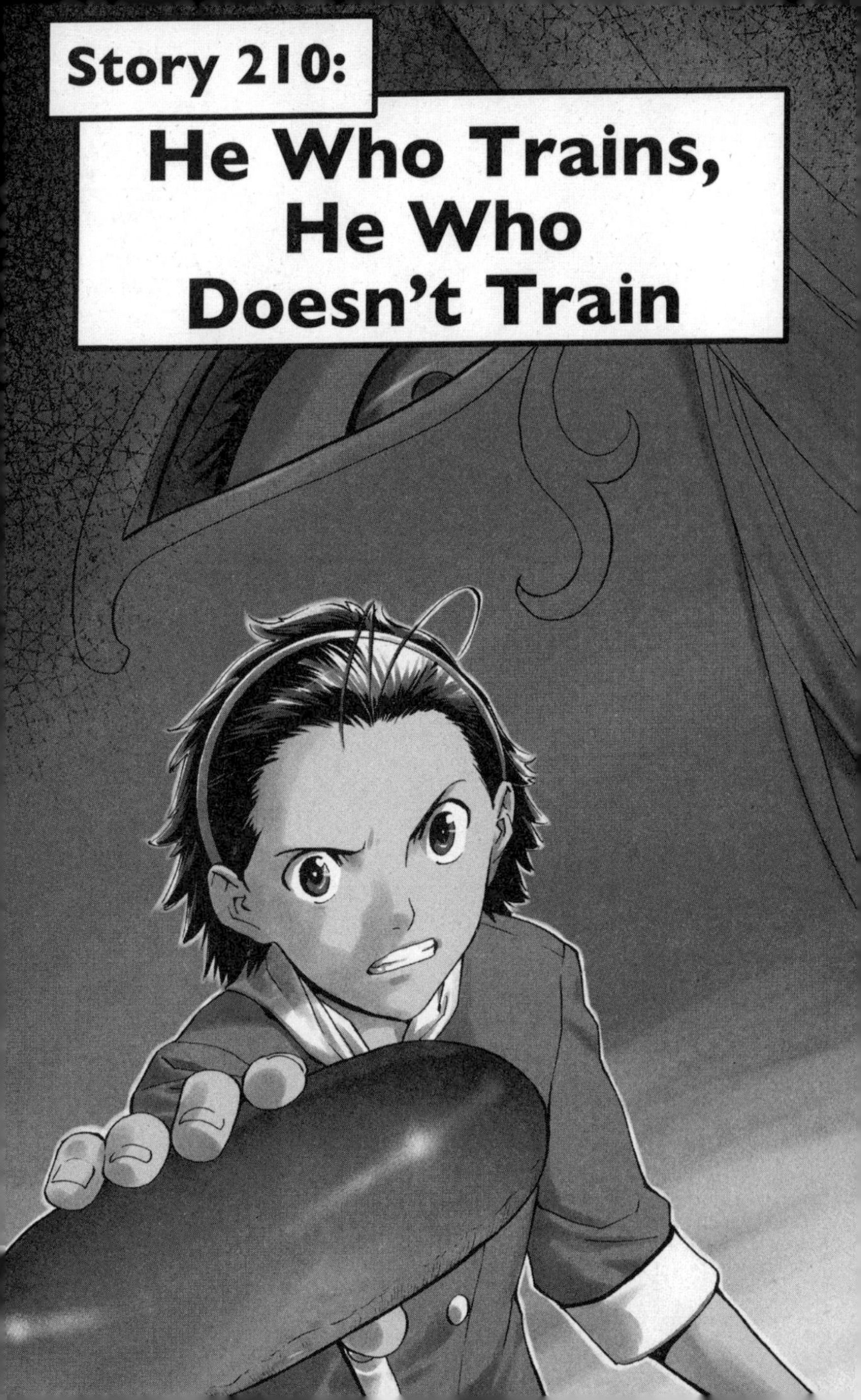
Story 210:
He Who Trains, He Who Doesn't Train

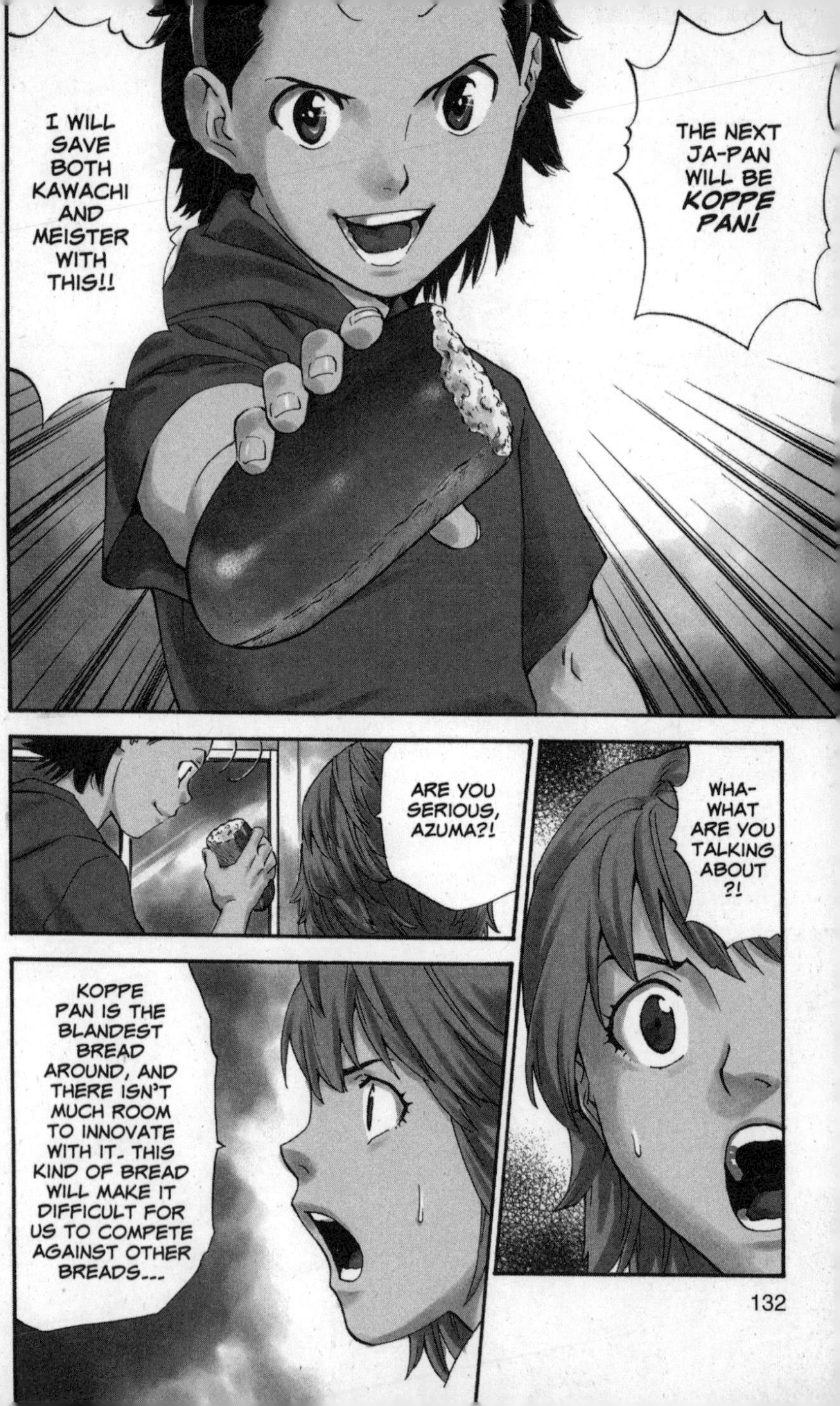
THE NEXT JA-PAN WILL BE KOPPE PAN!
I WILL SAVE BOTH KAWACHI AND MEISTER WITH THIS!!
WHA- WHAT ARE YOU TALKING ABOUT ?!
ARE YOU SERIOUS, AZUMA?!
KOPPE PAN IS THE BLANDEST BREAD AROUND, AND THERE ISN'T MUCH ROOM TO INNOVATE WITH IT. THIS KIND OF BREAD WILL MAKE IT DIFFICULT FOR US TO COMPETE AGAINST OTHER BREADS...

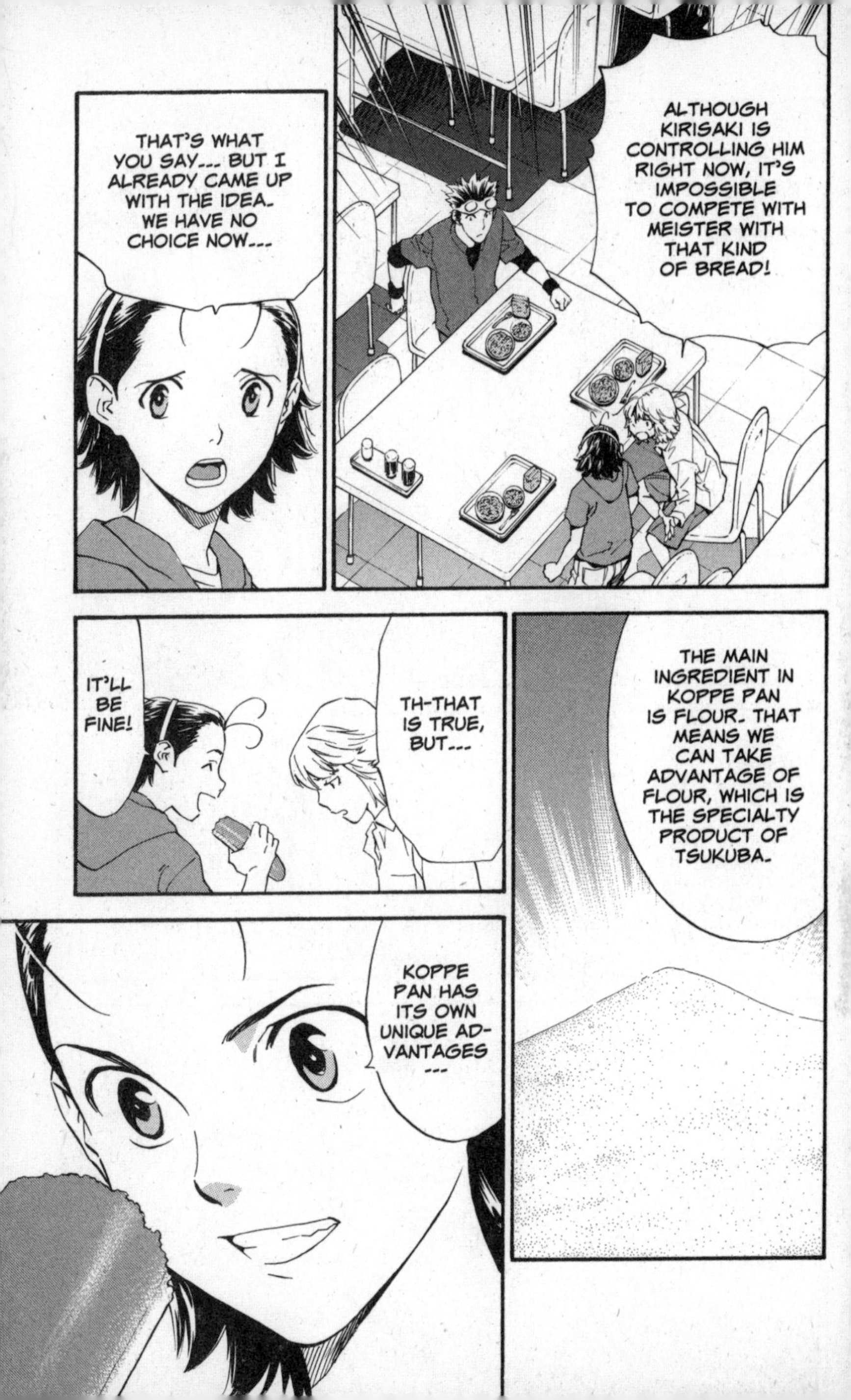
ALTHOUGH KIRISAKI IS CONTROLLING HIM RIGHT NOW, IT'S IMPOSSIBLE TO COMPETE WITH MEISTER WITH THAT KIND OF BREAD!
THAT'S WHAT YOU SAY... BUT I ALREADY CAME UP WITH THE IDEA. WE HAVE NO CHOICE NOW...
THE MAIN INGREDIENT IN KOPPE PAN IS FLOUR. THAT MEANS WE CAN TAKE ADVANTAGE OF FLOUR, WHICH IS THE SPECIALTY PRODUCT OF TSUKUBA.
TH-THAT IS TRUE, BUT...
IT'LL BE FINE!
KOPPE PAN HAS ITS OWN UNIQUE ADVANTAGES...

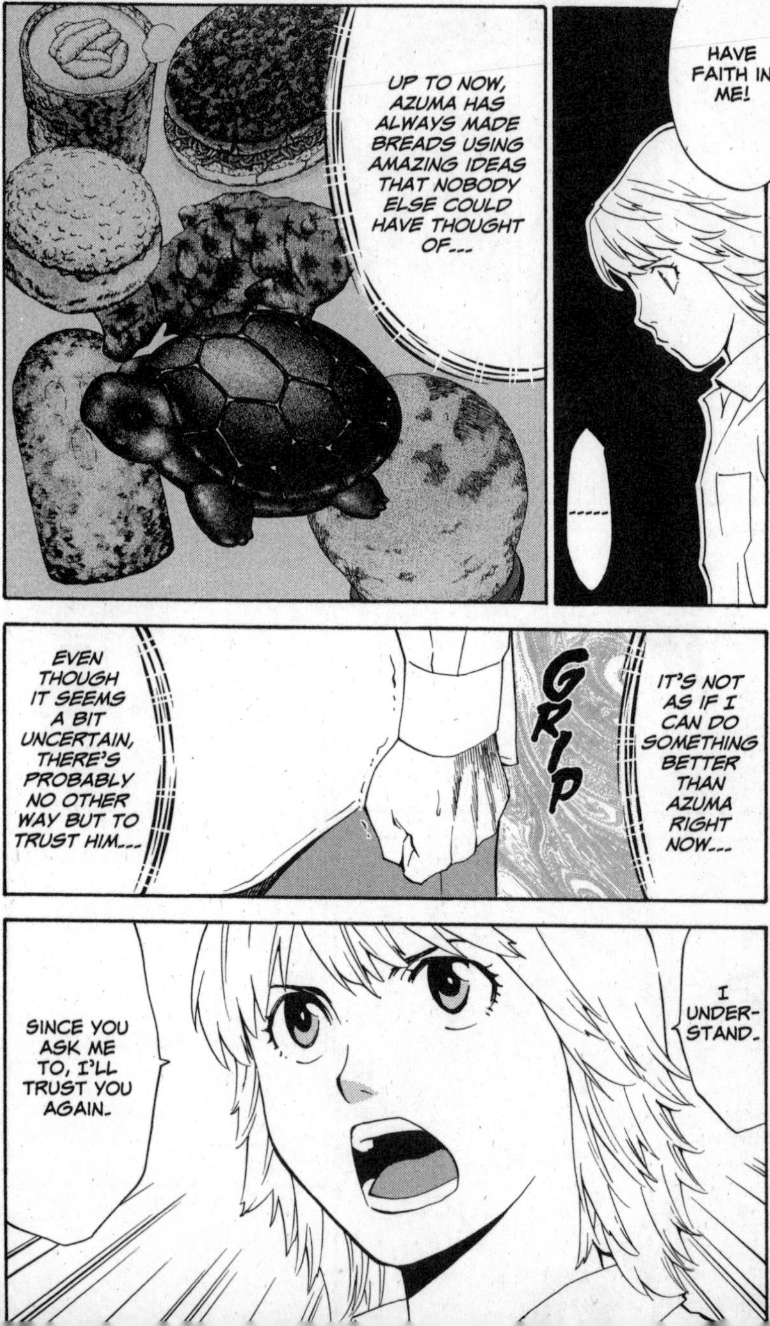
HAVE FAITH IN ME!
.....
UP TO NOW, AZUMA HAS ALWAYS MADE BREADS USING AMAZING IDEAS THAT NOBODY ELSE COULD HAVE THOUGHT OF...
IT'S NOT AS IF I CAN DO SOMETHING BETTER THAN AZUMA RIGHT NOW...
GRIP
EVEN THOUGH IT SEEMS A BIT UNCERTAIN, THERE'S PROBABLY NO OTHER WAY BUT TO TRUST HIM...
I UNDERSTAND.
SINCE YOU ASK ME TO, I'LL TRUST YOU AGAIN.

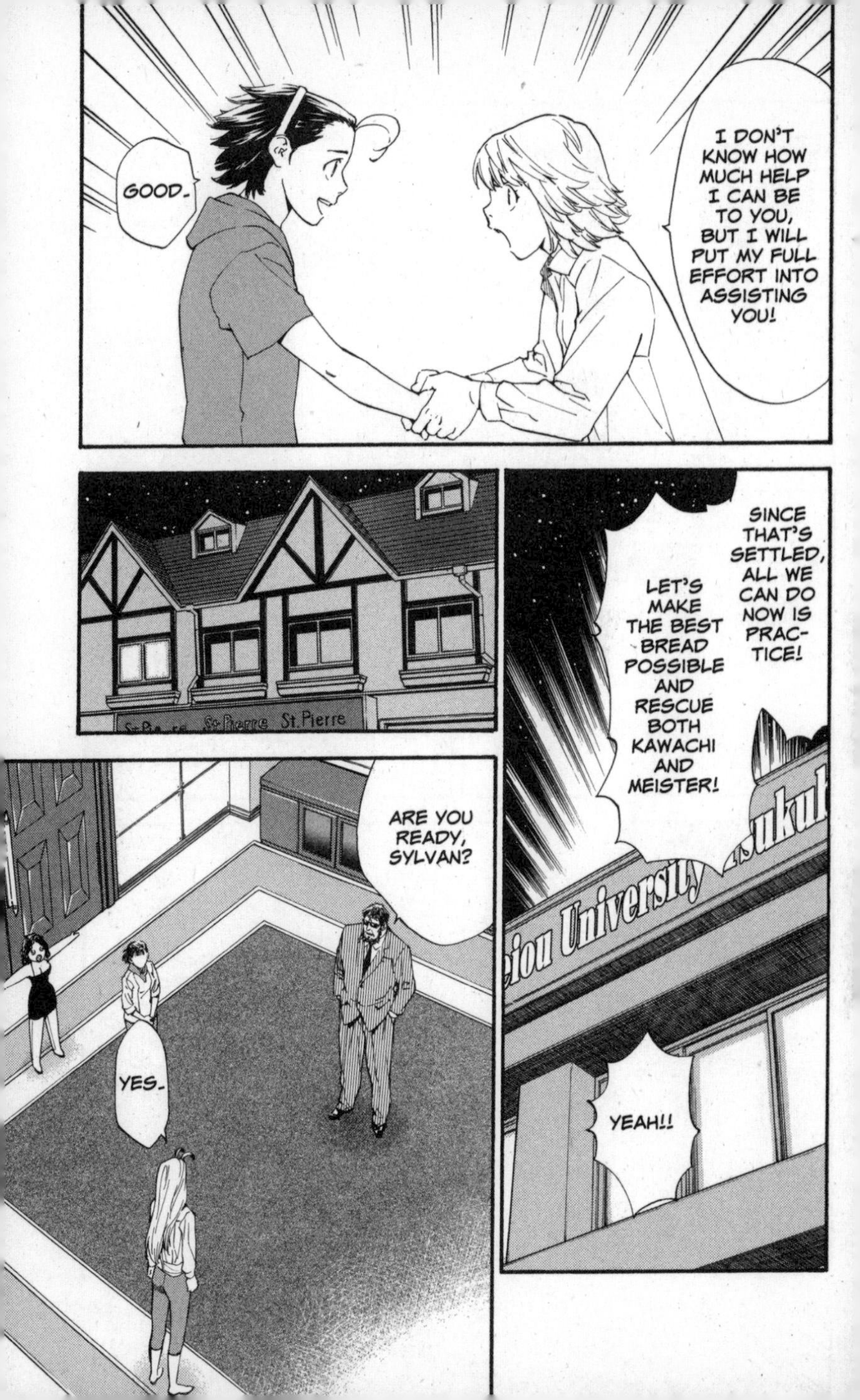
I DON'T KNOW HOW MUCH HELP I CAN BE TO YOU, BUT I WILL PUT MY FULL EFFORT INTO ASSISTING YOU!
GOOD...
SINCE THAT'S SETTLED, ALL WE CAN DO NOW IS PRAC-TICE!
LET'S MAKE THE BEST BREAD POSSIBLE AND RESCUE BOTH KAWACHI AND MEISTER!
YEAH!!
St. Pierre
ARE YOU READY, SYLVAN?
YES...

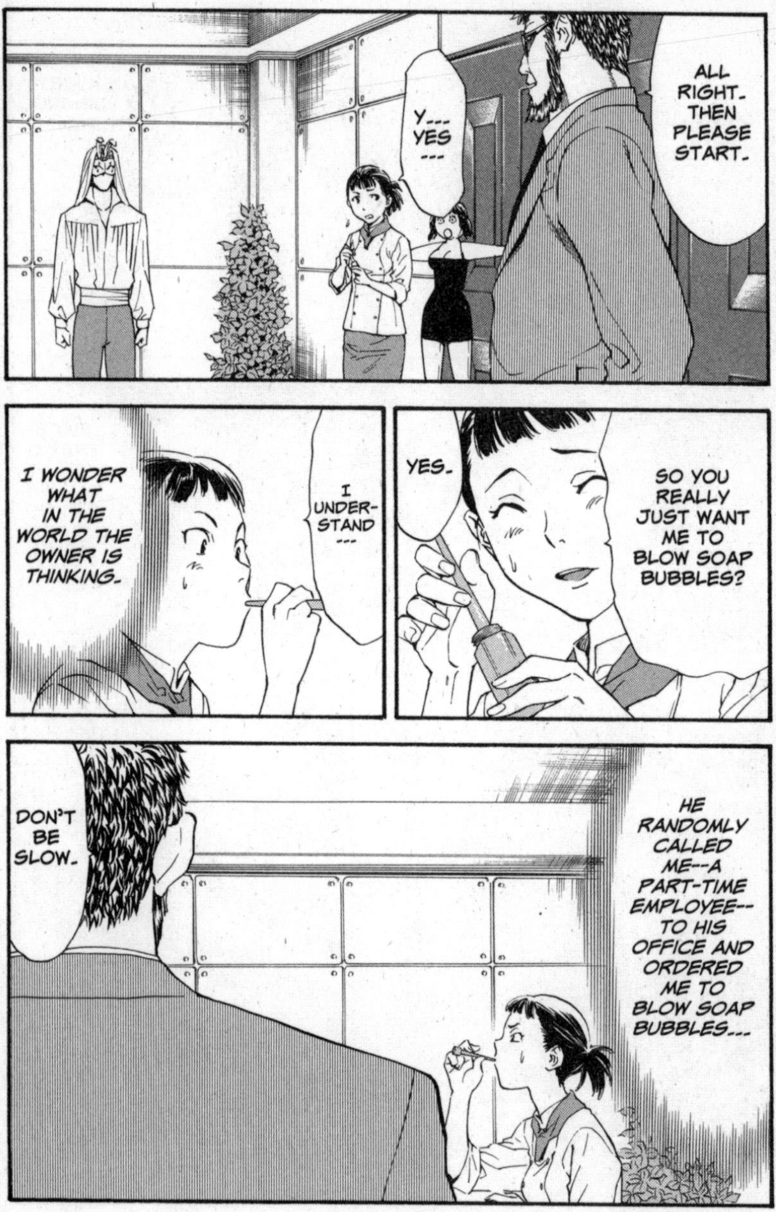
ALL RIGHT. THEN PLEASE START.
Y... YES...
SO YOU REALLY JUST WANT ME TO BLOW SOAP BUBBLES?
YES.
I UNDER-STAND...
I WONDER WHAT IN THE WORLD THE OWNER IS THINKING.
HE RANDOMLY CALLED ME--A PART-TIME EMPLOYEE--TO HIS OFFICE AND ORDERED ME TO BLOW SOAP BUBBLES...
DON'T BE SLOW.

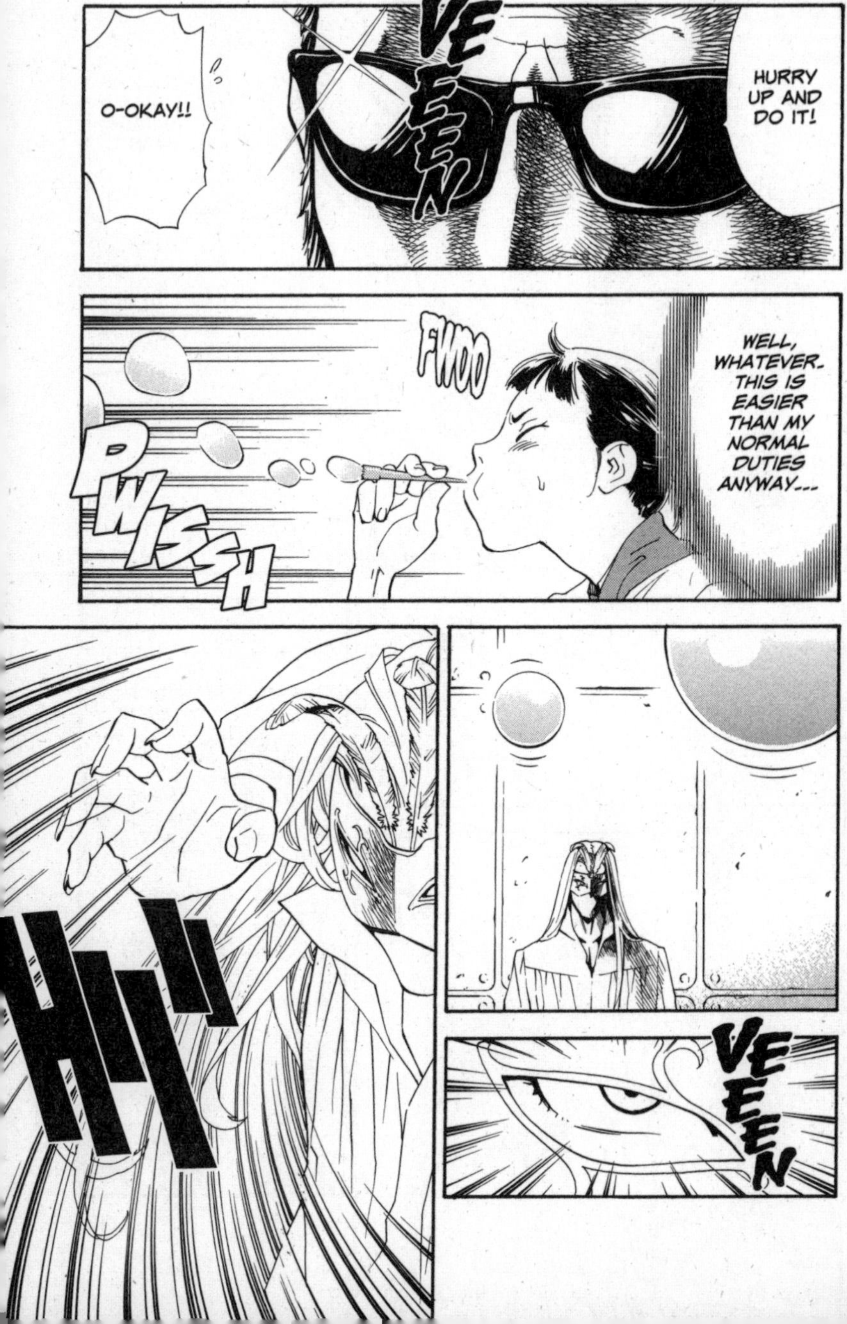

HURRY UP AND DO IT!
VEEEN
O-OKAY!!
WELL, WHATEVER. THIS IS EASIER THAN MY NORMAL DUTIES ANYWAY...
FWOO
PWISSH
VEEEN
HIII

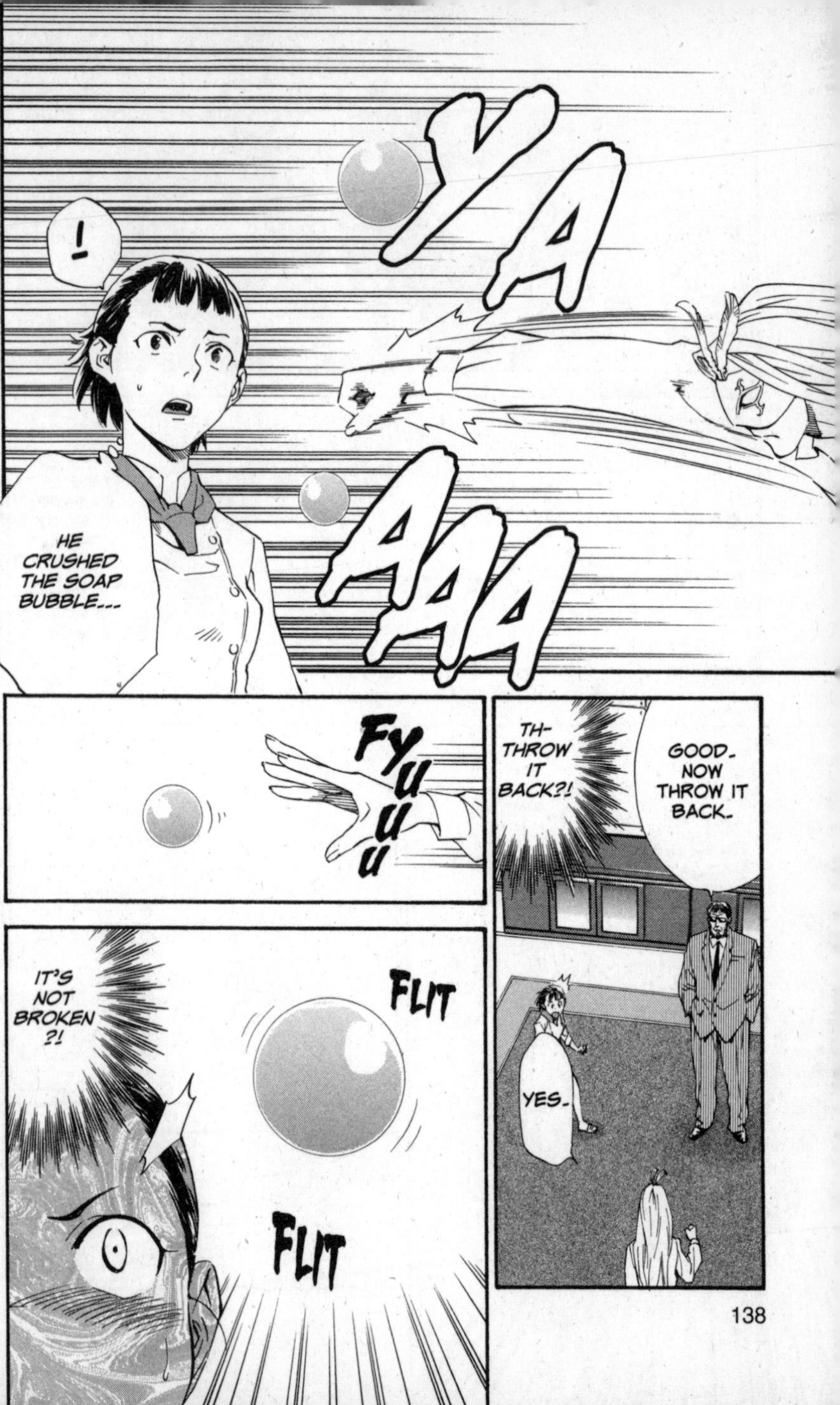
YAAAAA
!
HE CRUSHED THE SOAP BUBBLE...
GOOD. NOW THROW IT BACK.
TH-THROW IT BACK?!
YES.
Fyuuuu
FLIT
IT'S NOT BROKEN ?!
FLIT

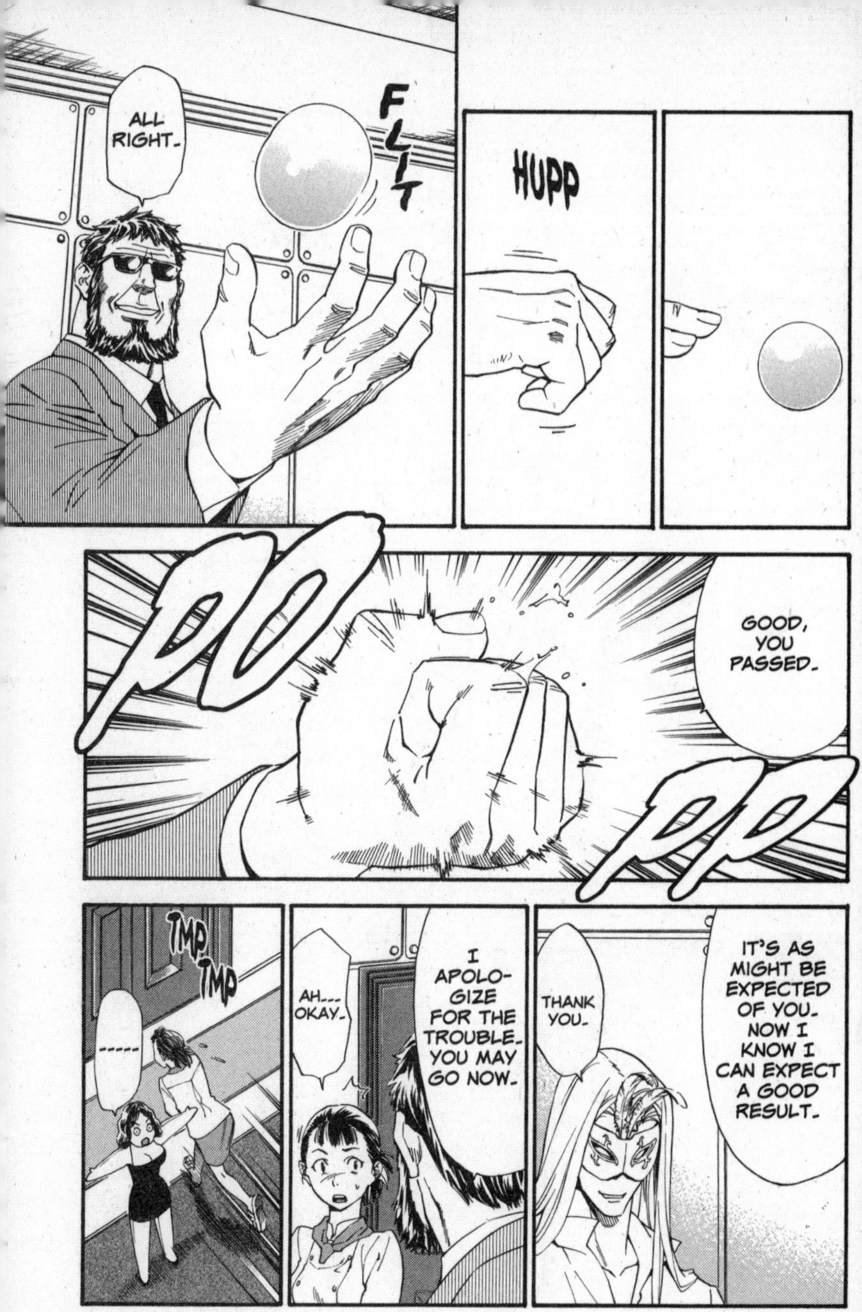
HUPP
ALL RIGHT.
FLIT
PO
GOOD, YOU PASSED.
PP
IT'S AS MIGHT BE EXPECTED OF YOU. NOW I KNOW I CAN EXPECT A GOOD RESULT.
THANK YOU.
I APOLOGIZE FOR THE TROUBLE. YOU MAY GO NOW.
AH... OKAY.
TMP TMP
.....

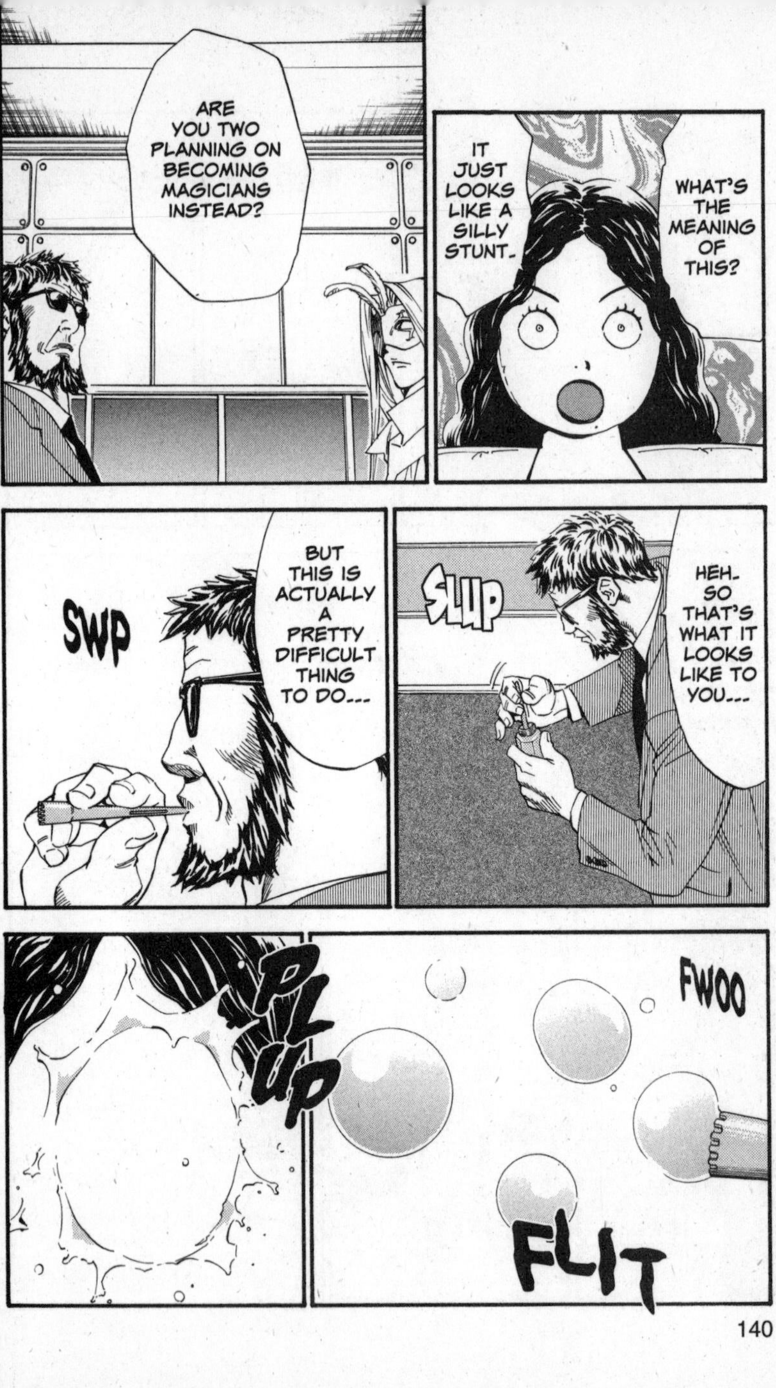
WHAT'S THE MEANING OF THIS?
IT JUST LOOKS LIKE A SILLY STUNT...
ARE YOU TWO PLANNING ON BECOMING MAGICIANS INSTEAD?
HEH. SO THAT'S WHAT IT LOOKS LIKE TO YOU...
SLUP
BUT THIS IS ACTUALLY A PRETTY DIFFICULT THING TO DO...
SWP
FWOO
FLIT
PLUP

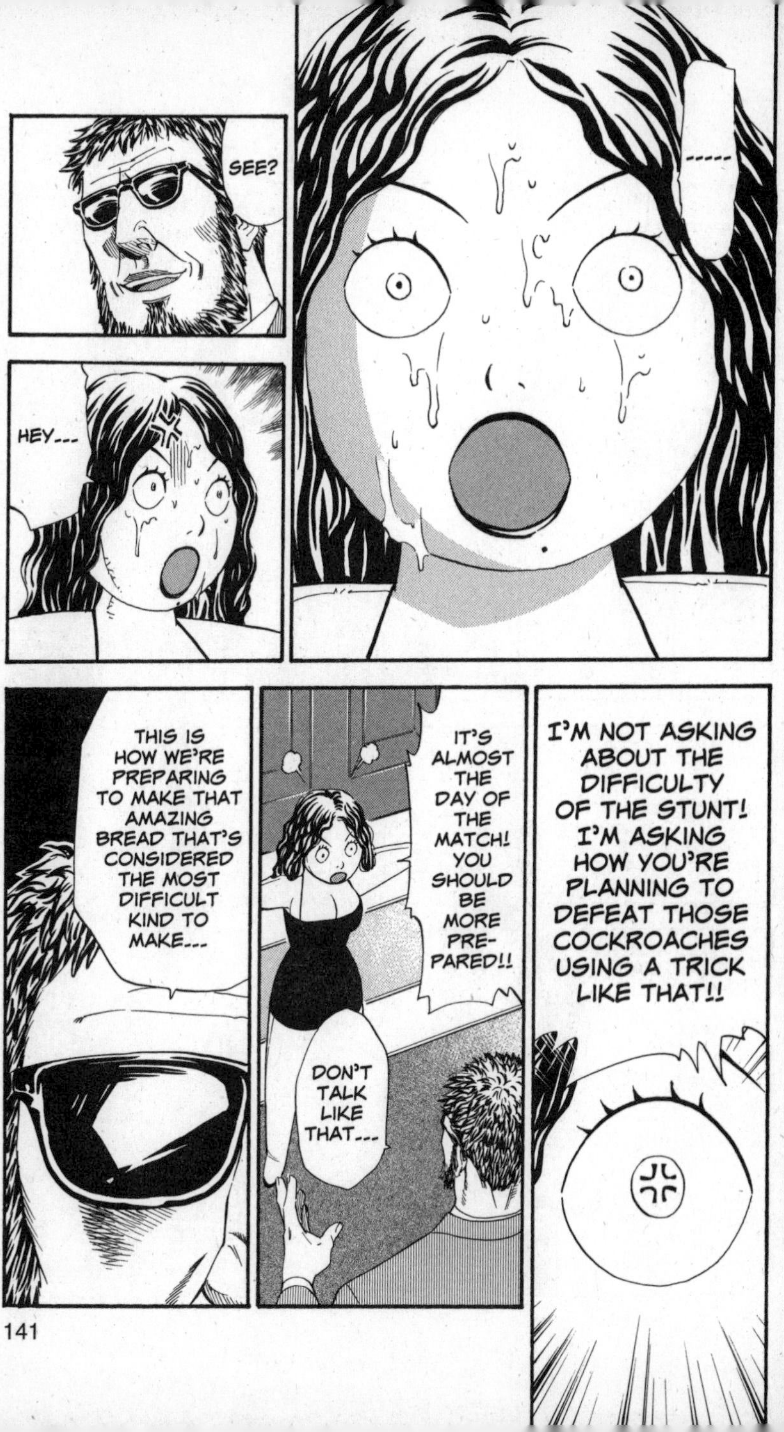

SEE?
HEY---
I'M NOT ASKING ABOUT THE DIFFICULTY OF THE STUNT! I'M ASKING HOW YOU'RE PLANNING TO DEFEAT THOSE COCKROACHES USING A TRICK LIKE THAT!!
IT'S ALMOST THE DAY OF THE MATCH! YOU SHOULD BE MORE PRE-PARED!!
DON'T TALK LIKE THAT---
THIS IS HOW WE'RE PREPARING TO MAKE THAT AMAZING BREAD THAT'S CONSIDERED THE MOST DIFFICULT KIND TO MAKE---

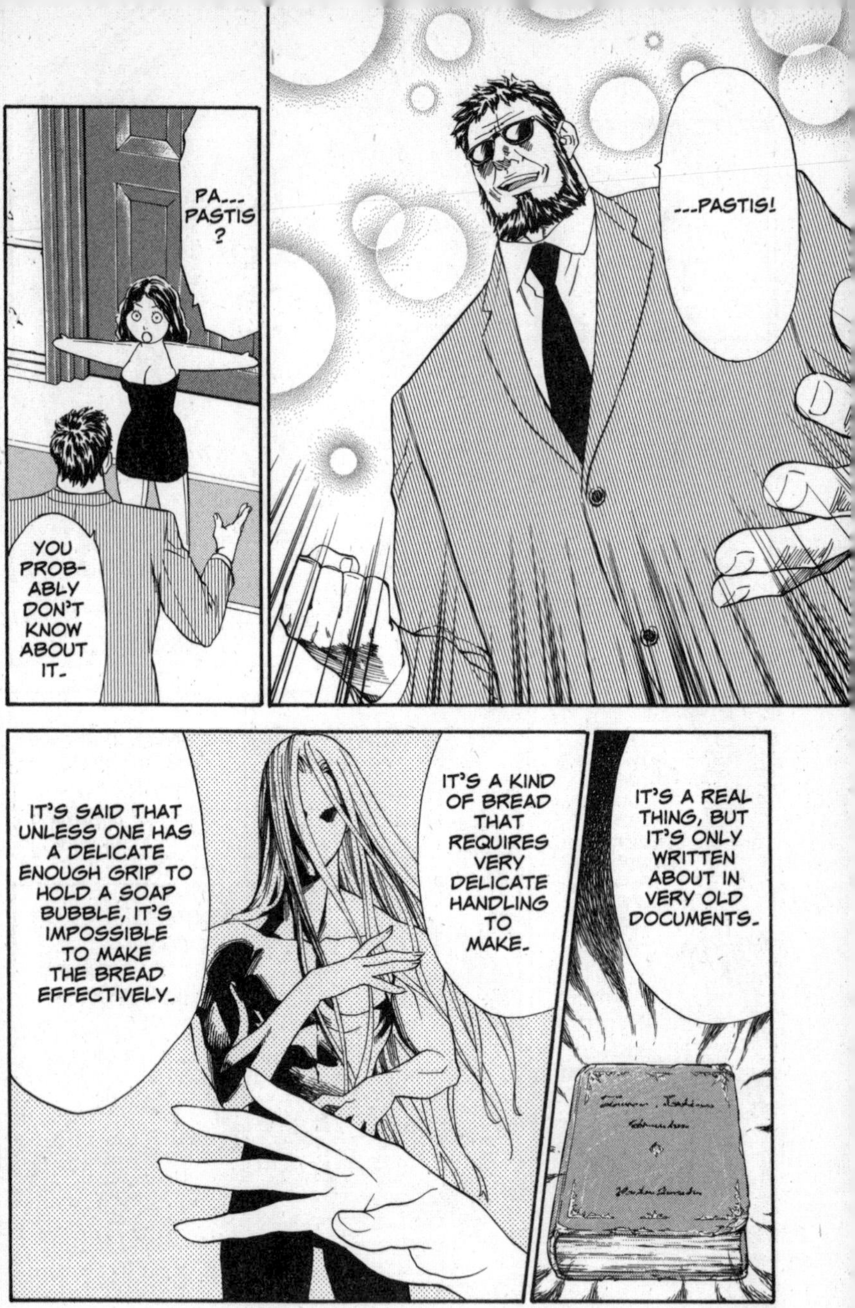
...PASTIS!
PA... PASTIS?
YOU PROBABLY DON'T KNOW ABOUT IT.
IT'S A REAL THING, BUT IT'S ONLY WRITTEN ABOUT IN VERY OLD DOCUMENTS.
IT'S A KIND OF BREAD THAT REQUIRES VERY DELICATE HANDLING TO MAKE.
IT'S SAID THAT UNLESS ONE HAS A DELICATE ENOUGH GRIP TO HOLD A SOAP BUBBLE, IT'S IMPOSSIBLE TO MAKE THE BREAD EFFECTIVELY.

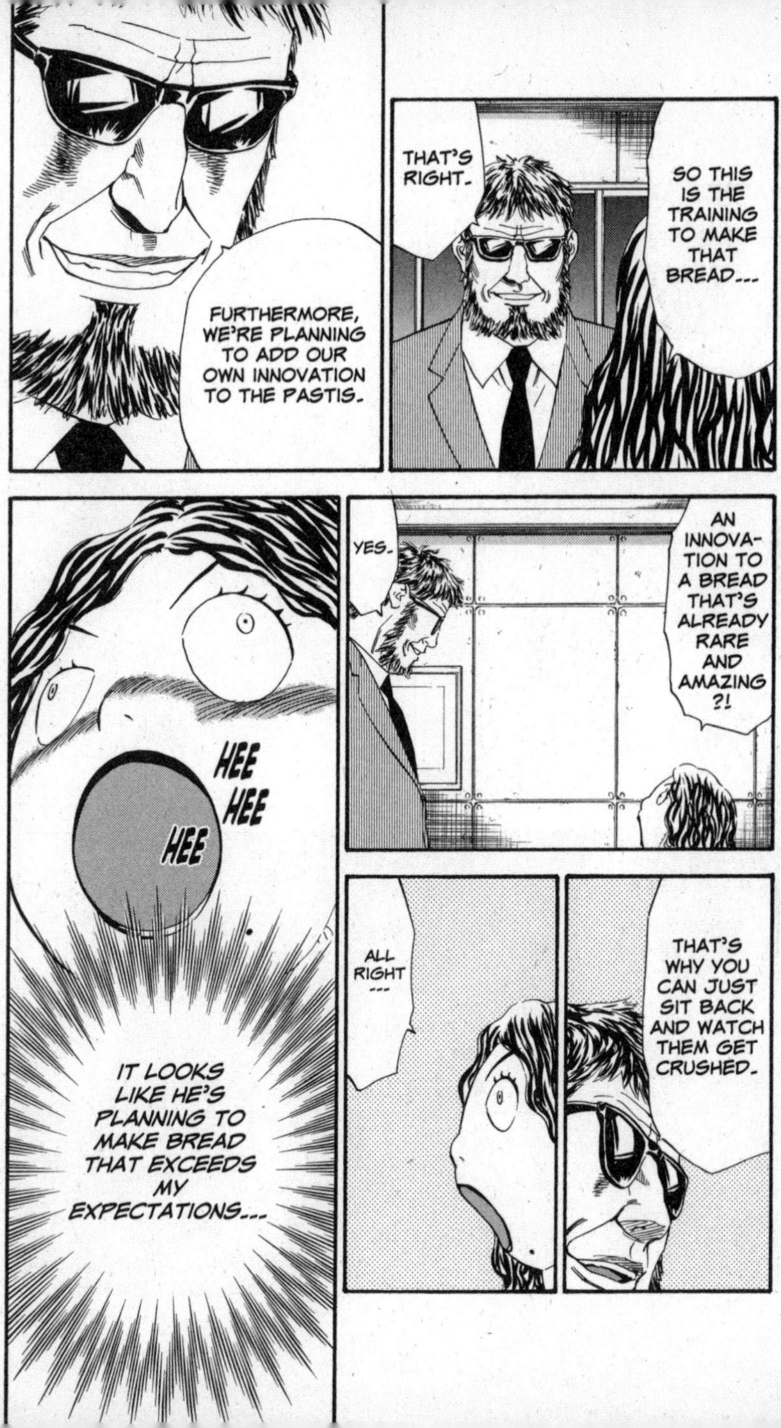
SO THIS IS THE TRAINING TO MAKE THAT BREAD...
THAT'S RIGHT.
FURTHERMORE, WE'RE PLANNING TO ADD OUR OWN INNOVATION TO THE PASTIS.
AN INNOVATION TO A BREAD THAT'S ALREADY RARE AND AMAZING ?!
YES.
THAT'S WHY YOU CAN JUST SIT BACK AND WATCH THEM GET CRUSHED.
ALL RIGHT ...
HEE HEE
HEE
IT LOOKS LIKE HE'S PLANNING TO MAKE BREAD THAT EXCEEDS MY EXPECTATIONS...

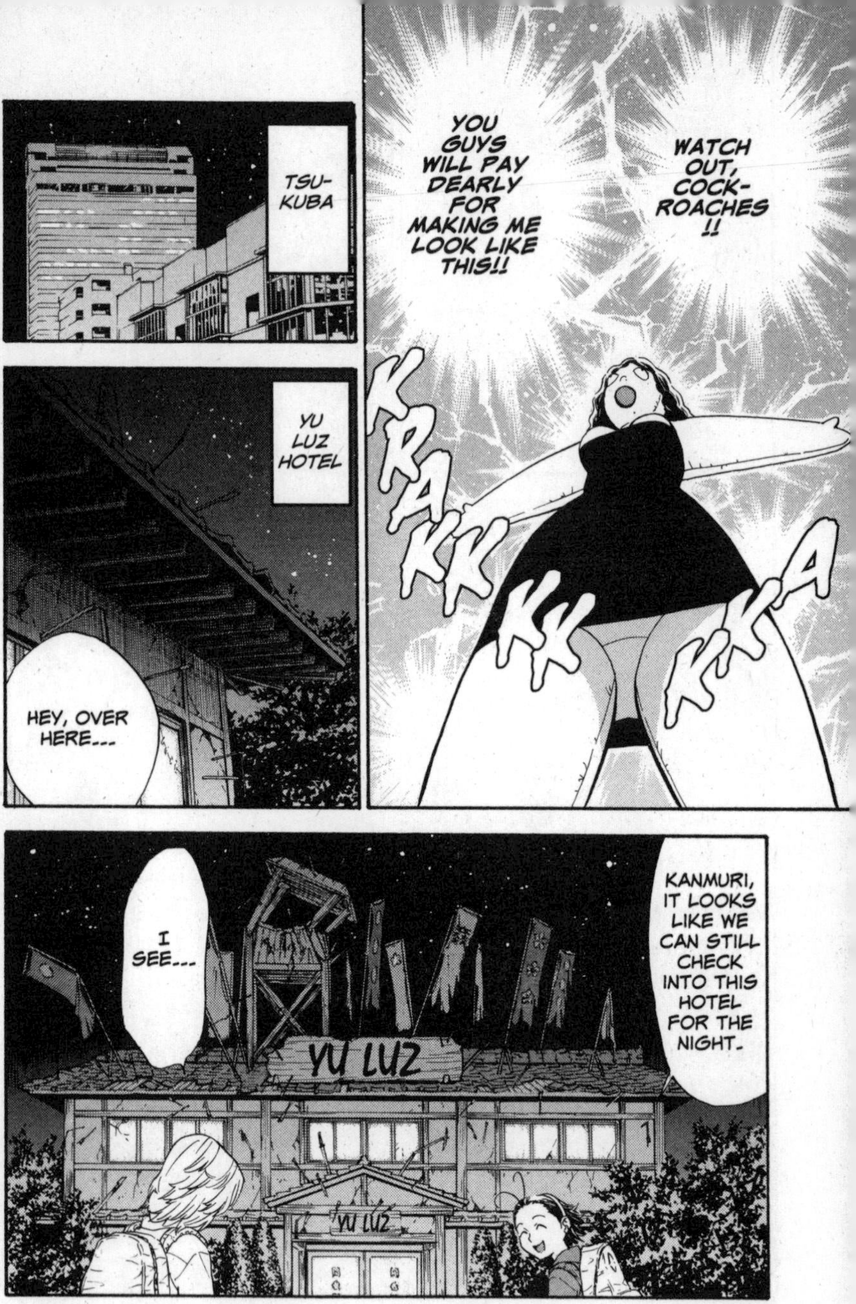
WATCH OUT, COCK-ROACHES!!
YOU GUYS WILL PAY DEARLY FOR MAKING ME LOOK LIKE THIS!!
KRAKKKKKKA
TSU-KUBA
YU LUZ HOTEL
HEY, OVER HERE...
KANMURI, IT LOOKS LIKE WE CAN STILL CHECK INTO THIS HOTEL FOR THE NIGHT.
I SEE...
YU LUZ
YU LUZ

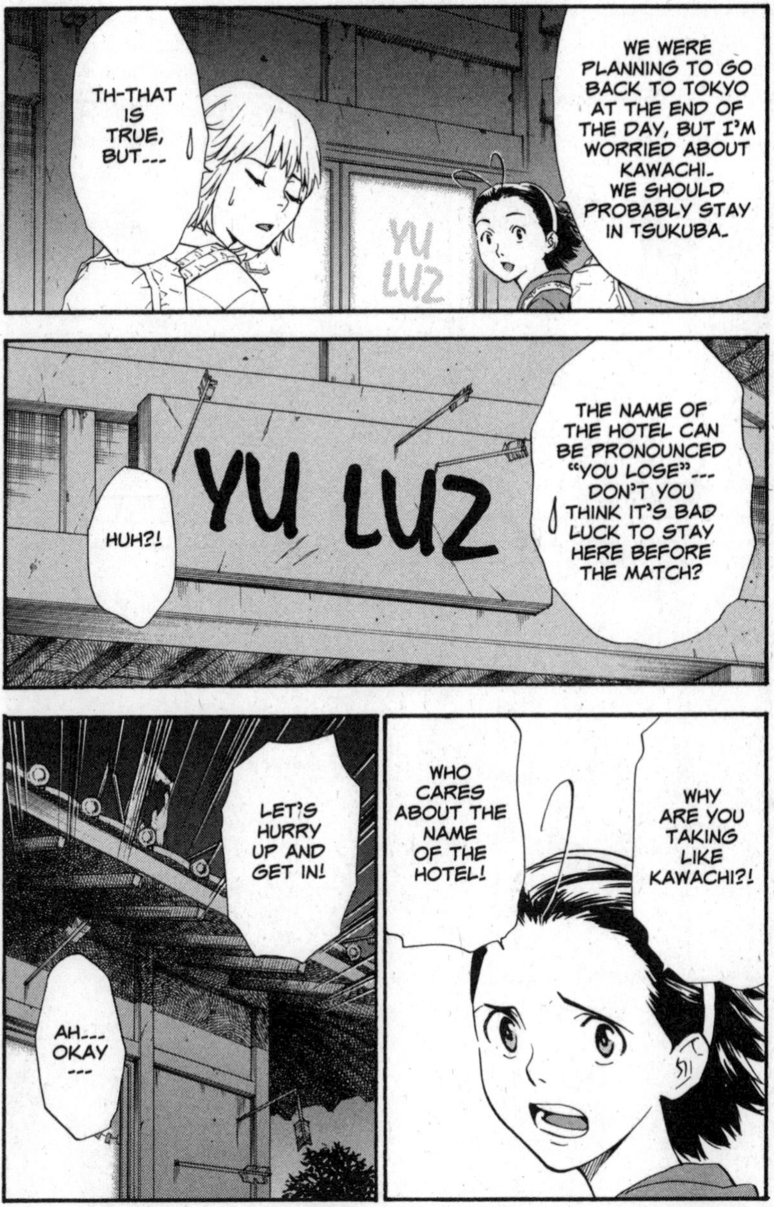
WE WERE PLANNING TO GO BACK TO TOKYO AT THE END OF THE DAY, BUT I'M WORRIED ABOUT KAWACHI. WE SHOULD PROBABLY STAY IN TSUKUBA.
YU LUZ
TH-THAT IS TRUE, BUT...
THE NAME OF THE HOTEL CAN BE PRONOUNCED "YOU LOSE"... DON'T YOU THINK IT'S BAD LUCK TO STAY HERE BEFORE THE MATCH?
YU LUZ
HUH?!
WHY ARE YOU TAKING LIKE KAWACHI?!
WHO CARES ABOUT THE NAME OF THE HOTEL!
LET'S HURRY UP AND GET IN!
AH... OKAY ...

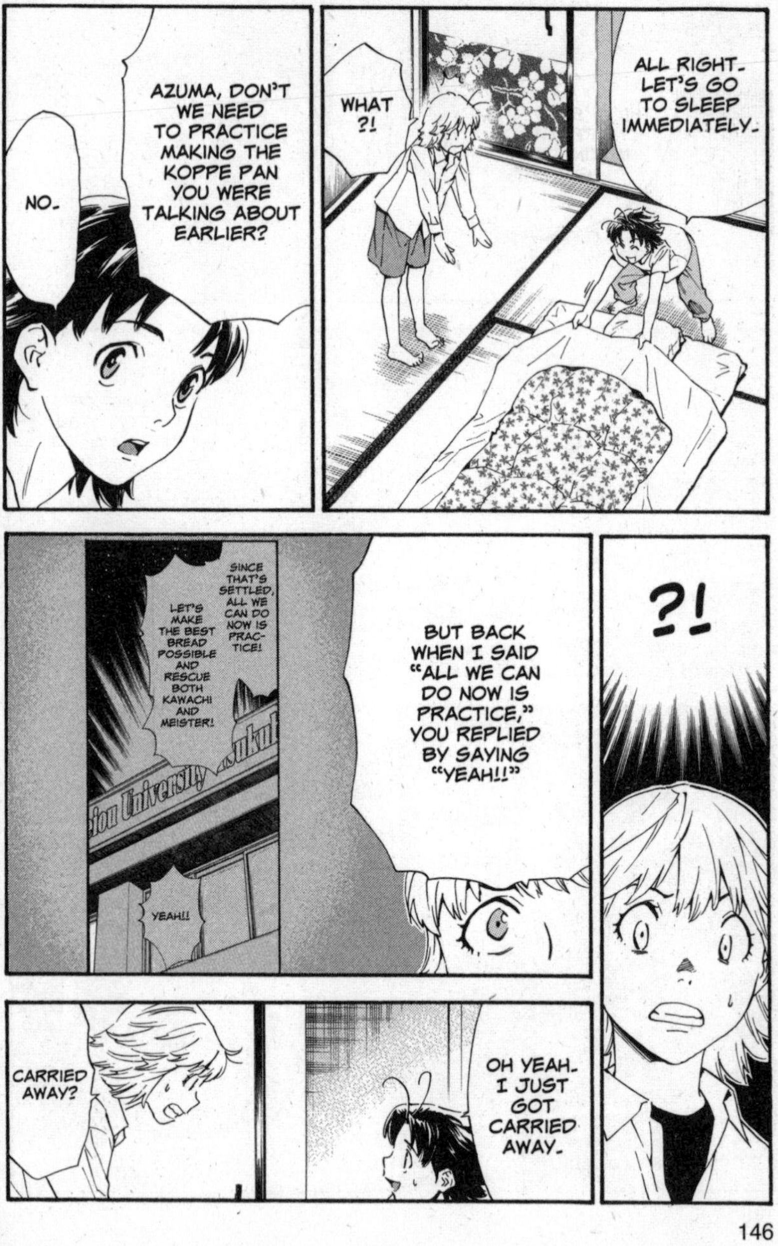
ALL RIGHT. LET'S GO TO SLEEP IMMEDIATELY.
WHAT ?!
AZUMA, DON'T WE NEED TO PRACTICE MAKING THE KOPPE PAN YOU WERE TALKING ABOUT EARLIER?
NO.
?!
BUT BACK WHEN I SAID "ALL WE CAN DO NOW IS PRACTICE," YOU REPLIED BY SAYING "YEAH!!"
SINCE THAT'S SETTLED, ALL WE CAN DO NOW IS PRAC-TICE!
LET'S MAKE THE BEST BREAD POSSIBLE AND RESCUE BOTH KAWACHI AND MEISTER!
YEAH!!
OH YEAH. I JUST GOT CARRIED AWAY.
CARRIED AWAY?

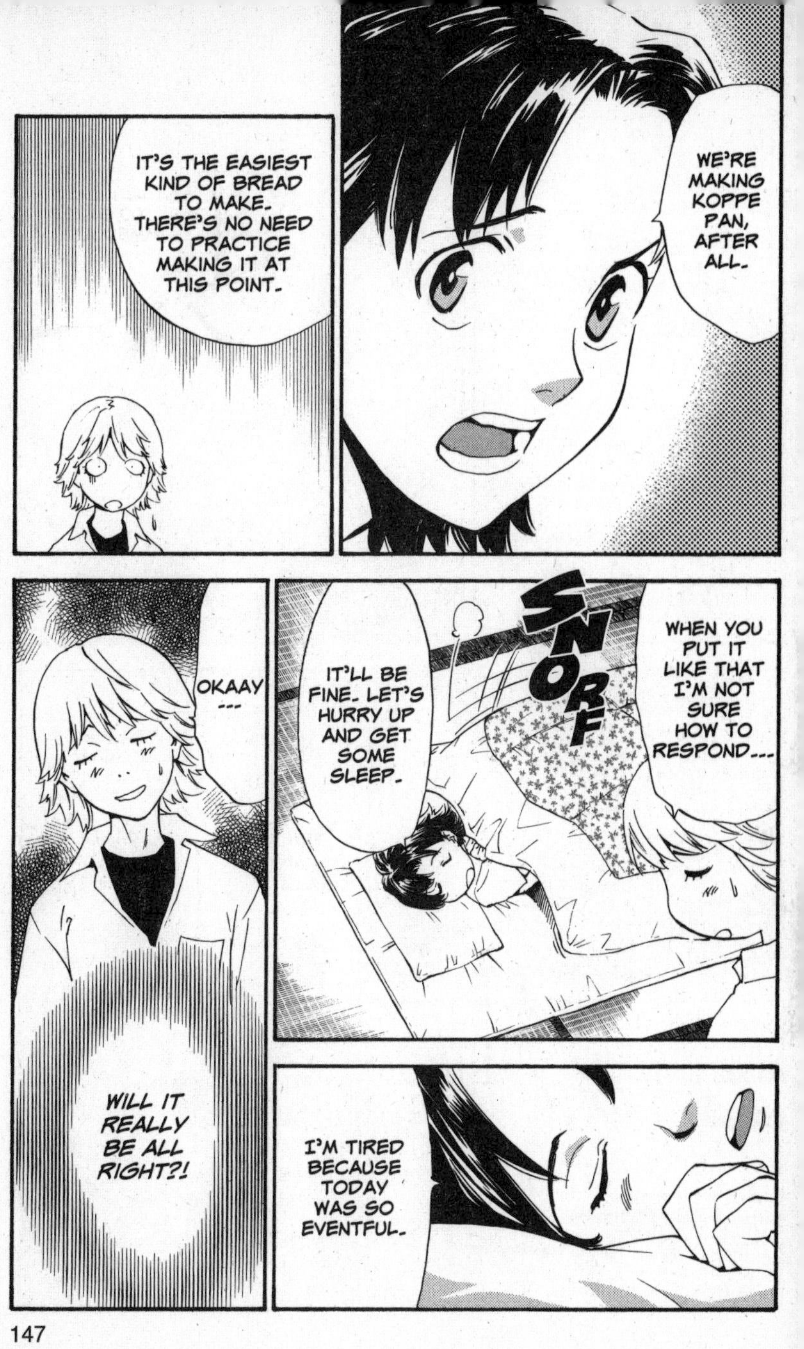

WE'RE MAKING KOPPE PAN, AFTER ALL.
IT'S THE EASIEST KIND OF BREAD TO MAKE. THERE'S NO NEED TO PRACTICE MAKING IT AT THIS POINT.
WHEN YOU PUT IT LIKE THAT I'M NOT SURE HOW TO RESPOND...
SNORF
IT'LL BE FINE. LET'S HURRY UP AND GET SOME SLEEP.
I'M TIRED BECAUSE TODAY WAS SO EVENTFUL.
OKAAY...
WILL IT REALLY BE ALL RIGHT?!

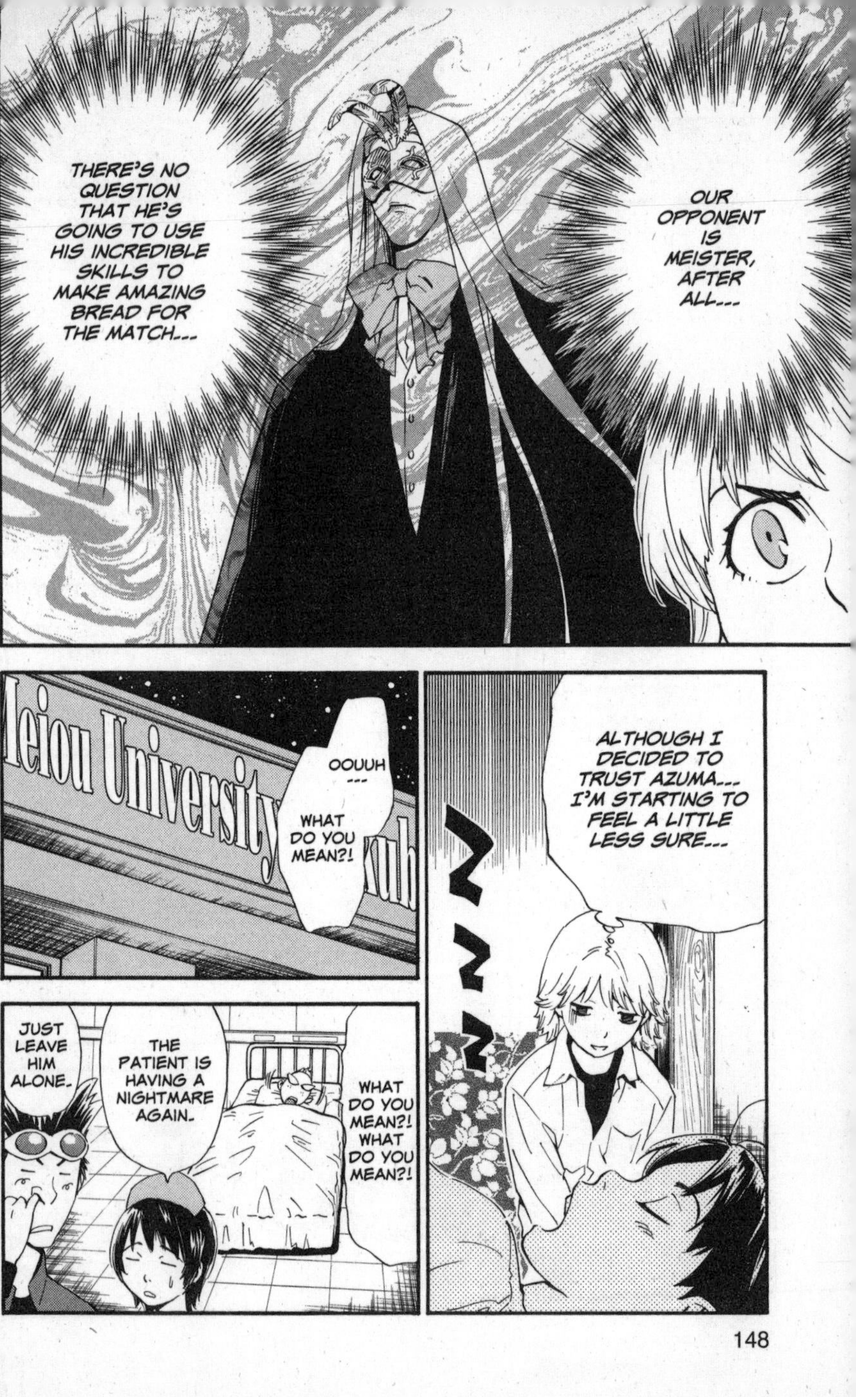
OUR OPPONENT IS MEISTER, AFTER ALL...
THERE'S NO QUESTION THAT HE'S GOING TO USE HIS INCREDIBLE SKILLS TO MAKE AMAZING BREAD FOR THE MATCH...
ALTHOUGH I DECIDED TO TRUST AZUMA... I'M STARTING TO FEEL A LITTLE LESS SURE...
ZZZ
OOUUH ...
WHAT DO YOU MEAN?!
WHAT DO YOU MEAN?! WHAT DO YOU MEAN?!
THE PATIENT IS HAVING A NIGHTMARE AGAIN.
JUST LEAVE HIM ALONE.

Story 211:
Meister's Magic

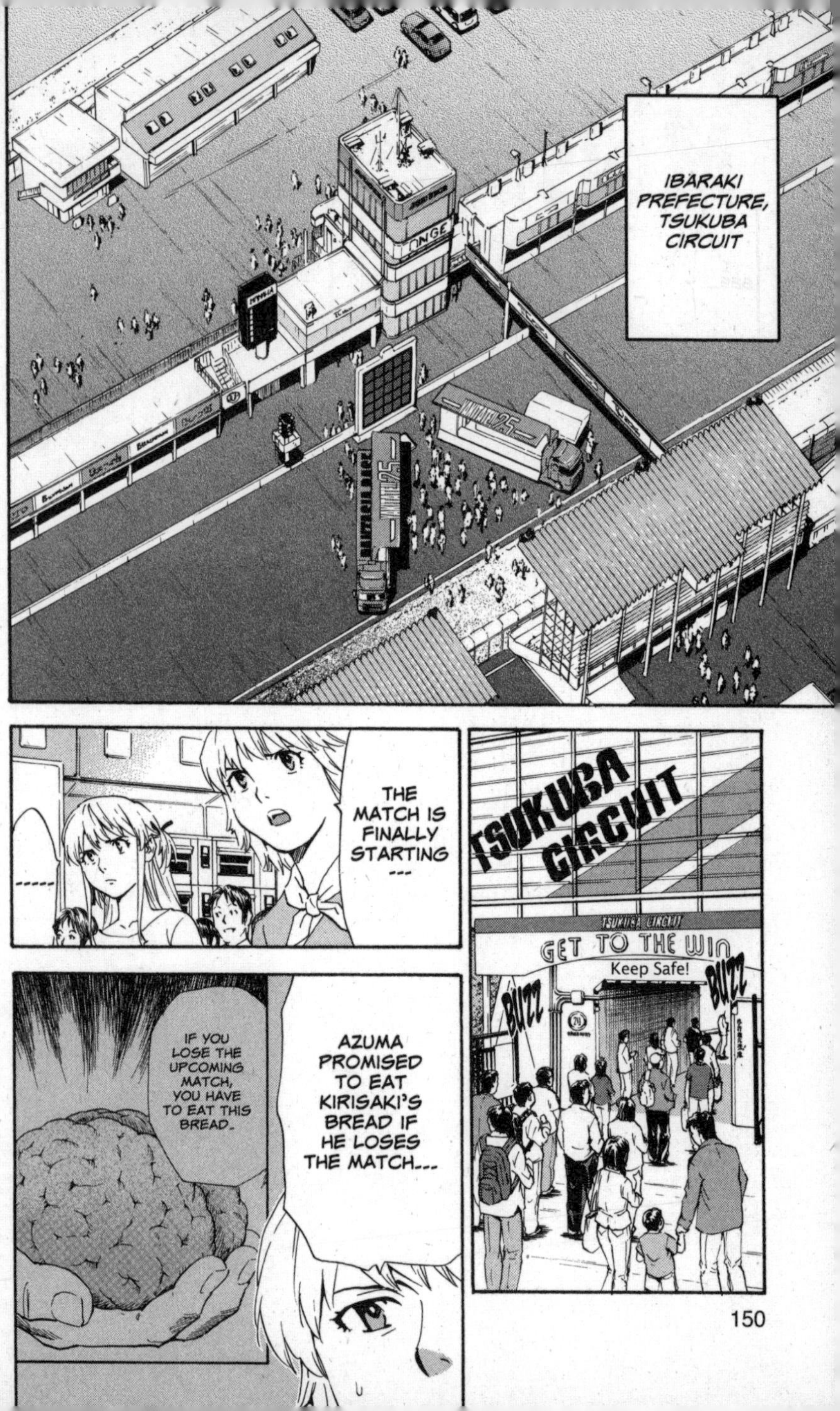
IBARAKI PREFECTURE, TSUKUBA CIRCUIT
TSUKUBA CIRCUIT
TSUKUBA CIRCUIT
GET TO THE WIN
Keep Safe!
BUZZ
BUZZ
THE MATCH IS FINALLY STARTING ---

AZUMA PROMISED TO EAT KIRISAKI'S BREAD IF HE LOSES THE MATCH...
IF YOU LOSE THE UPCOMING MATCH, YOU HAVE TO EAT THIS BREAD.

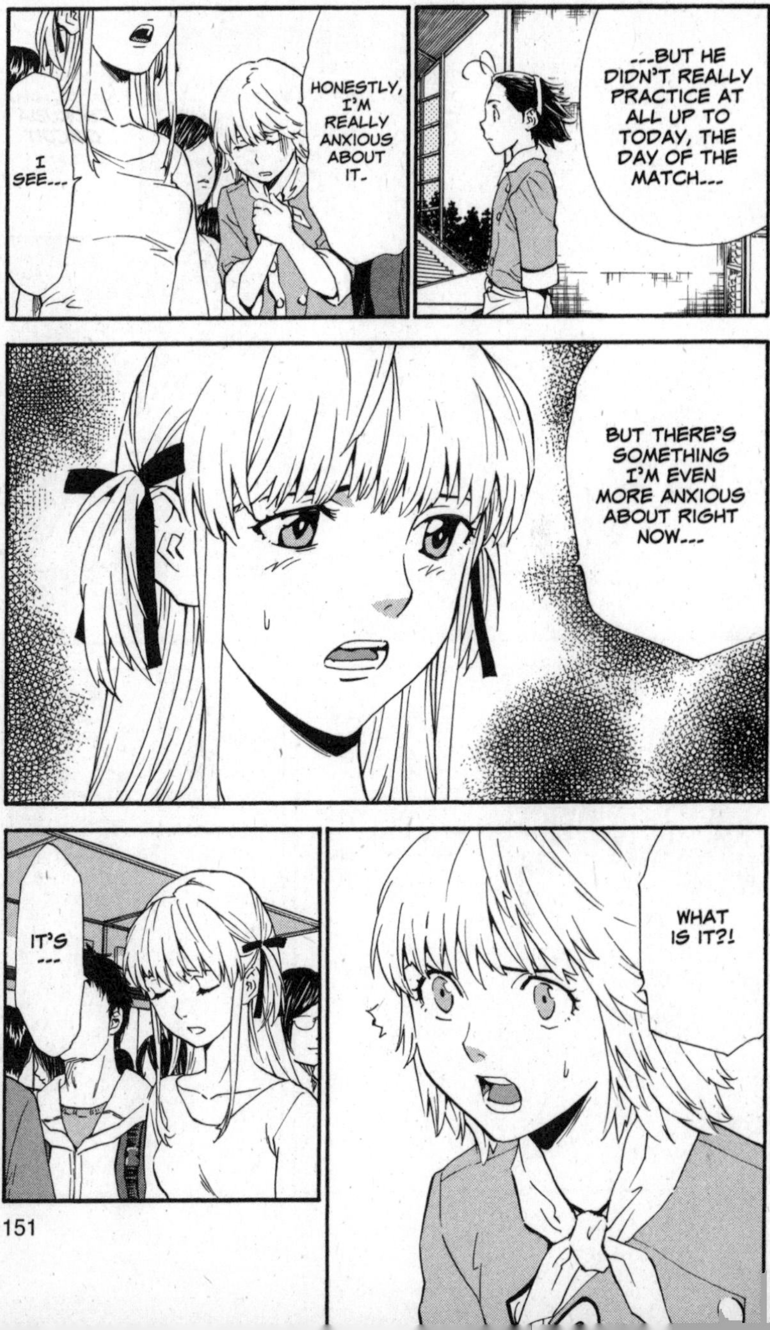
---BUT HE DIDN'T REALLY PRACTICE AT ALL UP TO TODAY, THE DAY OF THE MATCH---
HONESTLY, I'M REALLY ANXIOUS ABOUT IT.
I SEE---
BUT THERE'S SOMETHING I'M EVEN MORE ANXIOUS ABOUT RIGHT NOW---
WHAT IS IT?!
IT'S ---

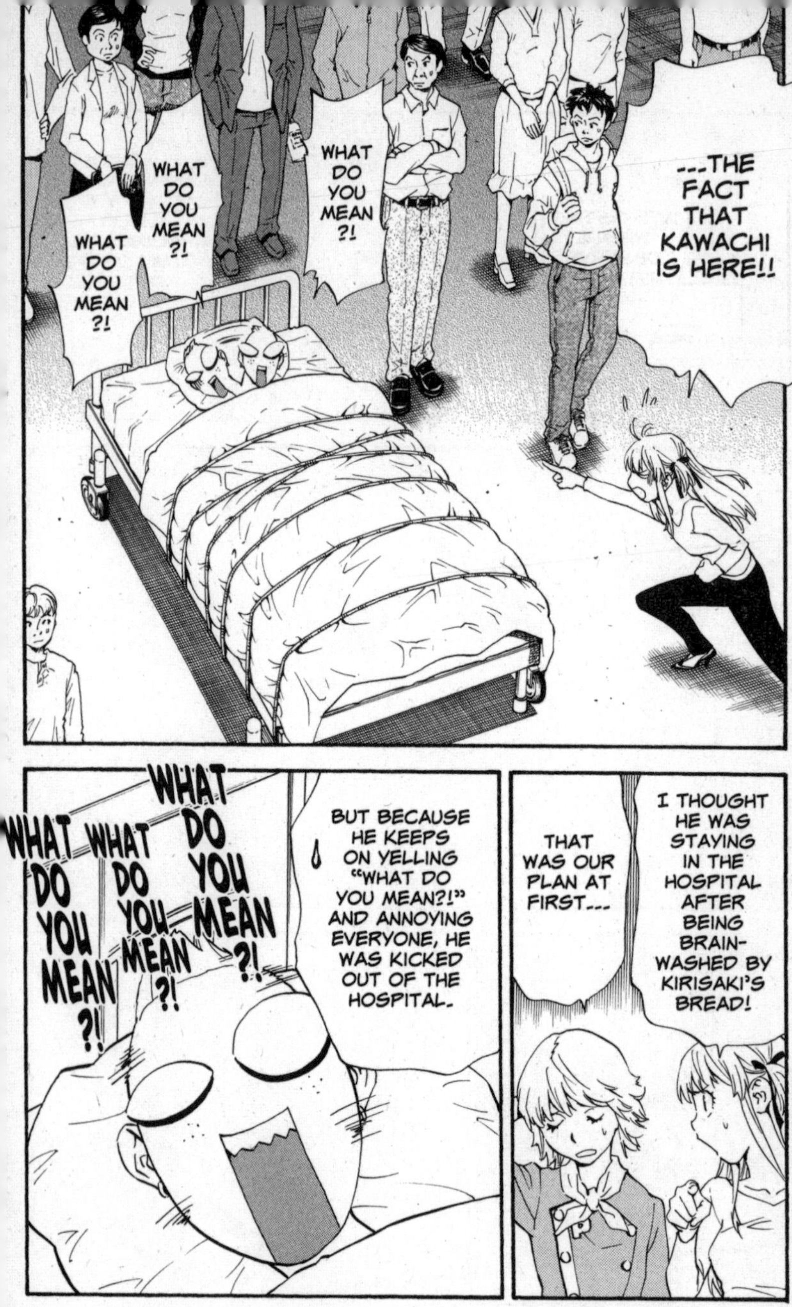
---THE FACT THAT KAWACHI IS HERE!!
WHAT DO YOU MEAN ?!
WHAT DO YOU MEAN ?!
WHAT DO YOU MEAN ?!
I THOUGHT HE WAS STAYING IN THE HOSPITAL AFTER BEING BRAIN-WASHED BY KIRISAKI'S BREAD!
THAT WAS OUR PLAN AT FIRST...
BUT BECAUSE HE KEEPS ON YELLING "WHAT DO YOU MEAN?!" AND ANNOYING EVERYONE, HE WAS KICKED OUT OF THE HOSPITAL.
WHAT DO YOU MEAN ?!
WHAT DO YOU MEAN ?!
WHAT DO YOU MEAN ?!

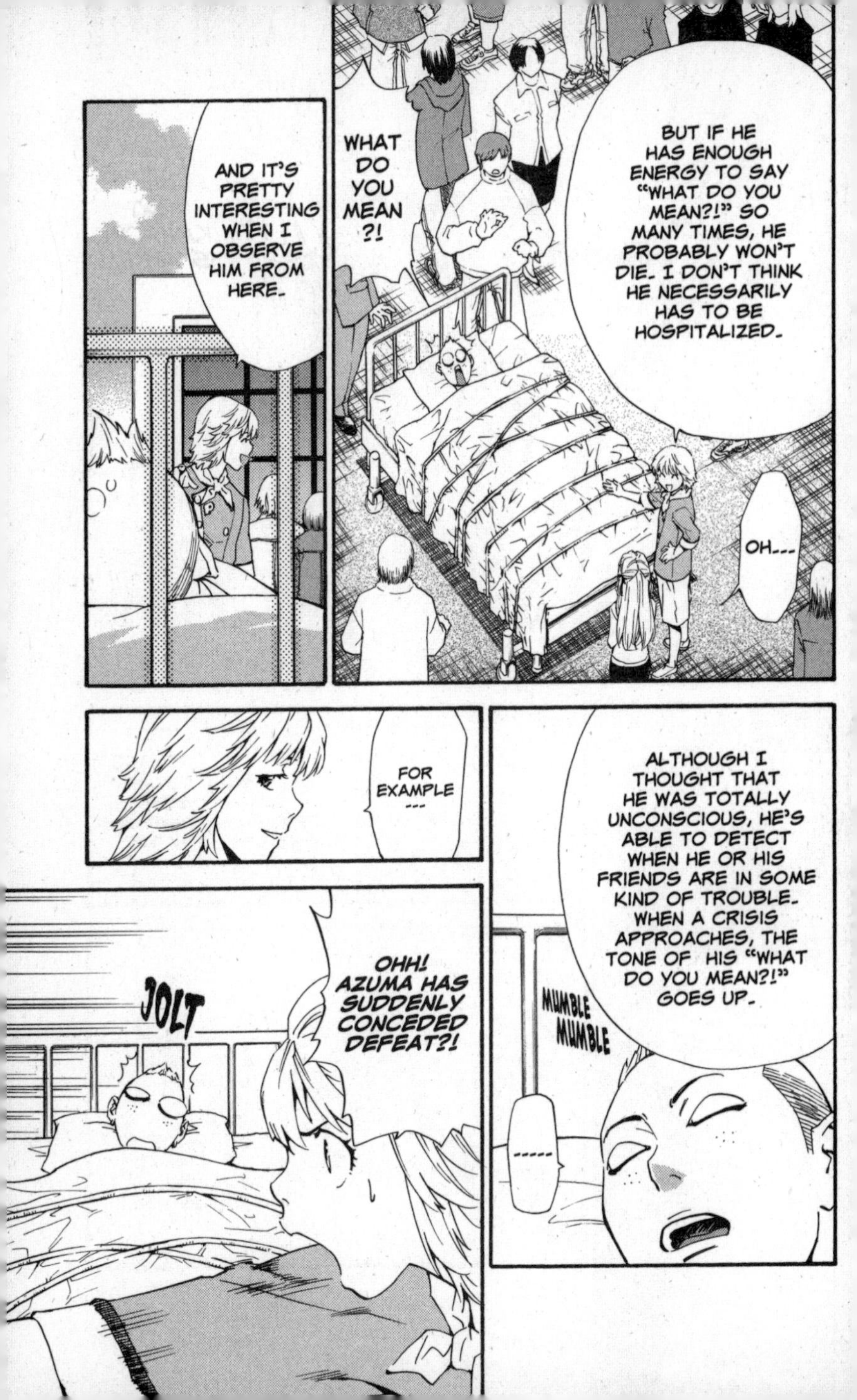
BUT IF HE HAS ENOUGH ENERGY TO SAY "WHAT DO YOU MEAN?!" SO MANY TIMES, HE PROBABLY WON'T DIE. I DON'T THINK HE NECESSARILY HAS TO BE HOSPITALIZED.
WHAT DO YOU MEAN?!
OH...
AND IT'S PRETTY INTERESTING WHEN I OBSERVE HIM FROM HERE.
ALTHOUGH I THOUGHT THAT HE WAS TOTALLY UNCONSCIOUS, HE'S ABLE TO DETECT WHEN HE OR HIS FRIENDS ARE IN SOME KIND OF TROUBLE. WHEN A CRISIS APPROACHES, THE TONE OF HIS "WHAT DO YOU MEAN?!" GOES UP.
MUMBLE MUMBLE

FOR EXAMPLE ---
OHH! AZUMA HAS SUDDENLY CONCEDED DEFEAT?!
JOLT

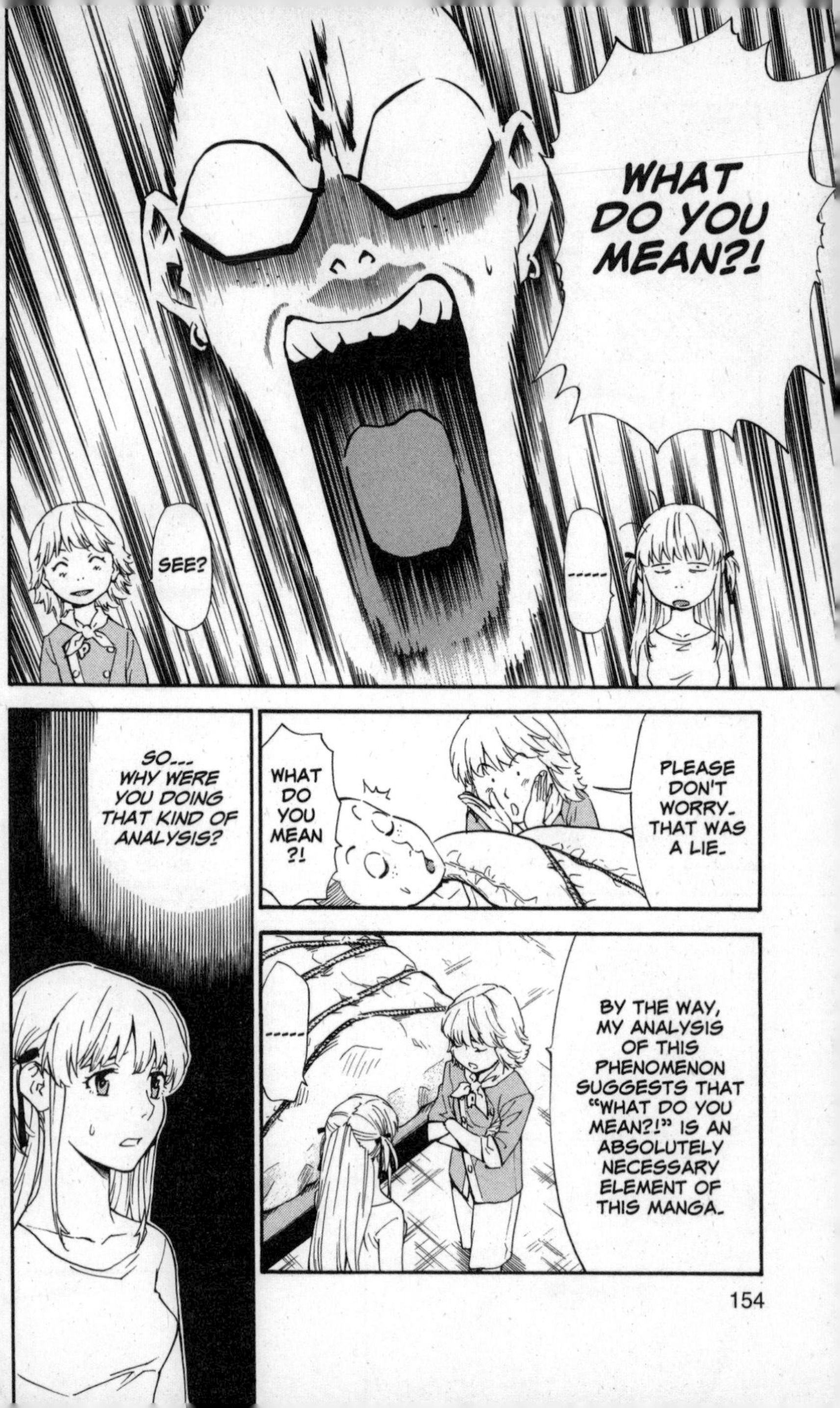
WHAT DO YOU MEAN?!
.....
SEE?
PLEASE DON'T WORRY. THAT WAS A LIE.
WHAT DO YOU MEAN ?!
BY THE WAY, MY ANALYSIS OF THIS PHENOMENON SUGGESTS THAT "WHAT DO YOU MEAN?!" IS AN ABSOLUTELY NECESSARY ELEMENT OF THIS MANGA.
.....
SO... WHY WERE YOU DOING THAT KIND OF ANALYSIS?

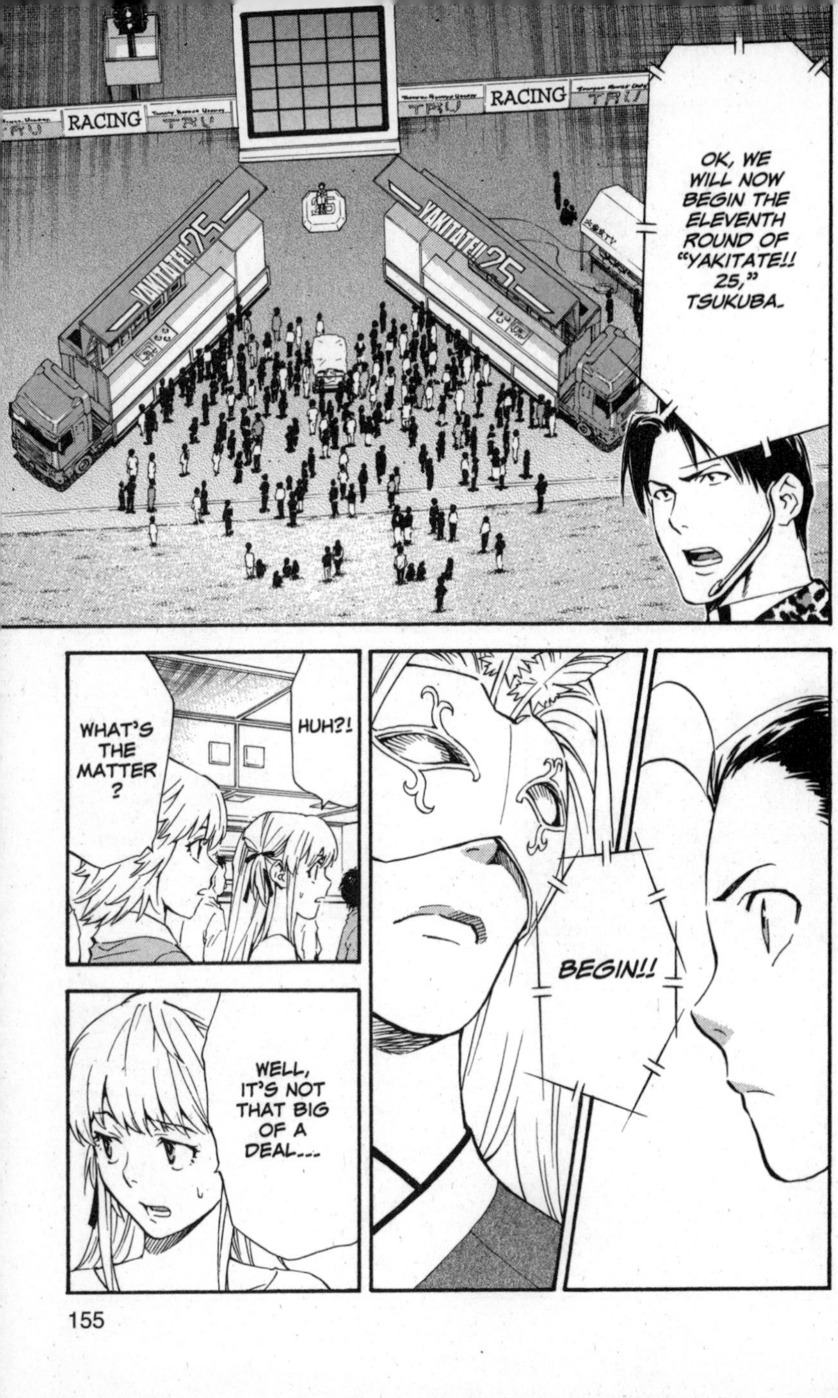
RACING
TRU
RACING
TRU
YAKITATE!! 25
YAKITATE!! 25
OK, WE WILL NOW BEGIN THE ELEVENTH ROUND OF "YAKITATE!! 25," TSUKUBA.
BEGIN!!
HUH?!
WHAT'S THE MATTER?
WELL, IT'S NOT THAT BIG OF A DEAL...

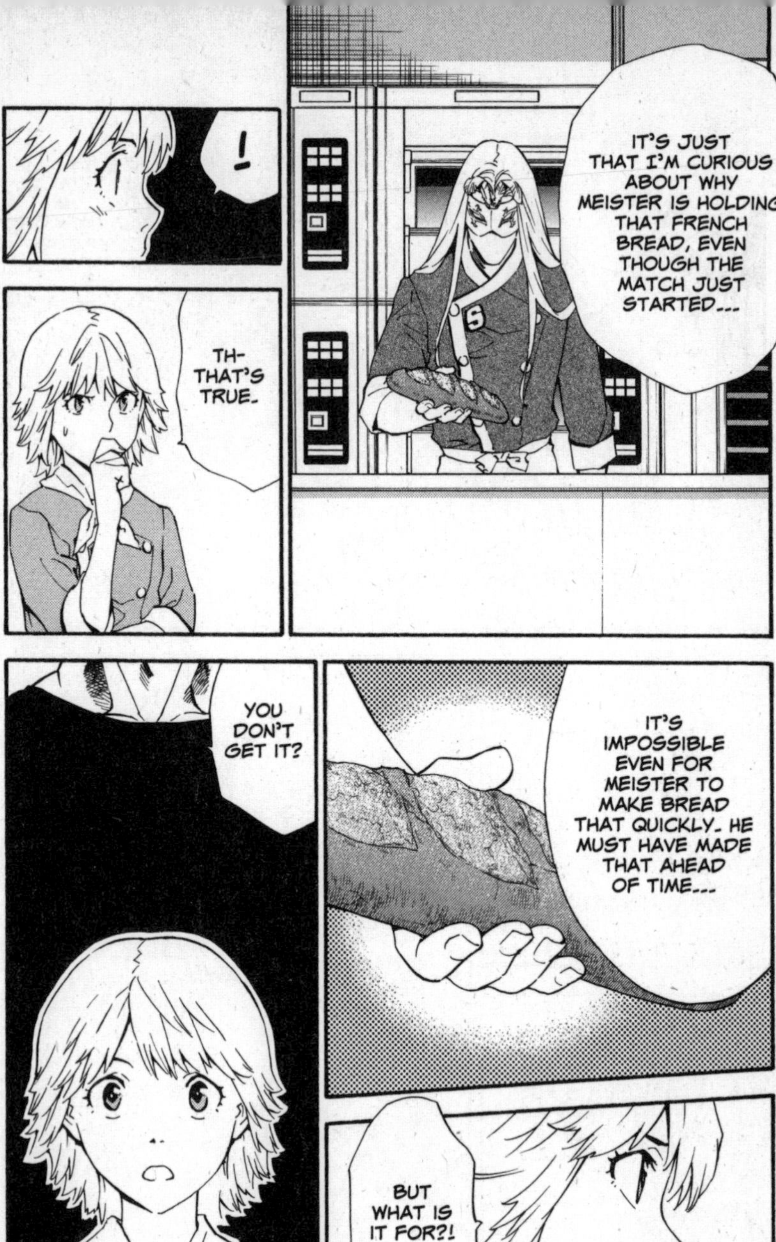
IT'S JUST THAT I'M CURIOUS ABOUT WHY MEISTER IS HOLDING THAT FRENCH BREAD, EVEN THOUGH THE MATCH JUST STARTED...
!
TH- THAT'S TRUE.
IT'S IMPOSSIBLE EVEN FOR MEISTER TO MAKE BREAD THAT QUICKLY. HE MUST HAVE MADE THAT AHEAD OF TIME...
BUT WHAT IS IT FOR?!
YOU DON'T GET IT?

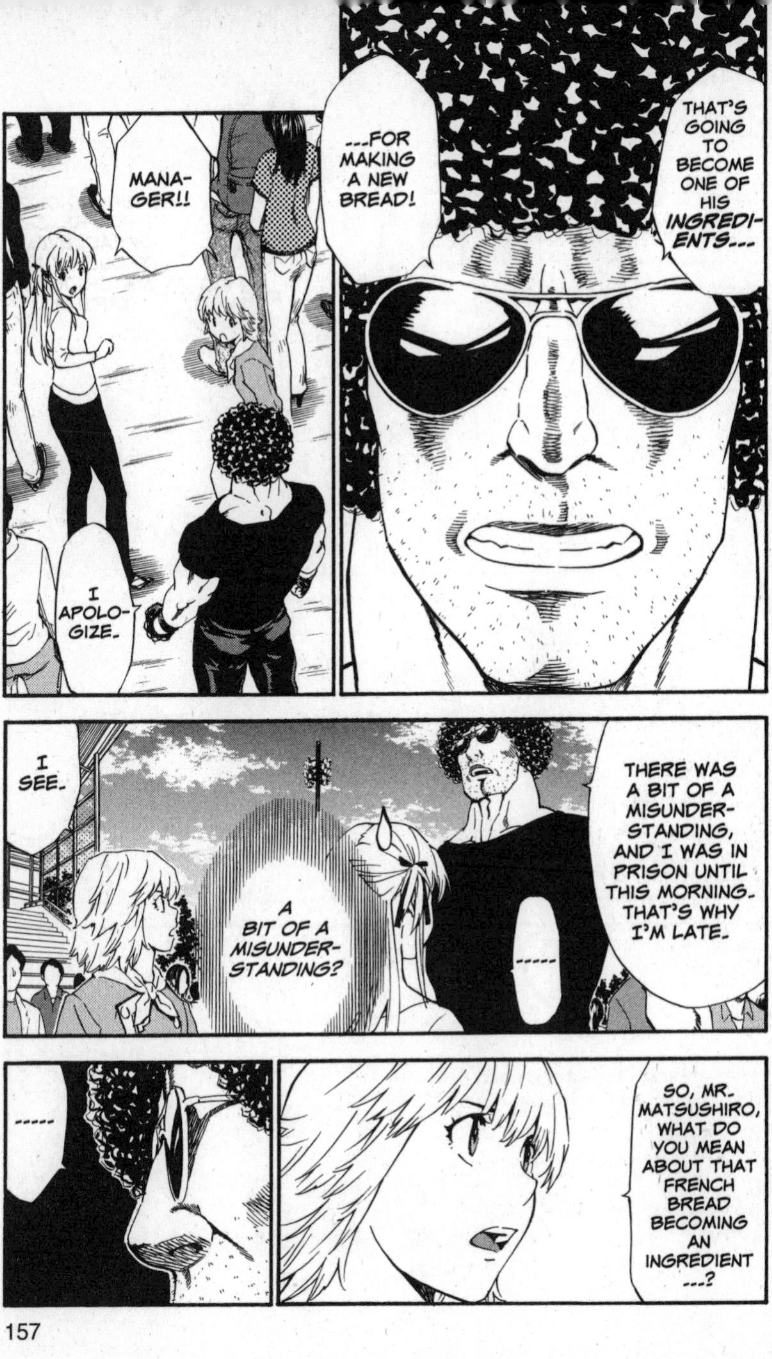
THAT'S GOING TO BECOME ONE OF HIS INGREDIENTS...
...FOR MAKING A NEW BREAD!
MANAGER!!
I APOLOGIZE.
THERE WAS A BIT OF A MISUNDERSTANDING, AND I WAS IN PRISON UNTIL THIS MORNING. THAT'S WHY I'M LATE.
.....
A BIT OF A MISUNDERSTANDING?
I SEE.
SO, MR. MATSUSHIRO, WHAT DO YOU MEAN ABOUT THAT FRENCH BREAD BECOMING AN INGREDIENT...?
.....

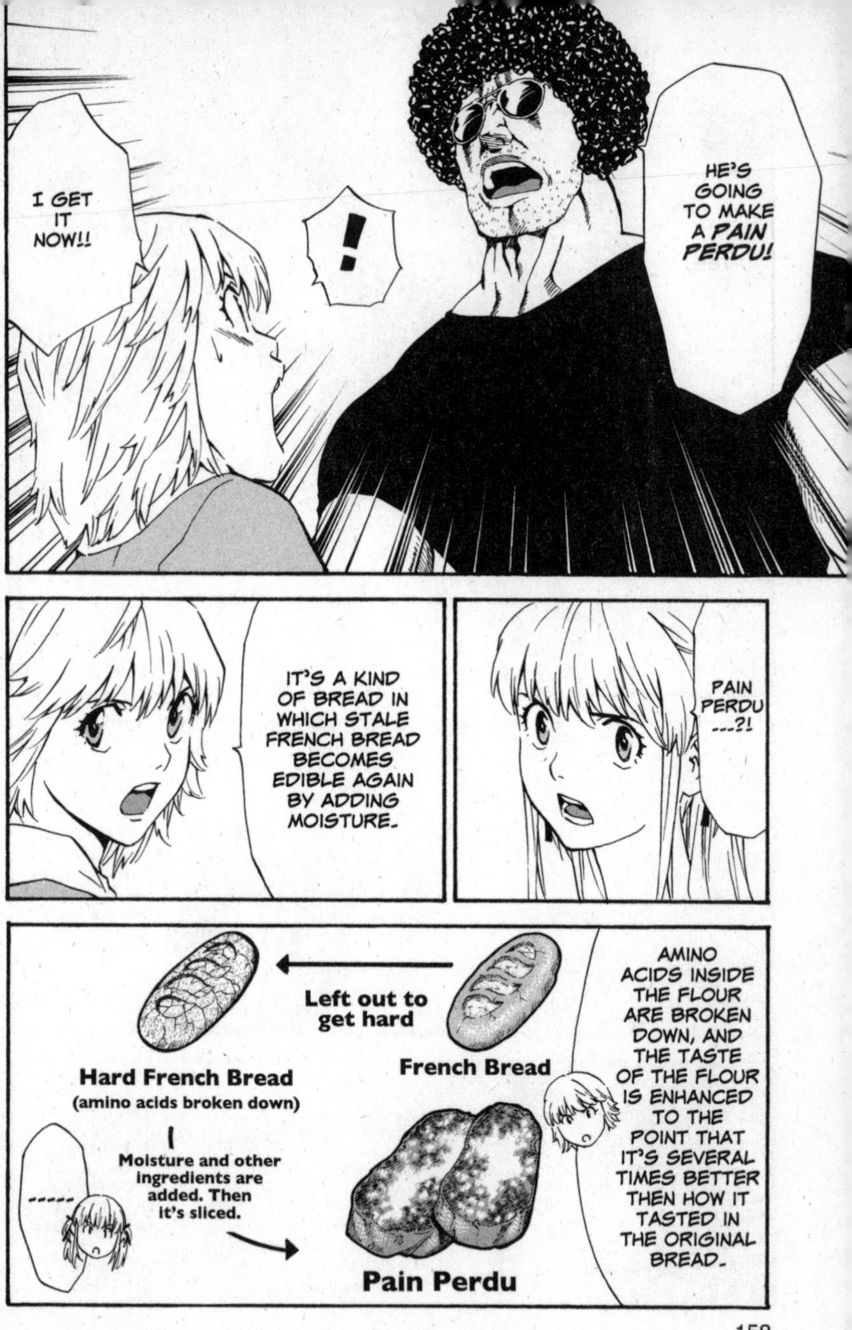
HE'S GOING TO MAKE A *PAIN PERDU!*
!
I GET IT NOW!!
PAIN PERDU ---?!
IT'S A KIND OF BREAD IN WHICH STALE FRENCH BREAD BECOMES EDIBLE AGAIN BY ADDING MOISTURE.
AMINO ACIDS INSIDE THE FLOUR ARE BROKEN DOWN, AND THE TASTE OF THE FLOUR IS ENHANCED TO THE POINT THAT IT'S SEVERAL TIMES BETTER THEN HOW IT TASTED IN THE ORIGINAL BREAD.
French Bread
Left out to get hard
Hard French Bread
(amino acids broken down)
Moisture and other ingredients are added. Then it's sliced.
Pain Perdu

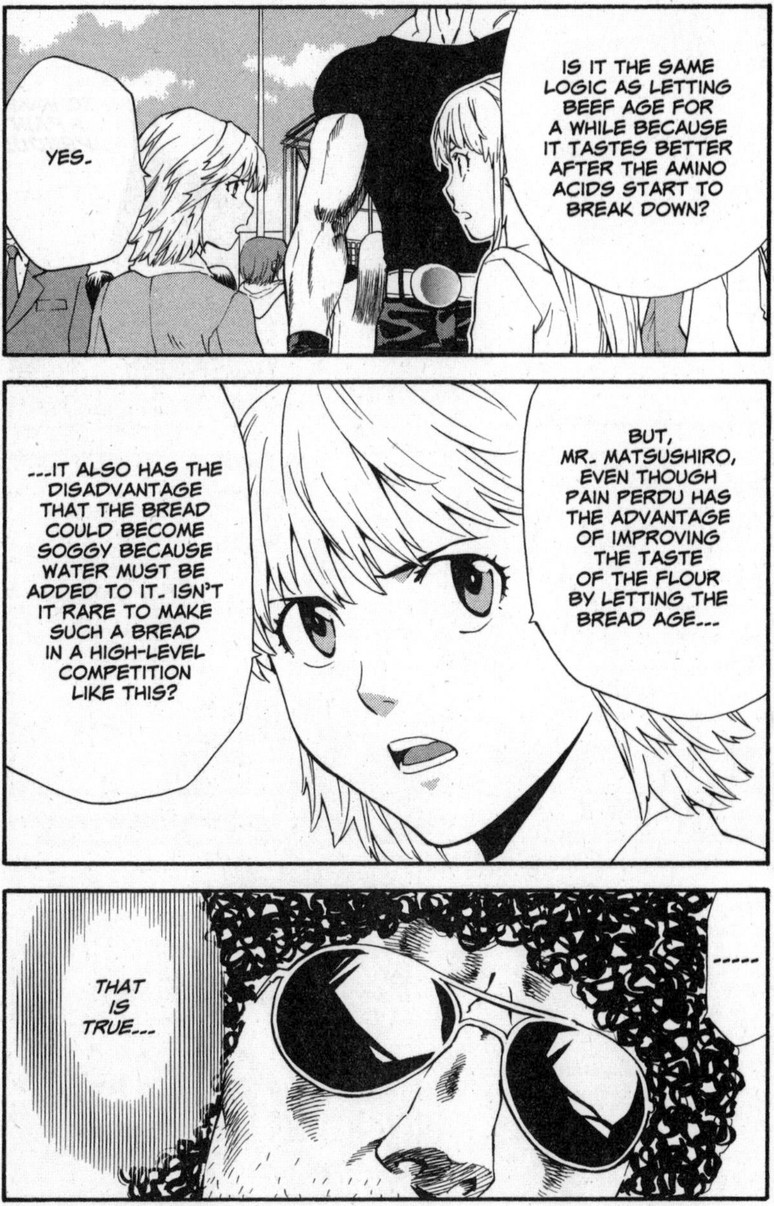
IS IT THE SAME LOGIC AS LETTING BEEF AGE FOR A WHILE BECAUSE IT TASTES BETTER AFTER THE AMINO ACIDS START TO BREAK DOWN?
YES.
BUT, MR. MATSUSHIRO, EVEN THOUGH PAIN PERDU HAS THE ADVANTAGE OF IMPROVING THE TASTE OF THE FLOUR BY LETTING THE BREAD AGE...
...IT ALSO HAS THE DISADVANTAGE THAT THE BREAD COULD BECOME SOGGY BECAUSE WATER MUST BE ADDED TO IT. ISN'T IT RARE TO MAKE SUCH A BREAD IN A HIGH-LEVEL COMPETITION LIKE THIS?
.....
THAT IS TRUE...

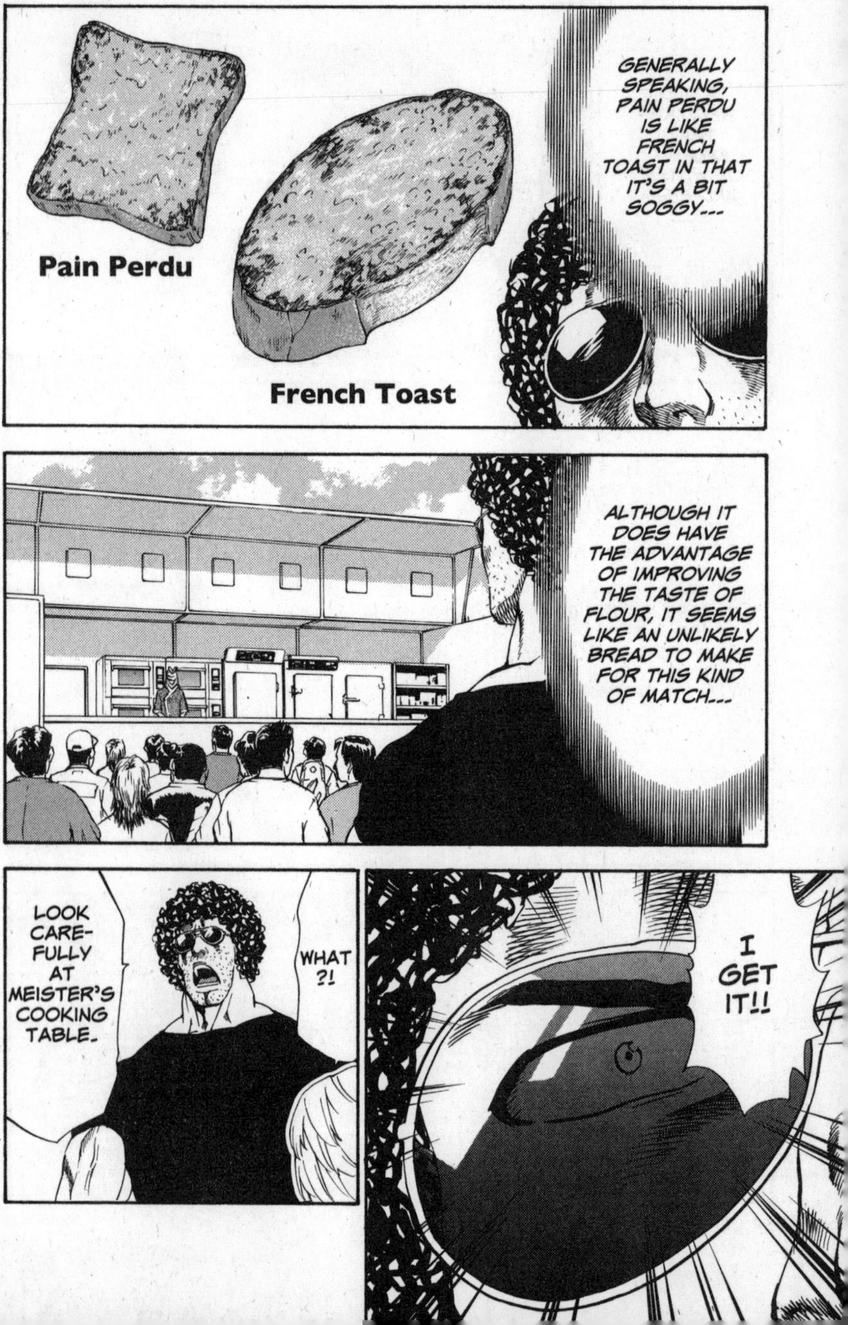
GENERALLY SPEAKING, PAIN PERDU IS LIKE FRENCH TOAST IN THAT IT'S A BIT SOGGY...
Pain Perdu
French Toast
ALTHOUGH IT DOES HAVE THE ADVANTAGE OF IMPROVING THE TASTE OF FLOUR, IT SEEMS LIKE AN UNLIKELY BREAD TO MAKE FOR THIS KIND OF MATCH...
I GET IT!!
WHAT?!
LOOK CAREFULLY AT MEISTER'S COOKING TABLE.

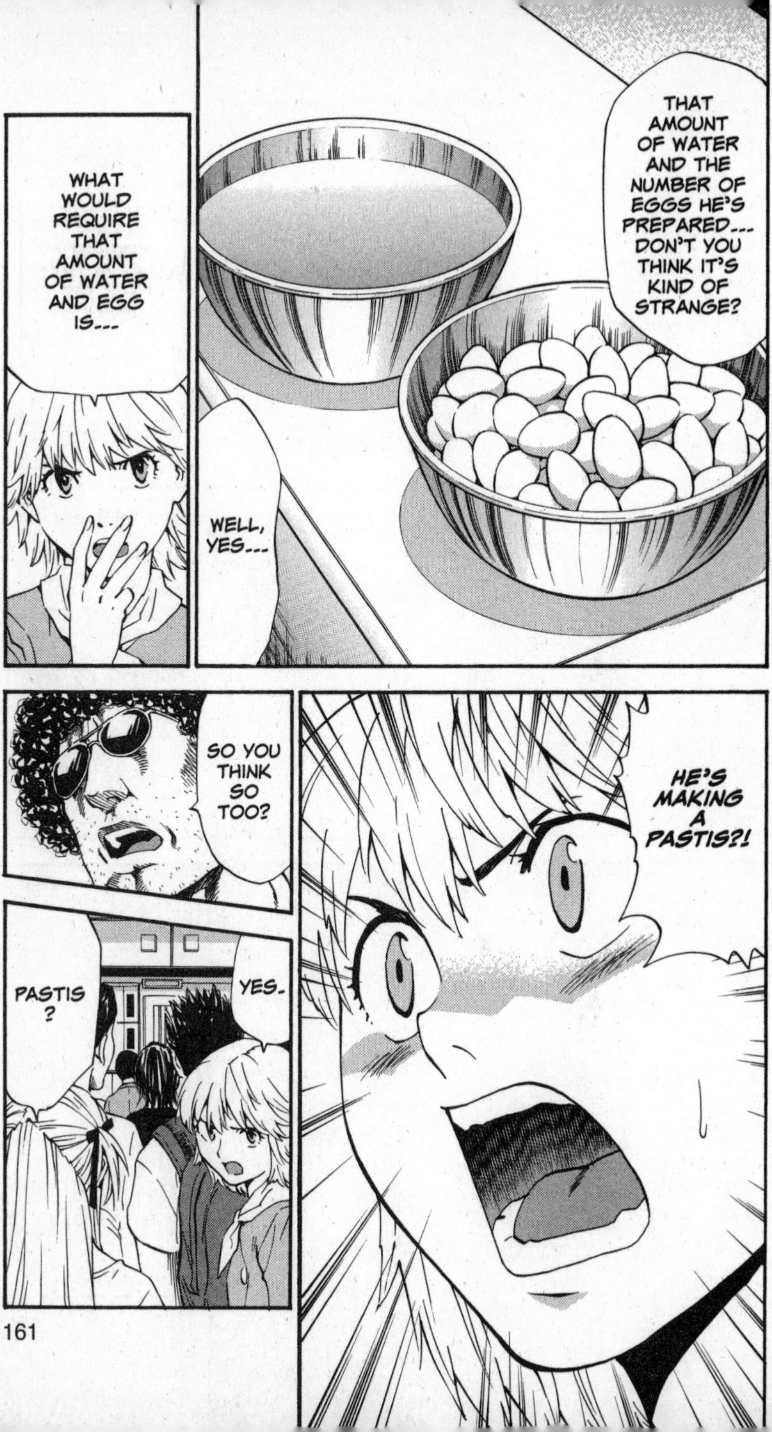
THAT AMOUNT OF WATER AND THE NUMBER OF EGGS HE'S PREPARED... DON'T YOU THINK IT'S KIND OF STRANGE?
WELL, YES...
WHAT WOULD REQUIRE THAT AMOUNT OF WATER AND EGG IS...
HE'S MAKING A PASTIS?!
SO YOU THINK SO TOO?
YES.
PASTIS?

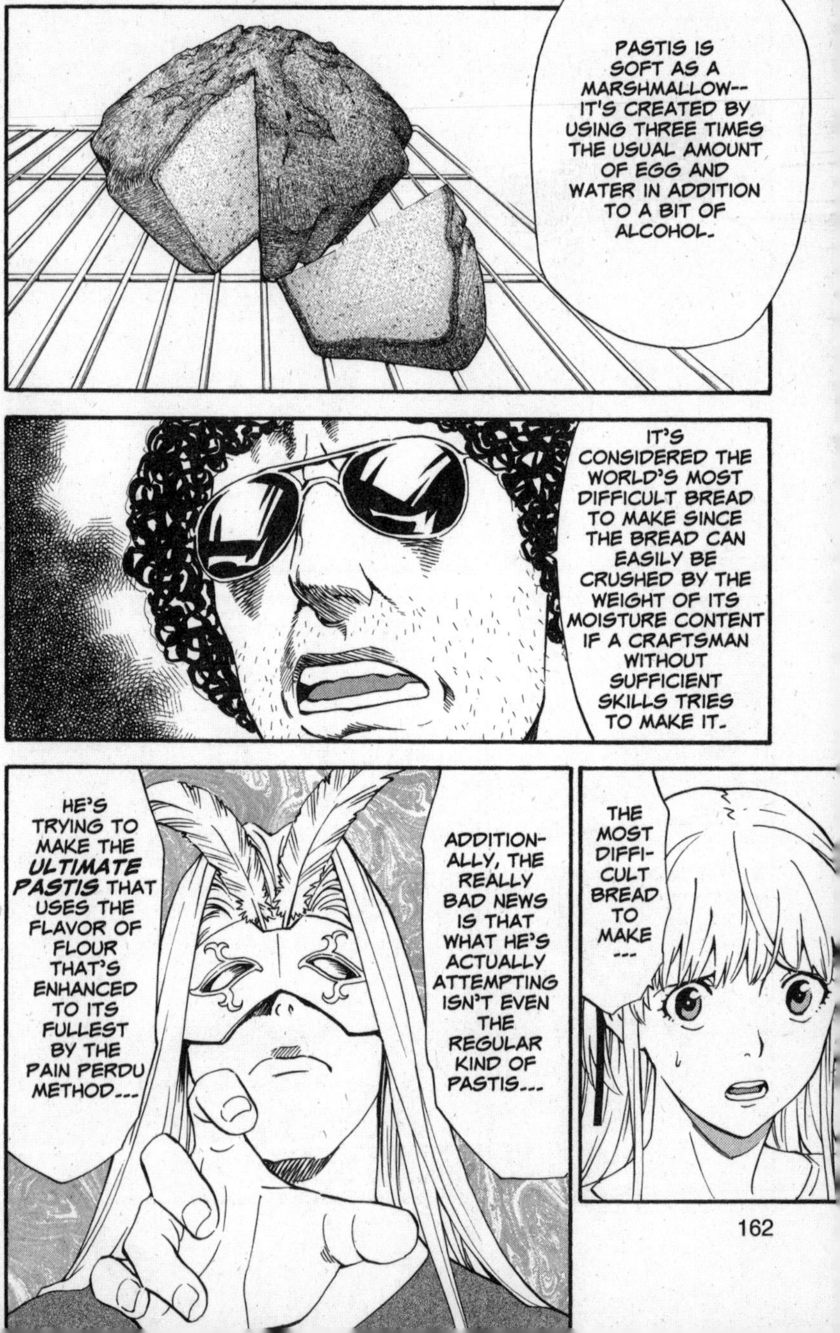
PASTIS IS SOFT AS A MARSHMALLOW-- IT'S CREATED BY USING THREE TIMES THE USUAL AMOUNT OF EGG AND WATER IN ADDITION TO A BIT OF ALCOHOL.
IT'S CONSIDERED THE WORLD'S MOST DIFFICULT BREAD TO MAKE SINCE THE BREAD CAN EASILY BE CRUSHED BY THE WEIGHT OF ITS MOISTURE CONTENT IF A CRAFTSMAN WITHOUT SUFFICIENT SKILLS TRIES TO MAKE IT.
THE MOST DIFFI-CULT BREAD TO MAKE ---
ADDITION-ALLY, THE REALLY BAD NEWS IS THAT WHAT HE'S ACTUALLY ATTEMPTING ISN'T EVEN THE REGULAR KIND OF PASTIS...
HE'S TRYING TO MAKE THE *ULTIMATE PASTIS* THAT USES THE FLAVOR OF FLOUR THAT'S ENHANCED TO ITS FULLEST BY THE PAIN PERDU METHOD...

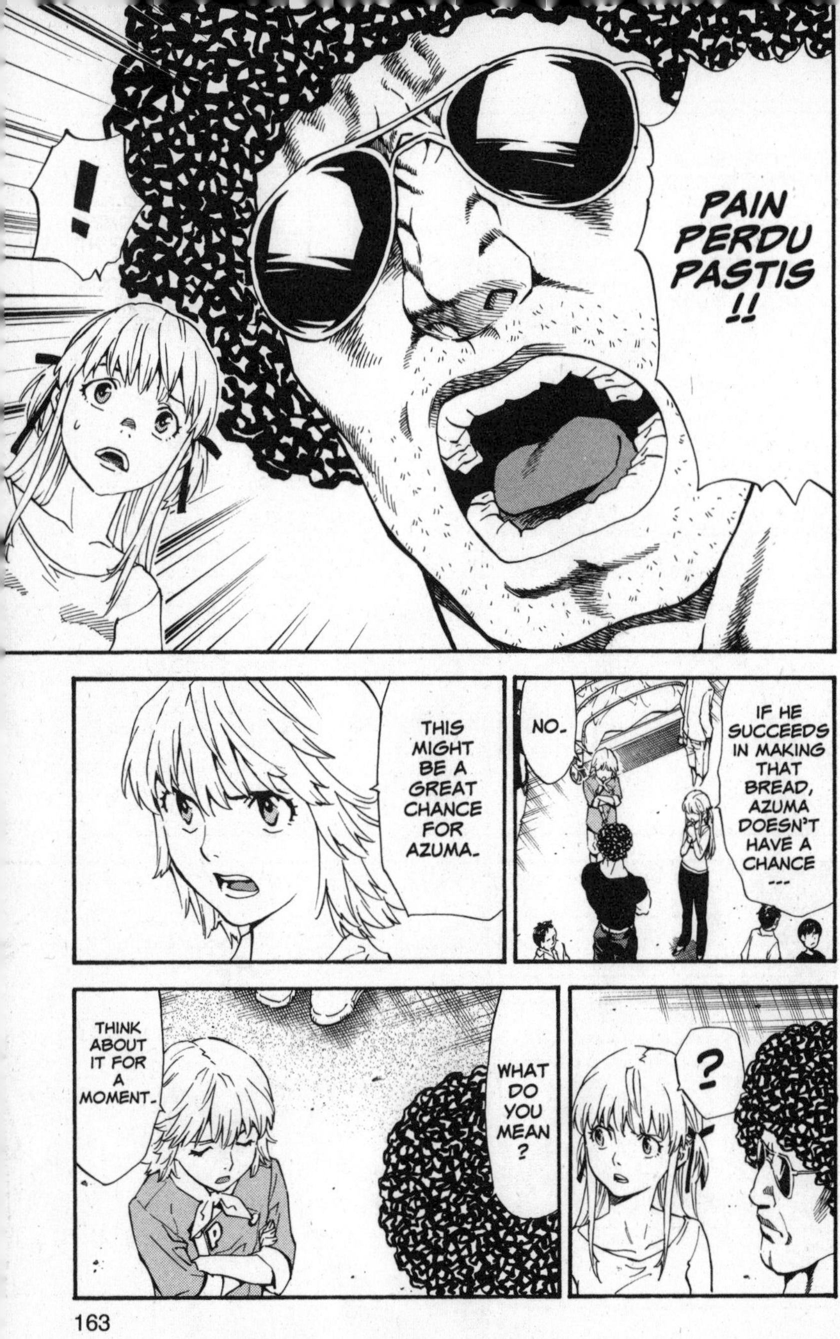
PAIN PERDU PASTIS !!
!
NO...
IF HE SUCCEEDS IN MAKING THAT BREAD, AZUMA DOESN'T HAVE A CHANCE ...
THIS MIGHT BE A GREAT CHANCE FOR AZUMA...
?
WHAT DO YOU MEAN ?
THINK ABOUT IT FOR A MOMENT...

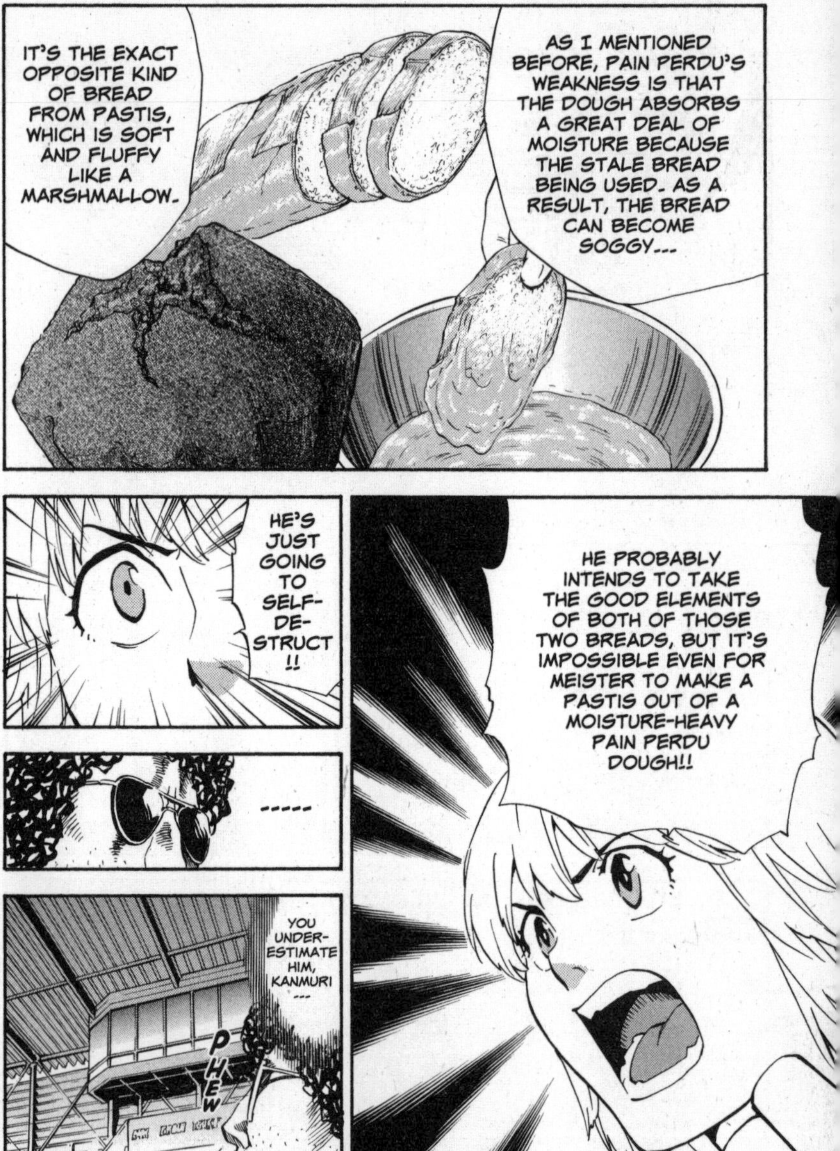
AS I MENTIONED BEFORE, PAIN PERDU'S WEAKNESS IS THAT THE DOUGH ABSORBS A GREAT DEAL OF MOISTURE BECAUSE THE STALE BREAD BEING USED. AS A RESULT, THE BREAD CAN BECOME SOGGY...
IT'S THE EXACT OPPOSITE KIND OF BREAD FROM PASTIS, WHICH IS SOFT AND FLUFFY LIKE A MARSHMALLOW.
HE PROBABLY INTENDS TO TAKE THE GOOD ELEMENTS OF BOTH OF THOSE TWO BREADS, BUT IT'S IMPOSSIBLE EVEN FOR MEISTER TO MAKE A PASTIS OUT OF A MOISTURE-HEAVY PAIN PERDU DOUGH!!
HE'S JUST GOING TO SELF-DESTRUCT!!
.....
YOU UNDER-ESTIMATE HIM, KANMURI...
PHEW

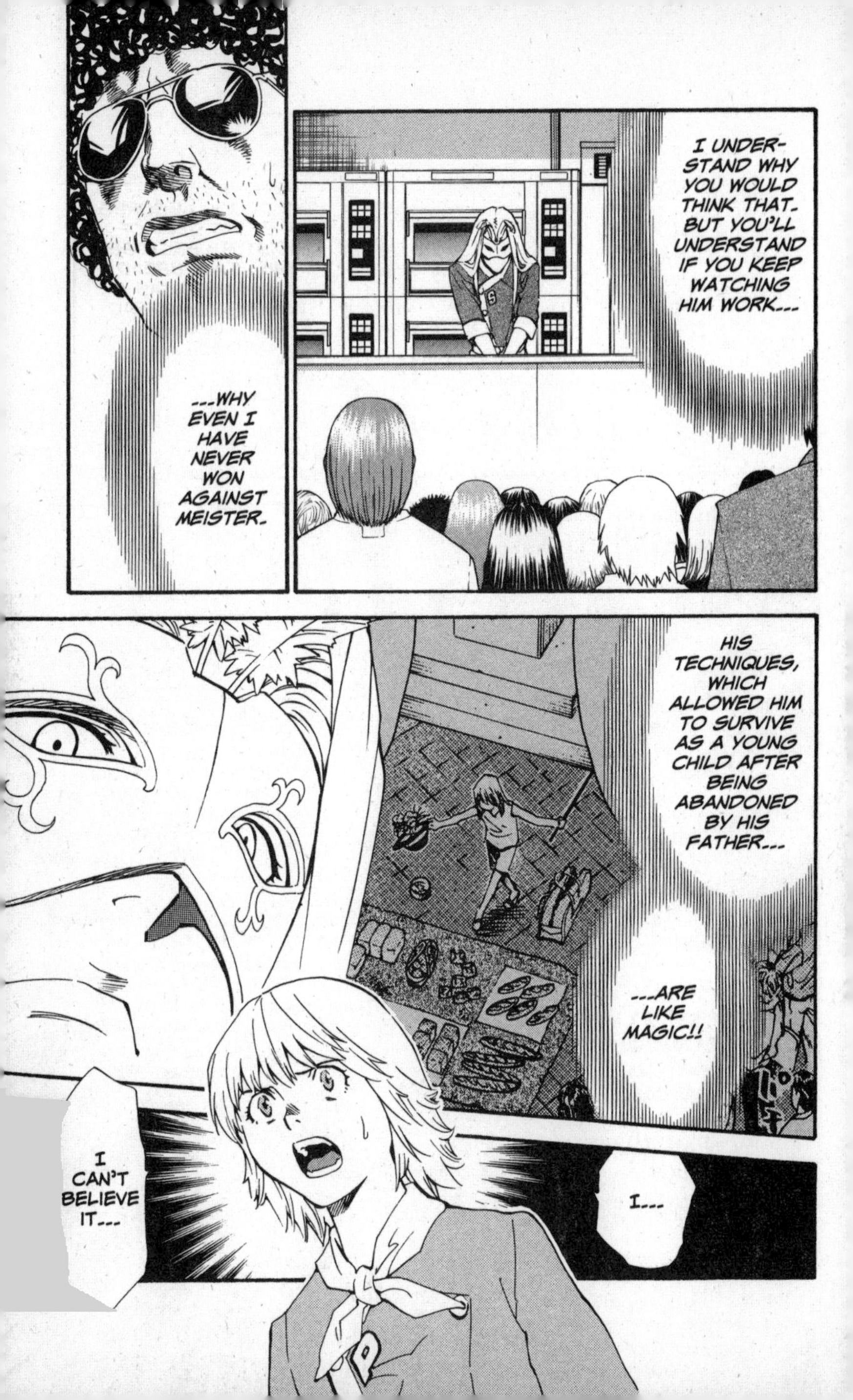
I UNDERSTAND WHY YOU WOULD THINK THAT. BUT YOU'LL UNDERSTAND IF YOU KEEP WATCHING HIM WORK...
...WHY EVEN I HAVE NEVER WON AGAINST MEISTER.
HIS TECHNIQUES, WHICH ALLOWED HIM TO SURVIVE AS A YOUNG CHILD AFTER BEING ABANDONED BY HIS FATHER...
...ARE LIKE MAGIC!!
I...
I CAN'T BELIEVE IT...

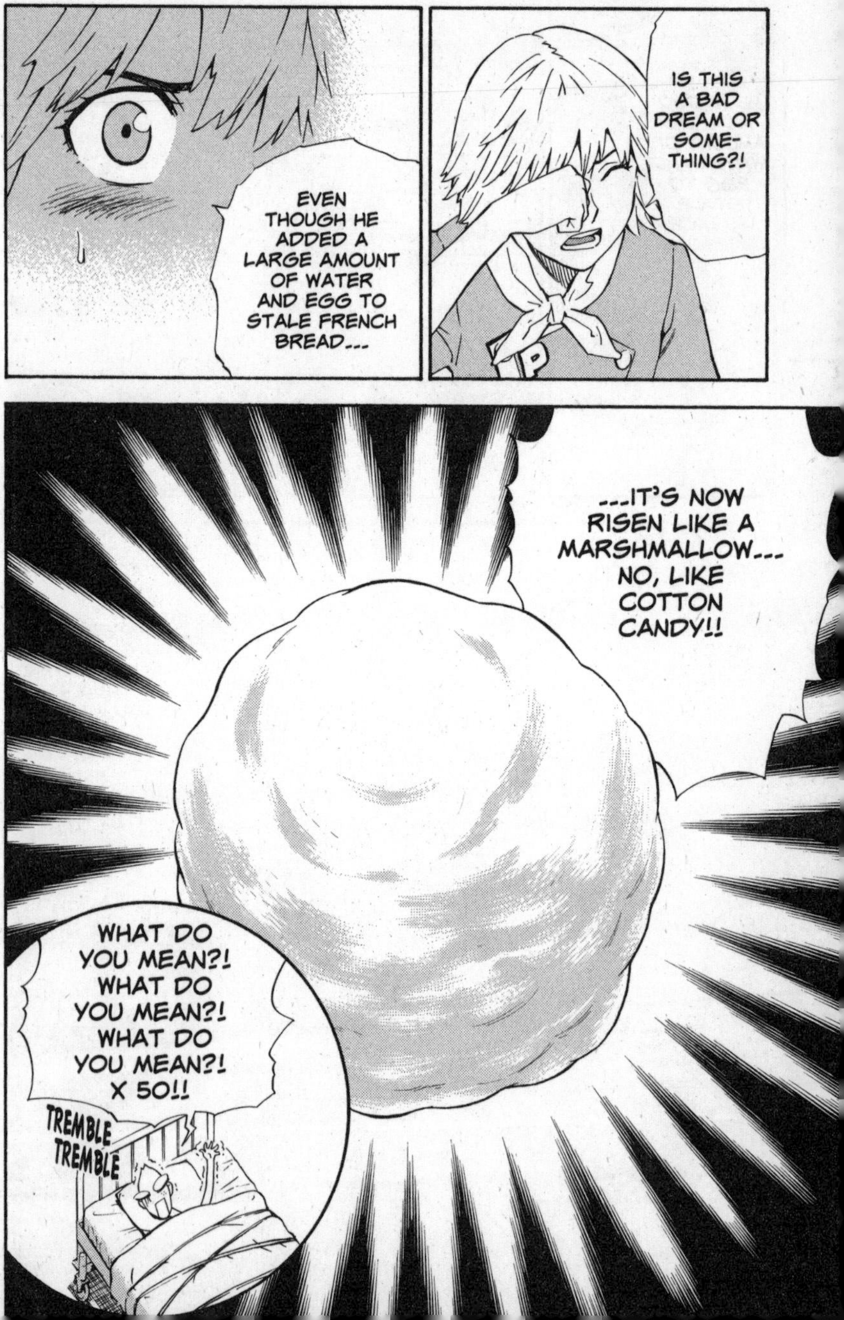
IS THIS A BAD DREAM OR SOME-THING?!
EVEN THOUGH HE ADDED A LARGE AMOUNT OF WATER AND EGG TO STALE FRENCH BREAD...
...IT'S NOW RISEN LIKE A MARSHMALLOW... NO, LIKE COTTON CANDY!!
WHAT DO YOU MEAN?! WHAT DO YOU MEAN?! WHAT DO YOU MEAN?! X 50!!
TREMBLE TREMBLE

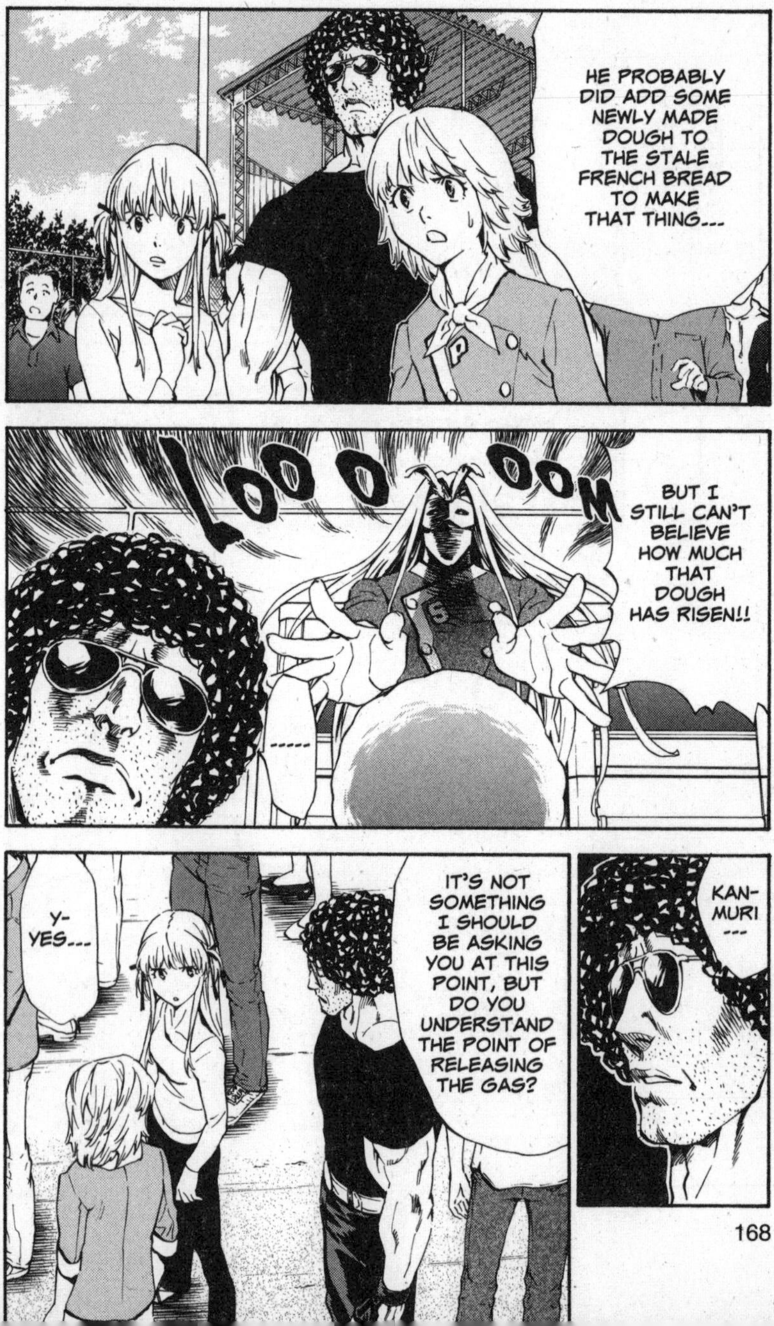
HE PROBABLY DID ADD SOME NEWLY MADE DOUGH TO THE STALE FRENCH BREAD TO MAKE THAT THING...
LOOO OOM
BUT I STILL CAN'T BELIEVE HOW MUCH THAT DOUGH HAS RISEN!!
.....
KAN-MURI...
IT'S NOT SOMETHING I SHOULD BE ASKING YOU AT THIS POINT, BUT DO YOU UNDERSTAND THE POINT OF RELEASING THE GAS?
Y-YES...

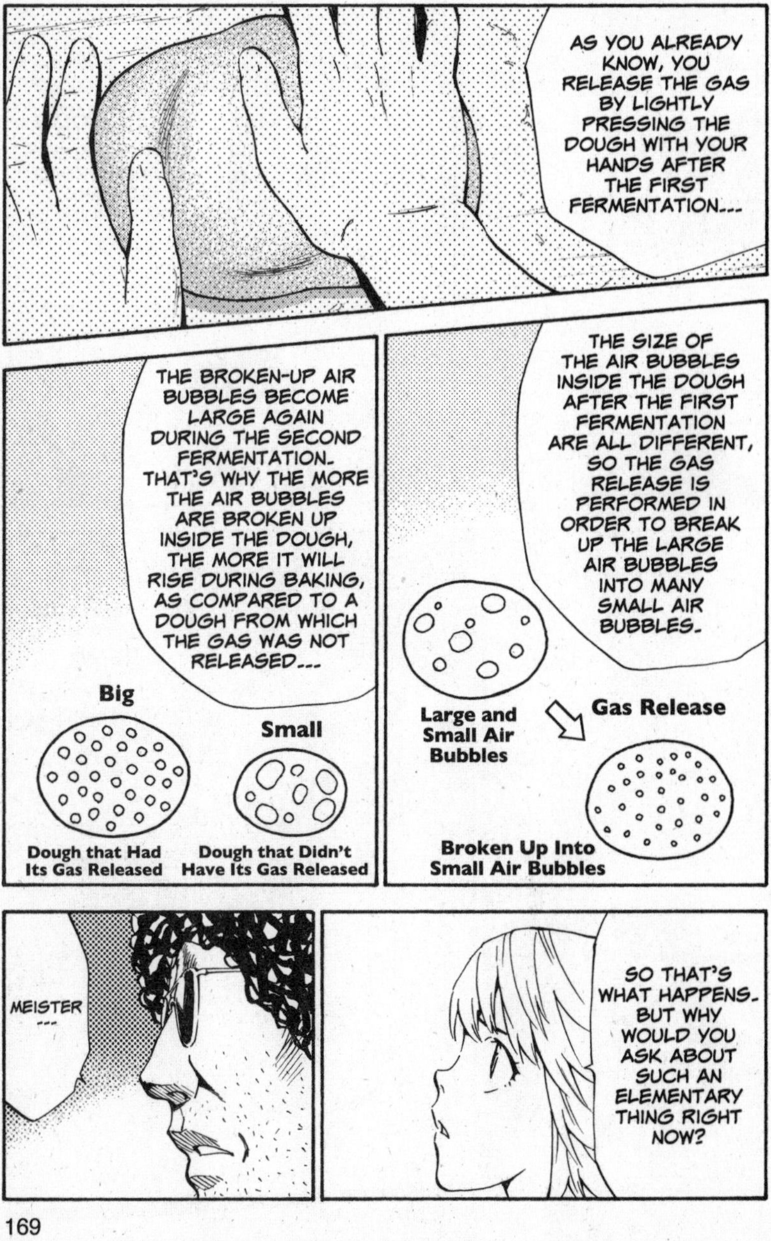
AS YOU ALREADY KNOW, YOU RELEASE THE GAS BY LIGHTLY PRESSING THE DOUGH WITH YOUR HANDS AFTER THE FIRST FERMENTATION...
THE SIZE OF THE AIR BUBBLES INSIDE THE DOUGH AFTER THE FIRST FERMENTATION ARE ALL DIFFERENT, SO THE GAS RELEASE IS PERFORMED IN ORDER TO BREAK UP THE LARGE AIR BUBBLES INTO MANY SMALL AIR BUBBLES.
Large and Small Air Bubbles
Gas Release
Broken Up Into Small Air Bubbles
THE BROKEN-UP AIR BUBBLES BECOME LARGE AGAIN DURING THE SECOND FERMENTATION. THAT'S WHY THE MORE THE AIR BUBBLES ARE BROKEN UP INSIDE THE DOUGH, THE MORE IT WILL RISE DURING BAKING, AS COMPARED TO A DOUGH FROM WHICH THE GAS WAS NOT RELEASED...
Big
Small
Dough that Had Its Gas Released
Dough that Didn't Have Its Gas Released
SO THAT'S WHAT HAPPENS. BUT WHY WOULD YOU ASK ABOUT SUCH AN ELEMENTARY THING RIGHT NOW?
MEISTER...

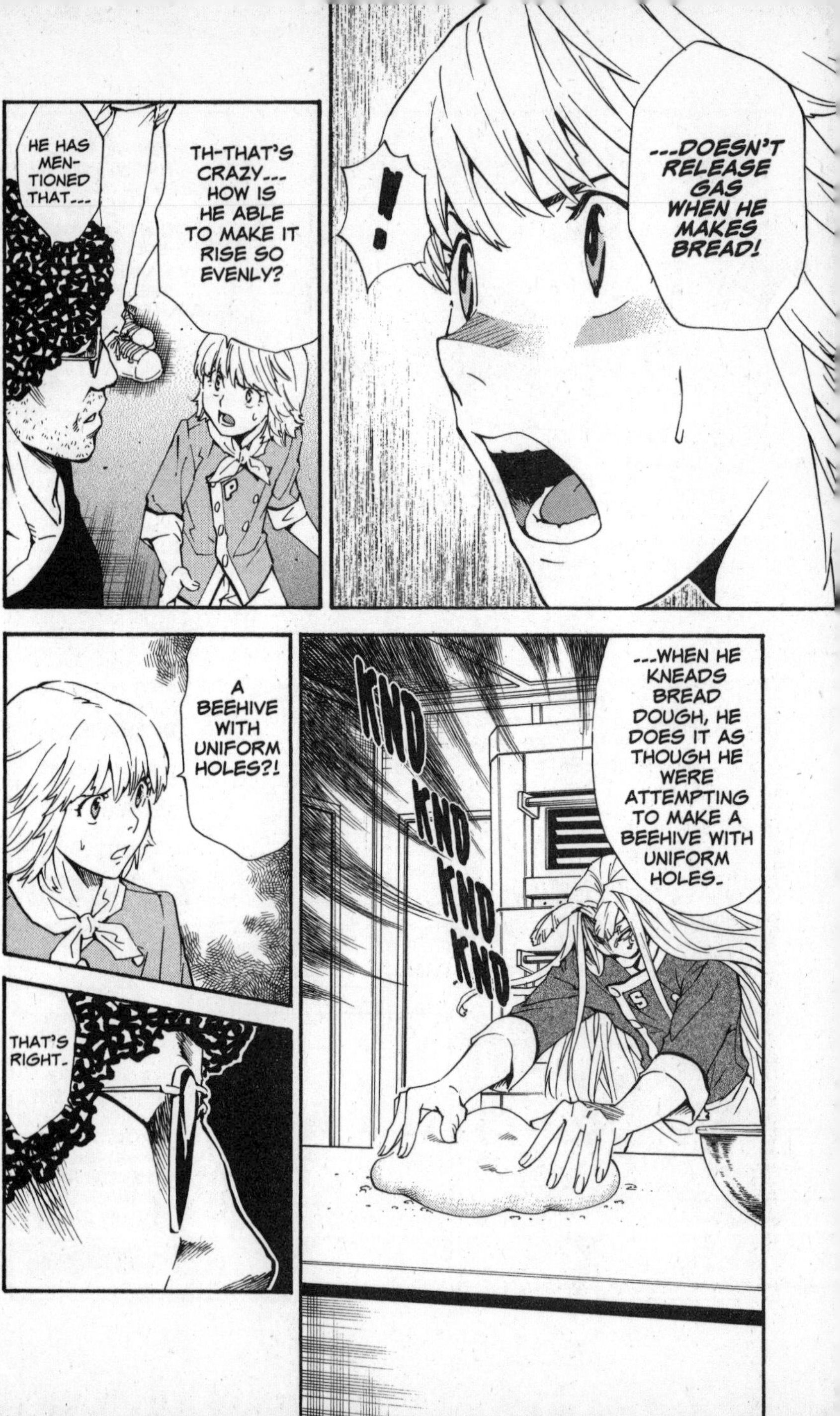
!
...DOESN'T RELEASE GAS WHEN HE MAKES BREAD!
TH-THAT'S CRAZY... HOW IS HE ABLE TO MAKE IT RISE SO EVENLY?
HE HAS MENTIONED THAT...
...WHEN HE KNEADS BREAD DOUGH, HE DOES IT AS THOUGH HE WERE ATTEMPTING TO MAKE A BEEHIVE WITH UNIFORM HOLES.
KND KND KND KND
A BEEHIVE WITH UNIFORM HOLES?!
THAT'S RIGHT.

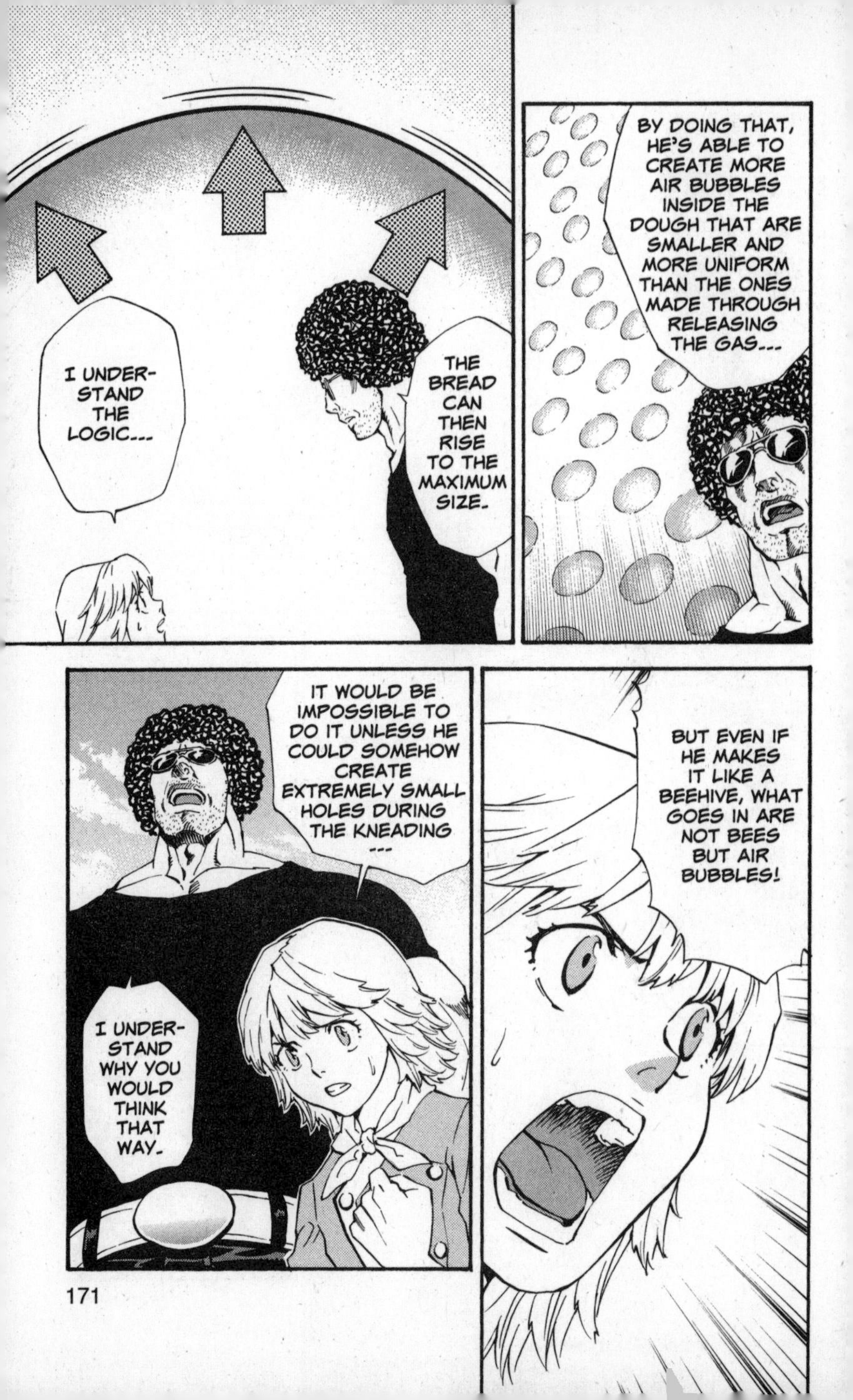
BY DOING THAT, HE'S ABLE TO CREATE MORE AIR BUBBLES INSIDE THE DOUGH THAT ARE SMALLER AND MORE UNIFORM THAN THE ONES MADE THROUGH RELEASING THE GAS...
THE BREAD CAN THEN RISE TO THE MAXIMUM SIZE.
I UNDER-STAND THE LOGIC...
BUT EVEN IF HE MAKES IT LIKE A BEEHIVE, WHAT GOES IN ARE NOT BEES BUT AIR BUBBLES!
IT WOULD BE IMPOSSIBLE TO DO IT UNLESS HE COULD SOMEHOW CREATE EXTREMELY SMALL HOLES DURING THE KNEADING ...
I UNDER-STAND WHY YOU WOULD THINK THAT WAY.

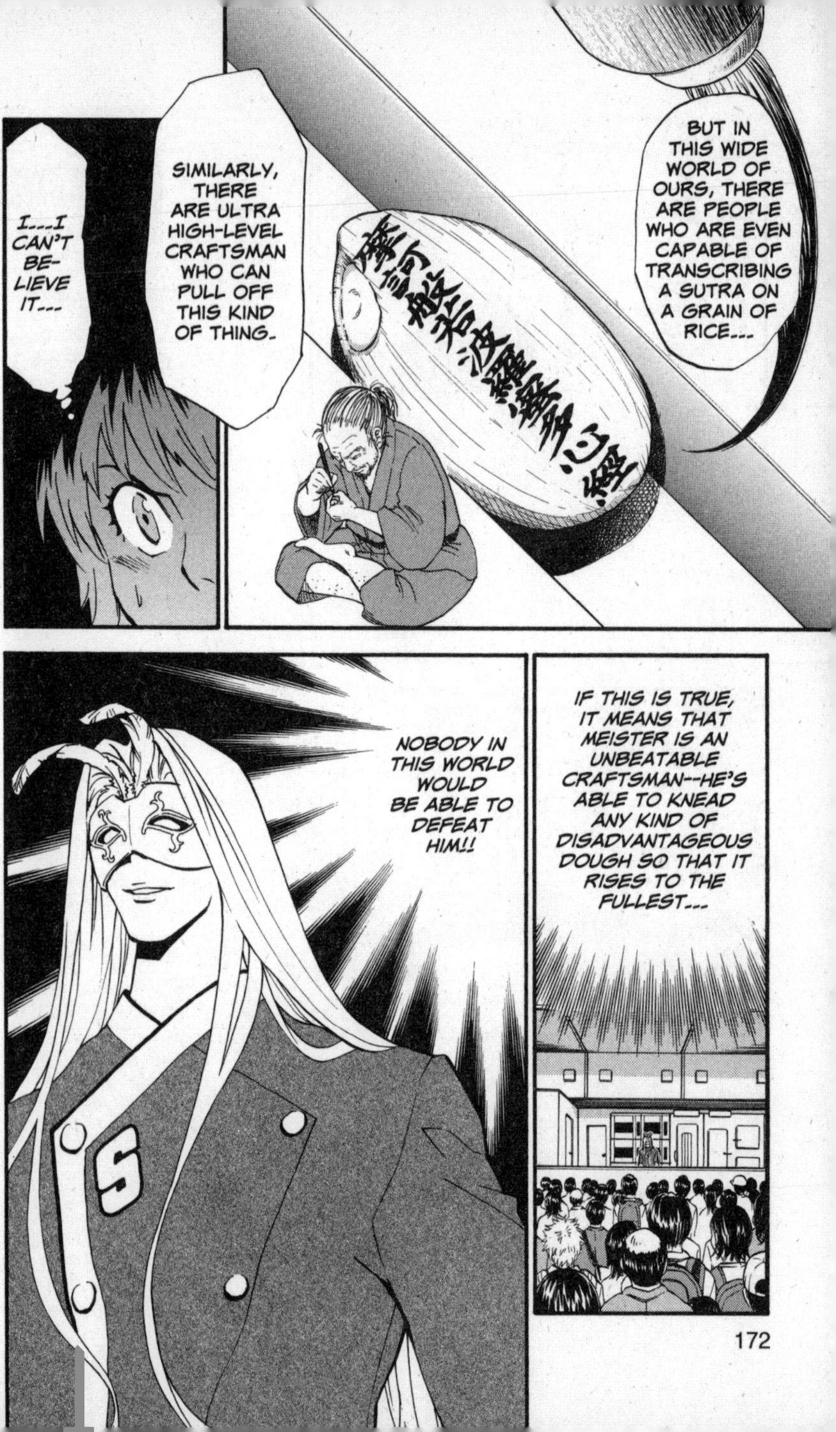
BUT IN THIS WIDE WORLD OF OURS, THERE ARE PEOPLE WHO ARE EVEN CAPABLE OF TRANSCRIBING A SUTRA ON A GRAIN OF RICE...
摩訶般若波羅蜜多心經
SIMILARLY, THERE ARE ULTRA HIGH-LEVEL CRAFTSMAN WHO CAN PULL OFF THIS KIND OF THING.
I...I CAN'T BE-LIEVE IT...
IF THIS IS TRUE, IT MEANS THAT MEISTER IS AN UNBEATABLE CRAFTSMAN--HE'S ABLE TO KNEAD ANY KIND OF DISADVANTAGEOUS DOUGH SO THAT IT RISES TO THE FULLEST...
NOBODY IN THIS WORLD WOULD BE ABLE TO DEFEAT HIM!!

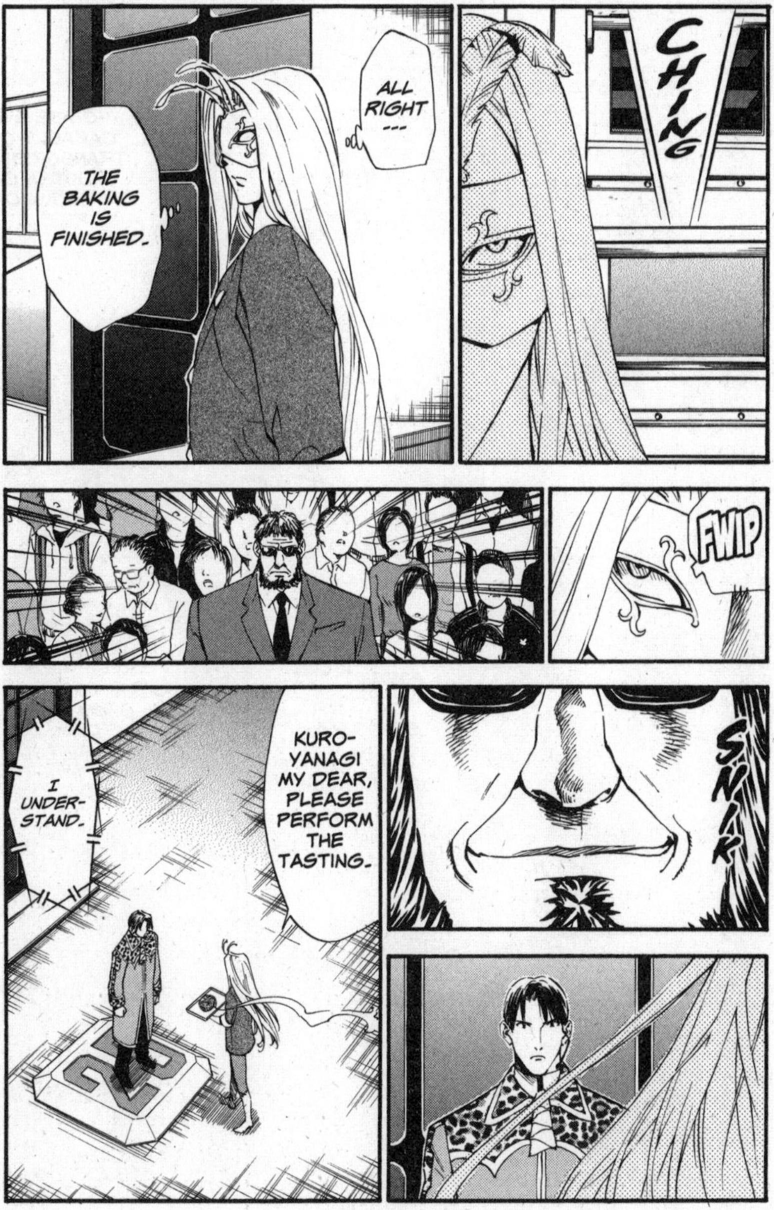
CHING
ALL RIGHT ---
THE BAKING IS FINISHED.
FWIP
SNIK
KURO-YANAGI MY DEAR, PLEASE PERFORM THE TASTING.
I UNDER-STAND.

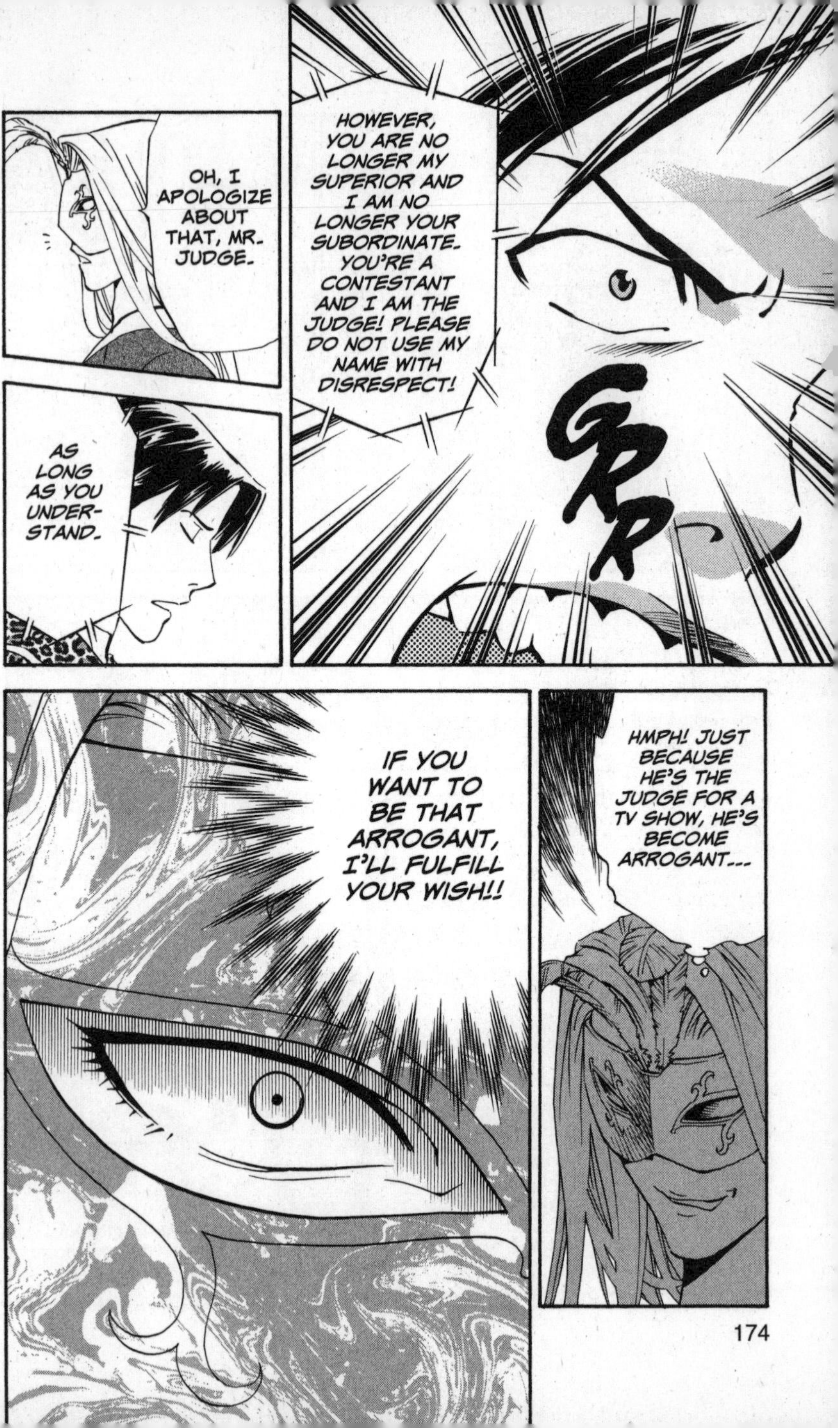
HOWEVER, YOU ARE NO LONGER MY SUPERIOR AND I AM NO LONGER YOUR SUBORDINATE. YOU'RE A CONTESTANT AND I AM THE JUDGE! PLEASE DO NOT USE MY NAME WITH DISRESPECT!
GRR
OH, I APOLOGIZE ABOUT THAT, MR. JUDGE.
AS LONG AS YOU UNDER-STAND.
HMPH! JUST BECAUSE HE'S THE JUDGE FOR A TV SHOW, HE'S BECOME ARROGANT...
IF YOU WANT TO BE THAT ARROGANT, I'LL FULFILL YOUR WISH!!

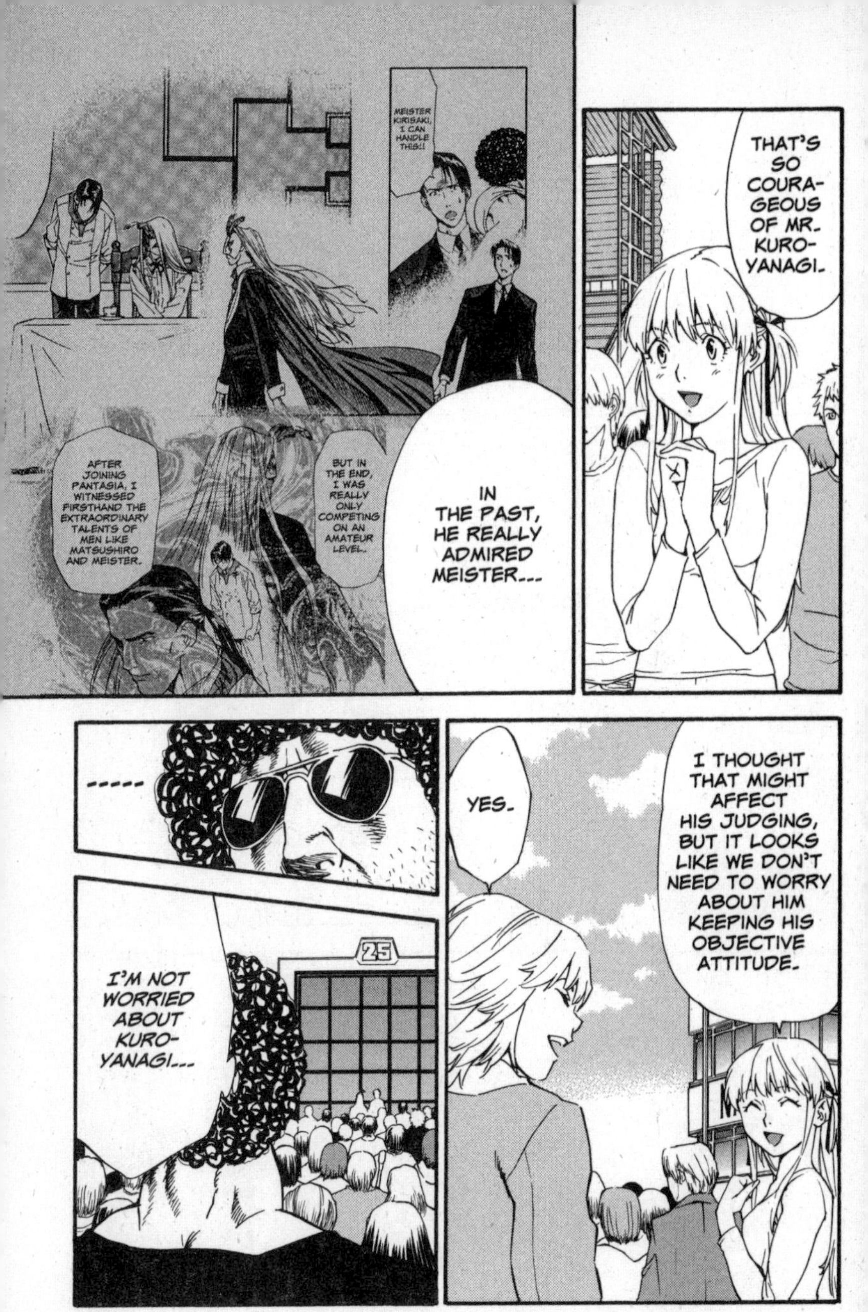
THAT'S SO COURAGEOUS OF MR. KUROYANAGI.
IN THE PAST, HE REALLY ADMIRED MEISTER...
MEISTER KIRISAKI, I CAN HANDLE THIS!!
AFTER JOINING PANTASIA, I WITNESSED FIRSTHAND THE EXTRAORDINARY TALENTS OF MEN LIKE MATSUSHIRO AND MEISTER.
BUT IN THE END, I WAS REALLY ONLY COMPETING ON AN AMATEUR LEVEL.
I THOUGHT THAT MIGHT AFFECT HIS JUDGING, BUT IT LOOKS LIKE WE DON'T NEED TO WORRY ABOUT HIM KEEPING HIS OBJECTIVE ATTITUDE.
YES.

I'M NOT WORRIED ABOUT KUROYANAGI...

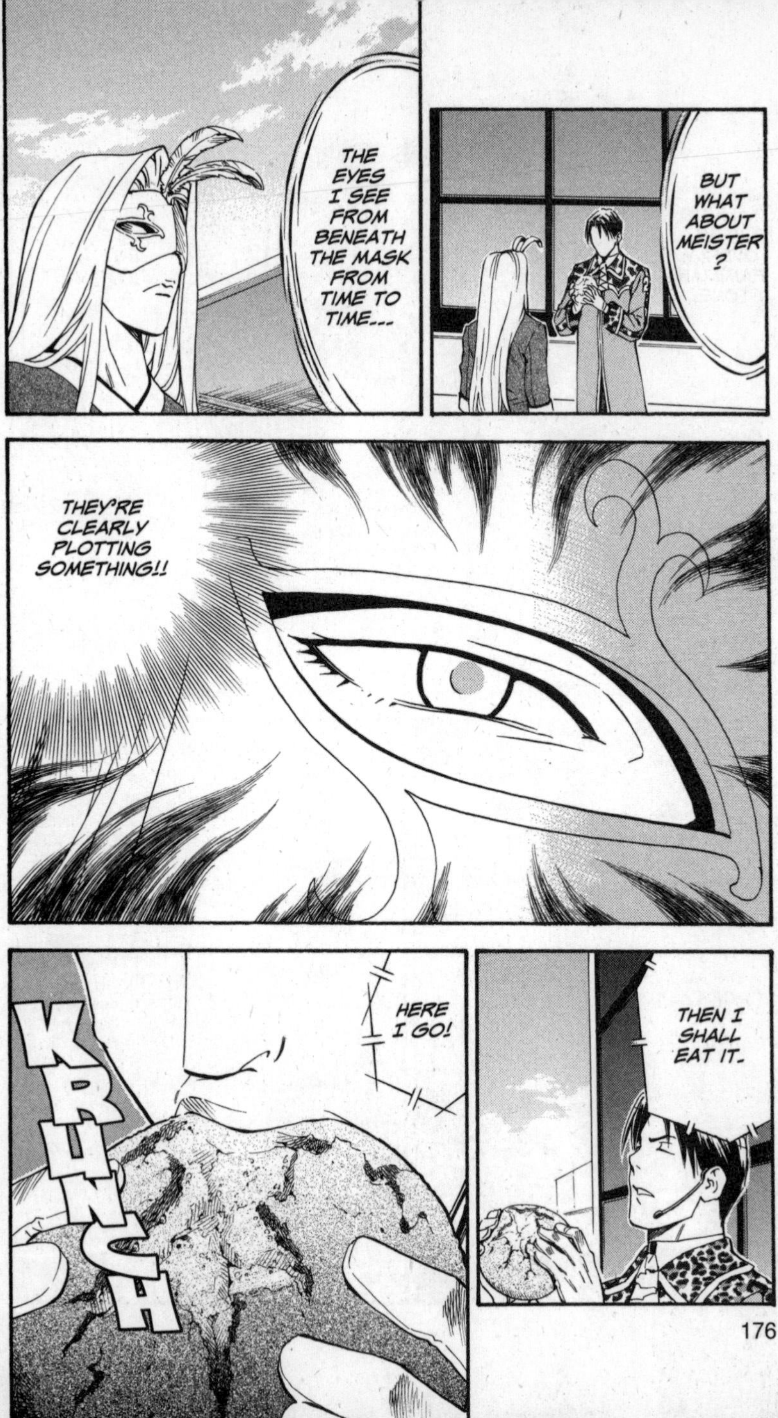
BUT WHAT ABOUT MEISTER?
THE EYES I SEE FROM BENEATH THE MASK FROM TIME TO TIME...
THEY'RE CLEARLY PLOTTING SOMETHING!!
THEN I SHALL EAT IT.
HERE I GO!
KRUNCH

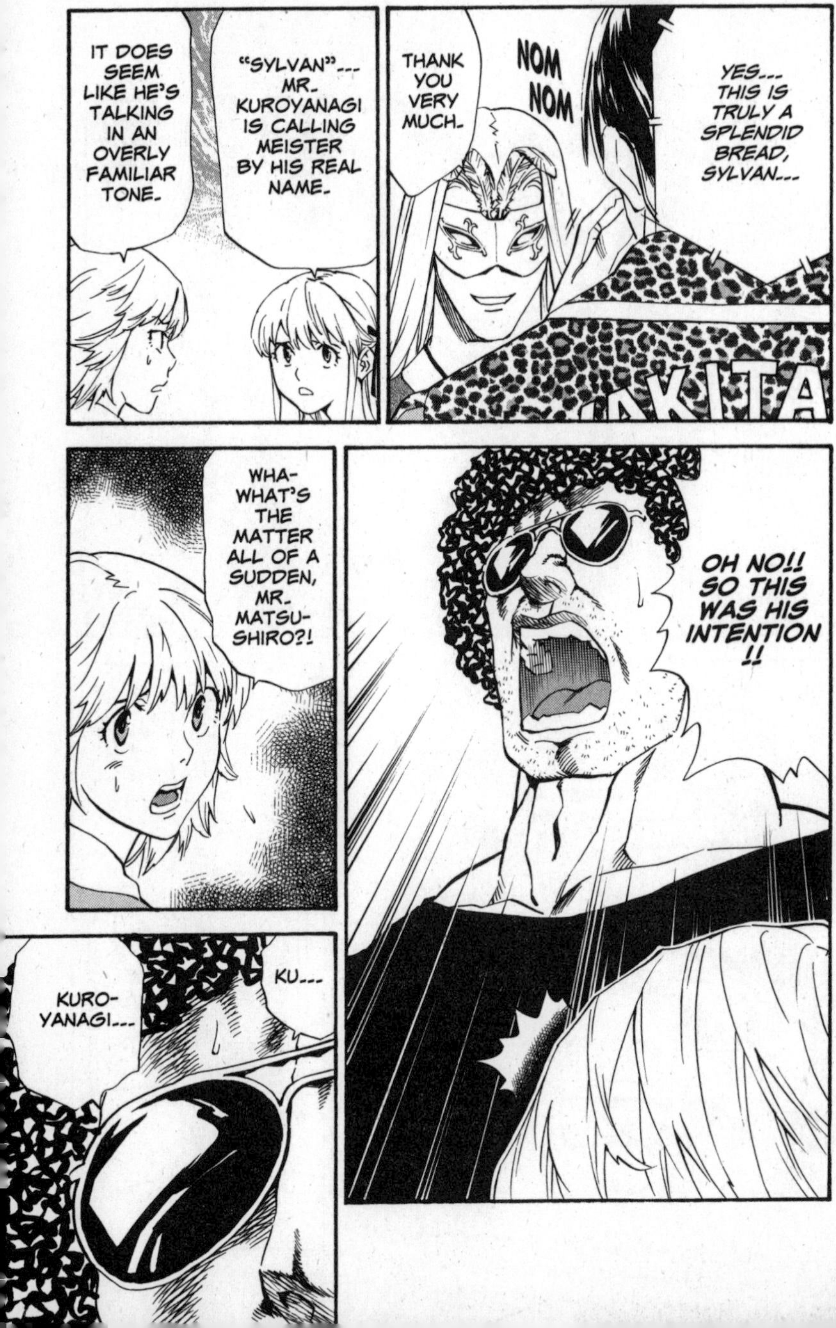

YES... THIS IS TRULY A SPLENDID BREAD, SYLVAN...
NOM NOM
THANK YOU VERY MUCH.
AKITA
"SYLVAN"... MR. KUROYANAGI IS CALLING MEISTER BY HIS REAL NAME.
IT DOES SEEM LIKE HE'S TALKING IN AN OVERLY FAMILIAR TONE.
OH NO!! SO THIS WAS HIS INTENTION!!
WHA-WHAT'S THE MATTER ALL OF A SUDDEN, MR. MATSUSHIRO?!
KU...
KURO-YANAGI...

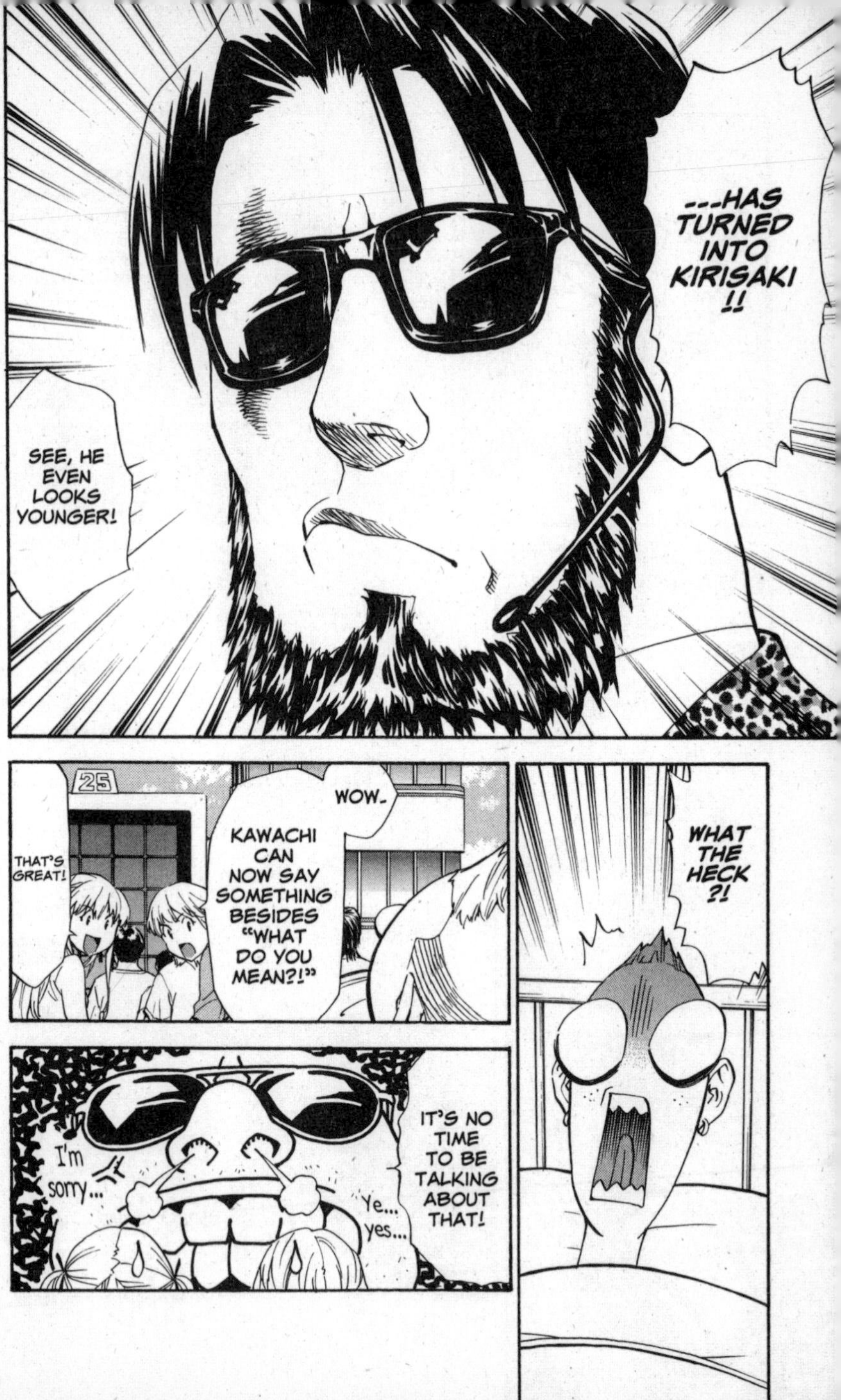
---HAS TURNED INTO KIRISAKI !!
SEE, HE EVEN LOOKS YOUNGER!
WHAT THE HECK ?!
WOW-
KAWACHI CAN NOW SAY SOMETHING BESIDES "WHAT DO YOU MEAN?!"
THAT'S GREAT!
IT'S NO TIME TO BE TALKING ABOUT THAT!
Ye... yes...
I'm sorry...

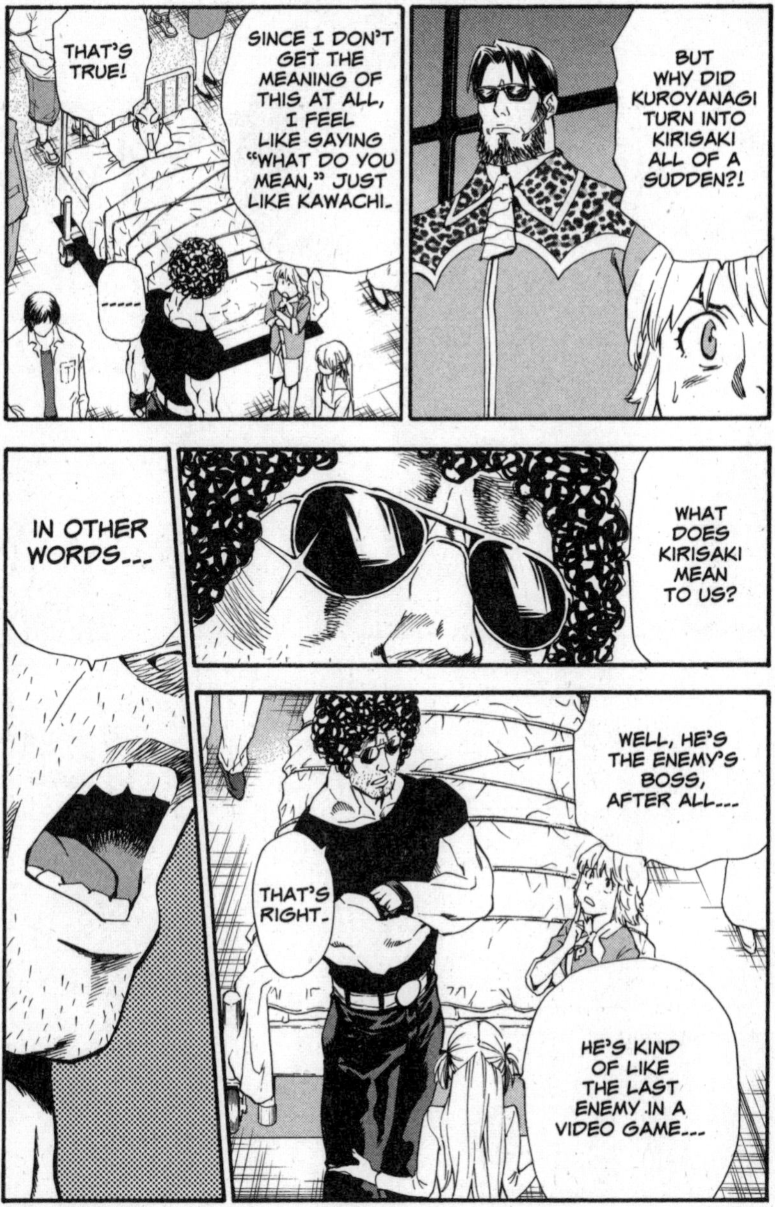
BUT WHY DID KUROYANAGI TURN INTO KIRISAKI ALL OF A SUDDEN?!
SINCE I DON'T GET THE MEANING OF THIS AT ALL, I FEEL LIKE SAYING "WHAT DO YOU MEAN," JUST LIKE KAWACHI.
THAT'S TRUE!
.....
WHAT DOES KIRISAKI MEAN TO US?
WELL, HE'S THE ENEMY'S BOSS, AFTER ALL...
THAT'S RIGHT.
HE'S KIND OF LIKE THE LAST ENEMY IN A VIDEO GAME...
IN OTHER WORDS...

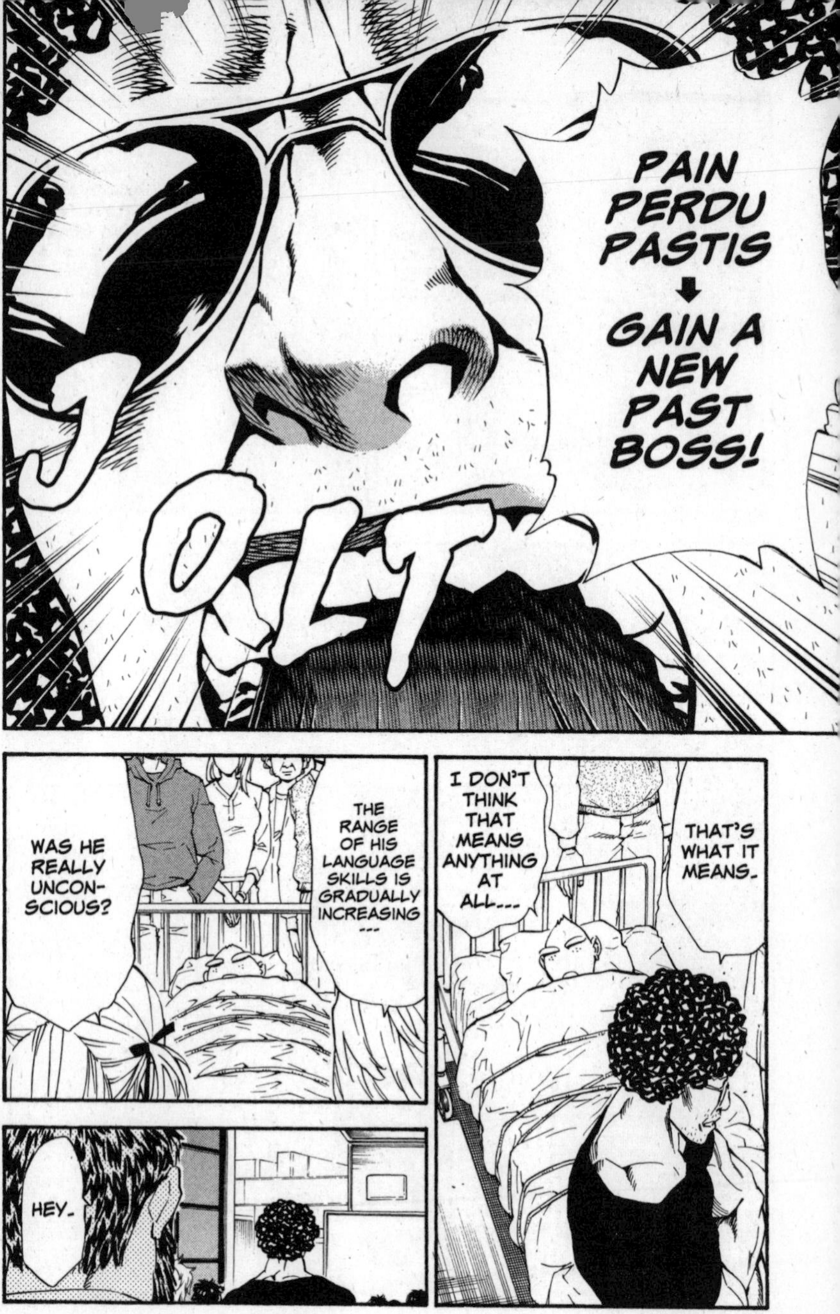
PAIN PERDU PASTIS ↓ GAIN A NEW PAST BOSS!
JOLT
THAT'S WHAT IT MEANS.
I DON'T THINK THAT MEANS ANYTHING AT ALL...
THE RANGE OF HIS LANGUAGE SKILLS IS GRADUALLY INCREASING...
WAS HE REALLY UNCON-SCIOUS?
HEY.

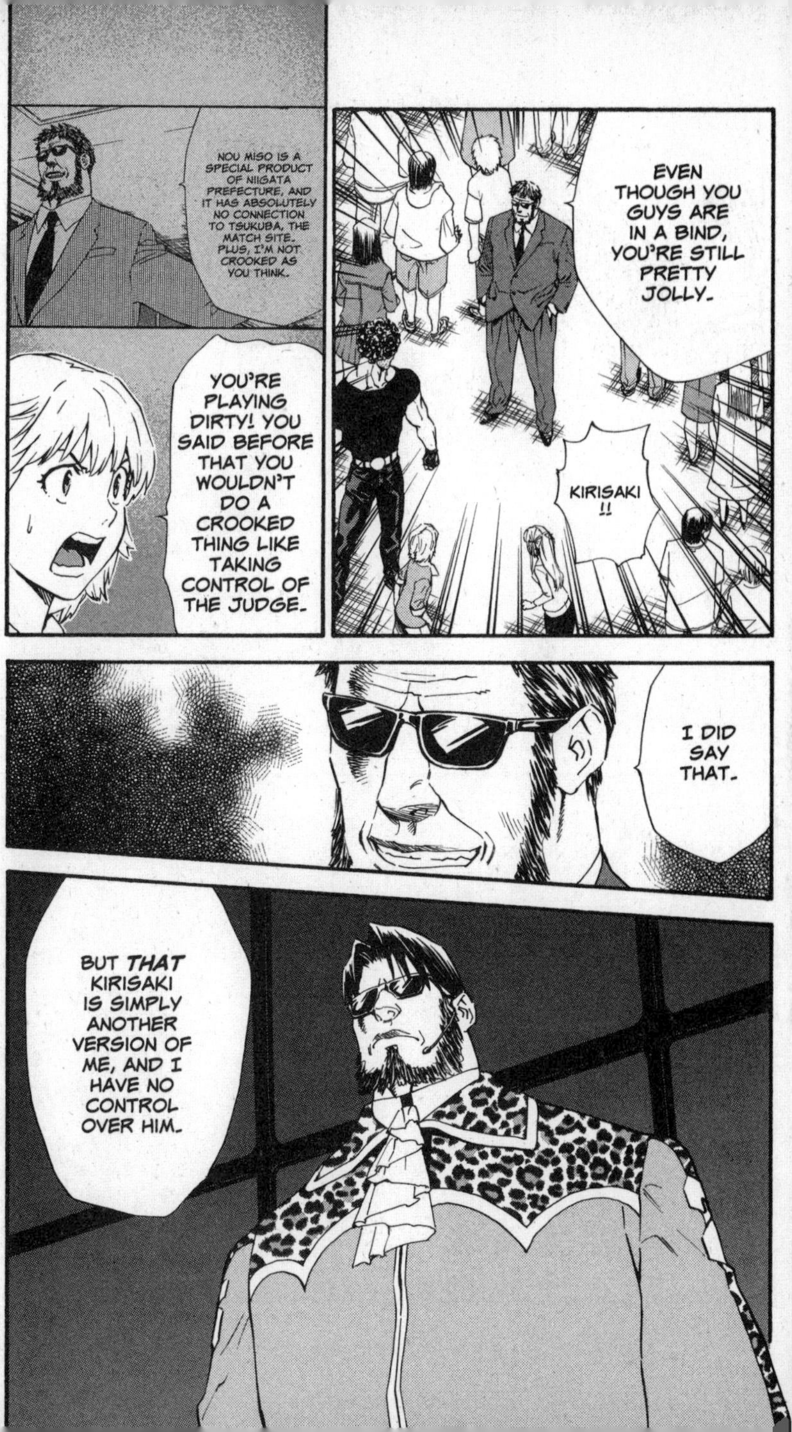
EVEN THOUGH YOU GUYS ARE IN A BIND, YOU'RE STILL PRETTY JOLLY.
KIRISAKI!!
NOU MISO IS A SPECIAL PRODUCT OF NIIGATA PREFECTURE, AND IT HAS ABSOLUTELY NO CONNECTION TO TSUKUBA, THE MATCH SITE. PLUS, I'M NOT CROOKED AS YOU THINK.
YOU'RE PLAYING DIRTY! YOU SAID BEFORE THAT YOU WOULDN'T DO A CROOKED THING LIKE TAKING CONTROL OF THE JUDGE.
I DID SAY THAT.
BUT *THAT* KIRISAKI IS SIMPLY ANOTHER VERSION OF ME, AND I HAVE NO CONTROL OVER HIM.

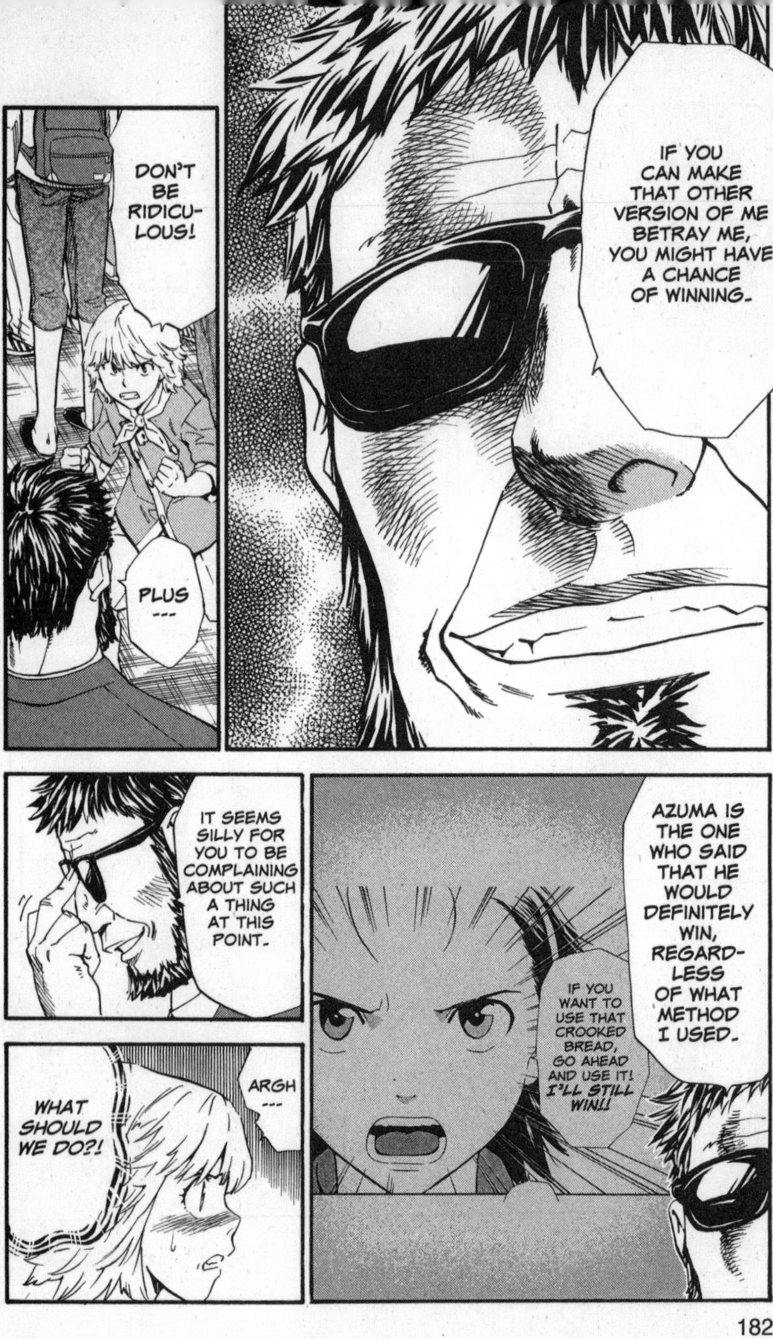
IF YOU CAN MAKE THAT OTHER VERSION OF ME BETRAY ME, YOU MIGHT HAVE A CHANCE OF WINNING.
DON'T BE RIDICULOUS!
PLUS ---
AZUMA IS THE ONE WHO SAID THAT HE WOULD DEFINITELY WIN, REGARDLESS OF WHAT METHOD I USED.
IF YOU WANT TO USE THAT CROOKED BREAD, GO AHEAD AND USE IT! I'LL STILL WIN!!
IT SEEMS SILLY FOR YOU TO BE COMPLAINING ABOUT SUCH A THING AT THIS POINT.
ARGH ---
WHAT SHOULD WE DO?!

IN ADDITION TO MAKING AN AMAZING BREAD LIKE PAIN PERDU PASTIS, MEISTER HAS TURNED KUROYANAGI INTO KIRISAKI...

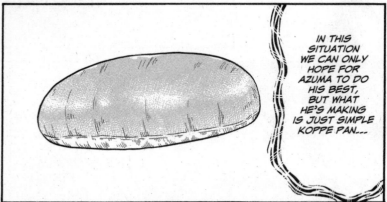

IN THIS SITUATION WE CAN ONLY HOPE FOR AZUMA TO DO HIS BEST, BUT WHAT HE'S MAKING IS JUST SIMPLE KOPPE PAN...

IT'S DONE!

THERE'S NO WAY NOW THAT...

HEY!

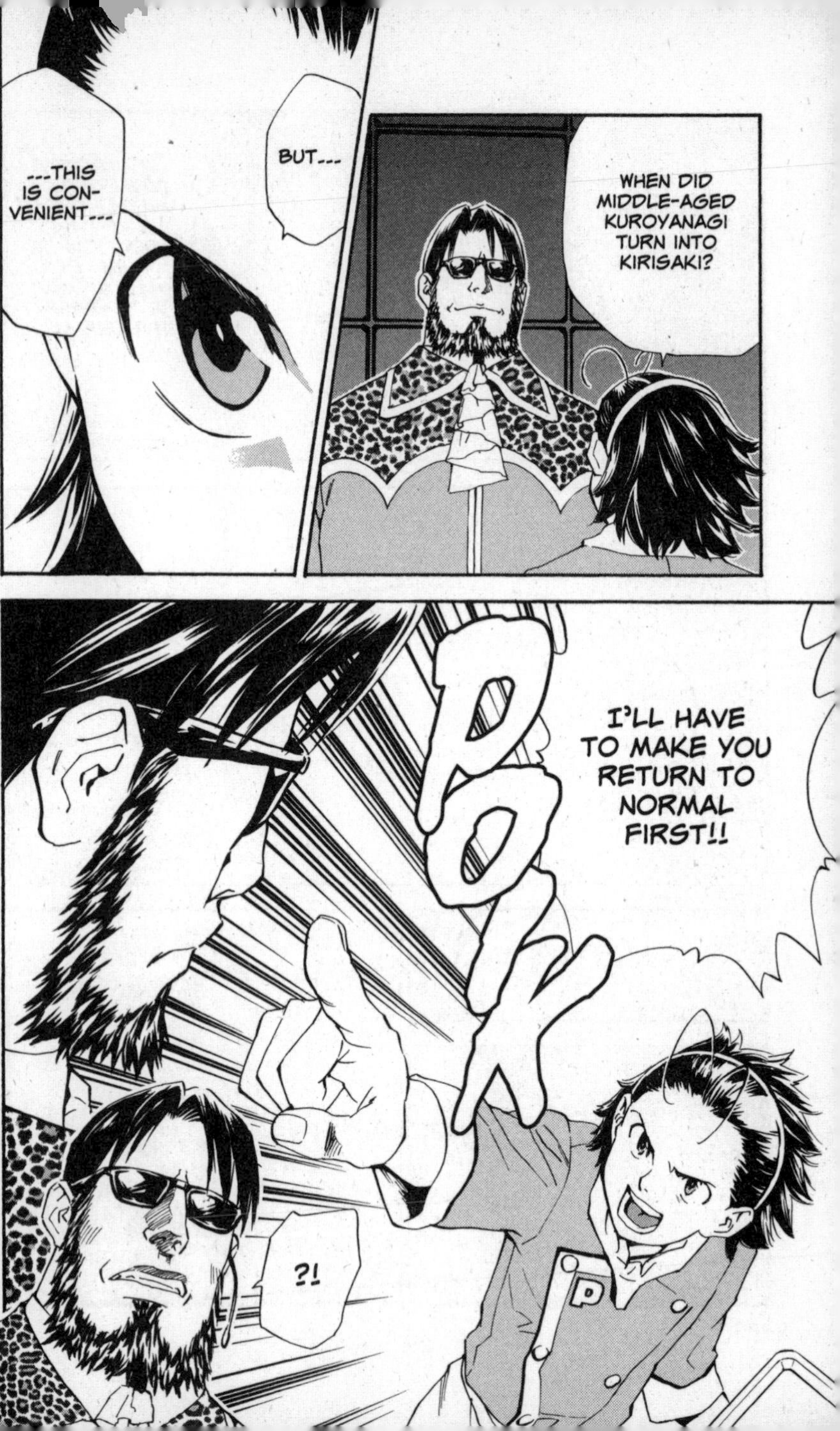
WHEN DID MIDDLE-AGED KUROYANAGI TURN INTO KIRISAKI?
BUT---
---THIS IS CON-VENIENT---
I'LL HAVE TO MAKE YOU RETURN TO NORMAL FIRST!!
?!

— o be continued! —

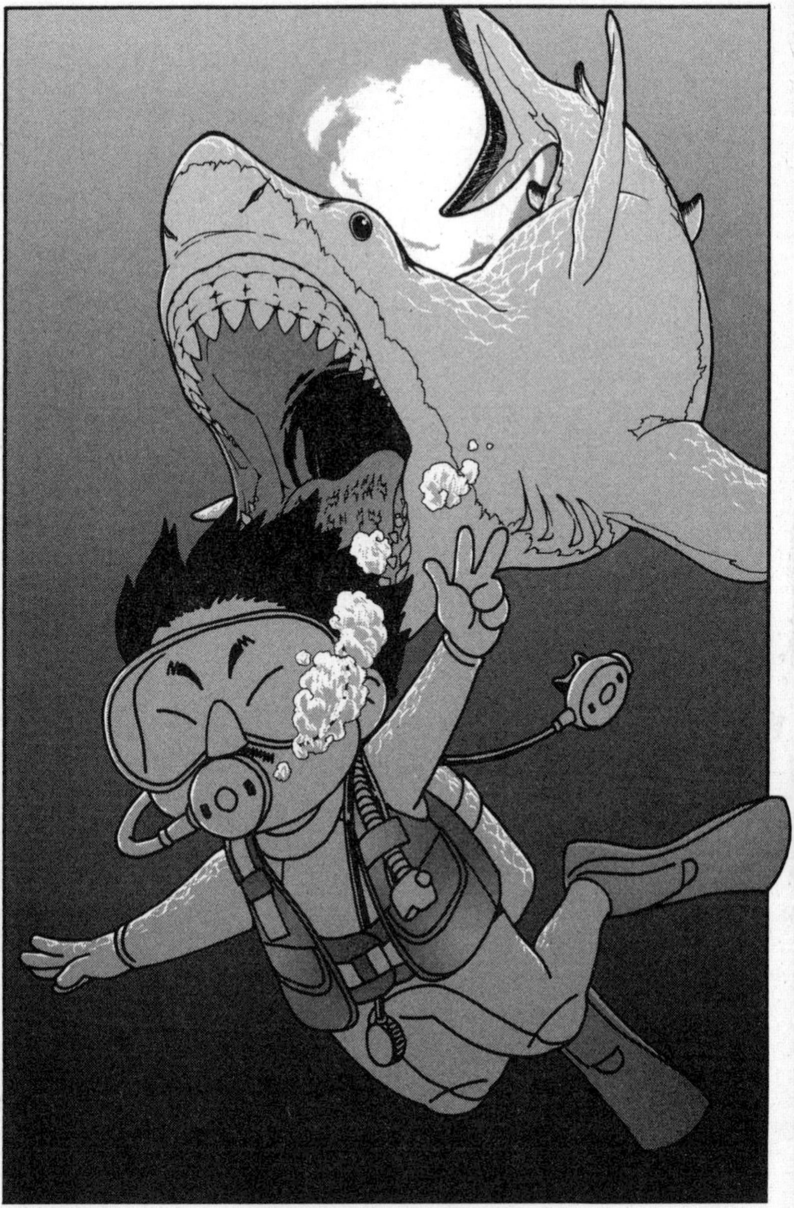

Bonus! ♡

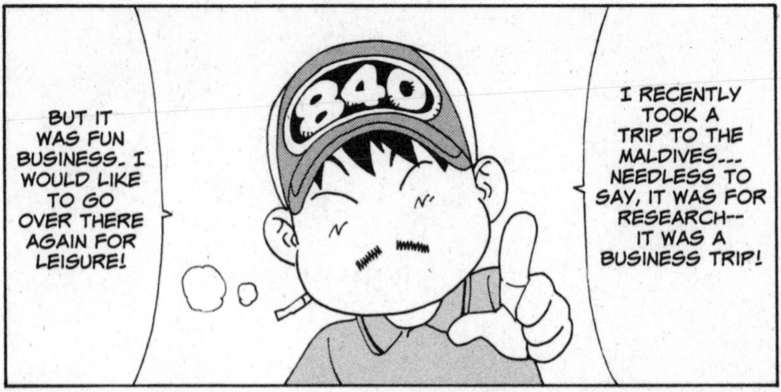
I RECENTLY TOOK A TRIP TO THE MALDIVES... NEEDLESS TO SAY, IT WAS FOR RESEARCH-- IT WAS A BUSINESS TRIP!
BUT IT WAS FUN BUSINESS. I WOULD LIKE TO GO OVER THERE AGAIN FOR LEISURE!

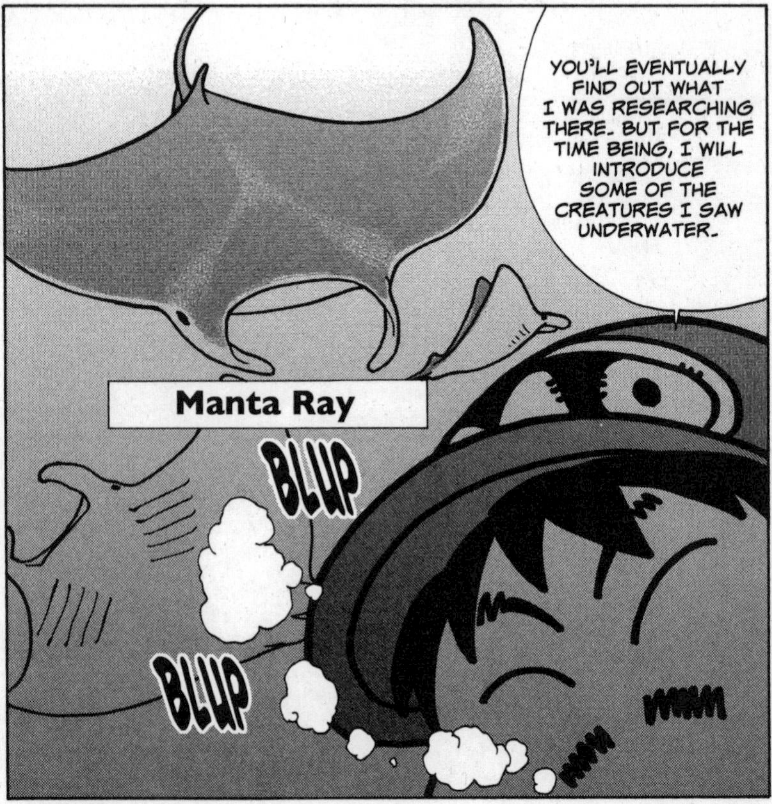
YOU'LL EVENTUALLY FIND OUT WHAT I WAS RESEARCHING THERE. BUT FOR THE TIME BEING, I WILL INTRODUCE SOME OF THE CREATURES I SAW UNDERWATER.
Manta Ray
BLUP
BLUP

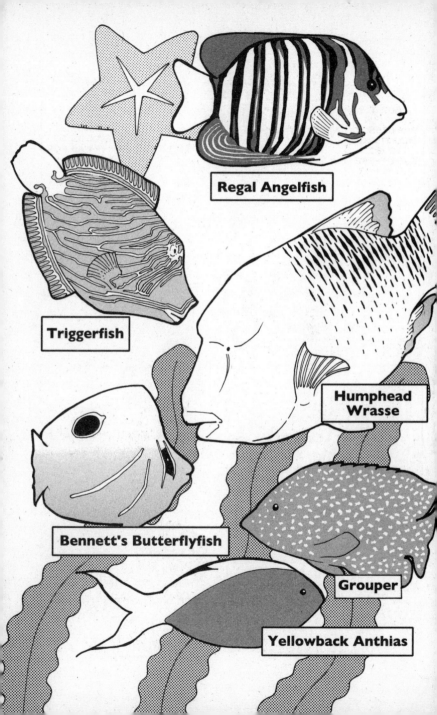

Regal Angelfish

Triggerfish

Humphead Wrasse

Bennett's Butterflyfish

Grouper

Yellowback Anthias

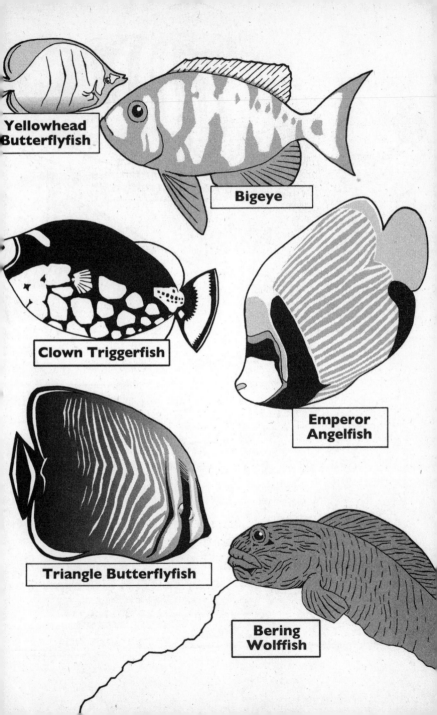

Yellowhead Butterflyfish

Bigeye

Clown Triggerfish

Emperor Angelfish

Triangle Butterflyfish

Bering Wolffish

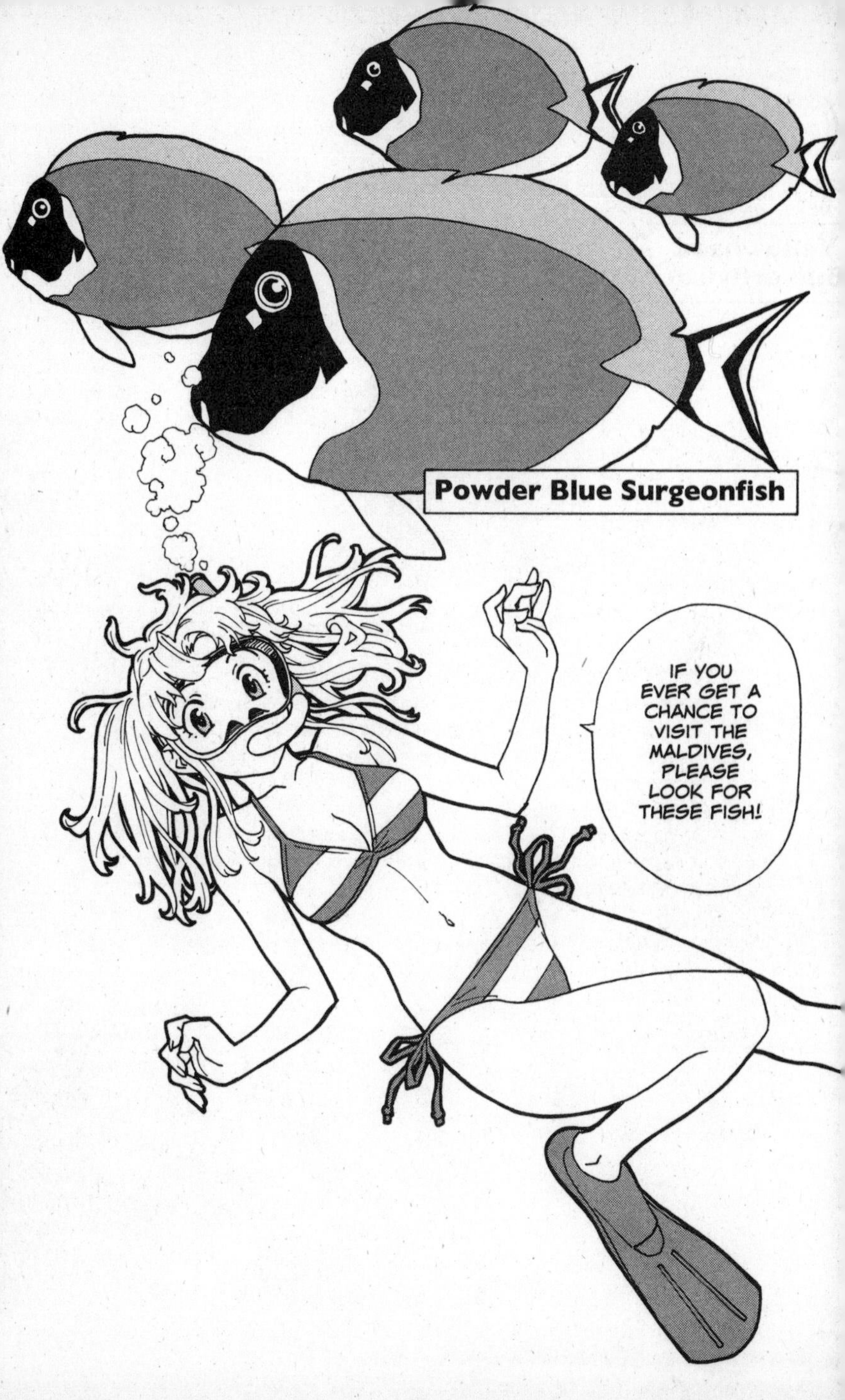
Powder Blue Surgeonfish
IF YOU EVER GET A CHANCE TO VISIT THE MALDIVES, PLEASE LOOK FOR THESE FISH!

Freshly Baked!!
Mini Information

Miso

Photograph by Masatoshi Hirose

Back in the old days of Japan, it was considered to be shameful to buy miso outside of the house, and each family was expected to make their own miso. As a result, families were very proud of the miso they produced, and this pride in one's own labor led to the birth of the phrase temae miso.

By the way, wasn't it a wonderful idea to have a wordplay with Nou Miso and nomiso (brain)? Although this is just me singing my own praise (hahaha).

The phrase "temae miso" roughly means to sing one's own praises (or to praise one's own miso!) and the words for Nou Miso and "brain" (nomiso) sound the same in Japanese. --Editor